Handcraft
ILLUSTRATED

~ 1998 ~

Published by
Boston Common Press Limited Partnership
17 Station Street
Brookline MA 02445

ISBN: 0-936184-33-7
ISSN: 1072-0529

To get home delivery of future issues of
Handcraft Illustrated magazine, call 800-526-8447. To order any of
the book titles from the *Handcraft Illustrated Library*,
call 800-611-0760, or write to the address above.

$29.95

NUMBER NINETEEN   WINTER 1998

Handcraft

ILLUSTRATED

Glass Mosaic
Made Easy

Make-at-Home
Bath Tablets
Mix-and-Mold Fragrant Disks
with Honey and Sea Salt

Three-Panel Dutch
Townscape
Folding Screen from Balsa Wood
and Paper Hinges

Cutout Valentine
Use Your Stencils to Create an
Elegant Multilayered Card

Secrets of Sewing
with Plastic
Forget Pins and Hems.
All You Need Is Painter's Tape

Handpainted Poppy
Bowl in 5 Easy Steps
Transform any Wooden Bowl with
a Georgia O'Keeffe-Style Design

ALSO
Quick-Cut Paper Collage Tray
Ten-Minute Box from Ribbon
Pyramid-Shaped Pillows
Fast and Easy Lace Cookies

PLUS: Annual Mail-Order Directory

Contents

Cutout Valentine, page 12

Beaded Butterflies, page 14

Paper Collage Tray, page 24

COVER PHOTOGRAPH:
Carl Tremblay

STYLING:
Melissa Gulley

Create this faux masterpiece in an afternoon. See page 31.

Handcraft
ILLUSTRATED

EDITOR
Carol Endler Sterbenz

ART DIRECTOR
Amy Klee

CORPORATE MANAGING EDITOR
Barbara Bourassa

SENIOR EDITOR
Michio Ryan

DIRECTIONS EDITOR
Candie Frankel

COPY EDITOR
Amy Finch

EDITORIAL ASSISTANT
Melissa Nachatelo

EDITORIAL INTERNS
Carmit Delman
Jordan Salvatoriello

❧

PUBLISHER AND FOUNDER
Christopher Kimball

MARKETING DIRECTOR
Adrienne Kimball

CIRCULATION MANAGER
David Mack

FULFILLMENT MANAGER
Larisa Greiner

CIRCULATION MANAGER
Darcy Beach

MARKETING ASSISTANT
Connie Forbes

CIRCULATION ASSISTANT
Steven Browall

❧

VICE PRESIDENT PRODUCTION AND TECHNOLOGY
James McCormack

EDITORIAL PRODUCTION MANAGER
Sheila Datz

DESKTOP PUBLISHING MANAGER
Kevin Moeller

PRODUCTION ARTIST
Robert Parsons

PRODUCTION ASSISTANT
Daniel Frey

❧

CONTROLLER
Lisa A. Carullo

SENIOR ACCOUNTANT
Mandy Shito

STAFF ACCOUNTANT
William Baggs

OFFICE MANAGER
Livia McRee

Handcraft Illustrated (ISSN 1072-0529) is published quarterly by Boston Common Press Limited Partners, 17 Station Street, Brookline, MA 02146. Copyright 1998 Boston Common Press Limited Partners. Second-class postage paid at Boston, MA, and additional mailing offices, USPS #011-895. For list rental information, please contact List Services Corporation, 6 Trowbridge Drive, P.O. Box 516, Bethel, CT 06801; (203) 743-2600; Fax (203) 743-0589. Editorial office: 17 Station Street, Brookline, MA 02146; (617) 232-1000, FAX (617) 232-1572, e-mail: hndcftill@aol.com. Editorial contributions should be sent or e-mailed to: Editor, *Handcraft Illustrated*. We cannot assume responsibility for manuscripts submitted to us. Submissions will be returned only if accompanied by a large, self-addressed stamped envelope. Subscription rates: $24.95 for one year; $45 for two years; $65 for three years. (Canada: add $6 per year; all other countries add $12 per year.) Postmaster: Send all new orders, subscription inquiries, and change of address notices to *Handcraft Illustrated*, P.O. Box 7450, Red Oak, IA 51591-0450. Single copies: $4 in U.S.; $4.95 in Canada and other countries. Back issues available for $5 each. PRINTED IN THE U.S.A.

From the Editor

I can't remember Spring. I can't seem to summon the sense of earthy fragrance that rises from moist soil warmed by morning sunshine, at least not today, when a chaotic wind pushes me along the sidewalk, now shovelled clear and dry after a heavy snowfall. I hurry to the train hidden under Boston's Arlington Street in the well-constructed subterranean labyrinth of rail transportation known as the "T".

I descend the stairway, relieved briefly of the bitter cold by a burst of hot air that rushes up the stairway corridor as an oncoming train pushes its way through the underground tunnel. The air smells like coal ash, perhaps a vestige of the old coal-fueled engines. I don't know, but its warmth is welcome. Today is Saturday and I am going to the office to catch up on some work. I am looking forward to reducing the stack of paper that forms and reforms during my frequent absences from the office when I am on the road for *Handcraft Illustrated*.

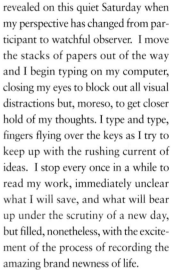

There will be a great deal more to do when I return next week, and I want be ready for the tasks, each made more complicated and sadly less inspired, by the onslaught of ringing telephone, chiming e-mail bell, and the disruptive clanking of radiator pipes which stretch the full length of my office. I actually like being in the office now. I find comfort in the unfamiliar quiet.

Shafts of early sun come through the venetian blinds in thick bars that brand the wall with dusty stripes, and I notice a little shower of gold particles in the air. My perspective has definitely shifted, perhaps as a result of the seeming barrenness of the space, yet, the furniture is placed as before—the door glass casts back a reflection of me sitting at my desk, a polished slab of honey-colored pine dotted with the usual objects—a lamp, a telephone, some photographs, my computer, and several neat piles of paper. No, the change has been created by the unexpected silence, and it causes me to feel like a stranger in my own office. It is this change that compels me to notice familiar things and to configure in them new meaning.

I remember the same sense of being in a familiar place but feeling strangely shifted in perspective when I was in college, spending an extra day in the dormitory

> It was not that the space itself had changed overnight, it was that I was seeing the room from a different perspective.

preparing for my last exam after all the students on my floor had left for Spring break. I walked from my room to a large common area that days before had been filled with students studying for exams. As I looked inside the space, it suddenly looked shabby and lifeless. It was not that the space itself had changed overnight, it was that I was seeing the room from a different perspective.

Now, sitting in my office, I wonder what might be revealed on this quiet Saturday when my perspective has changed from participant to watchful observer. I move the stacks of papers out of the way and I begin typing on my computer, closing my eyes to block out all visual distractions but, moreso, to get closer hold of my thoughts. I type and type, fingers flying over the keys as I try to keep up with the rushing current of ideas. I stop every once in a while to read my work, immediately unclear what I will save, and what will bear up under the scrutiny of a new day, but filled, nonetheless, with the excitement of the process of recording the amazing brand newness of life.

When I look up, I see the day has disappeared, and I am exhilarated by the sense of accomplishment I feel. I have developed a fruitful list of new books, together with a plan for new Fall projects. I leave the office and, as I walk past the mounds of snow shovelled into high piles along the curbs near the "T" stop, I am reminded of M.E. Mason's words, when he wrote of the coming Spring:

> *The frost lies soft—and thick—and white*
> *Upon the fields and in the air…*
> *On poplar trees—as if in prayer*
> *And orchard—mystical—apart—*
> *The unborn Spring within her heart.*

It seems clear that we can attach new meaning to even a long and arduous winter, when we realize that the changes it brings can cause us to be aware of our lives and bring new meaning to our world. It is certainly this possibility that is stored in each moment if we stop and accept the changes that inevitably come our way.

Notes from Readers

Learn how to imitate the look of burned wood, custom design a memory album, create a zesty fruit centerpiece, and give a sandy finish to terra-cotta pots.

🦃 COMPILED BY MELISSA NACHATELO

Woodburn Without Worry

I don't have the necessary tools to burn into wood, but I want to add a woodburned effect to a jewelry box I'm working on. Is there some way to do this?

JANET SHERRY
PORTLAND, OR

We came across a new product, Paper Etch, made by Silkpaint, that imitates the look you want. Although its name specifies etching on paper, the product also works on wood. We took a 5" x 7" plaque of soft basswood and tested the product's ability to create an authentic-looking woodburned effect. Here's how we did it:

We traced a child's initials and small drawings onto the wood with light pencil. Following the pencil marks for reference, we applied the Paper Etch dissolving gel onto the wood. The bottle's fine, narrow tip allowed easy maneuvering and thin, even lines, unlike a bulky electrical tool. After tracing the outline of the initials and filling in the block letters with the clear gel, we dried the gel with a blow dryer to prepare it for heating and preheated the oven to 170 degrees. The woodburned effect appeared on the wood within the first 5 to 10 minutes in the oven. When the outlines turned a dark shade of brown, we decided to remove the plaque. You can remove the project at any point, depending on the look you want: The longer it remains in the oven, the darker the images become. When we inspected the plaque we noticed a few of the outer lines seemed smudged. After talking to the manufacturer, we determined the problem was caused by two factors: applying a thick coat of gel to a porous wood. If you select a soft wood, such as basswood or pine, apply a thin coat of gel.

Be sure to use Paper Etch in a well-ventilated work space, and wear protective gloves and glasses at all times. Paper Etch costs $9.95 per 2-ounce bottle and is available from Silkpaint, 18220 Waldron Drive, P.O. Box 18, Waldron, MO 64092; 816-891-7774.

Animate Your Memories

I have a special book I'd like to paste my vacation photos in. The problem is that some photos overlap, expanding the book's binding capacity. I don't want to cut any of the photos, because I don't have the negatives, and I have my heart set on using this beautiful book as an album.

SARA MCNAMARA
ST. LOUIS, MO

The new craze for memory albums has the craft market teeming with great new ways to decorate albums of cherished photos. To increase your book's capacity, you need thinner pages with fewer overlapping photos. We suggest an easy and proven method to help you: laser color copies. Color photocopies of photographs give you the opportunity to enlarge or decrease the size of the original picture without distorting its details. You have the creative control to edit a photo: If you accidentally capture another tourist in a candid shot of your family, enlarge the print and cut the tourist out of the picture. Or, shrink a photo to incorporate more visually appealing scenes. The photocopy paper reduces bulkiness. Tell your own story of a favorite trip or family holiday by writing captions with colored markers, or add stickers, stamps, and other decorative memorabilia to the page. For more project ideas using color copies, *see* The Perfect Gift, page 7.

A New Durable Paint Line

What kind of paint do you suggest for decorating the outside of ceramic mugs? The paints that I've used in the past either wash off or fade dramatically when oven baked.

JENNY HARDEN
TRENTON, NJ

We recommend Pebeo's new line of Porcelaine 150 paints. Designed for use on ceramics, glass, porcelain, and other heat-stable surfaces, these water-based glazes come in 47 colors, including 28 transparent, 12 opaque, and 7 semi-opaque. You can stencil a design onto solid-color mugs and paint them with the colors of your choice. If you plan to use a mug for drinking, you will want to avoid painting the inside or too close to the lip. Let the paint dry for a full 24 hours before oven baking. To ensure the new design will be dishwasher-safe, place the mugs in a cold oven and heat to approximately 300 degrees for 35 minutes.

We found the finished glaze stayed true to its original color after being oven baked. Testing its claims, we vigorously hand-washed the mugs and placed them in a dishwasher. The paint did not wash off, chip, or fade in either washing. You can purchase Pebeo's Porcelaine 150 paints via mail order from Dick Blick, P.O. Box 1267, Galesburg, IL 61402-1267; 800-828-4548. Prices start at $3.69 per 1.5-ounce jar.

Zesty Centerpieces for the Table

My kitchen table needs a centerpiece. I really love fresh fruit, but a bowl of fruit is not enough for a decorative centerpiece. Any ideas?

SHAWNA LANGSTROM
DALLAS, TX

Fresh fruit enlivens any table immediately with its vivid color. For a new approach to the "still life" centerpiece, forget the traditional apples, bananas, grapes, and pears. You can create an elegant and fun citrus centerpiece with a fruit zester, oranges, lemons, limes, and grapefruits.

A fruit zester looks and acts much like a peeler. Specially designed to remove the zest, the outermost rind of citrus fruit, a zester makes grooved designs in the fruit. Take a thick-skinned orange and use the tool to groove spirals, circles, lines, or stars into the skin to reveal the white pith underneath. (Watch out for squirting citrus juices.) We made our own citrus centerpiece and found it lasted two weeks. The first week we displayed it, the scent of the citrus and colors were strong. The second week, the decorated fruit hardened, but still looked attractive. To enhance the fruit arrangement in the second week, surround the grooved fruit with greens, like lemon leaves.

Pom-Pom Passion

With some of my sewn projects, I like to add a decorative pom-pom here and there. Regular pom-poms are so easy to find at any store, but do you know where I can locate unique pom-poms?

BETH LINCOLN
CONCORD, NH

We found a company in Paterson, NJ, that adds an innovative twist to ordinary pom-poms. Aldastar Corp. recently introduced Pom Beadz (patent still pending), an acrylic pom-pom with a plastic tube center for easy stringing. We used the ¾"-tubed pom-poms along with 4-ply cotton yarn and made a sophisticated pom-pom fringe. Stringing the pom-poms onto the yarn with an embroidery needle was fast and easy (the thin tube allowed the pom-poms to slide easily on the yarn, anchored by a knot on either side). Aldastar carries Pom Beadz in a range of decorative colors and sizes. They also carry pom-poms without tubes. For more information or to order, write Aldastar, 70 Spruce Street, Building 8, Paterson, NJ 07501; 800-782-3622. Retail prices begin at $2.99 for a mixed package of 75 Pom Beadz.

Tracing Made Easy

My friend suggested I invest in a light table because I trace my own designs and patterns. This seems like an expensive option. What's the price range, and is it worth it?

CLARE WILLIAMS
TUCSON, AZ

Sax Arts & Crafts sells light boxes and tables ranging in price from $16.95 for a 6" x 9" box to $272 for an 18" x 24⅜" table. Portable light boxes averaging 15-22 watts tend to be less expensive than professional light tables and take up little space on a countertop. Oak or decorated tables can start as high as $900. So, before making an investment, decide if the frequency of use and the convenience is worth the expense.

If not, we have a no cost homemade method for tracing easily. If you have a glass-top table in your home, you can make your own "light box." Place a low-watt lamp underneath the glass table. Be sure to check the light's wattage and heat to avoid any heat hazards, exchanging any high-wattage bulbs for lower-wattage ones. To trace a pattern, tape the design to the top of the table and place tracing paper over it. The light source will allow you to see your design easily.

Write or call Sax at P.O. Box 510710, New Berlin, WI 53151-0710; 800-558-6696 to investigate options for light boxes and tables.

Create a Sandy Finish
I saw some amazing flower pots on a recent trip to New York City. They were terra-cotta and painted light yellow and blue, and finished with what appeared to be a separate layer of sand. They were relatively expensive, yet they looked easy to make.

JAMES DARCY
CHICAGO, IL

Terra-cotta pots with a sand/paint finish cost little and are fun to make yourself. Using a single color of acrylic paint (we chose lemon green), paint the interior of the pot, including the rim. Let it dry completely. Paint the exterior and bottom of the pot a second color. We applied two coats of baby blue to completely cover the terra-cotta. While the paint is still wet, roll the pot in a fine sand. Let the coats of sand and paint dry, then apply a light coat of acrylic spray overall. This will ensure that the sand will stick to the painted surface. Avoid overspraying, as it could cause milky white blotches to form on the sandy surface.

Pots are available at local garden centers or craft stores. You can find marine sand for approximately $3.99 per 5-pound bag at your local pet and fish retailer.

Use Rubber Bands for a Clean Line of Color
I've been working on the footstool from the Spring 1997 issue, page 18. Every time I try to change the color on the legs, I'm left with a sloppy finish between colors. How can I make clean lines when I change from a rose to a beige?

BETTINA A. MIELKE
PEORIA, AZ

You'll find it easy to paint clean lines with one base coat and a few rubber bands. Start by painting the entire leg white. Then, stretch narrow rubber bands around the leg. With the bands in place, paint each section its respective color (as directed) up to the rubber band. When the coats are dry, carefully snip off the rubber bands with manicure scissors. The clean line will form a border between the color sections.

If you prefer to paint the leg without delineated borders, use the rubber bands as a straight edge for clear distinctions between the sections. This method requires a drying time for each color and careful attention to the rubber bands' alignment. Like the border method, the bands will help you achieve clean, professional lines.

How to Fix Etching Mistakes on Glass
I etched two different sets of glasses and plates. Most of the dishes came out wonderfully, but two long champagne glasses had streaks and patches where the cream didn't work as well. What happened?

DONNA BLAIR
DARTMOUTH, NH

Glass, like wood, comes in different grains, so higher-quality glass allows better etched results. For this reason, some glassware may not be suitable for etching. Unfortunately, you'll only know if you try to etch the glass. To determine if this is the case, try re-etching your champagne glasses. By applying more etching cream to the glass, you can fix any streaks or gaps in a design. Be sure to thoroughly clean the glass to remove any grease marks before re-applying the cream. Align the original design to the glass. For instance, if you used lettering, place the stick-

ers back in their original positions. Then, put on your gloves and protective eyewear, and apply the cream to the entire surface. Leave the etching cream on the glass for no more than 10 to 15 minutes. This will be enough time for the cream to work. Finally, rinse the cream from the glass under a stream of running warm water.

Soda Ash
It's used for dyeing, but what exactly does soda ash do? Where can I buy it?

JANE QUINN
SAN MARINO, CA

A fabric dye needs a fixative in order to chemically bond to a fabric's fibers. According to Lisa Hyman, of the Dharma Trading Co., a supplier specializing in fiber arts, soda ash serves as this chemical agent. A mild alkali, soda ash assists in the reaction between a dye and the cellulose fibers to make a fabric dye-fast.

For basic solid color dying, dye your fabric in a tub following manufacturer's instructions. Stir the fabric constantly for 10 to 20 minutes, depending on the color tone you want. With rubber gloves and a ventilation mask on for safety, fill a separate container with very hot water, says Hyman, and mix in the required amount of soda ash. Pour the dissolved soda ash solution into the original dye bath slowly over a period of 15 minutes. To avoid streaking, discoloration or damage, do not pour the soda ash directly onto the fabric. Instead, hold the dyed garment to the side of the tub while pouring. Stir the bath frequently, leaving the fabric in from 30 minutes for a lighter shade to one hour for a deeper color.

A one-pound bag of soda ash is available for $1.75 from the Dharma Trading Company. To order a free catalog, contact the company at P.O. Box 150916, San Rafael, CA 94915; 800-542-5227.

Essential vs. Fragrance Oils
What's the difference between essential oil and fragrance oil?

JACKIE NEWMAN
LONG ISLAND CITY, NY

Fragrance oils are a synthetic blend of essential and perfume oils, offering longer lasting scents at a cheaper cost than essential oils. Essential oils, used for aromatherapy, are all-natural blends that necessitate the use of fixatives to ensure that the

scent won't waft away. And, because they are natural, scents are limited, unlike fragrance oils, which can mix any synthetic oil. According to A World of Plenty, makers/suppliers of both types of oil, you can use either type for most applications. We prefer natural, essential oils for massage oils, soaps, and cosmetics, and fragrance oils for perfume, potpourri, and candles.

For more information or to order a catalog ($1, refundable with purchase), write or call A World of Plenty, P.O. Box 1153, Hermantown, MN 55810-9724; 218-729-6761.

Knowing Your Fabrics
When I shop at a fabric store, I first look in sale bins for good buys. But I'm still a novice at determining the kind of material. How do I recognize the fabric remnants?

AMY LOUIS
TAMPA, FL

We spoke to fabric suppliers about determining the fiber content of fabric remnants. Experts admit it is nearly impossible to determine exact fiber content of a piece with the many natural and synthetic fiber combinations available in a blend. Seek help from the store's personnel. Ask if they have any similar pieces, or if they know from which section the remnant originally came. Or, rely upon your knowledge of fabric and its "hand." The "hand" is the way the fabric feels, hangs, wrinkles, or stretches. Although you may not be able to determine exact fibers, a strong guess will let you know whether a material will work well for a project.

Quick Tips

USING WOODEN SKEWERS

To join Styrofoam shapes (or hold them steady for painting and decorating), Benedetta Colletti, of Monroe, Connecticut, recommends using wooden shish kabob skewers. The thin, sharply pointed skewers leave unobtrusive holes, and the long sticks are easy to maneuver and trim.

BRUSH HOLDER

To protect her expensive artist's brushes, Lori O'Callaghan, of Fox River Grove, Illinois, devised a coffee can holder.

1. **Make small X-shaped incisions in the plastic lid using an X-Acto knife.**

2. **Snap on the lid, then stand each brush upright in its own slot.**

STRAIGHT BRISTLES

Use the tiny rubber bands that come with orthodontic braces to tame freshly washed stencil brushes, writes Melissa Ward, of Putnam Valley, New York. Just slip one or two rubber bands around the wet bristles to hold them tight as they dry.

ATTENTION READERS

Calling All Crafters

Do you have a craft, sewing, or decorating technique that saves time or money? Send it our way! We'll give you a one-year complimentary subscription for each Quick Tip that we publish. Send your tip to:

Quick Tips

Handcraft Illustrated
17 Station Street
Brookline, MA 02146

Please include your name, address, and daytime phone number with all correspondence.

ILLUSTRATION:
Michael Gellatly

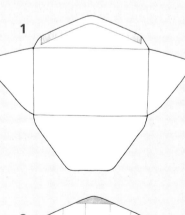

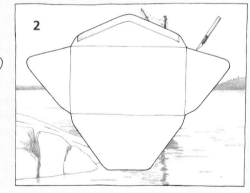

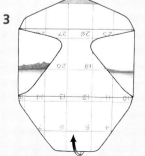

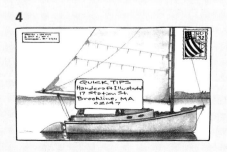

ARTISTIC ENVELOPES

Recycle last year's picture calendar to make unique envelopes, writes Cynthia St. John, of San Jose, California.

1. **Open the flaps of a sample envelope to make a template.**

2. **Cut a matching shape from a calendar page.**

3. **Fold in and glue the side and bottom flaps.**

4. **To address the envelope, use white self-adhesive labels.**

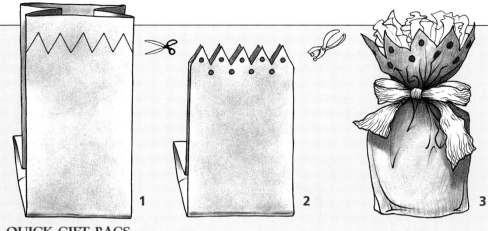

QUICK GIFT BAGS

Arianne Arreglado, of Long Island City, New York, turns plain brown lunch bags into gift packaging.

1. **Mark and cut the bag's open end in a zigzag pattern.**

2. **Make holes along the cut edge using a paper punch.**

3. **Complete the gift package with colored tissue and a raffia bow.**

PERFECT BUTTONS

Self-covered buttons look more professional when you use embroidery fabric spray, writes Mary Foley, of Larkspur, California. Spray the fabric circle for smooth, pucker-free adhesion to the pronged disk.

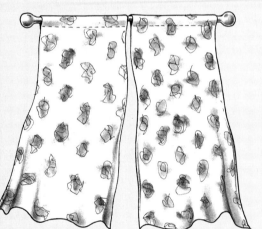
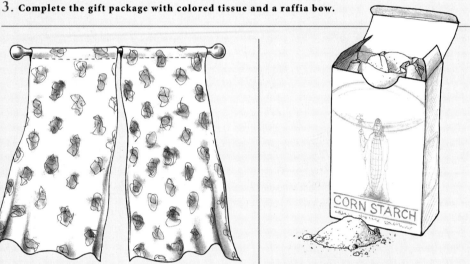
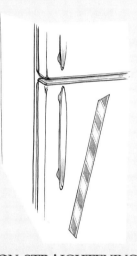

UPDATING SHEER CURTAINS

To revive old sheer curtains, try painting them. Lay the panels flat and apply acrylic craft paint with a sponge in a freeform design. Choose colors to match your updated decor. This tip comes from Debi Zukowski, of East Longmeadow, Massachusetts.

DECOUPAGE TIP

At the start of decoupage projects, Ilene Goldman, of Baltimore, Maryland, coats her hands with cornstarch. She finds that the powdery layer helps her fingers to retain their flexibility even when they become caked with glue.

RIBBON STRAIGHTENING

You don't need an iron to straighten a crinkled ribbon, writes Eileen Snell, of Pawley Island, South Carolina. Just wet the ribbon and stick it flat against a refrigerator or washing machine. It will dry smooth and flat overnight.

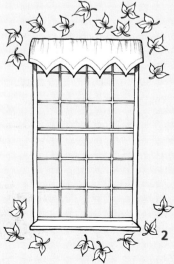

EASY WALL DESIGNS

Dale Craghead, of Park City, Utah, creates unique wall treatments using purchased wallpaper borders.

1. **Cut individual motifs from the border.**

2. **Paste the motifs around window and door openings, creating your own design.**

CONTROLLING STATIC

The effects of static electricity—foam peanuts that "dance," plastic vinyl that "purrs"—can make some projects difficult to tackle. To neutralize materials and tools that get overcharged, Samantha Riggert, of Portland, Oregon rubs them with an antistatic dryer sheet.

Quick Home Accents

Extend your home decorations beyond the table.

CHANDELIER DRESSINGS

COLOR PHOTOGRAPHY:
Carl Tremblay

DESIGN:
Dawn Anderson

STYLING:
Ritch Holben

For a lavish accent, we wrapped this chandelier in sheer organdy and suspended crystal beads from it to create an eye-catching focal point for any room.

To start, measure for fabric by interweaving a tape measure around each chandelier arm, suspending it loosely between adjacent arms. Double this measurement. Next, record the length from the cradle of one arm to the top, spiraling up (as shown), and add the two numbers together. Multiply by 45 percent, then add this number to the previous total and divide by two for the required fabric yardage.

Trim away selvages and cut the fabric in half lengthwise. Join the two strips in a French seam along the short sides. Hem the unfinished sides. To shrink and "texturize" the fabric, fill your washing machine with cold water, immerse the strip, and set on a gentle cycle for 2½ to 3 minutes. When finished, roll the strip in a towel to remove the excess water, and dry on medium heat. Press lightly with an iron to smooth the crinkles. Wrap the fabric loosely around the chandelier arms, similar to the pattern followed for measuring.

For the beaded accents, form a hook at the top of a short length 16-gauge brass wire using round-nose pliers. Trim the wire 1½" from hook and place bead onto wire. Form a loop under bead. Attach icicle beads or crystals to loop and hang from chandelier arms. As the finishing touch, suspend a gold chain by hooks across the chandelier. ◆

The Perfect Gift

Create a personalized calendar using your favorite photos and memory-album supplies.

COLOR COPY CALENDAR

Nowadays, most copying centers can make a calendar using twelve of your favorite photographs for about $20. It's more fun, however, to make your own using those same photos, a color copy machine, and a few memory-album supplies.

To make this calendar, we started by purchasing a 1998 calendar for the monthly pages. Although this is the easiest option, it's also possible to make your own monthly pages using a computer, or to draw your own pages. Next, we created images for each month using photos, colored paper, giftwrap, deckle-edge scissors, and memory album background paper. Glue or tape together the image and its month. If the calendar features captions, you can cover these with your own captions handwritten or typed on white labels, small secondary photos, or decorative stickers. Add birthdays, anniversaries and other special occasions to the individual days on the calendar using colored markers or rubber stamps.

Once the calendar is complete, find a copy shop with a color copy machine. Since prices for color copies vary consid-erably, shop around. (In the Boston area alone, prices quoted range from $1.50 to $4.00 per page.) After you copy and assemble the pages, trim them if neces-sary, and bind them together using one of the following methods: staple the pages at the center and fold the pages up each time you turn the month; spiral-bind the pages together; or use rivets and string the calendar pages together with ribbon or yarn. As a finishing step, decorate the individual days on the cal-endar with stickers, rubber-stamped images, or personalized messages. ◆

COLOR PHOTOGRAPHY:
Carl Tremblay

STYLING:
Ritch Holben

DESIGN:
Barbara Bourassa

Elegant Embossed Platter

Recreate the look of Chinese lacquerware using a leatherwork tool, paint, and crackle medium.

☙ BY DAWN ANDERSON

Display this stunning platter on a glass table or shelf, or let it bring simple elegance to your table setting as a centerpiece.

COLOR PHOTOGRAPHY:
Carl Tremblay

ILLUSTRATION:
Judy Love

STYLING:
Ritch Holben

I LOVE TO EXPERIMENT WITH NEW, inexpensive ways to reproduce classic designs from other regions of the world. Here, I found a way of recreating the look of Chinese lacquerware using items I already had in my home. Using a simple but unusual technique of stamping soft wood with a leatherwork tool, and decorating it with acrylic paints and crackle activator, I designed a platter that is useful, decorative, and faithful to an historic original.

You will find it easy to emboss the soft wood using several light taps of the hammer on a leatherworking tool whose end has a designed stamp. Pounding too hard may cause the wood grain to crack. To make a deeper impression, realign the stamp and tap with the hammer a couple of times.

Dawn Anderson, a writer and designer, lives in Redmond, Washington.

INSTRUCTIONS

1. *Mark platter for embossing.* Sand platter with 220-grit sandpaper. Wipe off dust with lightly misted paper towel. Using 1" flat brush, apply primer to platter front and back; let dry 30 minutes. To locate center of platter, set compass point at approximate center and adjust the pencil arm so pencil point touches platter lip. Rotate compass, testing to see if pencil point touches platter lip consistently all around. Adjust compass point as needed until you locate center. Using compass, draft one circle ⅛" beyond lip and a second circle ¼" inside outer rim (*see illustration A, next page*).

2. *Emboss platter lip.* Set Craftool stamp on lip circle. Using hammer, tap stamp three or four times to make scalloped impression in wood. Lift stamp, reposition it next to impression just made, and tap three or four times to make second impression. Repeat this process to emboss scalloped design on lip circle all around. As you near starting point, estimate the number of additional scallops needed to complete design. Adjust spacing as necessary on the last three or four impressions so design comes out even (illustration B).

3. *Emboss center medallion.* Tape metal button face down to center of platter. Tap button with hammer to impress wood. Untape and remove button. Center brass ring on platter, tape it down, and tap with hammer to make ring impression. Untape and remove ring. Using Craftool stamp, stamp scalloped motif six times around ring impression to complete center medallion (illustration C).

4. *Paint platter rim and back gold.* Protect work surface with newsprint.

MATERIALS

- **11½" round basswood platter**
- **2 ounces Delta Ceramcoat Tompte Red acrylic paint**
- **2 ounces DecoArt Dazzling Metallics, Glorious Gold acrylic paint**
- **Aleene's Mosaic Crackle Medium and Activator**
- **Aleene's All-purpose Primer**
- **Formby's Gold Leaf Pen**

You'll also need:
Craftool stamp #D438; metal button with raised design; ⅝" brass drapery ring; hammer; compass; ⅛", ⅜", and 1" flat brushes; 1" foam brush; paint palette or plastic lid; 220-grit sandpaper; newsprint; paper towels; spray mister; and transparent tape.

Embossing the Platter

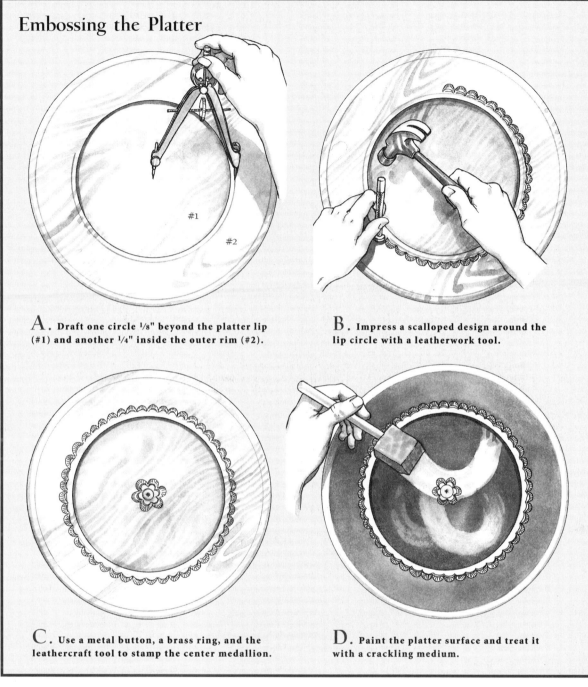

A. Draft one circle ⅛" beyond the platter lip (#1) and another ¼" inside the outer rim (#2).

B. Impress a scalloped design around the lip circle with a leatherwork tool.

C. Use a metal button, a brass ring, and the leathercraft tool to stamp the center medallion.

D. Paint the platter surface and treat it with a crackling medium.

DESIGNER'S TIP

It's easy to experiment with variations of this technique: stencil Greek Key or laurel leaf designs on the borders after embossing the inner lip of the platter. Or use alternative tools such as nails, screws, snaps, chains, zipper teeth, or the tip of a screwdriver to dent the wood in symmetrical patterns.

DESIGNER'S TIP

Be sure to allow crackle medium, paint, and crackle activator to dry thoroughly between coats or you may end up with a milky finish on your platter.

Using ⅜" flat brush, apply gold paint to outer edge and rim of platter, stopping at marked circle. Let dry 20 minutes. Using 1" flat brush, paint underside of platter gold. Let dry 30 minutes.

5. *Paint platter interior red.* Using 1" flat brush, apply red paint to platter interior bordered by gold rim; apply paint sparingly to embossed areas so they do not become caked with paint. Let dry 20 minutes. Paint a second red coat. Let dry 1 hour. In plastic palette, mix 1 part Mosaic Crackle Medium and 2 parts red paint. Using 1" flat brush, apply heavy coat of this mixture to red areas of platter. Move brush in a circu-

lar motion, following gold rim; do not paint with wood grain. Let dry overnight. Sand platter lightly and wipe off dust. Using 1" flat brush, apply one more coat of red paint over previously painted red areas, using light touch over embossed areas.

6. *Paint embossed designs.* Using ⅛" flat brush, apply gold paint to embossed border around platter lip. Brush paint even with outer edge of embossing and past penciled circle to inner edge of lip. Let dry 20 minutes. Paint center medallion in same way; let dry. Repeat steps 4 and 6 one more time, giving all gold areas a second coat. Let dry 1 hour.

7. *Complete crackling process.* Set Craftool stamp over previously stamped image, aligning crescent shape. Tilt stamp back slightly, then tap two or three times with hammer to deepen embossed image and bring out fine lines. Touch up gold paint, if necessary. Using foam brush, apply thin coat of Crackle Activator to red areas; brush in a circular motion, as in step 5 (illustration D). Let dry at least 4 hours, but preferably overnight; crackling will begin about 30 minutes after application and will continue as activator dries. Draw over embossed areas with gold leaf pen to bring out highlights. ◆

Flower Appliqué Place Mat and Napkin Ring

Quick-stitch a flower, stem, and leaf to a plain linen place mat, then slip in a rolled napkin.

✒ BY DAWN ANDERSON

This decorated, all-in-one place mat and napkin ring is reminiscent of the graphic florals of the '70s.

COLOR PHOTOGRAPHY:
Carl Tremblay

ILLUSTRATION:
Mary Newell DePalma

STYLING:
Ritch Holben

T HIS UNIQUE DESIGN KILLS TWO birds with one stone: the linen flower, leaf, and stem dress up an otherwise plain white place mat, and the stem loops around to create a built-in napkin ring.

To get started, you'll need 1⅞ yards of green linen for the stem and leaf, ⅜ yard of orchid linen for the flower, and ¼ yard of fusible tricot interfacing. Each of the pieces is sewn separately, then attached to the place mat during the final assembly.

For variation on this design, you can sew a button in the flower, then sew and button on flowers or other designs for dif-ferent holidays. Consider a poinsettia for Christmas, a bright yellow sun for summer picnics, or a white rose for bridal showers. The design could also be changed slightly to accommodate a valentine heart with an arrow through it for Valentine's Day, or a pair of baby booties or miniature sweater for baby showers. You could also change the fabric to suit the occasion: dressier fabrics for more formal settings, fun and lighthearted fabrics for more casual occasions.

Dawn Anderson is a writer and designer in Redmond, Washington.

MATERIALS
Yields four place mats with napkins

- **Four white linen hemstitched place mats**
- **1⅞ yards 45"-wide green linen**
- **⅜ yard 45"-wide orchid linen**
- **¼ yard 60"-wide fusible tricot interfacing**
- **Four 1" white shank buttons**
- **Sewing thread to match fabrics**

You'll also need:
flower and leaf patterns (*see* page 44); sewing machine; sewing shears; rotary cutter; quilter's acrylic grid ruler; self-healing cutting mat; iron; pins; seam ripper; point turner; chopstick; paper; pencil; tracing paper; scissors; and hand-sewing needle.

INSTRUCTIONS

1. *Prepare patterns.* Enlarge and trace flower and leaf patterns (*see* page 44). Cut out traced patterns with scissors.

2. *Cut fabrics.* Using rotary cutter, quilter's acrylic grid ruler, and cutting mat, cut four 21" squares, four 5" squares, eight 2¾" x 5" rectangles, and four 1¾" x 24" bias strips, from green linen (*see* cutting layout, page 44). From orchid linen, cut four 7" squares and eight 3¾" x 7" rectangles. From tricot interfacing, cut four 5" squares and four 7" squares. Following manufacturer's instructions, fuse interfacing squares to wrong side of same-size linen squares.

3. *Join linen rectangles.* Pin two orchid rectangles right sides together. Set machine for regular stitch length. Making a ¼" seam, machine-stitch along one 7" edge for 1½", then backtack. Change to longest stitch and machine-baste for 4". Change to regular stitch length, backtack, and stitch remaining 1½" to end (*see* illustration A, next page). Press seam open. Repeat process to join remaining orchid rectangles in pairs. Use same method to join green rectangles along 5" edges: sew for 1½", machine-baste for 2", then sew remaining 1½".

4. *Sew four orchid flowers.* Lay orchid square flat, right side up. Place seamed orchid piece on top, right side down. Position flower pattern on top so seam runs through flower center and two petals, then pin through all layers.

Set machine for closely spaced stitches. Machine-stitch around flower outline (illustration B). Remove pattern. Stitch again over previous stitching. Using scissors, clip to stitching between each flower petal, and trim fabric ⅛" from stitching around each petal. Using seam ripper, pick out machine basting along straight seam (illustration C). Turn flower right side out through opened seam, using rounded end of point turner to push out and shape petals. Steam-press. Hand-sew opening closed (illustration D). Repeat process to make four flowers total.

5. *Sew four green leaves.* Lay green square flat, right side up. Lay seamed green piece on top, right side down. Position leaf pattern on top diagonally, observing grain line and with seam running through leaf center. Stitch as for

flower, step 4. Clip across points, trim seam to ⅛", and turn right side out. Finish leaf as for flower (illustration E). Make four leaves total.

6. *Sew four green stems.* Fold green bias strip in half lengthwise, right side in. Machine-stitch down long edge and across one short edge, making ⅜" seam. Clip corners diagonally. Turn tube right side out using chopstick. Roll seam between index finger and thumb to smooth out bulk, and press well. Insert pin 6" from closed end. Beginning and ending at pin, edge-stitch down one side, across end, and up other side (illustration F). Repeat process to sew four green stems total.

7. *Assemble place mats.* Lay place mat right side up. From lower left corner, measure 2½" to right and 4¾" up; mark with pin. Set stem pin on this spot

and pin to secure. From upper right corner, measure 2¾" to left and 1¾" down; turn raw stem end under ¼" and pin it to this spot. Curve stem across place mat to take up slack, press well, and pin down. Topstitch stem to place mat along both long curving edges (illustration G). To make napkin ring, shape free end of stem into self loop and stitch down at first pin through all layers. Hand-tack flower to upper stem and leaf to napkin ring. Sew button to center of flower (illustration H). Repeat process for each place mat.

8. *Complete napkins.* Machine-stitch a scant ¼" from edge of napkin all around. Press edge ¼" to wrong side just beyond stitching line. Fold each edge ¼" to wrong side again, and topstitch. Repeat process to narrow-hem four napkins total. Insert each napkin into stem loop. ◆

PATTERNS

See page 44 for pattern pieces.

Making the Place Mat

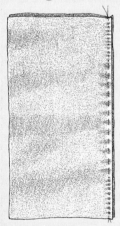

A. Sew the orchid rectangles in pairs, basting the seam in the middle.

B. To sew each orchid flower, stitch along the pattern outline.

C. Trim away the excess fabric, and open the basting stitches.

D. Turn the flower right side out, press, and stitch the opening closed.

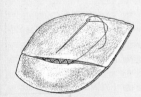

E. Follow the same method to sew each leaf.

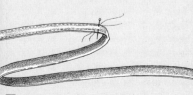

F. Make a bias tube. Edgestitch 6 inches at one end.

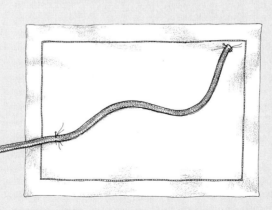

G. Position the tube on the place mat and topstitch the edges.

H. Loop the free end to make the napkin ring. Tack on the flower and the leaf.

Cutout Stencil Valentine Card

Cut a stencil in watercolor paper and glue colored scraps behind it for a multilayered valentine.

☙ BY ELIZABETH CAMERON

MATERIALS

- 5" x 7" ecru watercolor card
- 7" x 10" sheet of moss green stationery
- Scraps of red, blue, brown, and yellow paper

You'll also need:
teacup pattern (*see* page 45); X-Acto knife; self-healing cutting mat; quilter's acrylic grid ruler; glue stick; tracing paper; ballpoint pen; sharp #1 pencil; removable tape; and manicure scissors

Instead of colored paper scraps, try using textured paper or cloth behind the stencil. Accent your card with bits of felt, velvet, or fine silk left over from other projects.

COLOR PHOTOGRAPHY:
Carl Tremblay

ILLUSTRATION:
Mary Newell DePalma

STYLING:
Ritch Holben

Handmade cards, especially valentines, are wonderful alternatives to mass-produced greeting cards. For a fun design, start with a blank card made from watercolor paper (sold in art supply and craft stores). Instead of painting the card, cut a stencil in the card front, then glue different colored papers behind the cutouts to fill in the different sections of the design. For the liner, select a sheet of colored stationery so you can write a message or note inside. (Other papers might cause the ink to bleed, but stationery will not.)

This handsome valentine card is surprisingly simple if you follow these sure-fire directions. Use the traced pattern as a cutting guide (for both the card front and the bits of color) to avoid guesswork, and cut the design from inside the card to guarantee a crisp silhouette.

You'll find the process so easy, and the results so pleasing, that you'll be tempted to create your own innovative patterns for a whole series of personalized cards.

Elizabeth Cameron is a freelance writer in Brighton, Massachusetts.

INSTRUCTIONS

1. *Transfer teacup motif.* Using #1 pencil, trace entire teacup pattern onto tracing paper, including dash lines (*see* page 45). Open card flat on cutting mat. Turn tracing over. Using guidelines and ruler, center it on the inside front cover. Secure it with removable tape (*see* illustration A, next page). To transfer motif, press firmly with ballpoint pen to trace solid lines. Remove tracing and set aside.

2. *Cut out teacup motif.* Using X-Acto knife and cutting mat, cut teacup stencil on marked lines in the following order: hearts, rising steam, saucer, teacup (illustration B). For smooth cuts, press firmly and do not lift knife blade from surface until you reach end of cut. To cut deep curves, hold knife steady and rotate card. Set teacup cutout aside.

3. *Glue liner to card.* Using grid ruler, X-Acto knife, and cutting mat, trim moss green stationery to measure 6⅞" x 9 ⅞", or slightly smaller than open card. Fold liner in half, and test-fit it inside folded card (illustration C). To glue liner to card, open card flat, run glue stick on inside front cover along spine, slip liner in place, and press to adhere. The green liner will show through the stencil cutouts on the card front.

4. *Cut color blocks and ovals.* Place teacup tracing facedown on scrap of blue paper. Trace dashed outline for blue color block only. Referring to color key, repeat process to transfer yellow color block to yellow paper, red color block to red paper, large oval to brown paper, and small oval to ecru teacup cutout reserved in step 2. Cut out all pieces using manicure scissors (illustration D).

5. *Glue down color blocks and ovals.* Slip blue color block between green liner and card front so blue shows through saucer cutout, with no overlaps or protruding edges. Trim color block if necessary, then glue in position to green liner. Repeat process for red and yellow (illustration E). Referring to pattern, glue brown and ecru ovals to green teacup. To finish card, glue liner to inside front cover along outside edge (illustration F). ◆

Making the Valentine Card

A. Tape the tracing facedown to the inside cover. Transfer the design.

B. Cut the stencil on the marked lines, smallest shapes first.

C. Make a green folded liner to fit inside the card.

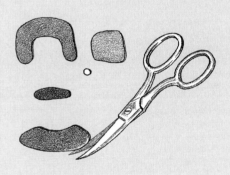

D. Cut blue, red, and yellow color blocks, and brown and ecru ovals.

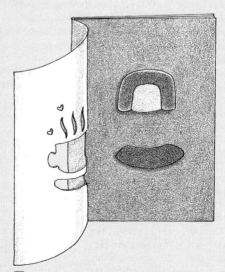

E. Glue the color blocks to the liner so they will peek through the stencil.

F. Glue the ovals to the teacup, then glue the cover and liner edges together.

DESIGNER'S TIP

Use cutouts to make a coordinating envelope. Match the envelope color to one of the card's color blocks, then cut tiny hearts on the envelope flap through both layers. The ecru card will show through the colored envelope wherever you've embellished it with heart cutouts.

PATTERNS

See page 45 for pattern pieces and enlargement instructions.

DESIGNER'S TIP

For a variation on this design, make patternless cutout cards featuring simple geometric shapes. Jazz up the presentation by using patterned and/or textured papers behind the simpler shapes. You could even create an antique quilt replica using small squares of patterned papers.

Beaded Butterflies

Use a simple thread-and-twist technique to make these sparkling accents for gift boxes, cards, and tags.

❧ BY NANCY OVERTON

Multiples of this butterfly are easy to make. To sort different sizes and colors of beads, use a cupcake tin or an ice cube tray.

COLOR PHOTOGRAPHY:
Carl Tremblay

ILLUSTRATION:
Mary Newell DePalma

STYLING:
Ritch Holben

THESE ELEGANT BEADED BUTTER-flies are so easy to make, you may want to use them all over your home. The design possibilities are endless: You can make the butterflies in any size, using any type of beads—from expensive crystal to plastic. In addition to decorating gift packages, use these beaded garden beauties on napkin rings, wreaths, or lamps, or as pins, ornaments, or party favors.

Nancy Overton of Oakland, California has designed and written about crafts for more than twenty years.

INSTRUCTIONS

1. *Make antennae and head.* Measure and cut one 12" length of wire. Using round-nose pliers, make a tiny loop at one end of wire. Thread three 3mm beads on wire and slide snug against loop. Cut second 12" wire and repeat process. Thread both antennae wires through one 8mm bead to form head. Bend both wires up at right angle to hold beads snug (*see* illustration A, above.)

2. *Make upper wings.* Thread eighteen 4mm beads (about 2¾") onto one wire. Form beaded section into a loop and secure by twisting once at base of head.

Repeat process for second wire (illustration B).

3. *Make lower wings.* Thread both wires through one 6mm bead for body. Bend both wires up at right angle to hold beads snug. Thread twelve 4mm beads (about 1¾") onto one wire. Form beaded section into a loop and secure by twisting once at base of body. Repeat process for second wire (illustration C).

4. *Complete body.* Thread both wires through two remaining 6mm beads until snug. Clip wires ½" beyond last bead. Using roundnose pliers, loop both ends to hold beads snug. ◆

MATERIALS
Yields one butterfly

- **Six 3mm faceted beads (for antennae)**
- **One 8mm bead (for head)**
- **Sixty 4mm faceted beads (for wings)**
- **Three 6mm faceted beads (for body)**
- **Two 12" lengths of 28-gauge wire**

You'll also need:
needlenose pliers; roundnose pliers; wire cutters; and ruler.

Beading the Butterfly

A. Make each antenna on a separate wire

B. Bead and loop each wire to form the upper wings.

C. Make the lower wings the same way

D. Run both wires through two large beads to complete the body.

Pyramid-Shaped Pillows

Sew these novelty, plush velvet pillows in less than an hour.

❧ BY DAWN ANDERSON

COLOR PHOTOGRAPHY:
Carl Tremblay

ILLUSTRATION:
Judy Love

STYLING:
Ritch Holben

LOOKING FOR A UNIQUE AND STYL-ish pillow for your bed or sofa? This pyramid-shaped pillow, made here from rich colors of cotton velveteen, works up quickly and easily.

The form I selected, which measures 14", is filled with feathers and down for especially sumptous loft. Pyramid forms are available in many sizes, from 14" to 34" (*see* Sources & Resources, page 48).

For finishing touches, consider adding tassels at each corner, embroidered crests and patches, or designer buttons. You can also enclose trims such as moss fringe in the seams.

Dawn Anderson is a writer and designer in Redmond, Washington.

INSTRUCTIONS

1. *Cut four velveteen triangles.* Lay velveteen fabric right side up on cutting mat. Determine fabric nap direction, then pin pattern to fabric to correspond. Cut out triangle using rotary cutter and acrylic grid ruler; mark XX edge with pin. Repeat process to cut three triangles total for pillow sides. Cut a fourth triangle in same way, except turn pattern 180 degrees so nap runs in opposite direction from arrow; mark XX edge with pin. Set fourth triangle (with nap running in opposite direction) aside for pillow base.

2. *Sew three pillow sides.* Place two "side" triangles right sides together and edges matching. Machine-stitch from X to Y along one edge only, backtacking at beginning and end (*see* illustration A). Flip top triangle back on itself to expose triangle underneath. Place third side triangle on exposed edge, right sides together and stitch from X to Y as before. Finally, sew two remaining free edges together from X to Y. Press seams open.

3. *Join pillow base.* Align XX edge of pillow base and one pillow side, right sides together. Stitch from X to X, backtacking at beginning and end. Pin one XY base edge to XX side edge, then stitch between dots on pattern, easing to fit. To join final edges, pin them right sides together, then stitch from each dot for 1½", backtacking at beginning and end; leave 11" middle section open for turning (illustration B). Press seams open.

4. *Enclose pillow form in cover.* Using scissors, clip off points of pillow cover diagonally at corners. Trim all seam allowances (except at opening) to ¼"; taper to ⅛" near points. Turn right side out and poke out points with point turner. Compress pillow form, insert into cover, and adjust fit at points. Pin opening closed, then slipstitch with matching thread (illustration C). ◆

For variation, make each side from coordinating shades of velvet.

MATERIALS
Yields one 12"-high pillow

- ½ yard 45"-wide cotton velveteen
- 14" three-dimensional triangle pillow form
- Matching thread

You'll also need:
triangle pattern (*see* page 45); sewing machine; iron; rotary cutter; quilter's acrylic grid ruler; self-healing cutting mat; scissors; hand-sewing needle; pins; and point turner.

PATTERNS
See page 45 for pattern pieces and enlargement instructions.

Sewing the Pillow

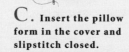

A. Join three triangles along the XY edges.

B. Join the base triangle, leaving an opening for turning.

C. Insert the pillow form in the cover and slipstitch closed.

Handpainted Wooden Poppy Bowl in Five Easy Steps

Turn a wooden bowl into a work of art with our Georgia O'Keeffe-style design.

≈ BY ESTHER KATZ

Once sealed, the poppy bowl is food-safe and can be used for tossed salads, fruit, popcorn, or other snacks. To clean the bowl, sponge it with warm soapy water, rinse, and dry immediately with a soft, absorbent cloth or paper towel.

COLOR PHOTOGRAPHY:
Carl Tremblay

ILLUSTRATION:
Mary Newell DePalma

STYLING:
Ritch Holben

PURCHASED IN A CRAFT GALLERY, a handpainted wooden salad bowl such as this one might cost upwards of $100. You can make your own, however, using a very easy and forgiving painting process.

The bowl's design, which features a large, loosely defined poppy blossom, makes the process simple. For starters, you only need two colors of acrylic craft paint: red and black. Second, the pattern provided on page 46 gives you the general petal shape as a guide; you can paint in and around the marked areas according to your own style. Creating the definition on the petals, which may appear difficult, is as easy as loading a brush with black paint, then stroking softly upwards along the petals. Finally, the bowl is sealed with water-based polyurethane.

Esther Katz is a landscape painter, decorative painter, and illustrator living in the Catskills.

MATERIALS

- **14"-15" unfinished wooden salad bowl**
- **2 ounces red acrylic craft paint**
- **2 ounces black acrylic craft paint**
- **Water-based satin polyurethane**

You'll also need:
poppy flower tracing paper pattern (see page 46); scissors; red chalk; 1" flat sabeline brush; ¼" round sabeline brush; 2" to 3" flat soft bristle brush; finest (#0000) steel wool; watercolor palette; paper towel; and 1-quart round plastic container.

INSTRUCTIONS

1. *Mark poppy pattern on bowl.* Using scissors, cut out poppy pattern on solid petal outlines, then cut five dash lines dividing petals. Center pattern on inside bottom of bowl; overlap petals to accommodate curves and let some petals extend onto bowl rim. Using chalk, trace poppy outline (*see* illustration A, next page). Remove pattern. Refine chalk lines as needed to show five distinct petals. Referring to pattern, sketch in additional dash lines.

2. *Paint red poppy design.* Transfer small amount red paint to palette and thin with water for creamy, not runny, consistency. Using 1" to 2" flat sabeline brush, paint each petal from outside edge down into center of flower (illustration B). Blot any paint that pools in center with paper towel. Let dry 20 minutes. Repeat process for three coats total, or until coverage is opaque.

3. *Paint black background.* Transfer small amount black paint to palette and thin with water until creamy. Using 1" flat brush and/or ¼" round brush and referring to dash lines on pattern, draw wet brush down into red petals in loose, easy motion to suggest crinkling. Paint rim and edge of bowl black, refining edges of flower petals as you go (illustration C). Let dry 20 minutes. Repeat process for three coats total, or until coverage is opaque.

4. *Paint center of poppy.* Transfer small amount thinned black paint to

Painting the Poppy Design

A. Fit the tracing pattern inside the bowl and outline with chalk.

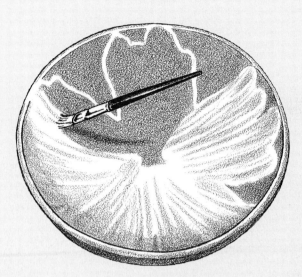

B. Paint the poppy portion of the design using red acrylic craft paint.

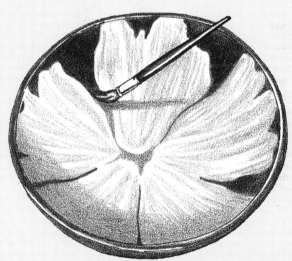

C. Paint the rim and background black, defining the petals as you go.

D. Draw black paint up from the center for realistic detailing.

center of bowl to make 1"-diameter pool. Using round brush, draw wet paint out from pool so edges are irregular. To further define the five petals, hold brush loosely, with bristles just barely touching surface, and draw brush up in jagged, irregular motion between petals (illustration D). Let dry at least 1 hour.

5. *Paint bowl underside and seal bowl.* Turn 1-quart container upside down; prop inverted bowl on top, so rim is elevated off surface. Using 1" flat brush, apply one coat black paint to bowl underside. Let dry 20 min-

utes. Repeat process for three coats total, or until coverage is opaque. Let dry overnight. To apply water-based satin polyurethane sealer, turn bowl right side up. Using 2" to 3" soft-bristled brush, apply thin coat of polyurethane sealer to rim and inside of bowl. Let dry 1 hour. Sand lightly with steel wool, and wipe out residue with paper towel. Repeat sealing and sanding process for three coats total. When inside of bowl is thoroughly dry, prop bowl upside down on plastic container and repeat process to seal underside. Let dry overnight. ◆

HISTORICAL TIDBIT

Georgia O'Keeffe (1887-1986), one of America's most popular artists, still captures the imagination of art lovers with her vivid colors and dramatically enlarged details. Her famous modernist paintings of desert skulls and fantasy flowers adorn the walls of the new Georgia O'Keeffe Museum, in Santa Fe, New Mexico. O'Keeffe said of her work, "I have things in my head that are not like what anyone has taught me... shapes and ideas so near to me."

PATTERNS

See page 46 for pattern pieces and enlargement instructions.

Padded Scented Hanger

Dress up your plain wooden hangers in ten simple steps.
Make these no-slip hangers in sets of three for a distinctive gift.

❧ BY DAWN ANDERSON

Consider gingham checks and tiny prints for the nursery, silk dupioni, velvet, or satin for evening gowns and lingerie.

PADDED HANGERS ADD A DISTINC-tive yet practical touch to any closet. In addition to bringing elegance to your wardrobe, they keep delicate garments from puckering at the shoulders when they are hung.

This classically designed padded hanger is so easy to assemble that you may want to make a set of three at once. All you need for each one is a wooden dress hanger, fabric and matching ribbon, cotton batting for the stuffing, and an herbal scented mixture. After cutting fabric pieces from a pattern that you make yourself, prepare scented strips of batting to pad the hanger. To assemble the pieces, you just glue and sew. For a creative touch, hang two scented strawberries from the hook.

I filled my hanger with an herbal moth repellent mixture (including cedar chips, rosemary, southernwood, lavender, and cardamom seed), but you can substitute dried lavender or use a tiny drop of essential oil to scent yours.

Dawn Anderson is a writer and designer in Redmond, Washington.

MATERIALS
Yields one hanger

- **Wooden dress hanger with screw-in hook**
- **2 cups mixed herbal ingredients**
- **1/2 yard 45"-wide checked fabric**
- **1/8 yard 45"-wide pindot fabric**
- **1/4 yard 45"-wide fleece**
- **12" x 45" piece of cotton batting**
- **1 1/4 yards 1/4"-wide ribbon**
- **Six 1"-long velvet leaves**
- **Sewing thread to match fabrics**
- **Upholstery thread**
- **Double-sided tape**
- **White craft glue**

You'll also need:
strawberry pattern (*see* page 45); sewing machine; iron; sewing shears; scissors; hand-sewing needle; pins; tracing paper; ruler; and pencil.

INSTRUCTIONS
Getting Started

1. *Prepare patterns.* Trace strawberry pattern (*see* page 45). To make custom hanger pattern, lay wooden hanger flat on tracing paper, and trace around wooden portion with pencil. Draft new line 1" beyond traced line, rounding off corners slightly (*see* illustration A, next page).

2. *Cut fabric and batting.* Fold checked fabric on bias. Place hanger pattern parallel to folded edge and pin (illustration B). Using scissors, cut along pattern outline through both layers. Also cut two hangers from fleece for the lining. Using strawberry pattern, cut four strawberries from pindot fabric and four from batting.

3. *Prepare scented batting strips.* Cut three 3" x 45" strips from batting. Split one strip into two plies by separating and peeling back the top layer. Sift through herbal mixture with your fingers, and discard any large or hard ingredients. Sprinkle half onto bottom ply of batting, then replace top layer to cover it (illustration C). Repeat process to layer remaining mixture inside second batting strip. Leave third strip as it is.

Covering the Hanger

1. *Glue ribbon to hanger hook.* Cut 12" length from ribbon and set it aside. Apply glue to tip of hook. Fold end of remaining ribbon yardage over tip, then wrap ribbon once around tip, concealing ribbon end. Apply glue to next 1/2" section of hook and wrap ribbon around it. Continue gluing and wrapping in 1/2" intervals (illustration D). When you reach wooden portion of hanger, trim ribbon 1/2" beyond hook and glue down.

2. *Pad hanger.* Affix double-sided tape

to front and back of wooden hanger. Starting at one end, wind one scented batting strip around hanger in a spiral wrap. When you reach middle of hanger, clip strip to accommodate hook and continue spiraling (illustration E). When you reach end, trim off and save excess strip. Wrap second scented strip over first strip. Finish padding hanger by wrapping plain strip around it.

3. *Sew hanger cover.* Lay one fleece hanger piece flat. Place checked hanger piece on top, right side up. Baste ¼" from raw edges all around through both layers. Repeat process to layer and baste second fleece/checked hanger pair. Place both pairs fabric sides together and pin. Beginning at one end, machine-stitch curved ends and long underside curve ¼" from edges (illustration F). Clip curves; turn right side out.

4. *Fit cover on hanger.* Stuff small wad of excess batting into each curved end of cover until firm. Insert hanger into cover through open top; fit should be snug but not tight. To increase padding, cut new 3" x 45" strip from batting, separate plies, and wrap one more ply around hanger, as in previous step. To decrease padding, remove final batting strip, separate plies, and rewrap hanger with one ply only. To finish upper seam, fold one edge under 1/4", lap it over other edge, and slipstitch closed; make firm stitches at base of hook (illustration G). Steampress seams.

Making the Strawberries

1. *Sew strawberries.* Lay one batting strawberry flat. Place pindot strawberry on top, right side up, and baste ¼" from raw edges all around. Repeat process for four strawberry shapes (two for each strawberry). Pin two strawberries fabric sides together, and machine-stitch between dots (illustration H). Clip curves; turn right side out. Repeat process for remaining pair of strawberries.

2. *Stuff strawberries.* Place one end of 12" ribbon even with top edge of strawberry, and machine-tack in place. Using upholstery thread, hand-sew gathering stitches ¼" from upper edge all around (illustration I). Stuff strawberry with leftover scented batting, then pull thread ends to cinch opening as tightly as possible. Using eraser end of pencil, push additional batting into cavity until strawberry is firm. Stitch securely, retacking ribbon if necessary (illustration J). Join second strawberry to opposite end of ribbon, gather edge by hand, and stuff it in same way.

3. *Glue leaves to strawberries.* Using scissors, trim stem end of six leaves at a 60-degree angle. Using white craft glue, affix three leaves to top of each strawberry, butting angled edges (illustration K). Allow outer edges near leaf tips to curl up for a natural look. To join strawberries to hanger, wind ribbon a few times around base of hook. ◆

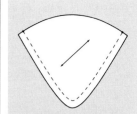

PATTERNS

See page 45 for pattern pieces and enlargement instructions.

Getting Started

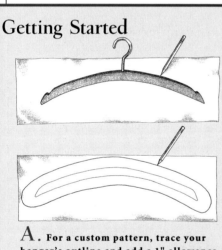

A. **For a custom pattern, trace your hanger's outline and add a 1" allowance all around.**

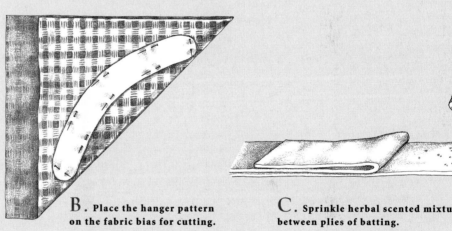

B. **Place the hanger pattern on the fabric bias for cutting.**

C. **Sprinkle herbal scented mixture between plies of batting.**

Covering the Hanger

D. **Wrap narrow ribbon around the hanger hook, gluing as you go.**

E. **Pad the hanger with the scented batting.**

F. **To make the cover, sew two fleece-lined pieces together.**

G. **Turn the cover right side out, fit the hanger inside, and stitch the open edge.**

Making the Strawberries

H. **Sew two fleece-lined strawberry pieces together to make a pocket.**

I. **Turn the pocket, tack on ribbon, and hand-gather the edge.**

J. **Stuff the strawberry and gather the edge closed.**

K. **Glue velvet leaves to the top to conceal the puckering.**

Mosaic Tile Candle Shades

Assemble these glowing pillar and hurricane candle shades using glass tiles, epoxy, and ordinary tile grout.

🍂 BY MICHIO RYAN

This mosaic technique works well with a variety of glass containers, such as cube-shaped votive candle holders, florists' vases, devotional candles, or jelly jars. The surface should be smooth and free of ridges.

MATERIALS

Pillar candle
- 3½"-diameter x 7"-high glass pillar

Hurricane shade
- 5½"-diameter x 14" glass hurricane shade

Other materials
- 1½ square feet of cathedral glass (assorted colors)
- 5-minute epoxy
- 8 ounces ready-mixed grout
- 1½-oz. tube "New Rose" Tints-All

You'll also need:
glass cutter; kerosene; diamond rasp or grinding stone; heavy canvas or rubber gloves; goggles; small dish; cotton balls; single-edged razor blade; flat, wide stiff-bristled brush; steel ruler with cork back; plastic grid ruler; 8" x 10" sheet of graph paper; fine-point permanent marker; pencil; paper plate; disposable plastic lid; toothpicks; craft sticks; and old newspaper.

DESIGNER'S TIP

To calculate the number of tiles needed to cover your project, multiply the total surface area you plan to cover by 85 percent. The result is the total area of glass tiles you will cut.

COLOR PHOTOGRAPHY:
Carl Tremblay

ILLUSTRATION:
Judy Love

STYLING:
Ritch Holben

YOU CAN CREATE THIS SHIMMERing votive candle shade in a weekend, using an ancient mosaic technique updated with modern shortcuts and materials. Start by covering the shade with small squares of cut colored glass, adhering them with 5-minute epoxy. Then fill the space between the squares with ordinary tile grout. When the shade is lit from inside, the multicolored tiles cast the light in different directions, and the thin grout lines form a fine web of tracery through which the lighted candle glows.

For the 7"-high pillar shown here, you will need approximately one hundred ¾"-square pieces of cathedral glass. For the hurricane shade, you'll need about 300 tiles of the same size. Cathedral glass is available wherever stained glass supplies are sold.

For this project, I cut the glass into squares myself, but you could also use irregular pieces of pre-cut glass, depending on the desired effect. While cutting your own glass requires a few additional pieces of equipment, it will give you more control over the color and size of the tiles.

You could select glass with swirling effects, different degrees of opacity, or marbled colors. It will probably also be less expensive—many places that sell glass for stained glass projects will sell several pounds of glass for a few dollars.

Cutting your own glass is a fast and relatively easy process, although it may seem intimidating at first. Crafters who have tried stained glass projects will be familiar with this process. You'll need a glass cutter (*see* illustration A, next page), a knife-like tool that features a small cutting wheel at one end. When the wheel is rolled along the glass surface, it etches a fine groove. The glass can then be gripped with both hands and snapped apart at the marked groove. Snap the glass immediately after making the groove or the break will be harder to make.

Instead of cutting each tile separately, the glass can be cut into strips and then cross-cut to make many tiles at once. Handling ready-made glass is not dangerous, as the edges will have been ground until dull. If you are cutting your own, however, you must wear goggles to protect your eyes, as small slivers can

Cutting Your Own Glass Tiles

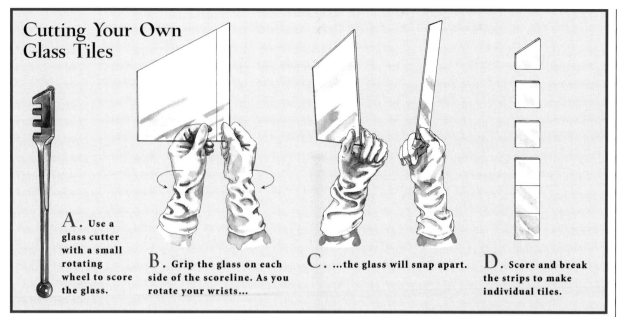

A. Use a glass cutter with a small rotating wheel to score the glass.

B. Grip the glass on each side of the scoreline. As you rotate your wrists...

C. ...the glass will snap apart.

D. Score and break the strips to make individual tiles.

flick off the edges while you are cutting. The cut-glass edge, while sharp, is small enough to be handled safely with bare hands. The freshly cut edges should be dulled with a grinding stone or diamond rasp, however, before gluing.

INSTRUCTIONS
Cutting the Glass Tiles

1. *Score glass strips.* Using fine-point marker and grid ruler, draft ¾" square grid on graph paper. Put on gloves and goggles. Place grid on thick layer of newspaper, then set glass on top, smoother side up, so grid is visible through it. Align straight edge of glass with straight edge of grid. Moisten cotton ball with kerosene and set it in small dish. Gently press wheel of glass cutter (*see* illustration A, above) into cotton ball to lubricate it, then immediately position wheel on glass surface ¾" in

from straight edge, using grid as a guide. Align steel ruler on glass parallel to and about ⅞" from straight edge, to butt edge of cutter. To score glass, draw cutter once firmly across surface from edge to edge.

2. *Break glass strips.* Grip glass on each side of scoreline between thumb and index finger, and fold each hand into a fist. Rotate both wrists up and out (illustration B). As you turn your thumbs outward, the glass will snap sharply in two (illustration C). Repeat steps 1 and 2 to score and break remainder of glass piece into strips. Lubricate cutter before each score and snap glass immediately. To dull tile edges, run them against diamond rasp or sharpening stone.

3. *Make individual tiles.* Lay glass strips side by side on grid. Align steel ruler on grid perpendicular to cut edges. Lubricate wheel and score glass surface as in step 2. Repeat process to score perpendicular lines ¾" apart across all strips. Immediately snap each strip at scorelines to make individual tiles (illustration D). For a better grip on small pieces, use notch on cutter. Repeat steps 1, 2, and 3 for each glass color to make approximately 100 tiles for pillar version and about 300 tiles for hurricane shade. File down sharp edges.

Tiling and Grouting the Pillar

1. *Glue tiles to base of pillar.* Stand glass pillar upright on paper plate. Spray pillar with glass cleaner, and wipe clean with paper towel. To maneuver pillar in steps that follow, rotate plate and avoid touching glass surface. Count out 13 glass tiles, or enough to fit around circumference at lower edge. Lay tiles flat, wrong side up, in random color sequence. Following manufacturer's

Tiling and Grouting the Pillar

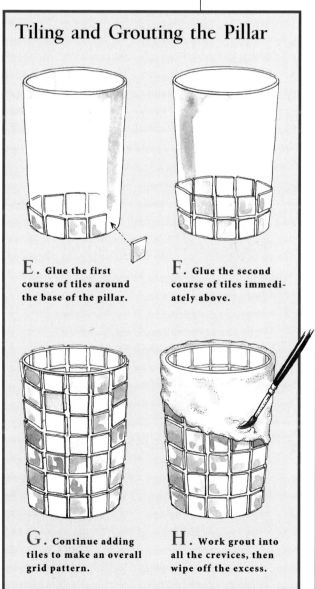

E. Glue the first course of tiles around the base of the pillar.

F. Glue the second course of tiles immediately above.

G. Continue adding tiles to make an overall grid pattern.

H. Work grout into all the crevices, then wipe off the excess.

directions, mix small amount of epoxy on disposable plastic lid with toothpick. Transfer pea-sized glob of epoxy to each tile. Press tiles, one by one, onto pillar around lower edge (illustration E). Before epoxy hardens (about 5 minutes), adjust tiles so spacing is even. Use clean toothpick to remove epoxy that oozes out between tiles. When first course of tiles is firmly set, proceed to step 2.

2. *Glue remaining tiles to pillar.* Count out 13 tiles and lay them flat. Mix epoxy and dab on tiles as before. Press one tile onto pillar directly above tile in first course. Repeat all around to create even grid pattern of tiles (illustration F). Leave approximately ⅛" space between rows for grout. Adjust spacing, then wait for epoxy to harden. Repeat process to add remaining tiles, for 7 rows total. Adjust the last three rows so that the final row lies about ¼" below top rim, to leave room for grout (illustration G).

3. *Apply grout.* Using craft stick, transfer half of grout to plastic container, and mix in one or two squirts of tint. To lighten color, mix in remaining grout; to darken color, add more tint, then add remaining grout. (Keep in mind that color will appear lighter once grout is cured.) Using brush, work grout into crevices between tiles and

along top rim (illustration H). Clean brush with water. Run craft stick over each crevice to smooth grout. Let grout cure 10 to 15 minutes, then wipe surface of tiles clean with damp sponge. Let cure 1 hour. Run single-edged razor blade along top rim at an angle to shave off excess grout and bevel the edge. Let grout cure at least 48 hours before using pillar to hold lighted candle.

Tiling and Grouting the Hurricane Shade

1. *Glue tiles to base of shade.* Stand glass hurricane upright on paper plate. Spray shade with glass cleaner, and wipe clean with paper towel. To maneuver shade in steps that follow, rotate plate and avoid touching glass surface. Count out 18 glass tiles, or enough to fit around circumference at lower edge. Lay tiles flat, wrong side up, in random color sequence. Following manufacturer's directions, mix small amount of 5-minute epoxy on disposable plastic lid with toothpick. Transfer pea-sized glob of epoxy to each tile. Press tiles, one by one, onto hurricane shade around lower edge (illustration I). Before epoxy hardens (about 5 minutes), adjust tiles so spacing is even. Use clean toothpick to remove epoxy that oozes out between tiles. When first course of tiles is firmly

set, proceed to step 2.

2. *Glue second course of tiles to shade.* Count out 18 tiles and lay them flat. Mix new batch of epoxy and dab glob onto each tile, as in step 1. Press one tile onto shade above first course, offsetting it from tiles directly below. Continue offsetting tiles all around, to create a brickwork pattern (illustration J). Adjust spacing, then wait up to 5 minutes for epoxy to harden.

3. *Complete remaining courses.* Repeat step 2 to add each new course of tiles in turn; continue to stagger placement. Note that you will use fewer tiles on courses where shade tapers in and additional tiles where shade fills out. Continue working up to top edge of shade. Run final course ⅛" to ¼" below top rim, to leave room for grout (illustration K).

4. *Apply grout.* Using brush, work grout into crevices between tiles and along top rim (illustration L). Run craft stick over each crevice to smooth grout. Let grout cure 10 to 15 minutes, then wipe surface of tiles clean with damp sponge. Let cure 1 hour. Run single-edged razor blade along top rim of hurricane at an angle to shave off excess grout and bevel the edge. Let grout cure at least 48 hours before placing shade over lighted candle. ◆

Tiling and Grouting the Hurricane Shade

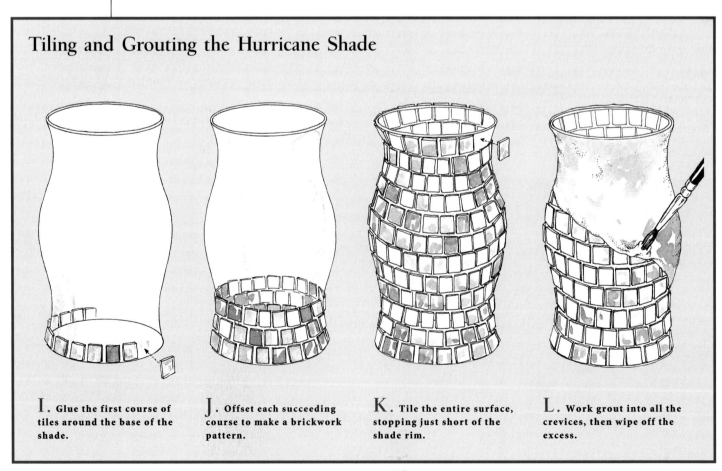

I. Glue the first course of tiles around the base of the shade.

J. Offset each succeeding course to make a brickwork pattern.

K. Tile the entire surface, stopping just short of the shade rim.

L. Work grout into all the crevices, then wipe off the excess.

The Secrets of Sewing with Plastic

Sew any custom-size plastic case with just a few simple materials.

COLOR PHOTOGRAPHY:
Carl Tremblay

ILLUSTRATION:
Mary Newell DePalma

STYLING:
Ritch Holben

BY ELIZABETH CAMERON

TIRED OF PAYING DESIGNER PRICES for plastic makeup bags? You can sew your own for a fraction of the cost using vinyl, available in most fabric stores for about $3/yard.

Although at first glance sewing with plastic may seem complicated, it's not. For starters, you won't need pins, as plastic's inherent static charges hold two layers together. Furthermore, because plastic will never fray, you can sew the entire project "wrong-side-out" and simply trim away the seam allowances.

The only "complication" is that the ordinary presser foot and sewing machine bed may cause the plastic to stick in place, making it difficult to move as you stitch. To remedy this, affix a small piece of painter's tape to the underside of your sewing machine's foot, or use a teflon presser foot.

Elizabeth Cameron is a freelance writer in Brighton, Massachusetts.

INSTRUCTIONS

Note: Sew vinyl pieces wrong sides together, so seams show on right side.

1. *Cut five pattern pieces.* Lay vinyl flat on gridded cutting mat. Using rotary cutter and acrylic cutting guide, cut following pieces: two 7½" squares, one 4" x 7½" rectangle, and two gussets (slip gusset pattern between vinyl and mat).

2. *Sew zipper to vinyl square.* At each end of zipper, butt tapes and zigzag them together across middle. Place zipper face down on one vinyl square, allowing ¼" between tape edge and vinyl edge. Machine-stitch other long edge of zipper tape through both layers. Turn square over. Using zipper foot, stitch as close to zipper teeth as possible on both sides (see illustration A, below). Cut opening in vinyl directly above zipper teeth; make

single continuous cut.

3. *Join squares and gussets.* Lay square with zipper right side down. Place gusset on one side edge, tapered end toward zipper; stitch ¼" from edge. Using scissors, trim seam allowance (including zipper tape) as close to stitching as possible. Repeat process to join second gusset to opposite side edge. Join second vinyl square to remaining gusset edges in same way (illustration B).

4. *Sew bottom and top.* Lay vinyl rectangle flat, and stand bag upright on it. Sew bag edges to corresponding base edges, long edges first, making ¼" seams; trim close to stitching as you complete each seam. At top of bag, align edges and press together. Stitch through all layers, catching top edge of zipper tape in seam. Trim vinyl seam allowance even with zipper tape (illustration C). ◆

To sew vinyl without sticking, use a Teflon presser foot.

MATERIALS
Yields one 7"-square bag

- ¼ yard 45"- to 60"-wide tinted vinyl plastic
- 7" zipper in coordinating color
- Matching sewing thread

You'll also need:
gusset pattern (*see* page 45); sewing machine; painter's tape or teflon presser foot; rotary cutter; self-healing cutting mat; quilter's acrylic grid ruler; and X-Acto knife with new blade.

PATTERNS
See page 45.

Making the Plastic Bag

A. Sew the zipper to one vinyl square.

B. Join the squares and gussets to make the bag walls.

C. Join the rectangular base and stitch the top closed.

Paper Collage Tray

Forget intricate cuts around detailed contours. Quick-cut bands of color for an updated, modern approach to decoupaging any flat surface.

👈 BY MARY NEWELL DEPALMA

Designed as you go along, paper strips are cut and glued in graphic blocks of color.

R EMEMBER THE PAPER COL-lages you made in grade school? This project works on the same principle—cut images and shapes from the pages of a magazine, then glue them to a wooden tray. To take this project to a more professional level, I coated the entire piece with Treasure Crystal Cote, a Xylene-based sealer, which creates a permanent, glossy barrier. *Note:* be sure to use this solvent-based material in a well-ventilated space.

The best part about this project is that you can make up the design as you go along. Simply flip through magazines looking for interesting images and photos revolving around a theme, or shapes cut from compatible colors. The tray shown here, for instance, uses a series of contrasting but compatible bright pastels: yellow and yellow-green accented with turquoise, peach, and lavender.

It's also fun and easy to personalize your tray, either for yourself, or to give as a gift. Create special interest by gluing down your initials (cut from magazines), postage stamps, ticket stubs, candy or gum wrappers, street and/or road maps of your neighborhood or city, invitations,

MATERIALS

- **Unfinished wooden tray (any size)**
- **Glossy magazines, catalogs, etc.**
- **Small papers or other items for personalizing**
- **Gesso**
- **Decoupage medium**
- **Xylene-based sealer (e.g., Treasure Crystal Cote)**

You'll also need:
220-grit sandpaper; several ¼" to 1" flat bristle brushes; old newspaper or telephone directory; newsprint; paper towels; dry cloth; lint-free rag; spray mister; scissors; four small wood blocks; Xylol (to clean brushes used with sealer); and latex gloves.

signatures, color xeroxes of favorite photos or paintings, or anything else that appeals to you.

This decoupage technique will also work well with other wooden items, such as boxes, vases, frames, and the like. Cover a vase with cut-out flowers or foliage, or make a holiday frame with images of evergreen and ornaments. For a man's gift, consider covering a wooden box with sports, fishing, or cigar-related images, then lining the inside with felt. For a children's gift, cover wooden letters with toy or children's images, then glue the letters to a wooden plaque for a special nameplate or wall hanging.

Mary Newell DePalma, a professional illustrator, lives in Boston.

INSTRUCTIONS

1. *Sand and prime tray.* Sand tray lightly, then wipe dust with lightly misted paper towel. Protect work surface with newsprint. Using lint-free rag, rub very thin layer of gesso over entire tray surface, including underside (*see* illustration A, next page). Prop tray on blocks at four corners and let dry 20 minutes. Repeat to apply second coat of gesso. Let dry overnight.

2. *Assemble color blocks for design.* Scan glossy magazines and catalogs, tearing out pages that feature blocks of solid color. Using scissors, cut colored areas into rectangular shapes of varying sizes (extreme precision is not necessary). Continue cutting out pieces until you have enough shapes to cover entire tray, including underside, plus several extra pieces for design flexibility.

3. *Glue down background.* Place one cutout face down on old newspaper or page of old telephone directory. Using flat brush, apply thin coat of decoupage medium across back of cutout and out beyond edges. Place cutout on tray (any position), and press down gently. To ensure good adhesion, gently pat surface and edges of piece with a dry cloth. Repeat process to glue down additional cutouts randomly over surface (illustration B). Position some pieces at irregular angles, to create variation. Change newspaper as needed to prevent wet glue from marring face of cutouts. Continue layering cutouts on tray, varying shapes and colors for design interest, until entire tray—front, underside, sides, and handles—is completely coated (illustration C).

4. *Glue down small paper items.* Select and arrange small papers and cutouts on color-blocked background, to personalize and finish collage. Glue down pieces one-by-one as in step 3 (illustration D). Prop tray on blocks and let dry overnight.

5. *Seal tray.* Work in well-ventilated area, preferably outdoors. Put on latex gloves. Prop tray on blocks so underside faces up. Using bristle brush, apply Xylene-based sealer to tray underside and sides. Let dry 20 minutes, or as manufacturer recommends. Repeat process for three coats total. Prop tray right side up on blocks. Apply three coats of sealer to top side in same way. Clean brush with Xylol. Let sealer cure until coat hardens. ◆

Making the Collage Tray

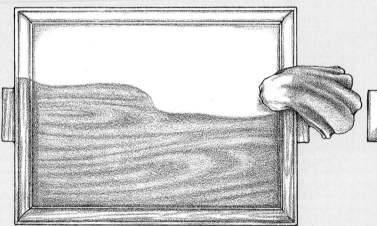

A. Using a lint-free rag, cover the tray with a thin layer of gesso.

B. Glue down colored paper rectangles cut from magazines.

C. Continue building the design until the entire surface is covered.

D. Add smaller cutouts of your choice for a personal touch.

Fleece Roll-Up Bed

Turn any couch into a comfortable spare bed with this fleece sofa mat. Unfasten the reversible strap and unroll the mat in an instant for overnight guests.

🐦 BY LILY FRANKLIN

The finished bedroll shown here measures 30" wide and 68" long and fits the top surface of most couches. To fit a larger couch, adjust the yardage accordingly.

COLOR PHOTOGRAPHY:
Carl Tremblay

ILLUSTRATION:
Judy Love

STYLING:
Ritch Holben

THERE ARE TIMES WHEN A FULL house means overnight guests must sleep on the sofa. This cozy fleece roll-up bed is designed to roll out on a couch, filling in the gaps between the sofa's cushions, and making a smooth, comfortable surface to sleep on. When not in use, the bed can be rolled up and secured with a 15"-wide reversible strap.

To make the bedroll especially thick and inviting, I sewed three layers of batting inside the fleece. Polar fleece is a perfect fabric for this project, as it is warm, lightweight, and washable. Many colors and types of fleece are available in fabric stores. I picked two contrasting but compatible colors—sage green and butter yellow. To add a touch of decoration, I embroidered simple cross-stitches on the bedroll using pale yellow yarn.

If you follow our two-color scheme, the following materials list provides enough fabric for two bedrolls and straps. If you want to make one solid-colored bedroll, you'll need just 2⅜ yards of fleece.

Lily Franklin is a designer and writer in Albuquerque, New Mexico.

MATERIALS
Yields two 30" x 68" bi-color bedrolls

- 2⅜ yards 60"-wide sage green fleece
- 2⅜ yards 60"-wide butter yellow fleece
- 72" x 90" polyester quilt batting
- 4-ply pale yellow acrylic yarn
- Four ⅞"-diameter self-covering buttons
- Monofilament thread

You'll also need:
sewing machine; rotary cutter; quilter's acrylic grid ruler; self-healing cutting mat; scissors; fabric marking pencil; tapestry needle; hand-sewing needle; seam ripper; and 2" quilter's pins.

INSTRUCTIONS

1. *Cut fleece.* Fold 60"-wide green fleece in half lengthwise. Using scissors, cut along fold to yield two 30"-wide pieces; do not separate layers. Using rotary cutter and grid ruler, cut across grain to yield two 30" x 68" bedrolls and two 30" x 15" straps (*see* illustration A, next page). Set aside straps and reserve (for buttons). Repeat process to cut yellow fleece.

2. *Assemble bedroll.* Lay one green fleece bedroll on flat surface. Fold batting in thirds, accordion-style, to measure 30" x 72", and set on fleece. Using scissors, trim edges of batting through all layers so fleece extends ⅝" beyond batting all around (illustration B). Turn assembled layers so batting faces down, and pin through all layers. Lay one yellow fleece bedroll flat. Set green fleece assembly on top, sandwiching batting between fleece, and pin raw edges every 5 or 6 inches. Using monofilament thread, zigzag fleece

DESIGNER'S TIP

Most polar fleece is made from recycled plastic, and various properties affect its use. Polar fleece should not be ironed, but it can be lightly smoothed—not stretched—into position. Because the cut edges do not ravel, polar fleece does not require hemming.

edges together all around (illustration C). Repeat process to assemble second bedroll from remaining green and yellow fleece.

3. *Cross-stitch ends.* At each end of bedroll, insert quilter's pins to mark two parallel lines 2" and 2¾" from edge. Insert series of perpendicular pins to divide space between lines into ¾" square. Thread tapestry needle with 48" length of yellow yarn. For reversible cross-stitch, work cross-stitch in every other square; use pins as guide, and remove pins on return pass (illustration

D). Repeat process to cross-stitch second bedroll.

4. *Tuft bedroll.* Lay bedroll flat, measure to locate center, and mark with two crossed pins. Measure and mark two more points evenly spaced along middle lengthwise axis and four points evenly spaced at either side, for 11 points total. Using hand-sewing needle and monofilament thread, take five stitches in place at each point; tie off in square knot and trim thread ends (illustration E). Repeat process to tuft second bedroll.

5. *Complete strap.* Lay one green strap

from step 1 flat; lay yellow strap on top, edges matching. Using monofilament thread, zigzag edges together. Following button manufacturer's instructions and using scrap fleece, cover one button with green fleece and one with yellow fleece. Machine-stitch buttonhole at each end of strap to fit button. Open buttonhole using seam ripper. Tie button shanks together and slip through one buttonhole (illustration F). Roll bedroll sleeping bag style, wrap strap around it, and button closed (illustration G). Repeat process for second bedroll. ◆

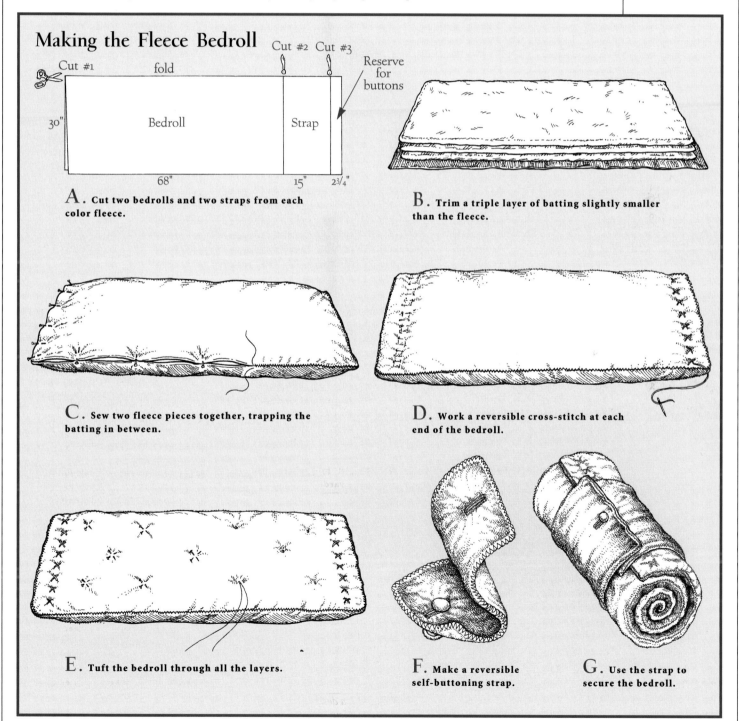

Making the Fleece Bedroll

A. Cut two bedrolls and two straps from each color fleece.

B. Trim a triple layer of batting slightly smaller than the fleece.

C. Sew two fleece pieces together, trapping the batting in between.

D. Work a reversible cross-stitch at each end of the bedroll.

E. Tuft the bedroll through all the layers.

F. Make a reversible self-buttoning strap.

G. Use the strap to secure the bedroll.

Lace Cookies

These wafers may look complicated, but the technique is simple: drop batter onto a baking sheet, where it spreads into lacy doilies.

🍃 BY ANNE TUOMEY AND ANN FLANIGAN

Shape cookies into rolls, fortune cookies, cones, and fluted baskets, then fill with ice cream, fruit, or toppings.

COLOR PHOTOGRAPHY:
Carl Tremblay

ILLUSTRATION:
Mary Newell DePalma

STYLING:
Myrosha Dzuick

WHEN WE WERE GROWING up, lace cookies were "special occasion" fare. Made from a dropped batter that spreads and separates as it bakes into brittle, lacy wafers, these fancy cookies crunch and then immediately melt in your mouth with the rich taste of butter and brown sugar. Though they look and taste like a specialty bakery item, they are easy to make with ingredients that you probably have on hand. Because there is no rolling or cutting of dough, they are also fast.

A basic lace cookie is flat and round,

about 5" in diameter. If you carefully gauge the timing and work efficiently, you can mold the cookies after baking, while they are still warm and soft. Let the cookies cool on the baking sheet for one or two minutes; after this time, just as they are starting to firm up, you should be able to handle them comfortably. Be sure to work within this limited time frame, otherwise the cookies will be too firm for shaping. If the cookie hardens before you've shaped it, however, you can soften it again by placing it back in the oven for a minute or two.

Until you get the hang of it, we recom-

MATERIALS
Yields 6 dozen 5" cookies

- **8 tablespoons unsalted butter**
- **¾ cup dark brown sugar**
- **½ cup light corn syrup**
- **1 teaspoon vanilla extract**
- **¼ teaspoon salt**
- **6 tablespoons all-purpose flour, sifted**
- **1 cup pecans or almonds, chopped fine**
- **1 tablespoon heavy cream**

You'll also need:
medium saucepan; wooden spoon; hand-held electric mixer; two teaspoons; measuring spoons; wet and dry measuring cups; sifter; cookie sheet(s) with baking sheet liner(s); metal spatula; wire racks; wine bottle; small bowl; and airtight storage container.

mend baking only one or two cookies at a time. After making each of the shapes shown on the next page, gently hold the cookie in place until it is set (about 10 seconds), then let it cool on a wire rack. If any of the cookies shatter after you have shaped them, save the crumbles to sprinkle on ice cream.

Humidity is the archenemy of lace cookies, so plan your baking for a dry day. If the cookies absorb too much moisture, they will be chewy instead of caramelized and brittle. To prevent sticking, use a nonstick liner or parchment paper on each baking sheet.

Anne Tuomey and Ann Flanigan are writers in Wellesley, Massachusetts. Reprinted with permission from the May/June 1997 issue of Cook's Illustrated.

INSTRUCTIONS

1. *Mix batter.* Adjust oven rack to center position; preheat oven to 350 degrees. Place butter, brown sugar, and corn syrup in medium saucepan. Bring just to boil over medium heat; cook 5 to 6 minutes, stirring frequently with wooden spoon. Remove saucepan from stovetop. Using electric mixer, beat in vanilla, salt, flour, nuts, and cream.

2. *Bake cookies.* Place baking sheet liner on each cookie sheet. Drop batter by rounded teaspoonful onto cookie sheet at 3" intervals (6 cookies per sheet). Bake 6 to 7 minutes, or until cookies are spread thin, color is deep golden brown, and bubbling has subsided.

3. *Shape cookies.* Let cookies cool and firm up slightly on baking sheet, 1 to 2 minutes. As soon as metal spatula slides under cookie without cookie's bunching or tearing, transfer cookies to wire rack

to complete cooling (for flat, round cookies), or follow one of the lace cookie shaping techniques illustrated below. As you complete a shape, hold it in position for 10 seconds until set, then place cookie on wire rack to finish cooling. Proceed immediately to shape next cookie. Cookies may be stored in airtight container up to one month. ◆

Lace Cookie Shaping Techniques

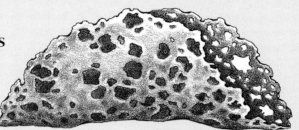

A. Cigarettes. Roll the cookie tightly around the handle of a wooden spoon.

B. Tuille. Lay a wine bottle on its side, and drape the cookie over the broad curved portion.

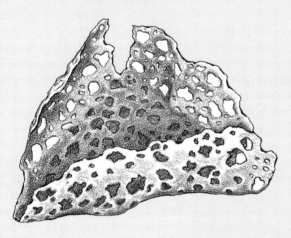

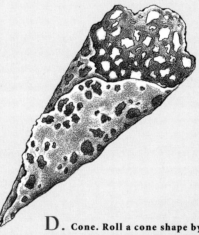

C. Tricorn hat. Press the cookie over the top of a wine bottle, then shape into three-sided "hat."

D. Cone. Roll a cone shape by hand, lapping one edge over the other.

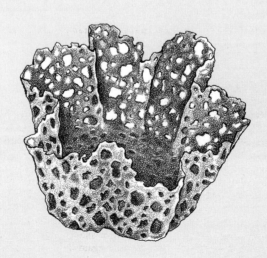

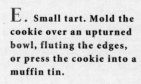

E. Small tart. Mold the cookie over an upturned bowl, fluting the edges, or press the cookie into a muffin tin.

Fragrant Bath Tablets

These mix-and-mold disks are made with honey. Dissolve one wafer in your bath for a welcome pick-me-up or wind-down.

❧ BY AMY JENNER

These tablets, which are mixed from natural ingredients and pressed into a mold, can be dissolved in water for a peaceful, aromatherapeutic bath.

COLOR PHOTOGRAPHY:
Carl Tremblay

STYLING:
Ritch Holben

S LIPPING INTO A WARM BATH scented with these dissolving bath tablets can leave you feeling either energized or relaxed. The recipe is so fast and easy, you may never buy off-the-shelf bath tablets again.

I made the tablets with five natural skin care ingredients: honey, used for centuries to restore moisture to skin; borax or Dead Sea salts, which soften your water, thereby enchancing the effects of other bath ingredients; sea salt, which heals and energizes; French white clay, used to draw impurities from the skin; and essential oil to add fragrance.

This recipe should not be doubled, as the ingredients must be molded while still warm. Use individual metal or plastic candy molds for shaping the tablets. Heat can mar some plastics, and after one or two pressings, plastic molds may lose their contour.

The tablets have a natural honey color. The addition of dried material—rose petals, cinnamon, mint—will add subtle color and texture.

Amy Jenner makes bath products at Stoney Hill Soap Works in Groton, Massachusetts.

MATERIALS
Yields six 1½"–2" tablets

- ½ cup borax or Dead Sea salts
- 1½ teaspoons sea salt
- 1 tablespoon French white clay
- 1 teaspoon dried ground herbs or flower petals
- ⅜ cup honey
- Essential oil (see "Aromatherapy Blends," below)

You'll also need:
food processor; six small candy or tart molds; mini saucepan; candy thermometer; wooden spoon; wet and dry measuring cups; measuring spoons; teaspoon; toothpick; paper towel; and airtight container.

INSTRUCTIONS
Note: Make tablets on clear, dry day.
1. *Combine dry ingredients and oil.* Place borax, sea salt, French white clay, dried material, and essential oil in food processor. Pulse several times to blend ingredients. Lay paper towel flat on counter and sprinkle surface with French white clay.

2. *Add honey.* Heat honey in mini saucepan over high heat, using candy thermometer to check temperature. When honey begins to boil, stir continuously with wooden spoon. When temperature reaches 300 degrees, immediately remove honey from heat, pour into processor, and pulse several times until well blended.

3. *Mold tablets.* Press small amount of mixture into individual candy or mini tart mold and pack firmly using back of teaspoon. Unmold immediately onto powdered paper towel, using toothpick to pry tablet free. Repeat process, working quickly while mixture is still warm, to make six tablets total. Let cure 24 hours. Store tablets flat in airtight container. ◆

AROMATHERAPY BLENDS

To make scented bath tablets, add any of the following essential oil blends to the six-tablet base recipe.

- **Relaxation:** 16 drops lavender, 13 drops marjoram, 8 drops chamomile, and 8 drops cypress.

- **Romance:** 18 drops sandalwood, 12 drops rosewood, 12 drops ylang-ylang, and 6 drops patchouli.

- **Joy:** 12 drops bergamot, 19 drops orange, and 3 drops basil.

- **Fatigue:** 9 drops rosemary, 6 drops sweet orange, 3 drops peppermint, and 1 drop thyme.

- **Calming:** 60 drops (1 teaspoon) lavender.

Faux Masterpiece Painting

Display stretched canvas without a frame, allowing brass tacks to convey the look of an oil painting straight from an artist's studio.

COLOR PHOTOGRAPHY:
Carl Tremblay

ILLUSTRATION:
Judy Love

STYLING:
Ritch Holben

&. BY NANCY OVERTON

THANKS TO MODERN CRAFT materials, it's now possible to make any new object look old. And, thanks to modern photocopying technology, it's also possible to "transfer" an illustration or painting onto fabric. When you combine these two possibilities, you can create this faux antique painting which looks quite authentic, yet costs only about $15 to make.

Nancy Overton, of Oakland, California, has designed and written about crafts for more than twenty years.

INSTRUCTIONS

1. *Photocopy image on transfer paper.* Read instructions provided by transfer paper manufacturer, and take instructions, transfer paper, and color artwork to copy center. Enlarge or reduce color artwork to print mirror image at least 8" x 10" on transfer paper. Copier operator should note that transfer paper prints on one side only and must be inserted correctly in the paper tray. Use X-Acto knife, straightedge, and cutting mat to trim to 8" x 10".

2. *Transfer image to fabric.* Drain all water from iron, preheat on hottest setting, then gently shake iron to release droplets. Turn steam feature off. Press out wrinkles. Center 12" x 14" polyester fabric on top. Press hot iron on fabric to preheat, then immediately center transfer face down on fabric. Press lightly for 20 seconds, then move iron slowly across transfer for 1 minute (*see illustration A, below*). To remove transfer paper, rotate iron in circular motion to reheat entire surface, then immediately peel up paper from one corner; if peeling is difficult, reheat and try peeling from a different corner.

3. *Glue fabric to canvas.* Place a small amount of white glue in palette, and dilute with a few drops of water for creamy consistency. Using 1" brush,

Create your own faux antique using two techniques: photo transfer and crackle finish.

apply diluted glue to surface and edges of artist's canvas. Drape printed fabric on canvas so image is centered, and press gently to adhere (illustration B). Smooth fabric onto edges, making hospital-style tucks at corners. To hold fabric flat, hammer tacks into edges every 1½"; fold excess fabric at corners to back and tack down. Trim off bulk with scissors.

4. *Add crackle finish to canvas.* Following manufacturer's instructions, apply Fragile Crackle Step 1 to surface of canvas, let dry to touch (30 to 60 minutes), then apply Fragile Crackle Step 2 (illustration C). Let dry overnight; crackling will occur as mediums dry. Place a small amount of cream or black paint in palette, and dilute with a few drops of water. Brush diluted black paint along edges of canvas to suggest dirt and aging; repeat process with cream paint. Let paints dry 1 hour. To seal, brush on single coat of satin varnish; let dry overnight. ◆

MATERIALS

- 8" x 10" prestretched artist's canvas
- 12" x 14" white polyester/cotton fabric
- 28 Copper or brass carpet tacks
- Anita's Faux Easy Fragile Crackle
- 2 ounces soft black acrylic paint
- 2 ounces cream acrylic paint
- White craft glue
- Acrylic satin-finish varnish

You'll also need:
color artwork (photograph, print, etc.), any size; photo transfer paper; access to copy center with laser color copier; X-Acto knife; straightedge; self-healing cutting mat; 1" flat brush; paint palette (or disposable plastic lid); iron; Teflon-covered ironing board; old, clean 100% cotton pillowcase; clean, lint-free rags; hammer; and scissors.

A. Transfer the photocopied image to fabric.

B. Glue the fabric to prestretched artist's canvas.

C. Treat the surface with crackle medium.

Beaded Napkin Pocket

To add a graceful touch to a table setting, replace your napkin rings with a set of quick-sew, beaded napkin slipcases.

❧ BY DAWN ANDERSON

A quick fold-and-stitch technique yields these elegant heirlooms for antique or new napkins.

COLOR PHOTOGRAPHY:
Carl Tremblay

ILLUSTRATION:
Judy Love

STYLING:
Ritch Holben

THIS LINEN NAPKIN POCKET IS AN elegant alternative to a napkin ring. It is also a great way to use favorite "stray" napkins—one linen napkin yields four napkin pockets.

To make the pocket, I purchased a 22"-square hemstitched linen napkin, then hand-stitched the floral design using beads. After you've discovered how easy it is to make these distinctive napkin pockets, you may want to devise your own beaded designs—perhaps one for each season. A simple holly leaf and berry would dress up a Christmas place setting, while a star and moon could be used for New Years. For extra inspiration, look at books of embroidery or appliqué designs, then transfer the design to beads.

Note: some glass beads have painted interiors, so be sure to test the washability of all beads before using them. To do this, soak them for an hour in a ½ water, ½ bleach mixture. Avoid using beads that are not colorfast, as they may leak color when the linen pocket is washed.

Dawn Anderson, a writer and designer, lives in Redmond, Washington.

MATERIALS
Yields four 5¾" x 4½" pockets

- 22"-square hemstitched ivory linen napkin
- 24 petal-shaped blue glass beads
- 8 leaf-shaped green glass beads
- 20 golden yellow opaque seed beads
- About 300 green silver-lined seed beads
- Ivory sewing thread
- Ivory beading thread

You'll also need:
beading pattern (*see* page 44); two beading needles; hand-sewing needle; 5" embroidery hoop; air-soluble marker; sewing machine; rotary cutter; self-healing cutting mat; quilter's acrylic grid ruler; scissors; pins; iron; point turner; and cotton dish towel.

INSTRUCTIONS

1. *Cut napkin.* Using rotary cutter, grid ruler, and mat, trim one edge from napkin just inside hemstitching. Repeat to trim opposite edge of napkin. Using air-soluble marker, mark midpoint of all four edges of napkin. Draft two lines to connect opposite midpoints, dividing napkin into quarters; each quarter will measure approximately 10" x 11". Cut napkin on marked lines. Follow steps 2 through 6 for each piece to make four pockets.

2. *Mark beading pattern.* Lay one piece wrong side up. Using iron, press edge opposite hem ¼" to wrong side. Fold this pressed edge up to meet hemstitching, and press again to set second crease. Lay piece flat, right side up, with hemmed edge at top. Using air-soluble marker and ruler, lightly draft line ⅜" in from each side edge. Draft three additional parallel lines to divide remaining area in fourths. Using lines as guide, position pattern under fabric so design is centered between hemstitching and crease; if design is not visible, hold pieces up to a window. Transfer pattern marking using air-soluble marker (*see* illustration A, facing page).

3. *Sew large beaded flower.* Secure fabric in embroidery hoop. Thread one beading needle with 24" of beading thread. Anchor thread to fabric by taking several small stitches at center of flower design, ending on right side. Referring to pattern (*see* page 48) and color photograph (*see* previous page), stitch down five golden yellow seed beads, one at a time, to make pistil. Stitch blue glass beads around yellow beads, then stitch again for secure hold. Draw thread to wrong side of napkin but do not cut.

4. *Couch long beaded stem.* Thread second beading needle with 8" of beading thread. Anchor thread to fabric where stem joins flower, string on about 3" of green seed beads, and slide beads down to flower head. Pull thread taut so beads

nearest flower head lie directly on marked stem line; do not try to conform beads to curve, but simply align beads on straight section of stem line. To keep thread taut and beads snug, lodge needle into fabric (as you would a straight pin), and wrap excess thread around needle shaft. To couch, or anchor, stem beads, use first beading needle. Draw needle up from underside between first and second beads and reinsert it, trapping stem thread in loop. Repeat between second and third beads, third and fourth beads, etc. (*see* couching detail, below). To round curves, reposition second needle in fabric so beads align with new section of stem line, pull thread taut as before, and continue couching. When you reach end, draw both threads through to wrong side, and end off.

5. *Attach remaining beads.* Working from bottom up, couch two remaining stems as for large stem. Tack one blue

bead and two green leaf beads in place, as indicated on pattern. Remove embroidery hoop. To press fabric, set beaded section face down on folded towel and press from wrong side.

6. *Assemble napkin pocket.* Fold beaded piece in half, right sides together and edges matching. Stitch ⅜" from raw edges to make tube (illustration B). Insert tightly rolled dishtowel inside tube and press seam open using iron. Remove towel, lay tube flat with seam centered, and pin to prevent shifting. Stitch through both layers along crease made in step 2, backtacking at beginning and end; if crease is faint, draft guideline and then stitch (illustration C). Turn beaded half of pocket right side out; remainder will slip inside to form self-lining. Poke out corners with point turner. To finish, slip-stitch lining to hemstitching all around; turn raw seam allowance under and stitch down (illustration D). ◆

PATTERNS
See page 44 for pattern pieces and enlargement instructions.

Making the Slipcase

A. Transfer the design, then sew on the beads.

B. Stitch the long edges together to make a tube.

C. Center the seam, then stitch the pocket bottom.

D. Turn right side out for a self-lined pocket.

Couching detail

Three-Panel Dutch Townscape

Make this tall, folding candle shade using balsa wood and paper hinges. For added decorative lighting, let the light from votive candles set its windows aglow.

🍂 BY MICHIO RYAN

MATERIALS

- 3/8" x 6" x 36"-long balsa sheet
- 1/8" x 4" x 12"-long balsa sheet
- 1/4" x 1/2" x 36"-long balsa stick
- 1/8" x 3/8" x 36"-long balsa stick
- Two 1/8" x 1/4" x 36"-long balsa sticks
- Two 1 1/2" mirror-image corner brackets
- 1" oval buckle
- 12 white map tacks
- Heavy-weight watercolor paper
- Scrap of 2-ply chipboard
- Scrap of 1-ply chipboard
- 2 ounces soft white acrylic paint
- Spray shellac
- Extra-tacky glue (e.g., Aleene's Thick Designer Tacky Glue)

You'll also need:
facade, stonework, door, and baroque pediment patterns (*see* pages 46 and 47); 1" soft flat brush; 1/4" stiff brush; X-Acto knife; quilter's acrylic grid ruler; self-healing cutting mat; emery board; spray adhesive; finishing nail; bone folder (or substitute); and map tacks.

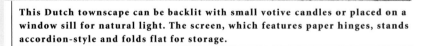

This Dutch townscape can be backlit with small votive candles or placed on a window sill for natural light. The screen, which features paper hinges, stands accordion-style and folds flat for storage.

PATTERNS

See pages 46 and 47 for pattern pieces and enlargement instructions.

COLOR PHOTOGRAPHY:
Carl Tremblay

ILLUSTRATION:
Michael Gellatly

STYLING:
Ritch Holben

THOUGH THIS MINIATURE FOLDing screen resembles a complicated woodworking project, it actually requires no heavy-duty tools, nails, or hardware. Instead, the panels are made from balsa wood, which can be cut with an X-Acto knife. I decorated each facade with small scraps of wood and chipboard, which also covers any rough or raw edges on the balsa wood. Last, borrowing technology from the world of bookbinding, I hinged the panels together using strips of paper. The entire project, from start to finish, costs about $15.

INSTRUCTIONS

1. *Cut three house facades.* Lightly apply spray adhesive to wrong side of three house facade templates. Adhere templates end to end to 6"-wide balsa strip. Using X-Acto knife and quilter's grid ruler, cut out each balsa facade on solid outline; make several passes of blade to cut clear through to mat. Cut window openings (solid lines) in same way. Remove templates and set aside. Rub emery board in circular motion over cut edges until smooth. Run tip of finishing nail along score lines on facade #2 to simulate planking. Score (do not cut through) three parallel lines on facade #2 (*see* illustration A, next page).

2. *Add window mullions.* Using X-Acto knife and grid ruler, cut several matchstick-width strips from 1-ply chipboard. Referring to template key (a), trim strips to span window openings, plus 1/8" on each side. Cut small notches in the back of the balsa so mullions lie flush with surface. On facade #2, make notches and fit mullions from back, so window appears recessed. Test-fit mullions, then glue in position (illustration B).

3. *Add balsa strip details.* Lay three balsa facades face up, side by side. Referring to templates, cut lengths of 1/8" x 3/8" balsa stick, and glue to all areas keyed (b). On facade #3, stack two (b) strips to create lower step; angle-cut (b) strips at top. In same way, cut and glue 1/4"-wide balsa strips to areas keyed (c). On facade #1, glue horizontal (c) strips first, then vertical strips. On facade #2, glue steps first, then cellar door framing and brickwork. Also cut two 1/4" x 1/2" strips to fit top and bottom of recessed window opening, and glue in place. To cap rooflines on facades #1 and #2, cut sections of ¼" x ½" balsa stick to fit each horizontal surface; cut piece for each roof peak slightly larger, to create side overhang. Glue down all roof pieces flush with panel back, to create front overhang (illustration C).

4. *Add balsa stonework to facade #3.* Using spray adhesive, affix three stonework templates to ⅛"-thick balsa sheet. Cut on solid lines using X-Acto knife and grid ruler (for straight edges). Remove template and separate balsa pieces. Referring to facade #3 template, glue pieces above and around windows to areas keyed (d). Top each pediment with keystone (illustration C).

5. *Add door to facade #3.* Using spray adhesive, affix door template to 2-ply chipboard. Using X-Acto knife and grid ruler, score as indicated, then cut on solid outlines. Remove template pieces. Peel up topmost plies of chipboard between scorelines to suggest stonework. Glue door to facade #3 above steps; glue thin strip of 1-ply chipboard above door opening to define triangular pediment (illustration C).

6. *Complete facade #3.* Cut baroque pediment from 2-ply chipboard as for door, and glue to top of facade #3. Glue oval buckle to center of pediment, adding 1-ply chipboard mullion to suggest four-paned oculus window. Glue remaining ⅜"-wide balsa strip across pediment, then glue ¼"-wide strip on top. From 2-ply chipboard, cut one ⅜" x 4¼" strip on crossgrain. Curl strip with your fingers, moisten with water, shape it to fit top arc, and glue down; hold in place with tape until dry, then remove tape. Glue two metal corner brackets to flank each side of pediment (illustration C). If necessary, support brackets from back with chipboard triangles cut to fit.

7. *Paint and join facades.* Apply two coats spray shellac to all surfaces, letting dry 10 minutes after each coat. Paint front of each panel soft white; do not paint edges. To make hinges, cut one 1½" x 7" strip and one 2½" x 7" strip from watercolor paper following the grain. Fold each strip in half lengthwise and crease with bone folder. Lay facade #2 and #3 face down on flat surface. Glue 1½" x 7" hinge to back of facade #2, aligning fold with left side edge; hold until glue sets. Lap free half of hinge onto back of facade #3 and glue down (illus-

tration D). Gently test hinge swing before glue sets. To join facades #1 and #2, hold facade #1 on its side, so edge to be hinged faces up. Glue 2½" x 7" strip to this edge, setting fold even with protruding balsa window trim. Fold excess onto back of facade, crease well, and glue down. Hold facade #1 and #2 right sides together and side edges even. Lap free

half of hinge onto side and back of facade #2, crease at edge, and glue down (illustration E). Let glue dry at least 1 hour, but preferably overnight.

8. *Finish screen.* Apply two coats white paint to all wood surfaces, letting dry 20 minutes after each coat. Insert map tacks every ¾" in roofline of facade #2. Stand finished screen upright (illustration F). ◆

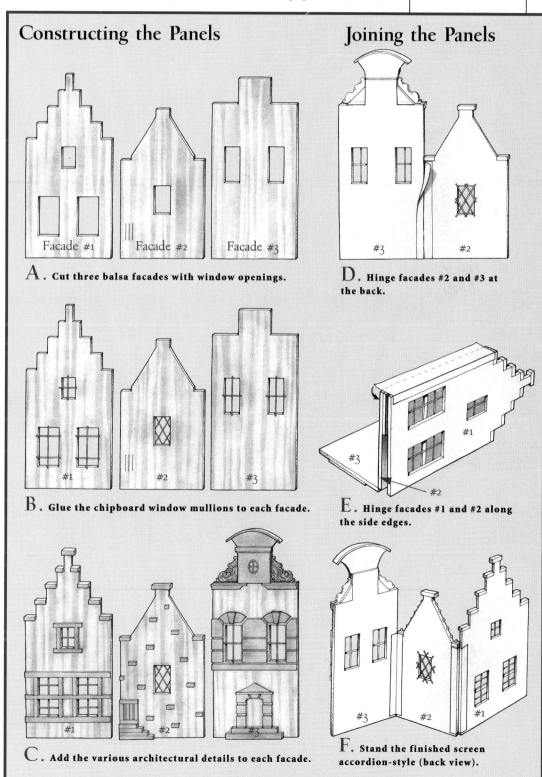

Constructing the Panels

A. Cut three balsa facades with window openings.

Facade #1   Facade #2   Facade #3

B. Glue the chipboard window mullions to each facade.

C. Add the various architectural details to each facade.

Joining the Panels

D. Hinge facades #2 and #3 at the back.

E. Hinge facades #1 and #2 along the side edges.

F. Stand the finished screen accordion-style (back view).

Two-Color Pillowcases

To create a matching set of linens, switch the hems on two pillowcases and join them with lace in between.

🐦 BY FRANCOISE HARDY

For a variation on this design, switch the hems on patterned pillowcases, then use a sheet from each pattern to create a full set of linens.

COLOR PHOTOGRAPHY:
Carl Tremblay

ILLUSTRATION:
Judy Love

STYLING:
Ritch Holben

L OOKING FOR A WAY TO COORDI-
nate two mismatched pillowcases? I did just that by inter-
changing the hems of each
pillowcase, with added trim in between.

I selected a white trim which resembles hemstitching, though it is actually made of narrow, crisscrossed ribbon. I backed the trim with pale lavender satin ribbon, which conceals the raw edges of the pillowcase on each side of the white trim.

For a variation on this design, try intermingling floral prints with solid-

colored designs, polka dots with stripes, or two different animal designs. You can also vary the trims used in between the pillows: substitute grosgrain ribbon, eyelet, lace, variegated ribbon, or the like. For a fast and simple version of this project, eliminate the lavender ribbon backing, and just use the open, criss-cross trim to attach the new hem to the body of the pillowcase.

Francoise Hardy is a Boston-based artisan and craftsperson.

MATERIALS
Yields two pillowcases

■ **20" x 30" key lime pillowcase**
■ **20" x 30" hydrangea pillowcase**
■ **2½ yards 1⅛"-wide white insertion trim**
■ **2½ yards 1¼"-wide lavender satin ribbon**
■ **Matching sewing thread**

You'll also need:
sewing machine; scissors; and iron.

INSTRUCTIONS

Note: Change the upper and bobbin threads as needed to match the fabric and trim colors being sewn.

1. *Cut off pillowcase hems.* Press key lime pillowcase to remove wrinkles. To start cut, clip into 4" double hem as close to topstitching as possible (*see illustration A, next page*). Continue cutting all around, so hem detaches as a continuous loop. Repeat process for hydrangea pillowcase.

2. *Apply insertion trim.* Machine-baste raw edges of key lime hem ⅛" from edge (illustration B). Place insertion trim on hem edge, right sides together. Leaving ¼" of trim free at start, stitch ³⁄₁₆" from edge all around (illustration C); clip excess trim, fold and overlap ends, and stitch down. Trim welting, if any, from cut edge of hydrangea pillowcase body. Place free edge of trim against hydrangea cut edge, right sides together, and side seams of hem and body aligned. Stitch trim to hydrangea body. On wrong side, press seams away from trim (illustration D). Repeat process to join hydrangea hem to key lime body.

3. *Apply ribbon backing.* Turn key lime pillowcase right side out, and lay flat. Fold back hydrangea hem to reveal hem/trim seamed edge (trim will be concealed underneath). Slip lavender ribbon under trim, letting it extend slightly beyond edge. Stitch through all layers over previous stitching (illustration E). Refold hem right side out. Topstitch hem ⅛" from fold through all layers (illustration F). Repeat process to sew ribbon to key lime body. Apply ribbon to remaining pillowcase in same way. ◆

Making the Pillowcases

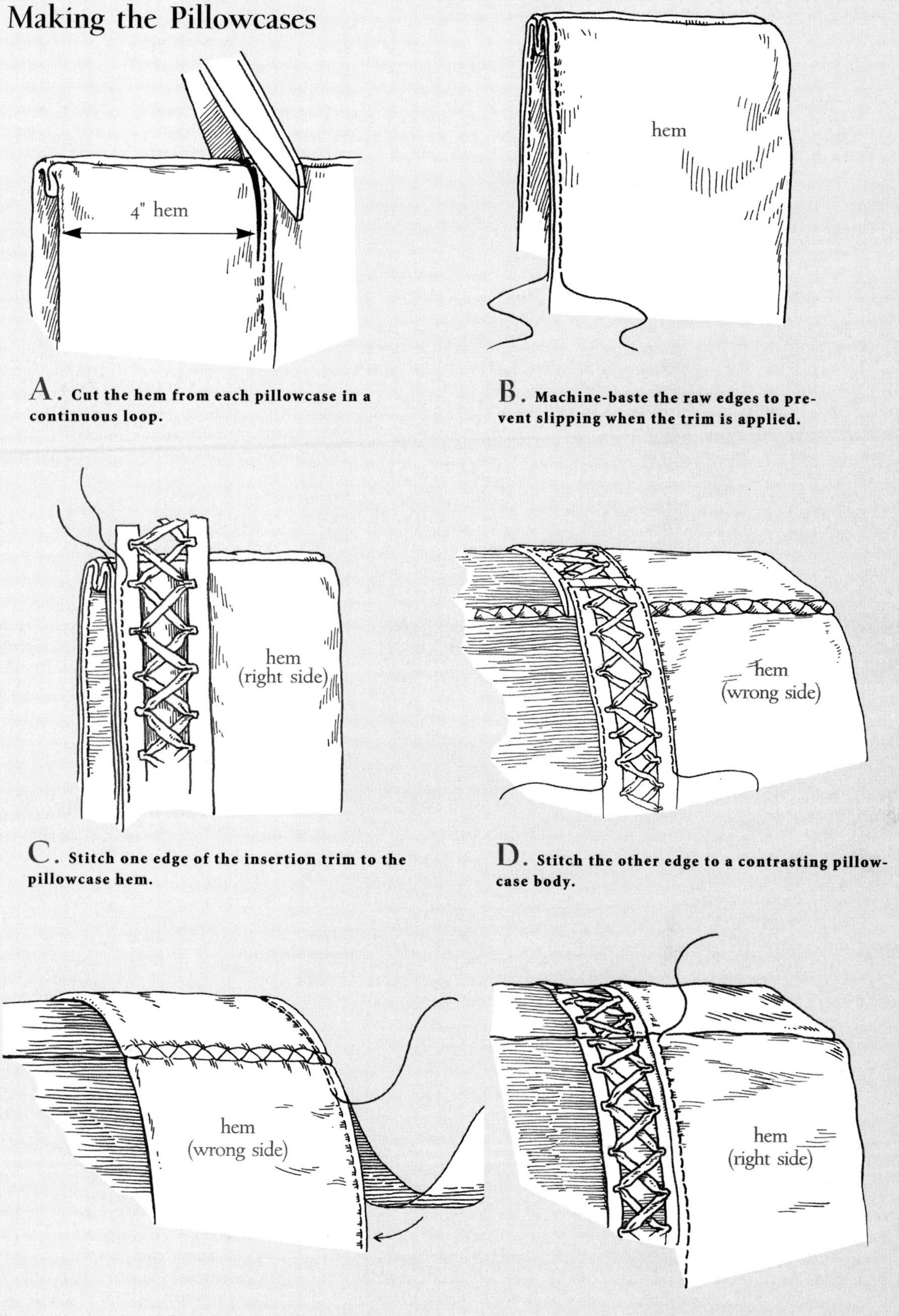

A. Cut the hem from each pillowcase in a continuous loop.

B. Machine-baste the raw edges to prevent slipping when the trim is applied.

C. Stitch one edge of the insertion trim to the pillowcase hem.

D. Stitch the other edge to a contrasting pillowcase body.

E. Attach a satin ribbon to back the insertion trim.

F. Topstitch through all the layers to complete the insertion.

4" hem

hem

hem
(right side)

hem
(wrong side)

hem
(wrong side)

hem
(right side)

DESIGNER'S TIP

For a modern version of this project, combine white and black pillowcases with checkerboard trim in between. For a holiday version, mix red and green pillowcases, then select a Christmassy trim.

Ten-Minute Box from Ribbon

Build a soft yet sturdy box for potpourri using one length of sheer, wire-edged ribbon.

🍂 BY MARIETTA VAN BUHLER

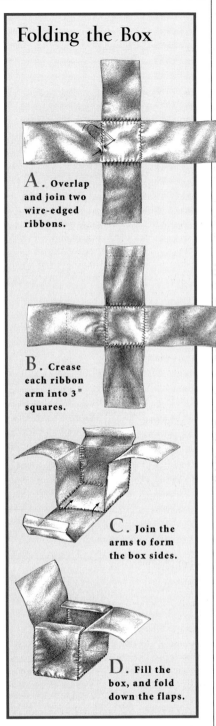

Made simply by overlapping two strips of ribbon, this box is also the perfect storage case for a single handmade ornament, love letter, or one-of-a-kind collectible.

MATERIALS
Yields one 3" box

- ¾ yard 3"-wide sheer wire-edged ribbon
- ¾ yard 1"-wide sheer ribbon
- 1" sheer ribbon rose
- Monofilament sewing thread

You'll also need:
sharp scissors; ruler; and hand-sewing needle.

COLOR PHOTOGRAPHY:
Carl Tremblay

ILLUSTRATION:
Mary Newell DePalma

STYLING:
Ritch Holben

THE WIRE IN WIRE-EDGED RIBBON is favored by floral designers, who can sculpt the ribbon to match any design. That same quality served me well in designing this box, which uses the soft but sturdy wire to hold the edges of a mesh gift box.

This box can be used to hold fragrant materials such as potpourri or lavender, or it can be sized for a particular object, such as jewelry or candy.

Marietta Van Buhler is a craft designer in Troy, Michigan.

INSTRUCTIONS

1. *Sew box bottom.* Using sharp scissors, cut wire-edged ribbon into one 15" and one 12" length. Lay both ribbons flat, overlapping them at center to form cross; measure to confirm placement. Using monofilament thread, whip overlapped sections together along edges for box bottom (*see illustration A, above*).

2. *Fold box sides.* Fold and crease one ribbon arm along edge of box bottom. Make parallel crease 3" away. Unfold arm and lay flat. Repeat process to crease each arm, forming 3" squares. Fold 1 ½"

excess at ends of shorter arms in half (illustration B).

3. *Sew box sides.* To form box, fold two adjacent arms up, perpendicular to box bottom, and whip butted edges together for 3". Repeat process to sew four seams total (illustration C).

4. *Fill and close box.* Place potpourri, confections, or other lightweight items inside box. Fold down inside flaps (shorter arms), then fold and overlap two top flaps to form cube (illustration D). Tie sheer ribbon bow around box. Attach ribbon rose to bow knot. ◆

Mail-Order Directory

Our Annual Mail-Order Supplier Directory

BY JORDAN SALVATORIELLO

Before running to your local craft store for etching cream or the "perfect" perfume bottle, consider a mail-order catalog. This directory, which lists over 100 catalogs, will help you locate hard-to-find items, order common supplies, or simply learn more about your most-used craft products.

Before you start ordering, however, keep these pointers in mind. Ask clear, concise questions to make sure you order what you want the first time around. Don't be rushed by mail-order operators who tend to move things quickly—instead, use them to answer your questions about the catalog and products. Start your order by supplying the item number, then verify the price, quantity, and quality of each. Catalogs come out in the beginning of the year, and prices are subject to change without notice. Smaller items, such as beads, may come in packages, so be sure you know how many you're receiving. Some companies may offer bulk discounts, so ask about any special offers.

If you don't have the catalog, but know exactly what you need, such as lavender oil for our Bath Tablets (page 30), search the "Florals & Naturals" section of the directory to locate an essential oil supplier. All operators have computer or catalog access to the products, and can give you any information to order. Be sure to inquire about convenient methods for payment and shipping costs. Minimum orders apply to some mail-order suppliers, so check their policy.

Art Supplies

AMERICAN TRADITIONAL STENCIL
442 First New Hampshire Turnpike
Northwood, NH 03261
Phone: 603-942-8100
Fax: 603-942-8919
Web site: www.amtrad-stencil.com
(password: wholesale)
Offers: An array of stencil designs consisting of classic dimension stencils, solid brass stencils, supplies, tools, books, and videos.
Catalog: $5

ANDREA DESIGNS
35673 Ashford Drive
Sterling Heights, MI 48312
Phone: 810-826-3404
Fax: 810-826-3621
Offers: Stencil designs, marked with registration holes for alignment, and a selection of stencil brushes. No minimum order. Return within 14 days for credit.
Catalog: $6

ART EXPRESS
P.O. Box 21662

Columbia, SC 29221
Phone: 800-535-5908
Fax: 803-750-1492
Offers: Assortment of paper, such as watercolor, printing, rice, pastel, and specialty papers. Also carries canvas, brushes, paints, oils, mediums, and art accessories.
Catalog: $3.50

ART SUPPLY WAREHOUSE
5325 Departure Drive
North Raleigh, NC 27616-1835
Phone: 800-995-6778
Fax: 919-878-5075
Web site: www.aswexpress.com
Offers: Wide range of artists' supplies, including paints, brushes, pencils, pastels, mat cutters, and frames. For orders under $100, add a $5.95 small order charge. Return for credit.
Catalog: $2

CHARRETTE
P.O. Box 4010
Woburn, MA 01888-4010
Phone: 800-367-3729
Fax: 800-626-7889
Web site: www.charrette.com
Offers: Art supplies such as paper, film and boards, portfolios, pens, pencils, markers, adhesives, tools, framing, fine art materials and more.
Catalog: $7.50

CHEAP JOE'S ART STUFF
374 Industrial Park Drive
Boone, NC 28607
Phone: 704-262-0793
Fax: 800-257-0874
Web site: www.artscape.com/cheapjoe/
Offers: Paint, brushes, drawing accessories, art supplies, frames, matboard, and more.
Free catalog.

CUTBILL & COMPANY
274 Sherman Avenue North
Unit 207
Hamilton, Ontario
Canada L8L 6N6
Phone: 905-547-8525
Fax: 905-547-8191
Offers: Block-printing supplies and materials, including kits, block-printing pads, and glazes.
Free catalog.

DANIEL SMITH
4150 First Avenue South
P.O. Box 84268
Seattle, WA 98124-5568
Phone: 800-426-6740
Fax: 800-238-4065
Offers: Artists' materials, such as paints, brushes, pens, etching supplies, print-making supplies, paper, frames, tools, metallic leafing supplies, and books. No minimum order. Returns in 90 days, full refund with the exception of custom products.
Catalog: $5 (includes $5 certificate). Free supplemental catalogs.

DICK BLICK ART MATERIALS
P.O. Box 1267
Galesburg, IL 61402-1267
Phone: 800-447-8192
Fax: 800-621-8293
Web site: www.dickblick.com
Offers: Large selection of artists' supplies, including paints, brushes, paper and boards, screen-printing materials, printmaking tools, craft supplies, ceramic tools, and software. No minimum order. Return for full refund.
Free catalog.

HOUSTON ART, INC.
10770 Moss Ridge Road
Houston, TX 77043-1175
Phone: 800-272-3804
Fax: 713-462-1783
Web site: www.houstonart.com

Offers: Mediums, gold leaf, gesso, finishes, paper, mirrors, squeeze bottles, glasschalk, wood cutouts, brushes, art accessories. Permission needed for returns.
Free catalog.

JANOVIC/PLAZA'S INCOMPLETE CATALOG FOR DECORATIVE AND SCENIC PAINTERS
30-35 Thomson Avenue
Long Island City, NY 11101
Phone: 800-772-4381
Fax: 718-361-7288
Web site: www.janovic.com
Offers: Brushes, tools, and materials for both home and commercial painting, as well as many specialty items used in restoration and preservation work. No minimum order. Return in 90 days with prior authorization for full refund, exchange, or credit.
Catalog: $4.95

JERRY'S ARTARAMA
P.O. Box 58638J
Raleigh, NC 27658-8638
Phone: 800-827-8478
Fax: 919-878-5075
Offers: Full line of art supplies, gifts, books, and furniture.
Free catalog.

NEW YORK CENTRAL ART SUPPLY, INC.
62 Third Avenue
New York, NY 10003
Phone: 800-950-6111
Fax: 212-475-2513
Offers: Fine art supplies, including paints, pastels, mediums, brushes, canvas, easels, and more. No minimum order. Returns in 5 days with prior authorization.
Free catalog.

OTT'S DISCOUNT ART SUPPLY
102 Hungate Drive
Greenville, NC 27858
Phone: 800-356-3289

Fax: 919-756-2397
Web site: www.otts.com
Offers: Discount art supplies from paints, brushes, calligraphy supplies, and palettes to drawing materials, canvas, markers, and varnish. No minimum order. Return within 30 days.
Free catalog.

PEARL PAINT CO., INC.
308 Canal Street
New York, NY 10013-2572
Phone: 800-221-6845 x2297
Fax: 212-431-5420
Web site: www.pearlpaint.com
Offers: Wide selection of art and craft supplies, including paints, mediums, canvas, framing materials, books, home decorating, furniture, drawing materials, paper, gold leaf, and accessories. Add $4.95 if order is under $50. Return within 30 days for credit.
Catalog: $1.50

PERMA COLORS
226 E. Tremont Street
Charlotte, NC 28203
Phone: 800-365-2656
Fax: 704-333-9201
Web site: members.aol.com/Anima1ia /index.html
Offers: Perma Color dry pigments: Standard, Bronze Powders, Metallic, Pearlescents, Iridescents and Fluorescents, as well as gesso, mediums, varnish, gold leaf, metallic powders, panels, and brushes.
Free catalog.

TEXAS ART SUPPLY CO.
2001 Montrose Blvd.
Houston, TX 77006-1299
Phone: 800-888-9278
Fax: 713-526-4062
Web site: www.texasart.com
Offers: Large variety of art supplies, frames, adhesives, projectors, ceramic supplies, fabric paints, and more. No minimum order, but $6 minimum shipping and handling fee. Returns within 30 days.
Catalog: $3

Craft Supplies

BOLEK'S CRAFT SUPPLY, INC.
P.O. Box 465
330 N. Tuscarawas Avenue
Dover, OH 44622-0465
Phone: 800-743-2723
Fax: 800-649-3735
Offers: Beads, dollmaking supplies, paint supplies, finishes, adhesives, cord, silk flowers, wood cutouts, flavoring oils, molds, stamps, and tools.
Catalog: $1.50

CIRCLE CRAFT SUPPLY
P.O. Box 3000
Dover, FL 33527-3000
Phone: 813-659-0992

Fax: 813-659-0017
Offers: Assorted craft supplies including beads, fabrics, jewelry findings, brushes, styrofoam, and wood products.
Catalog: $2

CRAFT CATALOG
P.O. Box 1069
Reynoldsburg, OH 43068
Phone: 800-777-1442
Fax: 800-955-5915
Web site: www.craftcatalog.com
Offers: Wide selection of craft supplies, including wood turnings, paint, jewelry findings, brushes, stencils, trims, and ribbons.
Free catalog.

CRAFT KING
P.O. Box 90637
Lakeland, FL 33804
Phone: 800-769-9494
Fax: 941-648-2972
Offers: Discount craft supplies covering a range of topics, including beads, books, doll parts, floral supplies, paint, ribbon, and wood items. No minimum order. Return in 30 days.
Free catalog.

EARTH GUILD
33 Haywood Street
Asheville, NC 28801
Phone: 800-327-8448
Fax: 704-255-8593
Web site: www.earthguild.com
Offers: Tools, materials, and books for handcrafts: basketry, dyeing, spinning, yarns, weaving, rug making, leatherwork, candle making, beading, and modeling clays. Orders under $10, 50 cents service fee. Return for full refund.
Catalog: $3 (free introductory catalog)

ENTERPRISE ART
P.O. Box 2918
Largo, FL 33779
Phone: 800-366-2218
Fax: 800-366-6121
Offers: Large assortment of beads, rhinestones, and findings, as well as assorted craft supplies.
Free catalog.

FLAX ART & DESIGN
240 Valley Drive
Brisbane, CA 94005
Phone: 415-468-7530
Fax: 415-648-1940
Web site: www.flaxart.com
Offers: Artist tools and supplies. No minimum order. Returns within 30 days.
Free catalog.

MAPLEWOOD CRAFTS
Humboldt Industrial Park
1 Maplewood Drive
Hazleton, PA 18201-0676
Phone: 800-899-0134
Fax: 717-384-2500

Offers: Wide range of seasonal craft kits, as well as beading and needlecraft supplies, books, tools, plastic, canvas, paint, dolls, and floral craft materials.
Free catalog.

MUNRO'S
3954 West 12 Mile Road
Berkley, MI 48072
Phone: 800-638-0543
Fax: 810-544-0357
Offers: Glass etching supplies, fabric paint, transfers, brushes, paints, glazes, finishes, crackle finish, beads, findings, clay, wood, lampshade accessories, and more. Shipping minimum of $25. Returns within 7 days with prior authorization.
Catalog: $5 (free with first order)

NASCO ARTS AND CRAFTS
901 Janesville Avenue
Fort Atkinson, WI 53538-0901
Phone: 800-558-9595
Fax: 920-563-8296
Web site: www.nascofa.com
Offers: Art supplies, such as paints, brushes, canvas, pencils, and paper. Also various craft supplies, knives, scissors, adhesives, wood, ceramics, molds, print making, stenciling, stained glass, and more.
Free catalog.

NATIONAL ARTCRAFT COMPANY HANDCRAFT VARIETY SOURCE BOOK
7996 Darrow Road
Twinsburg, OH 44087
Phone: 800-793-0152
Fax: 800-292-4916
Web site: www.nationalcraft.com
Offers: Wide variety of craft components, including miniatures, buttons by the bag, etching cream, dried flowers, picture frame supplies, tiles, hinges, tassels, and brushes.
Catalog: $1-$3.

S & S
P.O. Box 513
Colchester, CT 06415-0513
Phone: 800-243-9232
Fax: 800-566-6678
Web site: www.snswwide.com
Offers: Ornaments, decoupage and body art supplies, Christmas creations, star and heart boxes, stickers, stamps and craft punch cutouts, beads, foam hearts, poly clay, dylite molded shapes, art sand, silk and dried flowers, baskets, and more. Add $5 for orders under $25. Returns within 30 days.
Free catalog.

SAX ARTS & CRAFTS
P.O. Box 510710
New Berlin, WI 53151
Phone: 800-558-6696
Fax: 800-328-4729
Web site: www.artsupplies.com
Offers: Art supplies, tools, and materials, and books and gifts for the art enthusiast.

Return within 10 days.
Catalog: $5 (can be applied towards first purchase)

SUNSHINE DISCOUNT CRAFTS
P.O. Box 301
Largo, FL 33779-0301
Phone: 800-729-2878
Fax: 813-531-2739
Web site: www.hypernetusa.com/crafts/ sun.html
Offers: Large assortment of craft supplies, including modeling clays and accessories, beads, dolls, miniatures, brushes, and wood items. Add $2 for orders under $20. Returns within 30 days with fee.
Free catalog.

VANGUARD CRAFTS
1081 East 48th Street
Brooklyn, NY 11234
Phone: 800-662-7238
Fax: 718-692-0056
Offers: Clays, kits, fabric decorations, candle supplies, decoupage items, beads, finishes, baskets, and more.
Free catalog.

Specialty Supplies

BENJANE ARTS
P.O. Box 298
West Hempstead, NY 11552
Phone: 516-483-1330
Offers: An assortment of shells, including bi-valves, snail, clam, cut shells, coral, pearl, as well as starfish, teeth, bone, display stands, directions for projects, supplies, handcrafted shell jewelry, and gifts. Number in parentheses following price indicates minimum quantity you may order at that price.
Catalog: $5

CR BEAR AND DOLL SUPPLY CATALOG
Box 8
Leland, IA 50453
Phone: 515-567-3652
Fax: 515-567-3071
Web site: www.crscrafts.com
Offers: Teddy bear and dollmaking supplies, patterns, and kits. No minimum order. Returns with prior permission.
Catalog: $2

EASTERN ART GLASS
P.O. Box 341
Wyckoff, NJ 07481
Phone: 800-872-3458
Web site: www.etchworld.com
Offers: Glass and mirror etching, as well as decorating supplies.
Free catalog.

THE LAMP SHOP
P.O. Box 3606
Concord, NH 03302-3606
Phone: 603-224-1603
Fax: 603-224-6677

Offers: Wide variety of lampmaking supplies, including wire, bases, paper, frames, ribbon, fabric, tools, and parts.
Catalog: $3

MAINELY SHADES
100 Gray Road
Falmouth, ME 04105
Phone: 800-624-6359
Fax: 800-554-1755
Web site: www.maineguide.com/maine-shade
Offers: Lampshade crafting materials, including frames, fabrics, papers, and paints, lamp bases, and electrical supplies.
Catalog: $3

METALLIFEROUS
34 West 46th Street
New York, NY 10036
Phone: 212-944-0909
Fax: 212-944-0644
Offers: Large selection of wire, flat metals, jewelry supplies, and enameling supplies.
Catalog: $7.50

SURMA
11 East 7th Street
New York, NY 10003
Phone: 212-477-0729
Fax: 212-473-0439
Offers: Ukrainian Easter egg-decorating dyes, tools, kits, and supplies.
Free catalog.

THINGS JAPANESE
9805 N.E. 116th Street Suite 7160
Kirkland, WA 98034-4248
Phone: 425-821-2287
Fax: 425-821-3554
Offers: A variety of paints and dyes. Also Tire silk thread, double-sided silk satin ribbon, and silk embroidery ribbon.

TINKER BOB'S TINWARE
209 Summit Street
Norwich, CT 06360
Phone/Fax: 860-886-7365
Offers: A complete selection of reproduction colonial tinware.
Catalog: $3

Beads & Buttons

BALLY AND BEAD CO.
2304 Ridge Road
Rockwall, TX 75087-5101
Phone: 800-543-0280
Fax: 972-722-1979
Web site: www.ballybead.com
Offers: Beading and jewelry supplies, semi-precious gemstones, African trade beads, crystals, chains, charms, findings, and tools.
Catalog: $4.95 (refundable with first order)

BEADS GALORE INTERNATIONAL, INC.
2123 South Priest #201
Tempe, AZ 85282
Phone: 602-921-3949
Fax: 602-921-7549
Offers: Large selection of stone, glass, silver, and trade beads, as well as findings, pendants, and earrings. Minimum order $30.
Catalog: $5

BEADCATS
(The Universal Synergetics Inc., Bead Store)
P.O. Box 2840
Wilsonville, OR 97070-2840
Phone: 503-625-2323
Fax: 503-625-4329
Offers: An array of beads, different glass types, surface finishes of pressed glass beads, bugle beads, brass beads, pony beads, and more. Also needles, thread, and other supplies. Books, kits, bead cards, beading videos.
Catalog: $2

BEADWORKS, INC.
149 Water Street
Norwalk, CT 06854
Phone: 203-852-9108
Fax: 203-855-8015
Web site: www.beadworks.com
Offers: Beads of glass, ceramic, porcelain, clay, wood, stained horn, bone, metal, plastic, stones, pearls, Fimo, and cord. No minimum order. Returns within 10 days.
Catalog: $5

BOVIS BEAD CO.
P.O. Box 13345
Tucson, AZ 85732
Phone: 520-318-9512
Fax: 520-318-0023
Offers: Variety of beads, such as French glass beads, tin, silver, brass, and bone. Also buttons, shells, teeth, needles, thread, beaded tassels, beeswax, and more. Return fee $5.
Catalog: $5

ELVEE ROSENBERG
11 West 37 Street
New York, NY 10018-6235
Phone: 212-575-0767
Fax: 212-575-0931
Offers: Fashion beads, simulated pearls, glass cabochons, metal, crystals, adhesives, and wires. Returns within 5 days with prior authorization.
Free catalog.

ENTERPRISE ART
P.O. Box 2918
Largo, FL 33779
Phone: 800-366-2218
Fax: 800-366-6121
Web site: www.cousin.com
Offers: Large assortment of beads, rhinestones, findings, and assorted craft supplies, such as Fimo, Friendly plastic, kits, Western wear supplies, and paint. No minimum order. Return for full refund or credit.
Free catalog.

GARDEN OF BEADIN'
P.O. Box 1535
Redway, CA 95560
Phone: 800-232-3588
Fax: 707-923-9160
Web site: www.a1server.com/beadluv
Offers: A variety of beads in all shapes, colors, and sizes. Includes beading supplies, stone, wood, bugles, facetted and smooth glass seed beads and looms, metal findings, and crystals. Shipping $4. Return within 30 days.
Catalog: $3

GREY OWL INDIAN CRAFT SALES CORP.
132-05 Merrick Blvd.
P.O. Box 340468
Jamaica, NY 11434
Phone: 718-341-4000
Fax: 718-527-6000
Offers: Beads, jewelry/belt kits, thread, wire, needles, embroidery, metal spots, nails, clips, buttons, books, and music. Fine Native American crafts and supplies.
Catalog: $3

MORNING LIGHT EMPORIUM
Roxy Grinnell
P.O. Box 1155
Paonia, CO 81428
Phone/Fax: 800-392-0365
Web site: www.wic.net/mle/mle.htm
Offers: Beads: crow, pony, seed, hex, bone, metal, and glass. Also, jewelry supplies, wire, eye/head pins, clasps, and bells.
Free catalog.

ORNAMENTAL RESOURCES
P.O. Box 3010-HI
1427 Miner Street
Idaho Springs, CO 80452
Phone: 800-876-6762
Fax: 303-567-4245
Web site: www.ornabead.com
Offers: Wide variety of beads, findings, books, supplies, and tools. Minimum order $25. Return within 10 days.
Catalog: $15

TSI, INC.
101 Nickerson St.
P.O. Box 9266
Seattle, WA 98109
Phone: 800-426-9984
Fax: 206-281-8701
Offers: Beads, jewelry supplies, and tools. Glass, bone, painted wood, silver, terracotta, letter and number beads. Tweezers, files, saw blades, eye loupes, anvils, vises, and cords. $5 fee for orders under $25.
Free catalog.

Candle Making

BARKER CANDLE SUPPLIES
15106 10th Avenue S.W.
Seattle, WA 98166

Phone: 800-543-0601
Fax: 206-244-7334
Web site: www.barkerco.com
Offers: Candle decorations, wax and wax additives, wicks, scents, candle holders, thermometers, liters, wax remover, luster, metal and plastic molds, and more.
Free catalog.

CANDLECHEM COMPANY
32 Thayer Circle
P.O. Box 705
Randolph, MA 02368
Phone: 781-963-4161
Fax: 781-963-3440
Web site: www.alcasoft.com/candlechem
Offers: Basic scents, designer scents, dyes and pigments, wax additives, novelty molds, metal molds, acrylic molds, waxes, beeswax sheets, soapcasting supplies, equipment, and accessories. No minimum order. Returns subject to fee.
Free catalog.

POURETTE CANDLE MAKING SUPPLIES
1418 NW 53rd
P.O. Box 17056
Seattle, WA 98107
Phone: 800-888-9425
Fax: 206-789-3640
Web site: www.pourette.com
Offers: A complete selection of candle-making supplies, including wax, molds, and wicks.
Free catalog.

WALNUT HILL ENTERPRISE, INC.
2441 Wilson Avenue
P.O. Box 599
Bristol, PA 19007
Phone: 800-633-3929
Fax: 215-785-6594
Offers: Candle-making supplies and specialty waxes, such as beeswax, batix wax, and freeze-dry wax. Minimum order $75.
Free catalog.

Decorative Baking

A COOK'S WARES
211 37th Street
Beaver Falls, PA 15010-2103
Phone: 800-915-9788
Fax: 800-916-2886
Offers: Gourmet cooking and baking supplies, books, equipment, and ingredients.
Catalog: $2

GRAPEVINE TRADING COMPANY
59 Maxwell Court
Santa Rosa, CA 95401
Phone: 707-576-3950
Fax: 707-5676-3945
Offers: Dried berries and fruits, as well as crystallized edible flowers.
Free catalog.

KING ARTHUR FLOUR BAKER'S CATALOGUE
P.O. Box 876
Norwich, VT 05055-0876
Phone: 800-827-6836
Fax: 800-343-3002
Web site: www.kingarthurflour.com
Offers: Wide assortment of baking-related supplies and gifts, including breadmaking equipment and books, bakers' appliances, grains, yeasts, cake and pastry supplies, and pasta equipment.
Free catalog.

KITCHEN KRAFTS
P.O. Box 442
Waukon, IA 52172
Phone: 800-776-0575
Fax: 319-535-8001
Web site: www.kitchenkrafts.com
Offers: Food-crafting supplies, equipment, books, and ingredients.
Free catalog (with mention of this listing).

LITTLE FOX FACTORY
931 Marion Road
Bucyrus, OH 44820
Phone: 419-562-5420
Offers: Handmade cookie cutters for quilt patterns and other crafts. Hundreds of shapes, including dinosaurs, states, and animals.
Free catalog (with long SASE).

SUR LA TABLE
1765 6th Avenue South
Seattle, WA 98134-1608
Phone: 800-243-0852
Fax: 206-682-1026
Offers: Cooking equipment, housewares, and gifts, including cake-decorating supplies, Calphalon cookware, a large selection of copper cookware, and more.
Free catalog.

SWEET CELEBRATIONS, INC.
7009 Washington Avenue South
Edina, MN 55439
Phone: 800-328-6722
Fax: 612-943-1688
Offers: Wide assortment of dessert supplies and accessories, including baking equipment, bridal figures, cake-decorating tools, and candy-making supplies.
Free catalog.

WILLIAMS-SONOMA
P.O. Box 7456
San Francisco, CA 94120-7456
Phone: 800-541-2233
Fax: 415-421-5153
Offers: Large selection of housewares and cookware, including glasses, dinnerware, cooking and baking equipment, flatware, appliances, linens, chefs' clothing, and more. Also offers recipes, books, herbs, cleaning supplies, gifts, and specialty foods.
Free catalog.

Florals & Naturals

A WORLD OF PLENTY
P.O. Box 1153
Hermantown, MN 55810-9724
Phone/Fax: 218-729-6761
Offers: Potpourri and sachet ingredients, oils, herbs, teas, and tools. No minimum order.
Catalog: $1 (refundable)

COLORADO BLOSSOMS
1501 Rancho Way
Loveland, CO 80537
Phone: 970-669-4578
Fax: 970-669-4545
Offers: An assortment of pressed flowers, herbs, and foliage in packages and sheets. Minimum order $25. Returns within 15 days with fee.
Free catalog.

THE HERB SHOPPE
204 Azalea Box 395
Duenweg, MO 64841
Phone: 417-782-0457
Fax: 417-782-7733
Offers: A variety of herbs, spices, botanicals, ginsengs, oils, soaps, and sundries. No minimum order.
Catalog: $2

LAVENDER LANE
7337 #1 Roseville Road
Sacramento, CA 95842
Phone: 916-334-4400
Fax: 916-339-0842
Web site: www.choicemall.com/lavenderln/donna@ricp.com
Offers: An assortment of herbalware, including essential and fragrance oils, lotions, gels, powders, waxes, flowers, potpourri, candle and soap molds, plastic and glass bottles, how-to recipes, books, kits, and accessories. Returns within 15 days.
Free catalog.

NATURE'S HERB COMPANY
1010 46th Street
Emeryville, CA 94608
Phone: 510-601-0700
Fax: 510-601-0726
Offers: Herbs, spices, teas, potpourri, tinctures, extracts, oils, and containers. Returns within 30 days.
Free catalog.

NATURE'S HOLLER
15739 Old Lowery Rd. N.
Omaha, AR 72662
Phone: 501-426-5489
Offers: Grapevine wreaths, acorns, pods, cones, color-blushed wheat, dried assorted weeds and grasses, baby's breath, sunflowers, moss, bamboo, wood works, and more. No credit cards.
Catalog: $2

SAN FRANCISCO HERB COMPANY
250 14th Street
San Francisco, CA 94103
Phone: 800-227-4530
Fax: 415-861-4440
Web site: www.sfherb.com
Offers: Complete lines of spices for cooking, crafting, and potpourri recipes, ingredients, and essential oils. Minimum order $30. Sales final after 15 days.
Free catalog.

Home Decor

AMERICAN FRAME CORPORATION
Arrowhead Park
400 Tomahawk Drive
Maumee, OH 43537-1695
Phone: 800-537-0944
Fax: 800-893-3898
Web site: www.Americanframe.com
Offers: Design picture frames in woods or metals, mat boards and plexi-glass plus accessories: polyester film, corrugated corners, point drive, linen tape, and all assembly hardware such as screws, spring clips, hanging wire, and wall protectors. No minimum order. Returns within 60 days with fee.
Free catalog.

CALICO CORNERS
203 Gale Lane
Kennett Square, PA 19348-1764
Phone: 800-213-6366
Fax: 610-444-1228
Web site: www.calicocorners.com
Offers: A variety of fabrics for every room in the house. Returns for full refund.
Catalog: $2.50

FRAME FIT CO.
7353 Milnor Street
Philadelphia, PA 19136
Phone: 800-523-3693
Fax: 800-344-7010
Web site: www.netaxs.com/~framefit
Offers: Frames in different colors, sizes, materials, depths, and designs. All frames include necessary hardware for assembly. Also offers screw hangers, springs, corner hardware, and picture wire. No minimum order. Returns for credit or refund.
Free catalog.

GRAPHIK DIMENSIONS LTD.
2103 Brentwood Street #10002
High Point, NC 27263
Phone: 910-887-3700
Fax: 910-887-3777
Offers: Supplies and materials for do-it-yourself framing, and frames in modern metal, classic woods, linen or suede lines, also Oriental and European styles.
Free catalog.

POTTERY BARN
P.O. Box 7044
San Francisco, CA 94120-7044

Phone: 800-922-5507
Fax: 415-421-5153
Offers: Small selection of faux finishing products, including wood wash and distressing kit, crackle glaze, stencil kits, colorwash kit, and related books.
Free catalog.

Papers, Stamps, & More

EVERGREEN BAG COMPANY
22 Ash Street
East Hartford, CT 06108
Phone: 800-775-3595
Fax: 860-289-0081
Web site: www.alcasoft.com/everbag
Offers: Gift, jewelry, and apparel boxes, tissue paper, ribbons, and bows. A variety of bags such as cellophane, drawstring, poly, tintie, and more. Returns for full refund.
Free catalog.

FASCINATING FOLDS
P.O. Box 10070
Glendale, AZ 85318
Phone: 800-968-2418
Fax: 888-433-6537
Web site: www.fascinating-folds.com
Offers: Origami paper, artisan paper, rice paper, washi paper, napkins, quilling, card making supplies, marbling, calligraphy, paints, decoupage glues, finishes, box sets, X-acto knives, and more.
Catalog: $1 (free with first purchase)

GOOD STAMPS - STAMP GOODS
30901 Timberline Road
Willits, CA 95490
Phone: 800-637-6401
Fax: 707-459-5021
Web site: www.pacific.net/~gssg
Offers: Collection of rubber stamps: wildlife, fairies, seasonal, letters, sayings, and calligraphic expressions. Or, make your own stamp with hardwood wooden blocks, vulcanized rubber sheets, and rubber backing material.
Catalog: $4

MAINE STREET STAMPS
P.O. Box 14
Kingfield, ME 04947
Phone/Fax: 207-265-2500
Web site: www.mint.net/opdag/ms.html
Offers: Selection of rubber stamps including flowers, fairies, and holidays.
Catalog: $2 (refundable with first order)

Sculpting & Ceramics

GEORGIES CERAMIC & CLAY CO.
756 NE Lombard
Portland, OR 97211
Phone: 800-999-2529
Fax: 503-283-1387

Web site: www.georgies.com
Offers: Sculpture, jewelry, printing, candle making, and glass supplies, as well as kiln accessories, enamel, glaze, finishes, clay, porcelain, brushes, tools, and more.
Catalog: $6

CERAMIC SUPPLY OF NEW YORK AND NEW JERSEY, INC.
7 Route 46 West
Lodi, NJ 07644
Phone: 800-723-7264
Fax: 201-340-0089
Offers: Collection of ceramic supplies, including wheels, clay, glazes, sponges, brushes, tools, knives, bisqueware, and more.
Catalog: $4

Sewing Notions & Fabrics

THE AMERICAN NEEDLEWOMAN
2946-50 S.E. Loop 820
Fort Worth, TX 76140
Phone: 817-293-1229
Fax: 817-568-2859
Offers: Towels, tablecloths, needlepoint, yarn, glitter paints, ornaments, latch hook, quilting, ribbon, beads, frames, and handcraft accessories.
Catalog: $2

ARTEMIS
179 High Street
South Portland, ME 04106
Phone: 888-233-5187
Fax: 207-741-2497
Offers: Hand-dyed, colorfast, silk ribbons in a variety of colors, combinations and widths, and hand-sewn, silk ribbon roses.
Free catalog.

ATLANTA THREAD AND SUPPLY CO.
695 Red Oak Road
Stockbridge, GA 30281
Phone: 800-847-1001
Fax: 800-298-0403
Offers: Thread, sewing machines, notions, hook and loop tapes, drapery hardware, foam fabric adhesives, batting and pillowforms, lining and pocketing, chalks, hooks, eyes and snaps, seambinding and hem-facings, and other related supplies and equipment. Minimum order $20.
Free catalog.

CLOTILDE INC.
2 Sew Smart Way
Stevens Point, WI 54481-8031
Phone: 800-772-2891
Fax: 800-863-3191
Offers: Large selection of sewing supplies, notions, equipment, and tools, including sewing machine accessories, tables, books, patterns, and gifts.
Free catalog.

DHARMA TRADING COMPANY
P.O. Box 150916
San Rafael, CA 94915
Phone: 800-542-5227
Fax: 415-456-8747
Web site: www.dharmatrading.com
Offers: Procion dyes, silk and wool dyes, cotton, rayon, denim, hemp, brushes, painting tools, and more.
Free catalog.

THE FABRIC CENTER
485 Electric Avenue
P.O. Box 8212
Fitchburg, MA 01420-8212
Phone: 508-343-4402
Fax: 508-343-8139
Offers: Home-decorating fabrics, including lightweights for draperies and bedding, multipurpose fabrics suitable for almost any interior use, and heavyweight fabrics designed for upholstery applications.
Catalog: $2

FAY'S FASHIONS AND FABRICS
1155 Webster Drive
Pensacola, FL 32505-4553
Phone/Fax: 850-455-7866
Offers: A variety of fabrics and lace, as well as appliques, trims, elastics, hook-and-eye, tape, thread, notions, patterns, and more.
Catalog: $5 (refundable with first order)

HALCYON YARN
12 School Street
Bath, ME 04530
Phone: 800-341-0282
Fax: 207-442-0633
Web site: www.halcyonyarn.com
Offers: Specialty yarns, videos (available for sale or rental), books, and software, sewing notions, and looms. No minimum order. Returns within 1 month.
Free catalog.

HOME SEW
P.O. Box 4099
Bethlehem, PA 18018
Phone: 610-867-3833
Fax: 610-867-9717
Offers: Sewing and craft supplies, including thread, notions, glues, lace, ribbon, scissors, trims, and doilies.
Free catalog.

KEEPSAKE QUILTING
Route 25B
P.O. Box 1618
Centre Harbor, NH 03226-1618
Phone: 800-865-9458
Fax: 603-253-8346
Web site: www.keepsakequilting.com
Offers: Quilting and sewing supplies, including fabrics by the yard, patterns, books, and notions. No minimum order. Returns at anytime.
Free catalog.

M AND J TRIMMING CO.
1008 Sixth Avenue
New York, NY 10018
Phone: 212-391-9072
Fax: 212-391-1526
Web site: www.mjtrim.com
Offers: Assortment of ribbons, motifs, frogs, fringes, tassels, cordedges, Jacquards, cords, buttons, and more. Minimum order $50.
Free catalog.

NANCY'S NOTIONS LTD.
P.O. Box 683
Beaver Dam, WI 53916-0683
Phone: 800-833-0690
Fax: 800-255-8119
Web site: www.nancysnotions.com
Offers: Wide assortment of sewing supplies and notions, including fabric, patterns, lace, thread, books, and videos.
Free catalog.

NEWARK DRESSMAKER SUPPLY
6473 Ruch Road
P.O. Box 20730
Lehigh Valley, PA 18002-0730
Phone: 610-837-7500
Fax: 610-837-9115
Offers: Sewing, craft, and needlework supplies, including beads, bridal basics, fabric, jewelry findings, ribbon and silk flowers. No minimum order. Returns within 2 months.
Free catalog.

OPPENHEIM'S
P.O. Box 29
120 East Main Street
North Manchester, IN 46962-0029
Phone: 800-461-6728
Fax: 219-982-6557
Offers: Pillows, rag rugs, and quilt kits; country prints, mill remnants, denim, chambray, flannel, and broadcloth. Swatches upon request with SASE.
Free catalog.

OREGON TAILOR SUPPLY COMPANY
2123 SE Division Street
P.O. Box 42284
Portland, OR 97242
Phone: 800-678-2547
Fax: 503-232-9470
Offers: Sewing, dressmaking, and dry-cleaning supplies, including thread, buttons, zippers, shoulder pads, and pressing equipment.
Free catalog.

SARAH'S SEWING SUPPLIES
7267 Mobile HWY
Pensacola, FL 32526
Phone: 800-883-2348
Fax: 904-944-6106
Web site: www.wordsetc.com
Offers: Pattern paper, sewing

machine accessories, measuring devices, needles, marking aids, interfacing and stabilizers, and more. No minimum order. Return fee.
Free catalog.

SUPER SILK, INC.
P.O. Box 527596
Flushing, NY 11352
Phone: 800-432-7455
Fax: 718-886-2657
Offers: A variety of silk fabrics sold by the yard. Several colors offered. No minimum order.
Free catalog.

Soap Making

SUGAR PLUM SUNDRIES
5152 Fair Forest Drive
Stone Mountain, GA 30088
Phone: 404-297-0158
Web site: www.mindspring.com/~sugrplum
Offers: Soap-making supplies, bath oils, hand made soaps, and massage oils. No minimum order. 100% guarantee.
Catalog: $1

SUNFEATHER NATURAL SOAP CO.
1551 Route 72
Potsdam, NY 13676
Phone: 315-265-3648
Fax: 315-265-2902
Web site: www.electroniccottage.com/sunfeathersoaps/
Offers: Soap-making supplies, essential oils, powdered clay, pumice, molds, kits, soap-making video, and books. No minimum order. Returns for refund.
Catalog: $3

Unfinished Wood Products

WOOD-N-CRAFTS, INC.
P.O. Box 140
Lakeview, MI 48850
Phone: 800-444-8075
Fax: 517-352-6792
Web site: www.wood-n-crafts.com
Offers: Unfinished wood, such as animals, miniatures, boxes, dowels, balls, buttons, beads, candlesticks, fruit, stars, and hearts. No minimum order. Returns within 30 days. Free shipping for orders over $50.
Catalog: $2

THE WOODWORKERS' STORE
4365 Willow Drive
Medina, MN 55340
Phone: 800-279-4441
Fax: 612-478-8395
Web site: www.woodworkerstore.com
Offers: Lumber veneer, hardware, hinges, poles, door slides, and power tools.
Catalog: $2

Winter 1998 Patterns

Flower Appliqué Place Mats

(*see* article, page 10)

NOTE: PHOTOCOPY AT 100%

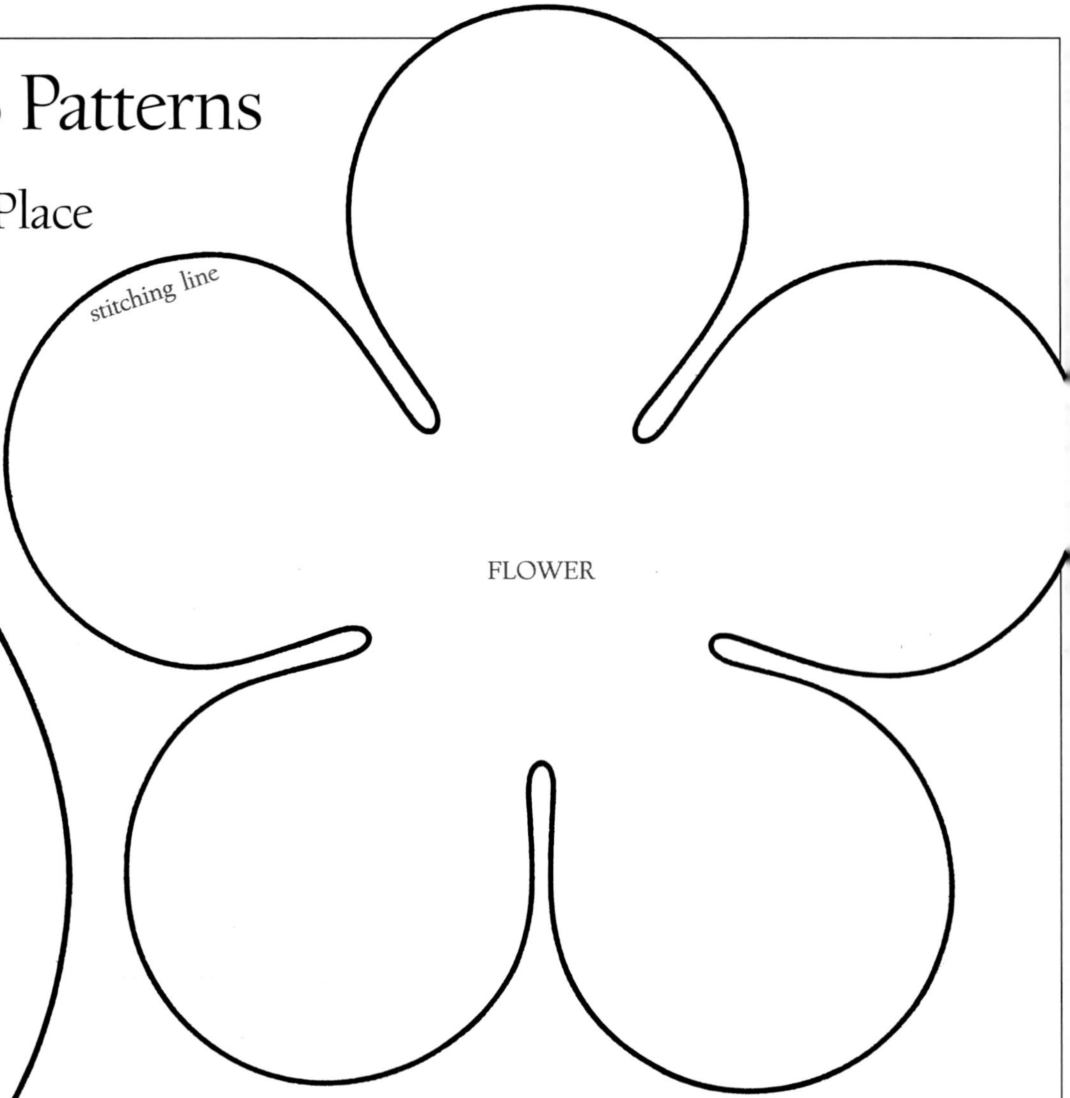

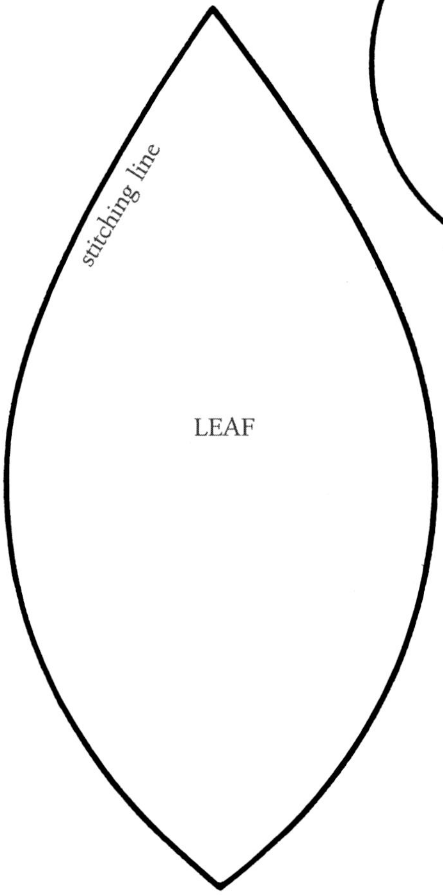

stitching line

LEAF

stitching line

FLOWER

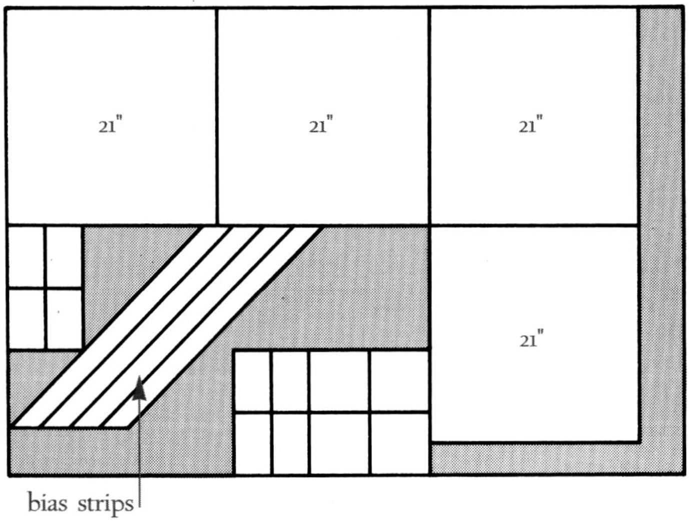

Beaded Napkin Pocket

(*see* article, page 32)

NOTE: PHOTOCOPY AT 100%

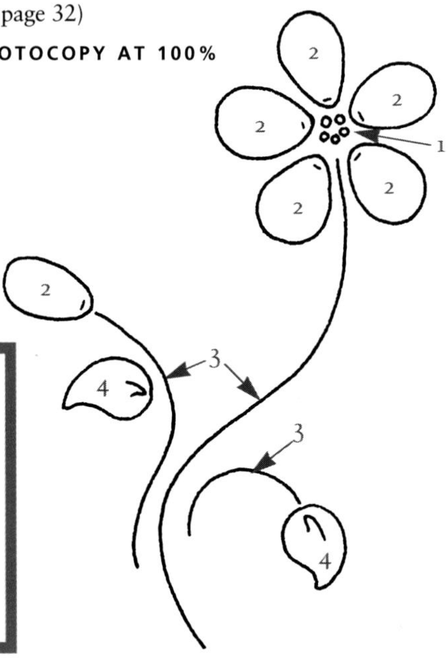

PLACE MAT CUTTING LAYOUT

21"	21"	21"
		21"

bias strips

COLOR KEY
1 = yellow
seed bead
2 = blue glass
petal
3 = green
seed bead
4 = green
glass leaf

Padded Scented Hanger

(*see* article, page 18)

NOTE: PHOTOCOPY AT 100%

The Secrets of Sewing with Plastic

(*see* article, page 23)

NOTE: PHOTOCOPY AT 200%

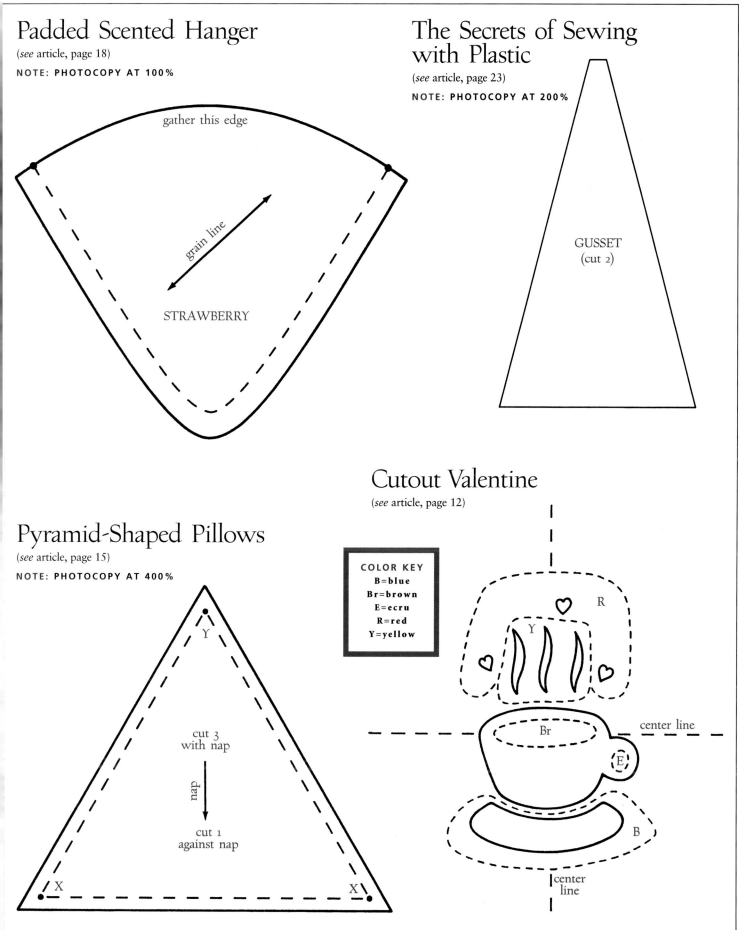

gather this edge

grain line

STRAWBERRY

GUSSET
(cut 2)

Pyramid-Shaped Pillows

(*see* article, page 15)

NOTE: PHOTOCOPY AT 400%

Cutout Valentine

(*see* article, page 12)

COLOR KEY
B=blue
Br=brown
E=ecru
R=red
Y=yellow

Y

cut 3
with nap

nap

cut 1
against nap

X   X

R

Y

Br

E

center line

B

center
line

Three-Panel Dutch Townscape

(*see* article, page 34)

NOTE: PHOTOCOPY ALL PIECES AT 100%

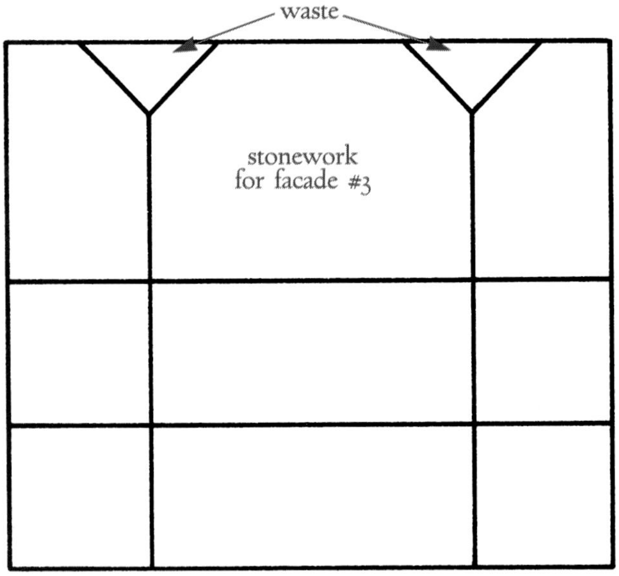

waste

stonework
for facade #3

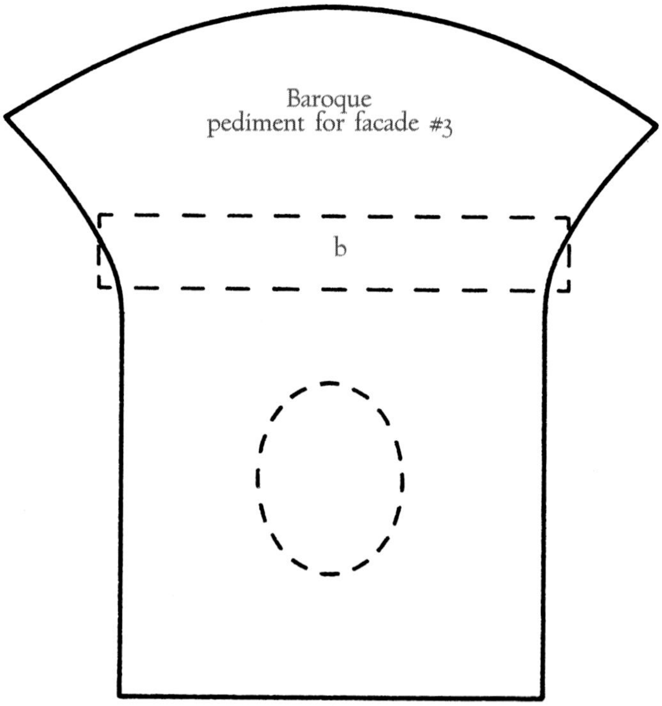

Baroque
pediment for facade #3

b

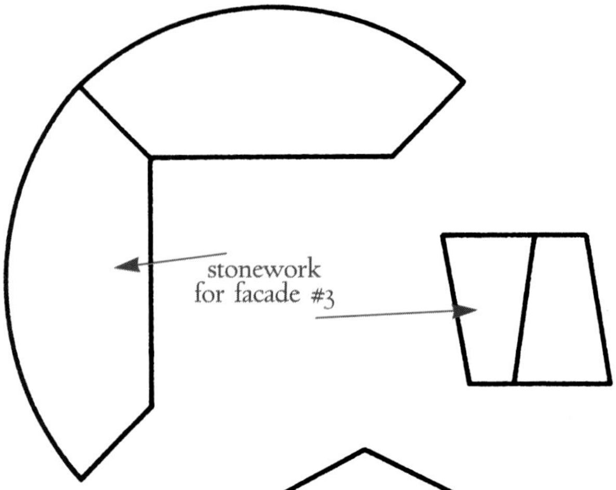

stonework
for facade #3

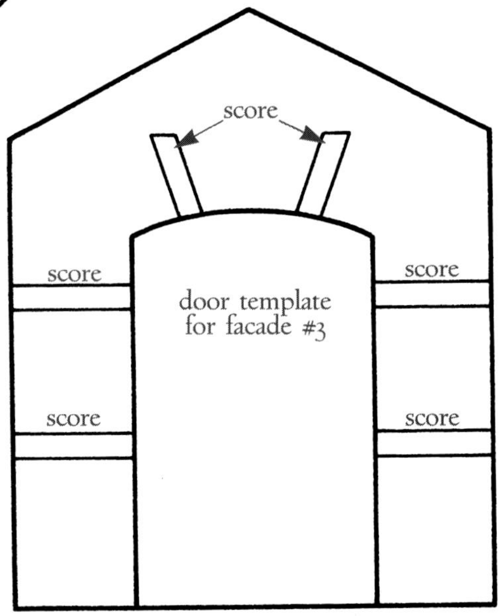

TEMPLATE KEY
a = 1-ply chipboard
b = ⅛" x ⅜" balsa
c = ⅛" x ¼" balsa
d = balsa "stonework"
e = 2-ply chipboard

Painted Poppy Bowl

(*see* article, page 16)

NOTE: PHOTOCOPY AT 400%

score

score   score

door template
for facade #3

score   score

Three-Panel Dutch Townscape

(*see* article, page 34)

NOTE: PHOTOCOPY ALL PIECES AT 200%

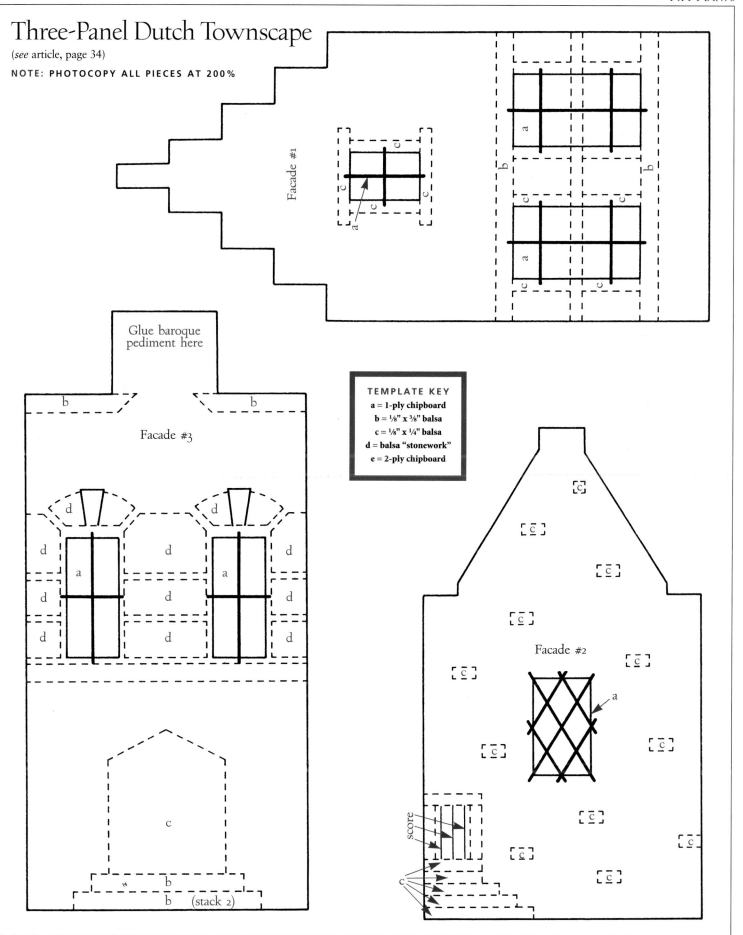

Facade #1

Glue baroque
pediment here

Facade #3

TEMPLATE KEY
a = 1-ply chipboard
b = ⅛" x ⅜" balsa
c = ⅛" x ¼" balsa
d = balsa "stonework"
e = 2-ply chipboard

Facade #2

(stack 2)

score

Sources & Resources

Following are the specific sources that offer mail-order for hard-to-find project items.

Most of the materials used in this issue are available at your local craft supply store, florist, fabric shop, hardware store, or bead and jewelry supply. Generic craft supplies can be ordered from catalogs such as Craft King, Pearl Paint Company, or Sunshine Discount Crafts. The following are specific sources for harder-to-find items, arranged by article. The suggested retail prices listed here were current at press time. Contact the suppliers directly to confirm prices and availability.

Home Accents, *page 6*
Metallic organza available for $10.25 per yard from Super Silk. Spiral icicle beads from Hands of the Hills.

Perfect Gift, *page 7*
Decorative paper books from $5.95 from Hot Off the Press.

Embossed Platter, *page 8*
Wooden round platter (item #3526) for $12.37 from Walnut Hollow.

Flower Place Mat, *page 10*
Linen ranging from $12-$30 per yard from Nancy's Sewing Basket. Four plain white linen place mats from $7.95 from David Moore's Table Top Shop.

Peekaboo Valentine, *page 12*
Watercolor 5"x 6⅞" card for $11.50 per 20, or watercolor sheets ranging from 90 cents to $3 each, both from Kate's Paperie.

Beaded Butterflies, *page 14*
Faceted 6mm and 8mm beads starting at 35 cents each from Beadworks.

Pyramid Pillows, *page 15*
"Three-D Triangle" pillow form starting at $15 for 14" from Down Decor.

Poppy Bowl, *page 16*
Unfinished 15" cullwood bowl for $16.70 from Granville Manufacturing.

Padded Hanger, *page 18*
Velvet leaves starting at 35 cents each from Nancy's Sewing Basket. "Moth-Be-Gone" moth-repellant herbs for $3.50 per 2-ounce bag from Cedarbrook Herb Farm.

Mosaic Tile Shades, *page 20*
Cathedral glass ranging from $5 to $12 per 12"x16" sheet from Delphi Stained Glass.

Sewing with Plastic, *page 23*
Vinyl plastic for $6.49 per yard from P&S Fabric.

Roll-Up Bed, *page 26*
Eskimo fleece for $9.95 per yard from Nancy's Notions.

Bath Tablets, *page 30*
Candy thermometer (#CE0978) for $3.50 from Kitchen Krafts. Natural essential oils starting at $2.50 per ¼-ounce bottle from Lavender Lane.

Faux Painting, *page 31*
Photo transfer paper for $5.95 for three 8-½" x 11" sheets from Hues, Inc.

Napkin Pocket, *page 32*
Petal and leaf beads available for 5 cents to 30 cents each (depending on style) from Beads and Beyond.

Three-Panel Dutch Townscape, *page 34*
Balsa sheet for $6.53 per sheet and basswood strips (item #8018) for $1.58 from Pearl Paint. Mirror-image metal corner brackets 75 cents each from Metalliferous.

Two-Color Pillowcases, *page 36*
Pillowcase set (#42-379859) for $40 for set of two 20"x 30" cases from Chambers.

Beaded Wastebasket, *Backcover*
Wire basket available for $24 (plus shipping & handling) from Black Ink.

🐚   🐚   🐚   🐚   🐚

The following companies are mentioned in the listing above. Contact each individually for a price list or catalog.

BEADS AND BEYOND
25 102nd Avenue NE, Bellevue, WA 98004; 425-462-8992

BEADWORKS, INC.
149 Water Street, Norwalk, CT 06854; 203-852-9108

BLACK INK
101 Charles Street, Boston, MA 02114; 617-723-3883

CEDARBROOK HERB FARM
1345 Sequim Avenue S., Sequim, WA 98382; 360-683-7733

CHAMBERS
P.O. Box 7841, San Francisco, CA 94120-7841; 800-334-9790

CRAFT KING
P.O. Box 90637, Lakeland, FL 33804; 800-769-9494

DAVID MOORE'S TABLE TOP SHOP
608 Bellevue Way NE, Bellevue, WA 98004; 425-454-7322

DELPHI STAINED GLASS
3380 E. Jolly Road, Lansing, MI 48910; 800-248-2048

DOWN DECOR
1910 South Street, Cincinnati, OH 45204; 800-792-3696

GRANVILLE MANUFACTURING
Route 100, P.O. Box 15, Granville, VT 05747; 800-828-1005

HANDS OF THE HILLS
3016 78th Avenue SE, Mercer Island, WA 98040; 206-232-8121

HOT OFF THE PRESS
1250 N.W. Third, Dept. B, Canby, OR 97013; 503-266-9102

HUES, INC.
936 Historical West 8th Street, Anderson, IN 46016; 800-268-9841

KATE'S PAPERIE
561 Broadway, New York, NY 10012; 212-941-9816

KITCHEN KRAFTS
P.O. Box 442, Waukon, IA 52172-0442; 800-776-0575

LAVENDER LANE
7337 Roseville Road #1, Sacramento, CA 95842; 888-593-4400

METALLIFEROUS
34 West 46th Street, New York, NY 10036; 888-944-0909

NANCY'S NOTIONS
333 Beichl Avenue, P.O. Box 683,
Beaver Dam, WI 53916-0683; 800-833-0690

NANCY'S SEWING BASKET
2221 Queen Anne Ave. N., Seattle, WA 98109; 206-282-9112

P&S FABRIC
355 Broadway, New York, NY 10013; 212-226-1534

PEARL PAINT COMPANY, INC.
308 Canal Street, New York, NY 10013-2572; 800-451-7327 (catalog) or 800-221-6845 x2297 (main store)

SUNSHINE DISCOUNT CRAFTS
P.O. Box 301, Largo, FL 33779-0301; 800-729-2878

SUPER SILK, INC.
P.O. Box 527596, Flushing, NY 11352; 800-432-7455

WALNUT HOLLOW
1409 State Road 23, Dept. CS, Dodgeville, WI 53533; 800-950-5101

UNITED STATES POSTAL SERVICE — Statement of Ownership, Management, and Circulation (Required by 39 USC 3685)

Quick Projects

Dress up your cabinet faces using these custom-designed drawer pulls.

Drawer pulls, shown clockwise from upper left: "Soap" type, clock face, embossed stamp, button, fruit basket, rhinestones, and pressed flower.

CUSTOM DRAWER PULLS

Spice up a cabinet or chest of drawers quickly and inexpensively by changing the face of the knobs. We used 2" wooden knobs for each of these designs, but they can be easily adapted to whatever type of knob your furnishings currently have. Begin by painting the knob a coordinating (or contrasting) color, then apply a decorative flourish.

■ **"Soap" type:** Paint knob with lavender acrylic. Starting with the letters "o" and "a", press adhesive letters to knob front.

■ **Clock face:** Paint knob with cream acrylic. Use photocopier to shrink clock face to just under 2" diameter; copy onto cream-colored paper. Cut out clock face and glue to knob surface with decoupage medium. Attach small clock hands to clock face with brass tack.

■ **Embossed stamp:** Paint knob with yellow acrylic paint. Use ink pad to stamp image onto knob face. Immediately sprinkle knob face with embossing powder. Shake off excess powder and heat knob face with heat gun (or hold over heated toaster) until powder "melts."

■ **Button:** Paint knob with green acrylic paint. Thread contrasting embroidery floss through embroidery needle. Holding end of thread at back of button, make 4-6 passes with needle and thread, ending at back of button. Remove needle and tie two ends in double knot. Hot-glue button in place.

■ **Decoupaged fruit basket:** Paint knob with coral acrylic paint. Use colored pencils to highlight selected areas of black and white image. Cut out image. Use decoupage medium to attach image to knob surface; second coat of decoupage medium onto entire knob surface.

■ **Rhinestones:** Paint knob with mustard yellow acrylic paint. Brush coat of contact cement across surface of knob. Beginning in center of knob, attach single large topaz rhinestone. Arrange medium-sized topaz rhinestones in concentric circles around central rhinestone. Finish edge of knob with smaller rhinestones.

■ **Pressed flower:** Paint knob with white acrylic paint. Cut out self-adhesive pressed flower image. Peel off backing and press flower to knob front. ◆

COLOR PHOTOGRAPHY:
Carl Tremblay

DESIGN:
Elizabeth Cameron

STYLING:
Ritch Holben

Beaded Wastebasket

To make the wastebasket, start by stringing the beads one by one onto a wire, then trapping them in place by wrapping a second, thinner gauge of wire around the original wire and the bead (see "Jeweled Cage Ornaments," Christmas 1997). The long strand of beaded wire is then wound around the belly of the wastebasket and secured with hidden medium-gauge wire.

To create the beaded wire, wrap a piece of 20-gauge wire five or six times around a basketball or large paint can, add 2", and clip with wire cutters. Unwind 10" of 24-gauge wire from a spool, but do not cut. Hold the two wire ends together, and twist the 24-gauge wire around the 20-gauge wire two or three times, for a spiral about 1/2" long. Slip the first bead onto the 20-gauge wire, and slide it down to the spiraled section. To lock the bead in place, twist the 24-gauge wire around the 20-gauge wire two or three times. Repeat the process with additional beads until you reach the end of the 20-gauge wire. To end off, spiral the 24-gauge wire around the 20-gauge wire for 1/2", then clip the wire from the spool. Create a second beaded wire of about the same length. Wind the beaded wires around the wastebasket.

To anchor the beaded wire to the wastebasket, first wind the twined ends of the wire around a vertical support. Cut a length of 24-gauge wire equal to the height of the wastebasket, plus 4" for each vertical support. Anchor the 24-gauge wires at the top of each vertical support. Wind the beaded wire around the wastebasket, securing it with the 24-gauge wires as it passes each vertical support. Weave the 24-gauge wire over and under the wastebasket's wire rings to hide it from view.

COLOR PHOTOGRAPHY: **Carl Tremblay**   STYLING: **Ritch Holben**   DESIGN: **Elizabeth Cameron**

NUMBER TWENTY

SPRING 1998

Handcraft
ILLUSTRATED

Spring!
**garden projects
baby gifts
fresh flower ideas
kitchen crafts**

Heirloom Eggs
A Unique Application for
Sealing Wax

Sand-Frosted
Flowerpots
The Secret: Paint is the Glue

The Easiest
Wildflower Wreath
Fresh Greens Circle a Frame

Mini Memory
Albums
Send Tiny Gift Books to Mark
Special Occasions

Folk Art Lamb
The Cutest Pompon Lamb
You'll Ever Make

Soft and Easy:

Lovely Painted Linens
Sheer Bedroom Canopy
Lace-Inset Towels
Daisy Shower Curtain
Striped Cotton Runner

Contents

Make beautiful egg candles to accent your Spring table. See page 13.

**Party Favor,
page 8**

**Apron and Mitts,
page 14**

**Miniature Memory
Album, page 16**

COVER PHOTOGRAPH:
Carl Tremblay

STYLING:
Ritch Holben

FEATURE STORIES

Handcraft
ILLUSTRATED

EDITOR
Carol Endler Sterbenz

SENIOR EDITOR
Mary Ann Hall

CREATIVE PROJECT DIRECTOR
Michio Ryan

RESEARCH AND TESTING EDITOR
Candie Frankel

CONTRIBUTING EDITOR
Elizabeth Cameron

ASSISTANT EDITOR
Melissa Nachatelo

❧

ART DIRECTOR
Amy Klee

CORPORATE MANAGING EDITOR
Barbara Bourassa

COPY EDITOR
Carol Parikh

❧

PUBLISHER AND FOUNDER
Christopher Kimball

MARKETING DIRECTOR
Adrienne Kimball

CIRCULATION DIRECTOR
David Mack

FULFILLMENT MANAGER
Larisa Greiner

CIRCULATION MANAGER
Darcy Beach

MARKETING ASSISTANT
Connie Forbes

PRODUCTS MANAGER
Steven Browall

❧

VICE PRESIDENT OF PRODUCTION AND TECHNOLOGY
James McCormack

EDITORIAL PRODUCTION MANAGER
Sheila Datz

DESKTOP PUBLISHING MANAGER
Kevin Moeller

PRODUCTION ARTIST
Robert Parsons

PRODUCTION ASSISTANT
Daniel Frey

❧

CONTROLLER
Lisa A. Carullo

SENIOR ACCOUNTANT
Mandy Shito

OFFICE MANAGER
Livia McRee

Handcraft Illustrated (ISSN 1072-0529) is published quarterly by Boston Common Press Limited Partners, 17 Station Street, Brookline, MA 02146. Copyright 1998 Boston Common Press Limited Partners. Second-class postage paid at Boston, MA, and additional mailing offices, USPS #011-895. For list rental information, please contact List Services Corporation, 6 Trowbridge Drive, P.O. Box 516, Bethel, CT 06801; (203) 743-2600; Fax (203) 743-0589. Editorial office: P.O.Box 470-509, 17 Station Street, Brookline, MA 02147; (617) 232-1000, FAX (617) 232-1572, e-mail: hndcftill@aol.com. Editorial contributions should be sent or e-mailed to: Editor, Handcraft Illustrated. We cannot assume responsibility for manuscripts submitted to us. Submissions will be returned only if accompanied by a large, self-addressed stamped envelope. Subscription rates: $24.95 for one year; $45 for two years; $65 for three years. (Canada: add $6 per year; all other countries add $12 per year.) Postmaster: Send all new orders, subscription inquiries, and change of address notices to Handcraft Illustrated, P.O. Box 7450, Red Oak, IA 51591-0450. Single copies: $4 in U.S.; $4.95 in Canada and other countries. Back issues available for $5 each. PRINTED IN THE U.S.A.

From the Editor

NATIVE AMERICANS HAVE A SAYING: Weave a mistake into a piece of work—it's a place to let the soul out. Unfortunately, our inclination seems to be the opposite. We struggle to control every aspect of our projects; as if what really matters is "perfection," what we fear most is our mistakes. Although most of the creative process is precarious, a path fraught with twists and turns that can lead us practically anywhere, crafters of all skill levels remain strangely on course, producing projects of uncommon beauty.

How do we account for this? Experience may explain some of this success. Outcomes are more predictable when we have worked in a certain medium than when we haven't, and practice gives us the confidence to further make the "right" choices. But if experience were the only foundation of artistic success, beginners would be doomed to filling drawers and closets with disappointing projects, even before they plugged in their glue guns for the first time. And this simply isn't the case. Beginning crafters consistently produce beautiful projects at first try, which is why I believe there is something more at work than practice and effort—something we can neither predict nor control—something I'm willing to call magic.

When beginners and experienced crafters alike talk about their work, they admit to moments of illumination, moments in which they experience a subtle shift from effortful participation to peaceful observation. They describe this sudden change as serendipity—unexpected, unpredictable, unbidden, and yet entirely welcome. And how else can we describe the high incidence of unexpected, satisfying, and appealing results accomplished by beginners?

Or by anyone. Goethe said, "Concerning all acts of initiative, and creation, there is one elementary truth—that the moment one definitely commits oneself, then Providence moves, too." In other words, there is a force that conspires with us in the creative process, bringing us moments of illumination that catalyze all our talent and all our efforts into something more than

There is something more at work than practice and effort—something I'm willing to call magic.

we had ever imagined. These moments aren't always remarkable; they can be so subtle as to escape our notice. And they don't always arrive on our schedule.

Illumination can come seconds or decades after we first set out to work. I have experienced this magic while I have worked, but I have also experienced the gift of illumination long after I have put my work aside. And more often than not, I have been amazed at how an answer to a design problem presents itself in a flash of insight when I am involved in doing something completely unrelated. It is as if the project continued to develop outside my awareness until that moment when it all fell together and brought me "a valuable gift not sought for." This is how M. Scott Peck defines "grace," that moment when something miraculous overrides our conscious choices and allows us to create a work that is so much more than we had first envisioned. Even if we ignore these moments of illumination, they will occur, but there is some benefit to keeping an innocent vigil, for you will find that if you expect these moments, they will arrive with greater frequency and imbue all your crafting of fabric, wood, paint, or any other material.

In the October/November 1989 issue of *American Craft* magazine, the following explanation of this component of the creative process was offered in the context of ceramics: "Ceramics, as meditation, as selfless concentration, requires the abandonment of anxiety and the perfection of skill to the point where it can be forgotten and one's consciousness become absorbed in the tactile sensations of the process. In this state, the work will form itself, and the potter may feel presumptuous even to take credit for the happenings which emerge from his kiln."

Who are we to reject our "mistakes," when it is their unplanned nature that can surprise us with an object of rare perfection?

Carol Endler Sterbenz

Notes from Readers

Learn to make rice paper napkins, discover the secrets to crackling finishes, color seashells with paint, and find a source for freeze-drying.

☙ COMPILED BY MELISSA NACHATELO

Antique-Crackle Success

I want to create a decoupage with a clear, crackled top glaze. I know the final step requires rubbing a top coat over the crackle medium. But I have tried several products with little success. Do you have any suggestions?

DAVID GORDINIER
ROCHESTER, NY

Finding a crackle medium for your project means choosing from a variety of crackling kits and mediums in the craft aisle. Almost every major brand has its own crackle medium. Each claims to give a crackling finish in a short amount of time and with relative ease. Unfortunately, not every brand works with every project. We tested more than five different brands, followed their directions, and found three to recommend.

In our Christmas 1997 issue, we used Anita's Fragile Crackle kit for the "Four-Panel Screen." This kit uses a two-step method and, unlike other crackle mediums, does not require an undercoat of acrylic paint to activate the crackle medium. Since it offers a clear finish, it works well on decoupage projects. As with most crackle mediums, the cracks can be emphasized further by applying a thin glaze as a topcoat.

We used Aleene's Mosaic Crackle Medium and Activator with a red acrylic paint on our "Embossed Platter" (Winter 1998). We liked this brand for its fine-crackle finish. With this product, the first step involves mixing one part crackle to two parts paint. In the second step, you apply the activator to the dried first layer. This activator layer then shrinks, forcing small, china-like cracks to appear.

The third crackle medium we suggest is DecoArt's Weathered Wood. We tested this medium with an undercoat of white acrylic paint. You can also use this on a decoupage surface. After allowing the crackle medium to dry for one hour, we brushed on a contrasting color.

Cracks showed immediately.

If you've tried these products and still have trouble achieving a crackle finish, re-evaluate your steps. Make sure to follow the directions carefully. Each label has detailed instructions on, for example, the amount of time given for drying between coats, and hints for creating small or large cracks. Generally, large cracks can be made by brushing on a thick coat of medium, while more intricate veins can be formed with a thinner layer. Most importantly, avoid going back and forth over an area repeatedly; you risk brushing out the crackles. Be sure to use long, sweeping brush strokes, covering an area with one stroke. In addition, crackle mediums will not activate in high humidity, so try to work in a cool, ventilated area.

Make Rice Paper Napkins

A friend told me about rice paper napkins and they seem perfect for a natural picnic setting. Do you know of a source?

CONNIE CALVERT
SAN LEANDRO, CA

Packaged napkins sold in Japanese grocery stores are generally made of rice paper. The napkins may not be labeled as such, but you can identify them by their texture and delicate designs, says Bren Riesinger, of Fascinating Folds, a paper company in Torrance, California. If a Japanese grocery market is not conveniently located in your area or you cannot find the napkins you need, making your own is easy.

We made a set of 12 full-sized napkins in under 10 minutes with a sheet of rice paper and scissors. Start by choosing a rice paper with a soft, almost clothlike texture. Make sure it is a composition that won't be too fragile or too rough. We bought a 24"x 36" sheet of soft *unryu* composed of 100% kozo (inner bark fiber) for $3. *Unryu* is available in an acid-free form, but the cost is significantly higher and since most paper napkins are not acid-free any-

way, we used a regular sheet.

To make the napkins, lay the paper out and fold it into squares to form the napkin size you want. (Cocktail-size squares will yield more napkins, but we decided to fold the sheet to form twelve 9"x 8" lunch napkins.) Next, cut along the folds. Straight cuts through the paper give the napkins a rustic, unfinished look, perfect for an outdoor picnic. We also tried cutting a deckle-edge with special shears, but since the kozo fibers tear like fabric, we don't suggest this. If you want a more finished appearance, scallop the edges using scissors.

Rice paper can be purchased at most art or craft stores. Fascinating Folds also carries 23"x 34" sheets of Thai soft *unryu* in a variety of colors. For more information or to order rice paper, call the company at 800-968-2418 or visit www.fascinating-folds.com on the Internet.

Choices for Project Fillings

I want to make the Terry Cloth Baby Animals (Christmas 1997) with the plastic pellets stuffing. I've never used this material before, and I was wondering what advantage it holds over beans, rice, or sand.

TRACY THAN
MODESTO, CA

We chose plastic pellets for their lightweight quality, smooth feel, easy clean up, and, above all, their flexible movement. Other fillings will work, but your choice depends on what kind of toy you want—one that will sit propped up on a shelf or one meant for play. The filling you use for a project should be determined by whether you will need to clean it, what weight it should be, and how much movement it needs.

Dry beans from the supermarket are a longtime favorite of many crafters. They are easy to find, ready to use, and come in many sizes. However, there are some disadvantages. Washing will fray the beans over time, and beans, like rice, will

ultimately attract insects. Sand is also a possibility for a project if you want a fine filling for a dense object. Sand works best when used for a doorstop or something stable, since one-half cup of sand weighs about 6.5 ounces, much more than navy beans, which weigh 3.5 ounces, and plastic pellets, which weigh 2.5 ounces (both per one-half cup). Another consideration is that sand must be wrapped within a toy or the grains will escape through the fibers as the fabric stretches.

For this project, we found pellets worked best and offered the characteristics we wanted. We thought beans would clog in the limbs and that sand would be too heavy. Pellets served us well, giving the baby animals a flexible slouch.

Crack Walnut Shells Easily

I teach a third grade class, and there is a walnut shell project my students enjoy. I've avoided this project because cracking the shells can be so difficult. They always break into little pieces. Is there a simple way to open a walnut that leaves the shell halves intact?

PATRICIA KELLY
TAUNTON, MA

For an easy solution, soak walnuts in a jar of salted water overnight. Use a jar with a tight-fitting lid, and add approximately ¼" teaspoon of table salt for each 10 ounces of water. Then, place untreated walnuts in the water and tighten the lid. Let it sit overnight. Remove the walnuts in the morning and let them dry. They will have a softened, more resilient shell. When the moisture is gone and you can grasp the shell easily, crack the shells lengthwise. Rather than cracking into little pieces, the two halves should snap apart intact. If the shell does not immediately break open, place a skewer or knife blade between the halves and gently pry apart. During our tests with this technique, about 80% of the shells stayed intact.

Velvet Fruit Patterns

I'm looking for patterns to make fabric fruits similar to the peaches made from stretched velvet in the Spring 1997 issue of Handcraft. *My own attempts to make velvet apples and pears have been unsuccessful.*

HARRIET ZIMMERMAN
LEXINGTON, NC

Butterick Company, Inc., carries a pattern that details apples, pears, and grapes, but the pattern comes only in a pincushion size. Measuring 2½" to 3¼", these fruity pincushions are not in proportion to the original velvet peach design in the Spring 1997 issue.

However, you can transform this pincushion miniature into a life-size version by enlarging the pattern. Begin by making a rough muslin sample of one of the original pincushion patterns. Then compare it to a real piece of fruit, and determine the differences in proportion. Photocopy the pattern and enlarge it by the percentage required. Ask your local sewing supply store for the Decorative Pincushions pattern #4795, or call Butterick at 800-678-8091.

We also recommend a comprehensive book, *A Patchwork Christmas* (Sedgewood Press, 1987), by Margit Echols. Although the book is no longer in print, look for a copy in your local library. The book contains a section of patterns for everything from apples, pineapples, and pumpkins to pears, grapefruits, and bananas.

Make Sure Memories Last

Can you suggest safe ways to preserve photos in an album?

JOSEPHINE LEWIS
ANN ARBOR, MI

We spoke with archival specialists from University Products, Inc., to determine the good methods for preserving precious photographic prints. They recommend sleeves made of polypropylene as the most protective method for displaying photos. Since the acid from hands can deteriorate any photo over time, these sleeves, detailed by dividers, protect photos by minimizing the amount of contact to a print. The sleeves also prevent yellowing and warping over time. Although sleeves with dividers aren't the most visually pleasing, you can dress them up with labels, written messages, and stickers placed on the top surface of the sheet.

The sheets come in a variety of dimensions to accommodate 3"x 5", 4"x 6", 5"x 7", or 8"x 10" photos. Prices range from $6.25 for 10 sheets to 50 sheets for $16.05. Call or write for a free catalog: University Products, Inc., 517 Main Street, P.O. Box 101, Holyoke, MA 01041-0101; 800-628-1912.

Accent Seashells with Paint

Collecting seashells and sea glass on the beach is one of my favorite hobbies. I always want to do something with the shells, but rarely have the time. Are there any quick ideas for decorating with these finds?

TARA NADIR
COTUIT, MA

After your next beach excursion, bring your sea treasures home and try some of these quick projects: Glue them to a picture frame or wooden box, display them in a vase, or simply showcase the shells on a platter for a table centerpiece.

If you're looking for ways to decorate the shells, try using watercolors and acrylic paints. We noticed that the porous nature of most shells allows a watercolor paint to seep into the grain and imitate the shell's natural texture. We began by removing the salt from the shells by boiling them in a pot of water for about five minutes. Next, we painted shades of blue, indigo, and salmon on whole clam shells and pieces of oyster and conch shells. The watercolor soaked into the shell quickly, leaving a subtle tint. Acrylics offer a fantasy-like appearance because the paint becomes an opaque skin over most of the shell. On certain shells, however, like clam shells, acrylic paint will simply seep into the crevices and contrast with the white ridges, which don't grab the paint.

We also experimented with glass paint on sea glass. It adheres, but we didn't think it added much to the natural beauty of the pieces. One way to add color to sea glass that we liked was to simply place the pieces over a colorful surface.

If you are interested in enhancing the natural colors of oyster shells or other varieties, apply an acrylic sealer. It will bring out the color and pattern and give the shell a finished shine.

Locating Freeze-Dried Fruits & Vegetables

Freeze-dried fruits and vegetables in a topiary look wonderful. Can you tell me how to make them or where to find them?

BEVERLY MANNING
PORTLAND, OR

Freeze-drying involves removing the moisture from the cells of fruits, vegetables, or flowers—without damaging the structure. This process requires special equipment, such as a freeze dryer, which costs anywhere from $5,000 to more than $50,000, and uses extremely low temperatures. For this reason, most people get freeze-dried items from a commercial source, such as a florist.

If you can't find a location near you, try mail-ordering. Lavender & Old Lace, a retail mail-order supplier, offers freeze-dried roses and flowers year-round, and fruits and vegetables during the summer. The fruits and vegetables come in slices or in halves. Glen Nelson, owner of Lavender & Old Lace, says you can bond halves together with glue to make a whole. Prices vary, so for information write or call Lavender & Old Lace, P.O. Box 4983, Missoula, MT 59806; 800-728-9244 .

Freeze-dried items can be planted in a topiary with ordinary floral wire and picks, but be sure to avoid direct sunlight, excessive heat, and moisture.

Age Your New Brick

We live in an old home and new brick was just used to replace the fireplace. Is there a way to give it an older finish?

LEORA TOWER
EDMONDS, WA

Bright red brick can be made to look worn, blackened, or antiqued in a number of ways. Make the brick appear worn down by using a hammer and cement chisel to carefully knock off corners of individual bricks (wear protective goggles). However, keep taps focused and do not disturb the mortar with the chisel. If this method is too extreme for you, focus on an applied finish.

For a "grayed" look, spot and spread thin layers of white plaster within the small dimples of the brick. Go over the dried plaster and brick with sandpaper to reduce the chaulky white areas. Or give the brick a darker, blackened appearance by covering the brick with a soaking wet cloth. Then, instead of spreading white plaster, use a commercially prepared black soot, available in most hardware stores, and lightly cover the surface of the fireplace brick. Acrylic paints in "stone" colors will also create an aged look. Paint soaks into the porous brick, but mistakes can still be quickly wiped away.

For any of these techniques, we suggest practicing on loose bricks or creating a mini-brick wall to test for the right finish. Although you can wipe away small mistakes, spreading soot or paint on the fireplace bricks can leave permanent color.

Gold Armature Wire

Is armature wire available in gold? I'd like to make armature sculptures to match the gold accents in my living room.

JOAN BENOCHI
TARRYTOWN, NY

Armature wire, a noncorrosive alloy wire, does not come in a gold or bronze tone, nor is there a counterpart made from brass or copper. The quickest way to turn the silver-toned wire into a gold metallic accent for your living room is with an acrylic-based gold spray paint. This method of spray painting the wire is not entirely permanent, but as long as your decorative piece is not handled much, it will probably do the trick.

Here are a few hints to make the gold paint hold. First, shape the wire into the sculpture form and remove any dangling pieces. Gently scrub the surface with steel wool and detergent to add "tooth" to the wire, creating a surface that paint will adhere to. Wipe the wire clean and let it dry. The sculpture should be set on newspaper in a well-ventilated work area. Spray the exposed surfaces thoroughly, let them dry, then turn the piece over and finish coating any unsprayed sections.

Quick Tips

POTPOURRI TIP

When arranging dried flowers, Mary Munnings of Alpharetta, Georgia, uses potpourri instead of florist foam. The dry potpourri mixture supports the stems without crushing them, emits a pleasant scent, and best of all, looks beautiful when viewed through a clear glass vase.

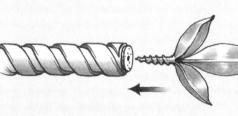

SCRATCH-FREE BEADS

Coat the tips of your craft tweezers with polish, writes Katherine Scott of Elkins, West Virginia. Now you can pick up beads and other small items without scratching them.

QUICK CURTAIN ROD

Plumbing and electrical hardware can be made into curtain rods, writes Heather Henderson of Sanford, Florida. Her favorite is electric conduit, which can pass for wrought iron.

1. **Spray-paint the conduit matte black, then add gold highlights.**

2. **Insert a wooden dowel for support, plugging each end with a cork.**

3. **Screw a lamp finial into each cork.**

ILLUSTRATION:
Michael Gellatly

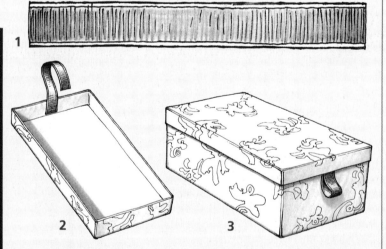

EASY OPEN

A ribbon tab makes box lids easier to open, writes Caroline Urban of Tarpon Springs, Florida.

1. **Cut a strip of grosgrain ribbon 2" longer than twice the box lid height.**

2. **Glue the ribbon ends to the inside lid.**

3. **To lift the lid, pull up on the ribbon loop.**

PAINT CAPS

For painting projects, double-welled plastic caps are indispensible, writes Jo Cabrera of Mustang, Oklahoma. Typical sources include spray starch, spray paint, and hairspray containers. Jo puts paint in the inner well and water in the outer ring for diluting and brush washing. When she needs a palette, she hot-glues several caps together.

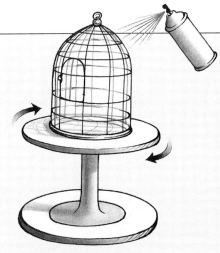

EVEN SPRAY PAINTING

If you spray paint small items frequently, a $15 potter's hand-building turntable is worth owning, writes Maureen Inman of Warner, New Hampshire. Just place the item to be painted on the turntable, spin with one hand (you control the speed), and spray with the other.

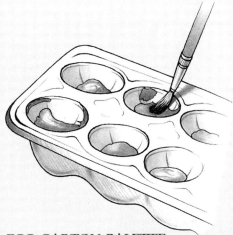

EGG CARTON PALETTE

Tani LeClair of Goodyear, Arizona, uses foam egg cartons for mixing paints. The compartments are roomier than commercial palettes, and used sections can be broken off and thrown away.

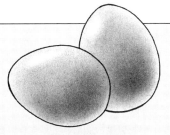

ANTIQUE EGG DYEING

Eggs colored in natural dye baths take on warm, earthy hues, like mustard yellow, olive green, and reddish brown. If you like the look, but don't want to spend hours boiling onion skins or berries, simply start with brown eggs instead of white. Use the same food color or kit dyes you would normally use. Thanks to Elaine Chabot of Tulsa, Oklahoma, for this tip.

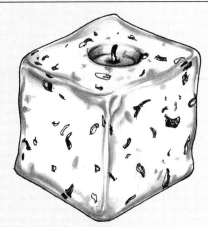

RECYCLING POTPOURRI

Don't throw out old or crushed potpourri, writes Sharon Wallace of Lawrence, Kansas. Even after the scent is long gone, the dried particles can add color and texture to handmade candles, soaps, and paper.

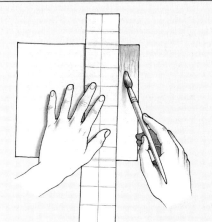

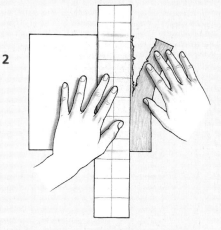

INSTANT DECKLE EDGE

To dress up plain rag paper or stationery, add a faux deckle edge, writes Caroline Mishure of Minneapolis, Minnesota.

1. **Using a plastic ruler as a guide, brush the paper edge with water.**

2. **Slowly pull the wet edge toward you at an angle, tearing it as you go.**

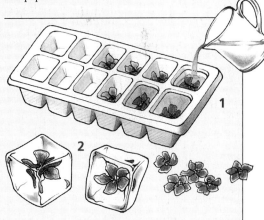

FLOWER PETAL ICE CUBES

Joan Parker of Carlisle, Masssachusetts, makes floral ice cubes that are perfect for iced teas, lemonades, and juices. Be sure to use edible flowers, such as roses or violets.

1. **Place a fresh blossom in each ice cube tray compartment. Fill the tray with water, making sure the petals are submerged.**

2. **Freeze overnight. Pop out the cubes as needed.**

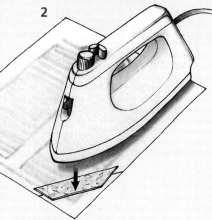

PAPER FIX

Before mounting torn cards or clippings in a memory album, try this repair tip from Jamie Fontaine of Tampa, Florida.

1. **Fit the torn edges together.**

2. **Apply lightweight fusible webbing to rejoin the pieces.**

Quick Home Accents

Snip single daisies off a yard of embroidery to transform a bed sheet into a custom shower curtain.

DAISY APPLIQUÉ SHOWER CURTAIN

Restyle your bathroom in an afternoon by turning a sheet and some sewing notions into a new shower curtain. We started with a green and white gingham sheet, added grommets along the top, and attached appliqué daisies. The daisies were clipped from appliqué trim that comes by the yard. We used two sizes: 1" and 1¾" daisies. A yard of daisies costs around $5—much less than the cost of individual appliqués.

Because the appliqué trim we found was solid white, we colored the daisy centers with yellow fabric paint and set them aside to dry. We cut a 76" square from the sheet and machine-stitched a 1" dou-

ble-fold hem along the lower edge and sides. Then we machine-stitched a 1¼" double-fold hem along the upper edge. We installed twelve ⁵⁄₁₆" grommets along the upper edge of the curtain, centering them on the seam allowance.

We clipped the daisy appliqués apart and pinned them onto the shower curtain in offset vertical rows, alternating between the two sizes. Instead of daisies, you may want to use another appliqué, or even ribbons or buttons. The size and shape of your accents may suggest different arrangements.

We used a small amount of Liqui-fuse fusible web on each daisy, heat-setting

each one onto the curtain. This product looks very much like ordinary white glue but behaves a little differently; if it sits for a few minutes without being heat-set, it becomes powdery. If this happens, don't worry—it can be lifted away and new glue applied.

To complete our custom curtain, we also painted the plastic shower curtain rings with yellow dots to echo the daisy appliqués. After roughing them up to ensure that the paint would adhere, we applied Delta CeramDecor Perm Enamel products—conditioner, paint, and a protective glaze—in an easy-to-follow sequence. ◆

COLOR PHOTOGRAPHY:
Carl Tremblay

DESIGN:
Dawn Anderson

STYLING:
Ritch Holben

The Perfect Gift

Create matching place mats and napkins by hand-painting simple patterns in bright colors onto linen.

PAINTED LINENS

These hand-painted linens make the perfect gift when packaged in their own coordinating gift tubes. Several tubes can be tied together with ribbon to make a set.

Use cocktail napkins and place mats with hemstitched borders; the well-defined borders make them easy to paint. You will also need mailing tubes, drawing paper to cover them, ribbon, and paint. We used Createx airbrush paints and mixed white paint into the colors to make pastels.

Prewash the linens to remove any sizing. Paint both sides of the border areas of the place mats and napkins.

■ **Painting the flowers:** Create a square pattern out of paper using dimensions of inside border of napkin. Randomly place six quarters on the pattern to mark flower placement. Draw circles around quarters with black marker. Cover pattern with waxed paper and lay napkin on top, aligning inside border. Circles should be visible. Cut six triangles from masking tape and place one triangle in center of each circle on right side of napkin. With ¼" shader brush, start at one point of triangle, paint a stroke, rotating brush one quarter turn. Repeat two more times for petals. Remove tape. Use eraser end of pencil to paint flower centers.

■ **Painting the leaves:** Using pointed round brush, paint shallow S–curve next to flower. Starting at top of S, paint curved line. Shade inside area lightly.

■ **Painting the wave pattern:** Load 1" shader brush with paint. With brush perpendicular to surface, paint wavy line, leaving some white showing through. For wide waves, paint additional strokes, overlapping preceding stroke. Alternate thick and thin waves, leaving 1" spaces between them where you can paint straight lines in a contrasting color.

To finish, heat-set paints and glue or tape paper around mailing tubes. Punch hole in corner of gift card for ribbon. Place linens in tubes and tie tubes together with ribbon. ◆

COLOR PHOTOGRAPHY:
Carl Tremblay

DESIGN:
Dawn Anderson

STYLING:
Ritch Holben

Easter Party Favor

Layer giftwrap silhouettes to create a seasonal gift bag.

🐚 BY DAWN ANDERSON

MATERIALS

Makes one gift bag

- 7" x 12" solid color giftwrap (for rabbit)
- 8" x 12" printed giftwrap (for egg)
- 12" x 18" gold-coated card stock
- 2" x 3¼" x 6"-high gold gift bag
- ⅜ yard ½"-wide gold mesh ribbon
- ⅜ yard ⅛"-wide gold mesh ribbon
- Four 9" x 12" sheets double-sided adhesive
- Gold pigment ink
- Gold embossing powder

You'll also need:
rabbit and egg templates (*see* page 47); X-Acto knife; self-healing cutting mat; quilter's acrylic grid ruler; rubber stamp with small motif; toaster (or other heat source); scissors; hole punch; white craft glue; and pencil.

Choosing complementary papers is the key to designing these decorative Easter table accents.

COLOR PHOTOGRAPHY:
Carl Tremblay

ILLUSTRATION:
Michael Gellatly

STYLING:
Ritch Holben

P ASS ALONG SMALL AND PRE- cious gifts this season in these easy-to-make party favors. The construction method is simple— all you do is cut the rabbit and egg silhouettes from giftwrap paper, add embossed designs to the rabbit, laminate each piece, and adhere them to a small gift bag.

You will need only a small amount of giftwrap for each party favor—about the size of a sheet of typing paper. A package or roll of giftwrap should be plenty to make a matched set, or you could save scraps to make an assortment.

For this Easter version, I chose a pastel and gold patterned paper for the "decorated" egg. Then I selected a solid lavender paper for the rabbit which matched the printed paper, and used gold accents all around to create harmony between the elements and add a festive flair.

The layering technique presented here can be used to create gift bags for other occasions as well. Just choose two appropriate symbols for the occasion, like a carriage and a rattle for a baby shower, or a star and a pine tree for Christmas, and follow the basic procedures.

Dawn Anderson is a writer and designer living in Redmond, Washington.

INSTRUCTIONS

1. *Rough-cut rabbit and egg papers.* For rabbits, rough-cut eight 6" x 7" rectangles: two from solid giftwrap, two from gold card stock, and four from double-sided adhesive. For eggs, cut six 6" x 8" rectangles: two from printed giftwrap, two from gold card stock, and two from double-sided adhesive. Prepare rabbit and egg templates (*see* page 47).

2. *Mark papers.* Lay printed giftwrap rectangles face up. For each, center egg template on top, and trace outline with sharp pencil. Repeat process to mark rabbit outline on solid giftwrap rectangles, flipping template so second rabbit is mirror image (*see* illustration A, next page).

3. *Emboss solid papers.* Lay two solid giftwrap rectangles flat, marked side up. Using rubber stamp and gold ink, stamp image once within rabbit outline. Immediately, while ink is still wet, sprinkle gold embossing powder over stamped image. Repeat process to stamp approximately nine images at random inside each rabbit outline (illustration B). Following manufacturer's instructions, hold paper over toaster (or substitute) to activate powder and raise designs.

4. *Laminate rabbit and egg papers.* Peel paper backing from one side of 6" x 7" adhesive rectangle. Press adhesive against wrong side of corresponding gold card stock. Smooth on both sides with palm. Peel off remaining backing. Position rabbit giftwrap along one edge, right side up, and press into position with palm (illustration C). Repeat process to laminate all four giftwrap rectangles to card stock.

5. *Join rabbits and eggs.* Using scissors for eggs, and X-Acto knife and cutting mat for rabbits, cut out each piece just inside pencil outline (illustration D). Using scissors, trim rabbit template just inside egg outline to remove paw, nose, and tail (illustration E). Place altered template on each remaining adhesive sheet, trace outline, and cut out with X-Acto knife. Peel off backing from one surface and adhere to gold side of giftwrap rabbit. Position rabbit on egg, referring to egg template for position, and mark outline lightly with pencil. Peel off remaining backing and adhere rabbit to egg (illustration F).

Repeat to join remaining egg and rabbit.

6. *Join eggs to bag.* Fold and crease top of bag 4" from bag bottom; trim off excess 1¼" above fold. Tuck 1¼" allowance inside bag and crease well. From double-sided adhesive, cut two rectangles 3⅛" x 3⅞", or slightly smaller than bag face surface. Peel backing from one rectangle and apply it to bag face. Peel off remaining backing and adhere to

gold side of egg, ¼" above lower edge. Join remaining egg to other side (illustration G).

7. *Add ribbons.* Cut ⅛" gold ribbon in half. Tie each piece into bow and glue to rabbit's neck. Align eggs at top of bag. Punch hole ⅛" from top center through both layers. Insert ½" ribbon through both holes (illustration H). Fill bag with party treats, then tie ribbon in bow. ◆

PATTERNS
See page 47 for pattern piece and enlargement instructions.

Make an Easter Party Favor

A. Mark two eggs and two rabbits on giftwrap.

B. Stamp and emboss each rabbit.

C. Laminate each giftwrap paper to gold card stock.

D. Cut out the rabbits and the eggs.

E. Trim the rabbit template.

F. Adhere each rabbit to an egg.

G. Adhere an egg to each side of a small gift bag.

H. Thread a gold mesh ribbon through the hole to tie the bag closed.

Piqué Bath Stool Slipcover

Quick-sew cotton towels into a cozy seat for the bath.

❧ BY CHIPPY IRVINE

Patches of hook-and-loop tape hold this piqué slipcover on its ordinary wooden stool. Hook and loop spots also connect the button-tufted cushion to the top of the slipcover.

COLOR PHOTOGRAPHY:
Carl Tremblay

ILLUSTRATION:

Mary Newell DePalma:
A, D, F, G, H, K
Judy Love:
B, C, E, I, J

STYLING:
Ritch Holben

A CCORDING TO A RECENT ARTI-cle, we have become a nation of shower people. I, however, am one of those who believe a bathroom should be a place for luxurious retreat. If you agree, then this slipcovered bath stool is for you.

The slipcover, which conceals a small wooden stool, is made from five white waffle piqué towels. Four towels make up the side panels and the top, while the fifth one forms the cover for a button-tufted cushion filled with washable batting.

Chippy Irvine is a designer living in Patterson, New York.

MATERIALS
Makes one slipcovered bath stool

- **Rectangular wooden stool, up to 17" high and 15" wide**
- **Five 17" x 28" waffle piqué cotton towels**
- **High-loft batting**
- **9" x ¾" white Velcro sew-on strip**
- **Nine ¾" self-covering buttons**
- **Sewing thread to match cotton towels**

You'll also need:
sewing machine; iron; rotary cutter; quilter's acrylic grid ruler; self-healing cutting mat; sewing shears; tape measure; point turner; hand-sewing needle; fabric-marking pencil; and paper.

INSTRUCTIONS

1. *Cut and press side panels.* Measure seat and height of stool. Sketch your stool and record its measurements, e.g., 15" x 11½" x 17" high (*see* illustration A, next page). Lay one 17" x 28" towel flat. Starting at hem edge, measure and mark stool height + ½", e.g., 17½". Using grid ruler, rotary cutter, and cutting mat, cut towel at mark parallel to hem edge. Repeat process to cut four panels total (illustration B). On two panels, fold and press side edges to wrong side to match seat width. On remaining two panels, fold and press side edges to equal seat length (illustration C). Set aside remaining fabric.

2. *Prepare seat panel.* Place two reserved pieces right sides together and cut edges matching. Sew ⅜" from cut edges to join pieces. Press seam open. With seam centered, cut one rectangle ½" larger all around than stool seat, e.g., 16" x 12½" (illustration D).

3. *Make four tabs.* Cut four 3½" squares from reserve. For each tab, fold square in half, right side in, and stitch ½" from raw edge on side parallel to fold. With seam centered, press tube open. Using corner of grid ruler as template, mark right-angle "point" at one end. Stitch on marked line. Trim across point, and trim remainder close to stitching. Turn tab right side out using point turner; press well. Stitch raw edges together to prevent ravelling (illustration E).

4. *Sew tabs to side panels.* Lay one wider side panel right side up. Slip a tab under each folded side edge 7" from top raw edge. Adjust so 2" of tab extends beyond fold. Pin in place. Topstitch folded edges, catching tabs in stitching (illustration F). Repeat for matching panel.

5. *Join side and seat panels.* Place seat panel and one wider side panel right sides together, raw edges matching; pin ½" from edges. Pin second wider panel to opposite edge. Double-check fit on footstool, adjust as needed, then machine-stitch both seams (illustration G). Pin the two remaining side panels to top panel, aligning pressed-in creases with corners of stool; unfold side edges so they extend around corners, and pin over previous stitching. Check fit on footstool. Machine-stitch to secure (illustration H).

6. *Cut cushion pieces.* Fold remaining towel in half crosswise on cutting mat. Using grid ruler and rotary cutter, cut two rectangles ¾" larger all around than stool top, e.g., 16½" x 13". Taper corners by ¼" to prevent flaring (illustration I). Cut three same-size pieces from batting. From

Velcro strip, cut nine 1" squares; separate five into hook and loop pieces. Place one towel rectangle (underside of cushion) face up on flat surface. Position five hook pieces on top—one 2½" from each corner and one at center; stitch in place (illustration I). Set remaining Velcro aside.

7. *Sew cushion.* Stack following pieces: three batting rectangles, plain towel rectangle right side up, and Velcro towel rectangle right side down. Machine-stitch ½" from edge all around, leaving 6" opening on one edge for turning (illustration J). Trim batting as close to stitching as possible; clip corners diagonally. Turn right side out. Slipstitch opening closed.

8. *Complete cushion and button detailing.* Following manufacturer's directions, cover nine buttons with reserved towel fabric. Sew five buttons to cushion front to correspond to Velcro placement on cushion underside; sew through all layers to create tufted effect. With slipcover on stool, mark narrow side panels and backs of tabs for Velcro placement. Sew Velcro hook piece to back of each tab; sew corresponding loop pieces to narrow panels. Sew five remaining loop pieces to slipcover seat—one in each corner and one in middle—to correspond to cushion underside. Sew remaining four buttons to tab fronts, concealing Velcro stitching. Set pillow on seat (illustration K).◆

Making the Slipcover

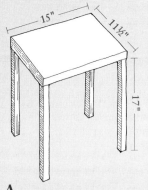

A. Measure the stool.

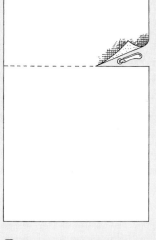

B. Cut four side panels, one panel per towel.

C. Fold and press the panel edges to match the stool dimensions.

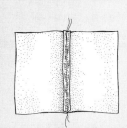

D. Sew a seat panel from the reserved toweling.

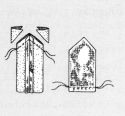
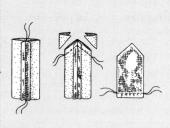

E. Sew four tabs from the reserved toweling.

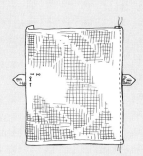

F. Join two tabs to each larger side panel.

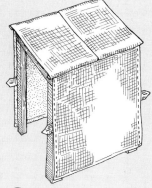

G. Sew the larger panels to the seat panel.

H. Add the remaining panels to hide the stool legs.

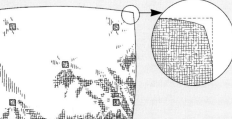
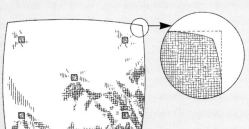

I. Sew Velcro patches to the cushion underside.

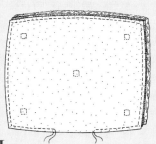

J. Assemble the cushion layers and sew around the edges.

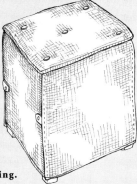

K. Tuft the cushion and complete the button detailing.

Floral Letter Seals

Trap pressed flowers between adhesive seals to make beautiful and unique stationery accents.

❧ BY ELIZABETH CAMERON

COLOR PHOTOGRAPHY:
Carl Tremblay

ILLUSTRATION:
Mary Newell DePalma

STYLING:
Ritch Holben

If your pressed flowers end up looking stark or bare, add an extra petal from another bloom.

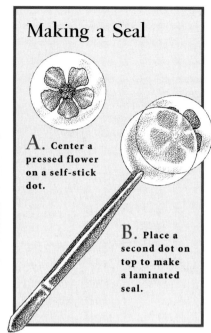

Making a Seal

A. Center a pressed flower on a self-stick dot.

B. Place a second dot on top to make a laminated seal.

MATERIALS
Makes 30 flower stickers

- **3 to 4 dozen fresh miniature flowers**
- **60 clear 1"-diameter self-adhesive seals**

You'll also need:
flower press; manicure scissors; tweezers; X-Acto knife; and masking tape.

THESE FLORAL SEALS LET YOU capture a sampling of spring to use year-round. All you do is press dried garden and field flowers between two clear 1"-diameter stationery seals. You can use them to brighten any envelope or to personalize wedding or party invitations.

I used Queen Anne's Lace and buttercups found near my house, but other blossoms and leaves press just as beautifully. The ones that work best are flat and have small petals, like African violets, miniature pansies, daisies, starflowers, and bachelor's buttons. If you have trouble finding small flowers, you can separate the petals from larger flowers to use individually. I used this technique on yellow orchids; the petals, with their veiny color and unusual shape, made very interesting seals. Tiny leaves also work and tend to be inexpensive and available in large quantities. You can cut new leaves from houseplants or use snippets of foliage from store-bought bouquets.

I used a microwave flower press made by Microfleur (*see* "Notes from Readers," Fall 1997) because it was so speedy—most small thin flowers dry in seconds. Of course, the type and number of flowers in the press, as well as the type of oven you have, can all impact the timing. You can use a conventional press, in which drying may take up to a week, or you can lay your flowers between paper towels and press them between the pages of a heavy book. Experiment with your drying technique: many flowers will change in color and size, and you should expect that some will be unusable after drying. The flowers must be dried thoroughly before you seal them between the stickers. If any moisture remains, the petals will bruise and discolor as you press the stickers together.

INSTRUCTIONS

1. *Press flowers.* Use manicure scissors to cut stems from flower heads, eliminating bulk. Arrange flowers in press as per manufacturer's instructions; press until flat and dry (up to one week for conventional flower press, less than one minute for microwave press). Examine pressed flowers, discarding any with damaged or discolored petals. From remainder, choose the 30 most perfect specimens.

2. *Laminate flowers to dots.* Lay one sheet of 15 dots face up on flat surface; tape down corners to prevent curling. Center one pressed flower face up on one dot (*see* illustration A, above). Using tweezers, lift dot from second sheet, center it adhesive side down over first dot, and lower it into place, matching edges (illustration B). Burnish top dot with your fingernail to create tight seal and remove air bubbles. Gently run X-Acto knife blade along edge of dot to trim off protruding petals and leaves, if any. Repeat process with remaining flowers and dots to create 30 unique stickers. To use a sticker, peel it off the paper backing. ◆

Egg Candles

The secret: Hollowed-out eggshells make the perfect molds.

COLOR PHOTOGRAPHY:
Carl Tremblay

ILLUSTRATION:
Mary Newell DePalma

STYLING:
Ritch Holben

✒ BY NANCY OVERTON

ADD A SOFT GLOW TO THE spring table by making egg-shaped candles. Though I had blown eggs and I had made candles before, I'd never put the two together. The method is simple: Blow out the shells, add a wick, and pour in melted wax. After the wax cools, the shell peels away easily.

To achieve soft colors, I dipped my white egg candles into hot colored wax once or twice for a very pastel look, or several more times for a vivid color. Using colored wax chunks will yield pale, translucent eggs. For more intense color, use candle-wax dyes.

Nancy Overton of Oakland, California, has designed and written about crafts for more than twenty years.

INSTRUCTIONS

1. *Blow eggs.* Use egg-blowing tool to pierce egg at each end and blow out contents. Enlarge hole at broader end to ½". Rinse shell and let air-dry. Repeat to blow 12 eggs total.

2. *Prepare wicks.* Cut 5" length of wick. Pass wick through small hole of eggshell and out larger hole, until wick extends 1½" beyond small hole. Work Play-Doh into ½"-diameter ball, roll into 1"-long sausage, and flatten slightly. Fold Play-Doh around the wick at the narrow end of the egg (*see* illustration A, below). Bend wick down and gently press Play-Doh onto shell, sealing wick against it. Set egg in carton, sealed end down. Repeat for 12 eggshells total.

3. *Fill eggshells with wax.* Following manufacturer's instructions, melt 12 ounces of white wax granules in boiling bag. Carefully pour hot liquid wax into each eggshell; do not fill shell completely, since a flat-bottomed egg candle will stand upright (illustration B). Return bag to saucepan; melt more wax crystals as

needed. As wax egg cools and area surrounding wick sinks down, pour more wax into shell to fill cavity. Continue until all eggs are filled. Let cool overnight.

4. *Overdip wax eggs.* Bring water to boil in teakettle. Peel shells from eggs beginning at broad end. Cut wick even with bottom of egg, and stand egg upright. If wobbly, shave bottom of egg with paring knife until level. Melt 6 to 8 ounces white wax and small chunk of colored wax or wax dye in boiling bag, as in step 3. Pour melted wax into mug, and set mug in pan. Pour boiling water into pan to keep wax in hot liquid state. Prepare additional colored waxes in same way. To overdip egg, hold wick and lower egg into colored wax (illustration C). Lift out and set on counter to cool. Let cool completely (about 1 minute) before redipping. You can dip an egg in the same color several times for a darker hue, or dip it into a different color to change the hue. ◆

Nest these eggs on a table to create a soft country accent, or stand them on candlesticks for a more dramatic look.

MATERIALS
Makes 12 egg-shaped candles

- 12 extra-large eggs
- 36 to 48 ounces white wax crystals
- Candle-wax dyes (assorted colors)
- 60" W-1 wire core wick

You'll also need:
empty egg carton; egg-blowing tool; Play-Doh; candle-making boil bags; 2-quart saucepan; 2"-deep baking pan; clear glass mugs or jars (one per dye color); scissors; paring knife; towel; and teakettle.

Making the Egg Candle

A. Secure a wick in the empty eggshell with Play-Doh.

B. Pour in the hot, melted wax.

C. Dye the egg candle in hot colored wax.

Fifties-Style Apron and Oven Mitts

Create designer kitchen apparel that really works: The mitts attach with Velcro.

❧ BY DAWN ANDERSON

Make kitchen apparel that is as stylish as it is clever by using fabric with bold prints and eye-catching colors.

PATTERN
See page 45 for pattern pieces, cutting template, and enlargement instructions.

COLOR PHOTOGRAPHY:
Carl Tremblay

ILLUSTRATION:
Judy Love

STYLING:
Ritch Holben

ANYONE WHO COOKS KNOWS the value of having your oven mitts available when you need them. This kitchenwear set ensures that luxury. The secret: Each oven mitt has a slender strip of Velcro attached to the wrist on the palm side. The facing Velcro sections are attached to the front of the apron where your hands naturally fall. When the oven mitts are not in use, they remain securely attached to the apron.

To make this designer set, I chose fabric with a retro-looking color and pattern, but any two coordinating cotton piqué fabrics will work—one for the apron and one for the oven mitts. For the lining of the oven mitts, I recommend using a heat-resistant batting. You can purchase batting that comes with a foil liner for around $10 per yard. The other option is to purchase aluminum sheeting which costs a few dollars a yard and which can be layered between regular cotton batting.

The construction is simple. The oven mitt layers are quilted by machine. If your machine has a quilting guide, you're saved from having to mark every quilt line. The apron pattern is a large rectangle, from which the armholes are cut using the curve of a dinner plate as a guide. The apron tie is a continuous cotton cord which is threaded through large eyelets at the two ends of the armhole.

The final step is placing the Velcro pieces. The positioning is key. With the apron on, have a friend mark the place where it will be easiest for you to slip your mitts off and on.

Dawn Anderson is a writer and designer living in Redmond, Washington.

MATERIALS
Makes one apron and two mitts

- 1 yard 45"-wide cotton piqué print (for apron)
- ½ yard 45"-wide coordinating cotton piqué print (for mitts)
- ½ yard 45"-wide muslin
- 1 yard 45"-wide Teflon-impregnated batting
- 2 yards extra-wide double-fold bias tape
- 3½ yards ³⁄₁₆"-diameter cotton cording
- ¾" x 8" Velcro tape
- Scrap of fusible interfacing
- Four 6mm eyelets (with tool)
- Sewing thread to match fabrics

You'll also need:
oven mitt pattern (*see* page 45); sewing machine with walking foot; rotary cutter; self-healing cutting mat; quilter's acrylic grid ruler; sewing shears; iron; hand-sewing needle; quilter's pins; air-soluble fabric-marking pen; scissors; dinner plate; 8½" x 11" paper; and pencil.

INSTRUCTIONS
Making the Oven Mitts

1. *Prepare fabrics and batting.* Cut sixteen 11" x 18" rectangles: four cotton piqué (mitt print), four muslin, and eight Teflon batting. Using air-soluble pen, mark oven mitt pattern on four cotton piqué rectangles (reverse two). Using grid ruler, extend lower straight edge 1" beyond mitt outline at each side. Referring to pattern, mark parallel lines every ¾" across mitt surface, extending them 1" beyond edge.

2. *Quilt mitt layers.* Layer one muslin rectangle, two batting rectangles, and one cotton piqué rectangle marked side up; pin every 3". Using walking foot, machine-stitch along marked lines through all layers (*see* illustration A, next page). Repeat process to make four quilted pieces.

3. *Assemble mitts.* Trim quilted pieces 1" beyond mitt outlines. Place two mitts right sides together, aligning lower edges and quilting lines, if possible; outer edges do not need to match. Position pattern on top and pin all layers. Stitch around edges of pattern, starting and stopping ⅜" beyond lower edge. Unpin pattern. Trim fabric ¼" beyond curved edge (illustration B). Zigzag curved edges; clip inside curve at thumb. Trim bottom ⅜" beyond straight stitching. Bind lower straight edge with bias tape following manufacturer's instructions. Repeat to sew second mitt.

Making the Apron

1. *Cut apron fabric.* Referring to template diagram (*see* page 45), set dinner plate facedown on corner of 8½" x 11" paper, and trace curved edge. Cut on marked line to make template. From apron fabric, cut one 28" x 34" rectangle, with longer edges parallel to selvage; fold in half lengthwise, right side in. Referring to cutting diagram (*see* page 45), position armhole template on top corner of fabric opposite fold; pin in place. Cut on curved line through both layers.

2. *Hem straight edges.* Fold and press bottom straight edge of apron 1" toward wrong side. Fold another 1" and press well. Topstitch along first fold through all layers. Double-fold and press top edge of apron in same way. Cut two ⅞" squares of interfacing, slip them between folds ¼" from each end, and fuse in place. Topstitch same as lower hem. Repeat process to hem each straight side edge, fusing ⅞" square of interfacing to top corner at armhole edge (illustration C).

3. *Prepare armhole binding.* Cut length of bias binding 1" longer than each curved armhole edge. Open center fold and press out crease. Set paper template on ironing board; place binding strip along curved edge, letting ends extend ½" at each end. Using template as a guide, press binding to match curve. Turn template over and repeat process, pressing second strip in mirror image. Unfold inside curve of bias binding and pin to corresponding armhole edge, right sides together and ends extending ¼". Stitch along binding fold line (illustration D).

4. *Install eyelets.* From each top corner of apron, measure ½" down and ½" in from binding seam; make dot with fabric marker. Mark top corners of each side edge in same way. Following manufacturer's instructions, install 6mm eyelet at each dot. From right side, thread cord through top eyelet and out lower armhole eyelet. Thread other end of cord through opposite side following same path. Knot cord ends (illustration E).

5. *Bind armhole edges.* Press binding facings to wrong side. Lay apron facedown and adjust cord length so facings lie flat. Pin each facing along free edge, trapping cord within. Stitch down facing, removing pins as you go. Turn ends to inside and slipstitch (illustration F).

6. *Sew on Velcro strips.* Cut Velcro strip in half. Separate each strip. Butt loop section against binding on palm side of mitt, and pin. Stitch down Velcro edges all around. Try on apron and oven mitts. Place hands comfortably at sides, and have someone mark apron for hook tape position. Remove apron and mitts. Stitch hook sections of tape to apron as marked (illustration G).◆

DESIGNER'S TIP

If you want the lower portion of the apron to have more coverage around your sides, increase the width of the rectangle. Take the number of inches that you have increased the width and divide it in half, then move the armhole template that number of inches toward the fold, extending the cutting line through the added fabric.

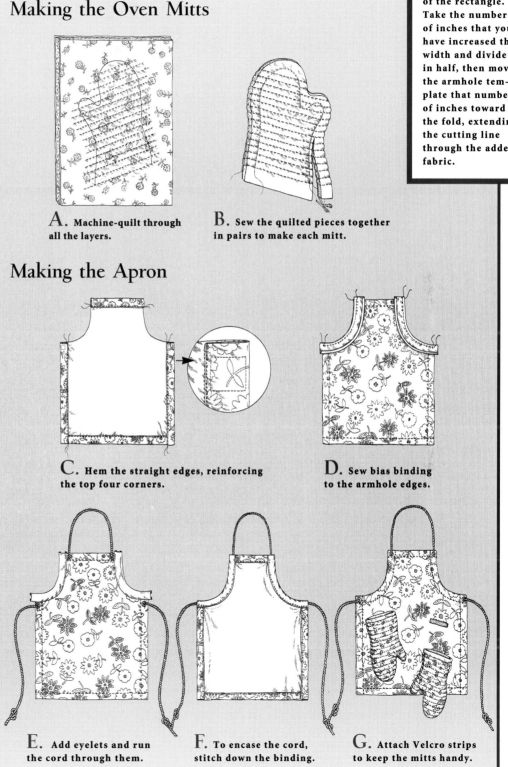

Making the Oven Mitts

A. Machine-quilt through all the layers.

B. Sew the quilted pieces together in pairs to make each mitt.

Making the Apron

C. Hem the straight edges, reinforcing the top four corners.

D. Sew bias binding to the armhole edges.

E. Add eyelets and run the cord through them.

F. To encase the cord, stitch down the binding.

G. Attach Velcro strips to keep the mitts handy.

Miniature Memory Album

Make fabulous albums fast using paper, ribbon, and photos.

BY DAWN ANDERSON

These albums are easy to compile assembly-line style to save time. From a 24" x 30" sheet of mulberry paper, you could cut 30 covers, or enough for 15 announcements.

COLOR PHOTOGRAPHY:
Carl Tremblay

ILLUSTRATION:
Mary Newell DePalma

SILHOUETTE PHOTOGRAPHY:
Daniel van Ackere

STYLING:
Ritch Holben

THESE MINIATURE ALBUMS, whether made for yourself or for someone close to you, are a wonderful way to commemorate a birth or other special occasion. The cover, cut from handmade paper, houses pages for a birth announcement, the baby's statistics, and photos.

The inside pages are printed on a computer, making the albums easy to produce in multiples.

I used acid-free mulberry paper, which has a soft, clothlike texture, for the cover, but you can use any soft, low-acid paper. Those made of bast (inner bark), like kozo, hemp, and flax, have long fibers and are usually strong and durable. You can also use "rag" papers, made from cotton and other textile fibers.

The inner pages are separated with sheets of striped vellum. Vellum, similar to and thicker than parchment paper, is made from calfskin, lambskin, or goatskin. Typically used for bookbinding, it protects the pages, adds strength to the book, and is pH-neutral, so it won't chemically react with the photograph over time.

Dawn Anderson is a writer and designer living in Redmond, Washington.

MATERIALS
Makes one 4⅛" x 5⅜" album

- **9" x 12" medium-weight mulberry paper**
- **Scrap of lightweight mulberry paper**
- **Two 8½" x 11" white card stock**
- **8½" x 11" striped vellum**
- **4½" x 5¾" white envelope**
- **⅝ yard ½"-wide organza ribbon**
- **6" length of ⅛"-wide gold mesh ribbon**
- **Four ¼" brass eyelets (with setting tool)**
- **Brass baby charm**
- **Four white photo corners**
- **White craft glue**
- **Hot glue**
- **Spray adhesive**

You'll also need:
computer with high-quality printer; rotary cutter; X-Acto knife; quilter's acrylic grid ruler; self-healing cutting mat; hammer; hole punch; scissors; pencil; and tracing vellum.

INSTRUCTIONS

1. *Make vellum page guide.* Using grid ruler, X-Acto knife, and cutting mat, cut 4⅛" x 5⅜" rectangle from tracing vellum. Measure ½" in from one short edge and draft line parallel to edge with pencil. Mark four dots 1" apart on line, and punch with hole punch. Draft second line 1" from same edge (*see illustration A, next page*).

2. *Type and print announcement.* Enter your birth announcement details on a computer, following format below. For title page, type:

Announcing
Robert Wesley

For second page, type:

Name: Robert Wesley Anderson
Born: June 5, 1997 at 2:33 a.m.
Weight: 8lb. 4oz. Length: 20¼"
Parents: Jeff & Karla Anderson

Using computer's software, select fonts and point sizes. Print sample announcement on scrap paper. Overlay page guide on each section to see if lettering fits within 4⅛" x 4⅜" rectangle, allowing 1" margin to left (illustration B). Change computer specifications as needed to adjust type, spacing, or typefaces. Continue until you obtain the desired look. Print final version on white card stock.

3. *Cut pages and covers.* Lay card stock flat, printed side up. Overlay page guide on each printed section, as in step 2, and lightly trace around edges. Using grid ruler and X-Acto knife and following pencil guidelines, cut 4⅛" x 5⅜" title page and second page. Also cut one blank white card stock and two striped vellum pages. For covers, cut two mulberry-paper rectangles, using rotary cutter instead of X-Acto knife to avoid tearing paper fibers (illustration C). Using page guide as template, punch four holes in each page and cover along left margin.

4. *Prepare photo page.* Using scissors, trim baby photo to fit within page guide, allowing at least ½" margin all around. Mount photo on blank card-stock page with white photo corners (illustration D).

5. *Assemble book.* Insert four eyelets through holes in front cover. Lay cover facedown, eyelets at right. Stack pages facedown onto eyelets in this order: striped vellum, title page, second page, striped vellum, photo page, back cover. Double-check page positions. Complete eyelet installation per manufacturer's instructions. Thread organza ribbon through bottom eyelet until ends are even. Draw one end through remaining

holes from back to front; lace other end from front to back (illustration E). Tie ends in bow at top of card; trim ends diagonally.

6. *Add label and trims.* Cut 2⅝" x 3⅛" rectangle from lightweight mulberry paper and 2⅞" x 3⅜" rectangle from card stock. Using spray adhesive, affix mulberry paper to card stock, then affix entire label to front cover. Slip narrow gold ribbon through charm loop, and tie ends in bow. Apply clear craft glue to wrong side of ribbon tails ¾" from knot; let dry. Cut ribbon ends diagonally through dried glue to prevent fraying. Attach charm to label using hot glue (illustration F). ◆

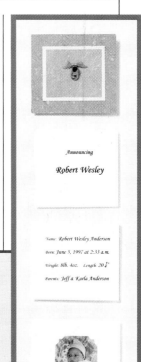

Making the Mini-Album

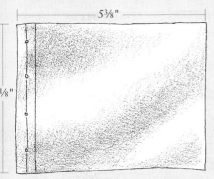

A. Make a page guide from see-through tracing vellum.

B. Use the guide to fine-tune your computer printout.

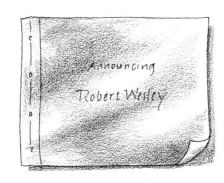

C. Cut two covers and five pages, including the two printed pages.

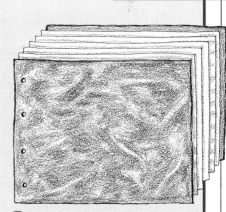

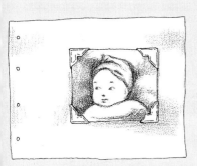

D. Mount the baby's photo on one blank page.

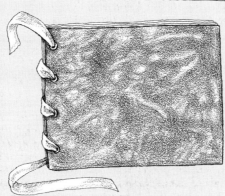

E. Bind the pages and covers together using eyelets and ribbon.

F. Glue a label and a brass charm to the front cover.

Mediterranean Flowerpots

Easy antique: Roll freshly painted clay pots in a bed of sand.

🐚 BY MARY ANN HALL

Sand Pots

A. Apply the paint mixture with a foam brush.

B. Soften the paint line with a damp sponge.

C. Roll the wet areas in sand to coat the pot.

To achieve a denser coat of sand, add some white tacky glue to the paint along with the extender medium.

MATERIALS
Makes one pot

- **Hand-thrown terra-cotta pot**
- **5 pounds clean, dry sand**
- **2 ounces acrylic paint (soft, muted shade)**
- **2 ounces acrylic extender medium**

You'll also need:
1" to 2" foam brush; palette or disposable container; cellulose sponge; craft stick; fork; tape measure; and newspaper.

COLOR PHOTOGRAPHY:
Carl Tremblay

ILLUSTRATION:
Mary Newell DePalma

STYLING:
Ritch Holben

TERRA COTTA, A HARD, FIRED clay, can add beauty to any room. I've seen many ideas for painting terra cotta, but I wanted an elegant, understated design. I decided to use subdued shades evoking the Mediterranean for color, and a sprinkling of sand for texture.

I chose rimless hand-thrown pots, but this technique works with other styles as well, including flowerpots with deep rims. Sand is available from several sources: pet supply stores, garden centers, craft stores, and lumberyards. I purchased a five-pound bag of marine sand, used in aquariums, for $3.50. I bought

paint in soft warm hues like celadon, apricot, lemon, ocher, and ocean blue, colors that accent the stuccoed villas of the Mediterranean.

I started by painting a 3" pot with acrylic paint. I had to work fast because the paint soaks into the terra cotta very quickly. Because I knew this drying effect would increase with larger pots, I mixed in a retarding medium to slow the drying time. I further increased my working time by painting on a dampened pot. Once the paint was applied, running a damp sponge around the rims exposed some of the deep brownish red terra-cotta and created a soft, fading color line. This

technique replicated the look of glazed pots fired in a kiln, where the glaze has been wiped away from the bottom to prevent the pot from sticking to the kiln.

After some experimentation with sprinkling, rubbing, and smoothing on the sand with my fingers, I decided that I most preferred the even coating I got from rolling. I poured a pile of sand onto newspaper and smoothed it out with my hand. I laid the pot on its side, and coated it in one roll along the sand.

INSTRUCTIONS

1. *Prepare sand bed.* Lay several layers of newspaper on work surface. Measure pot height and circumference, e.g., 5" x 13". Spread ½"-deep bed of sand slightly larger than pot area on newspaper.

2. *Apply paint.* Transfer small amount of paint to palette. Add up to one-third as much extender medium and blend thoroughly with craft stick. Wash terra-cotta pot in warm water; let drain. Turn damp pot upside down. Using foam brush, apply paint mixture to outside of pot in horizontal strokes; allow ¼" margin at top and bottom rims (*see* illustration A, above). Wipe edge of damp sponge around each rim to soften color transition (illustration B).

3. *Coat pot with sand.* Immediately, while paint is still wet, turn pot on side and set down on edge of sand bed. Handling pot at rims, roll firmly along sand bed to coat entire painted area (illustration C). To coat additional pots, rake sand bed with fork, then repeat steps 2 and 3. Stand pots upright on flat surface; let dry one hour. Tap surface gently with fingertip to remove loose grains. ◆

The Easiest Wildflower Wreath

Bind bouquets of fresh greenery around a frame and accent with flowers.

COLOR PHOTOGRAPHY:
Carl Tremblay

ILLUSTRATION:
Mary Newell DePalma

STYLING:
Ritch Holben

❧ BY CAROL ENDLER STERBENZ

THIS SPRING WREATH WAS inspired by our family trip to the south of France where wildflowers grow in colorful profusion along the road, on the hillsides, and in the fields. I wanted to design a wreath that was reminiscent of the exquisite beauty and vivid colors of this sun-drenched region.

Once home, I looked for varieties of fresh greenery that would give my arrangement a wide spectrum of color and texture. I found that I could use practically any sturdy plant material with woody stems, including weeds, since those kinds of plants don't require a constant water supply.

The technique for making the wreath is simple: gather a variety of greens, arrange them in graduated tiers, and bind them with wire into bouquets. The bouquets are then lashed to a wire wreath frame in overlapping bunches.

The appeal of this design is that you can add any number or variety of flowers once the wreath is bound. You simply insert the stems between the branches of the foliage, articulating the stems so that they resemble naturally growing wild flowers. I used silk flowers for this wreath, but you can also use fresh flowers—just insert each stem into an orchid vial filled with water.

Make this wreath for a special occasion like an anniversary party, a family reunion, or a wedding.

Making the Wreath

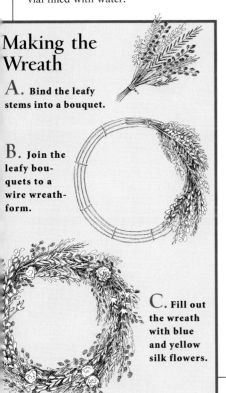

A. Bind the leafy stems into a bouquet.

B. Join the leafy bouquets to a wire wreath-form.

C. Fill out the wreath with blue and yellow silk flowers.

INSTRUCTIONS

1. *Make green bouquets.* Divide greens by type into separate piles. Select three or four stems from each pile and assemble into a leafy bouquet. Bind stems at base with florist wire (*see* illustration A, left). Make four to six bouquets, or enough to go around wreath form.

2. *Wire bouquets to wreath.* Lay one bouquet on wreath form. Using florist wire, bind bouquet to wreath form over previous binding. Position and bind second bouquet on form so its leaves overlap and conceal bound section of first bouquet (illustration B). Repeat process to bind remaining bouquets; conceal stems of final bouquet under leafy section of first bouquet. To further secure and contain bouquets, join end of spool wire to wreath form at any spot. Holding spool in one hand, wind wire around wreath in a loose spiral. When you reach starting point, twist wire ends together and clip off excess. Free individual sprigs so they conceal wire.

3. *Add silk flowers to wreath.* Insert stems of silk flowers into wreath at same angle as leafy stems. Fill in noticeably empty spaces first, then vary placement of remaining stems to carry out random wildflower look (illustration C). The wreath will last one to two weeks. Frequent misting will prolong display life. ◆

MATERIALS

Makes one 20"-diameter wreath

- 18"-long silk flower stems:
  5 yellow mini-chrysanthemums,
  4 blue cornflowers,
  3 yellow rununculus
- 18"-long leafy, woody stems:
  24 variegated pit,
  24 Italian ruscus,
  24 micro-eucalyptus
- 18" wire wreath form
- Green florist spool wire

You'll also need: pruning shears and wire cutters.

Mariner's Stool

Combine simple wood-burning and staining techniques to create a nautical design.

❧ BY ELIZABETH CAMERON

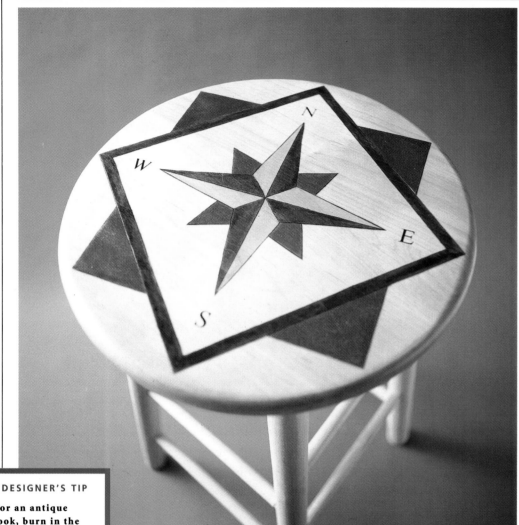

Choose a stool made of hardwood, like this maple one. Because hardwoods burn slower than soft woods, you will have more control over the wood-burning tool.

DESIGNER'S TIP

For an antique look, burn in the compass points— N, S, E, and W— instead of using press type. You can trace script lettering from books containing alphabets or calligraphy. Use the script point, which is standard with most woodburning tools.

COLOR PHOTOGRAPHY:
Carl Tremblay

ILLUSTRATION:
Judy Love

STYLING:
Ritch Holben

I WANTED TO ADD COLOR AND DEFInition to this stool without disguising the grain of the wood, so I knew I needed to work with stains, not paints. Because I wanted to make a design using three different stains, I needed to devise a way to keep them from bleeding into one another. A wood-burning tool helped me turn the lines of my design into moats that the various colors of stain could not cross.

Wood burning was much easier to master than I had anticipated. As I practiced on scrap wood, the lightweight tool, which is held like a pencil, quickly began to feel natural. The design for this stool uses only straight lines, which are made with a wedge-shaped tip. The tip cuts a trough in the wood as it burns, making it easy to retrace the lines if greater definition is needed.

I pressed down dry-transfer lettering to indicate the compass points. This kind of lettering, sometimes called press type, has been traditionally used by the advertising and graphics industries, and can be found in stationery and art stores. You transfer letters by applying pressure with a pencil tip to rub the letters from a piece of film and onto the final surface.

To color the design, I chose water-based wood stains because they can be thinned and cleaned up with water. Available in dozens of colors, they can be found at woodworking and home improvement stores. To apply these stains, which will naturally thin out as you brush them, I recommend placing your brush in the middle of the area to be painted and then brushing the stain outward to the wood-burned holding line. This will help keep the stains from running into neighboring surfaces.

I finished the stool with three coats of polyurethane. Though you can use an acrylic sealer, which has the advantage of cleaning up with water, I recommend polyurethane because it's more durable. To avoid having to clean your paintbrush in paint thinner, consider using disposable sponge brushes.

INSTRUCTIONS

1. *Transfer pattern.* Lay transfer paper facedown on stool seat; fold edges to seat underside and secure with tape. Tape compass pattern face up onto tracing paper. Using pencil and ruler, trace all pattern lines; bear down with pencil to impress wood surface (*see* illustration A, next page). Remove pattern and transfer paper. Draft a portion of same design on scrap wood for practice burning and staining.

2. *Burn design.* Read manufacturer's instructions for wood-burning tool (illustration B). If you have long hair, tuck it up under a cap. Insert wedge-shaped tip, plug in tool, and preheat 5-10 minutes. Holding tool like a pencil, practice burning lines in scrap wood by running tip of tool freehand

Burning and Staining the Design

A. Trace the pattern by pressing the design into the stool seat.

B. Read the safety instructions for your wood-burning tool.

standard tip   script tip

C. Work freehand to burn in the compass design.

D. Stain the designated areas one by one.

E. Add dry-transfer compass point letters. Finish with two or three coats of sealer.

over pencil lines. Do not use ruler, which can redistribute heat and cause scorch marks. Go over lines a second time to darken and deepen grooves. Once you are satisfied with your technique, burn compass design on stool seat in same way (illustration C). When you are through, unplug tool and let it cool. Sand off stray burn marks with emery board.

3. *Stain design.* Practice on your scrap piece. To prevent bleeding, load watercolor brush with stain, deposit deepest concentration of stain in center of design area, and then brush out to the burned-in holding line. Once area is filled, blot excess stain with paper towel to reveal wood grain; always wipe with a clean section of towel. When you are satisfied with your technique, stain compass design on stool seat, following color key (*see* page 47). Stain rosewood sections first, then teal, then golden oak (illustration D). (If using other colors, stain the darkest color first.) Let dry overnight.

4. *Apply dry-transfer letters and sealer.* Position lettering sheet flat on stool so a capital "N" is at end of one compass point. Rub blunt pencil point over film to transfer "N" to wood surface. Repeat process to transfer "S," "E," and "W" to appropriate remaining points. Spray each letter lightly with acrylic sealer; let dry 10 minutes. Seal entire stool with polyurethane following manufacturer's instructions; clean brush with paint thinner between coats (illustration E). ◆

PATTERNS

See page 47 for pattern and enlargement instructions.

Papier-Mâché Peppers

Use this simple layering technique to transform colored gift tissue into realistic chili peppers.

🍂 BY KATHRYN PHELAN

COLOR PHOTOGRAPHY:
Carl Tremblay

ILLUSTRATION:
Mary Newell DePalma

STYLING:
Ritch Holben

The chilies shown here accent a jar of jalapeño jelly—the recipe is given on page 23.

CHILI PEPPERS, WITH THEIR unique shapes and bright colors, have become the vegetable of choice for spicy decorating. The chilies shown here, made of papier-mâché, make beautiful accents for gift boxes or jars of homemade salsas and jellies. You can also string the chilis for kitchen or party decor, add them to wreaths, or put them in a bowl as a centerpiece.

These chilies are easily formed out of three layers of tissue paper. To save on paper costs, I made the first two layers, the core and the shoulders of the chili, with white tissue, which is usually less expensive than colored tissue. I used colored tissue only for the outer "skin" of the chili. To create realistic curves and folds in the chilies, you can use fresh or dried chilies as a guide. The more you crush and dimple the cone shape, the more dried your chili will look.

I recommend using giftwrap tissue, not arts and crafts tissue, which is lighter and may bleed or tear when wet. If the size of the tissue paper you purchase varies from the measurements listed here, you can easily adjust the size of the rectangles to fit the paper. The shapes don't need to be cut with extreme precision in order to work.

Once the papier-mâché shells dry hard and firm, you can turn your chilies into

MATERIALS
Makes two dozen 6"-long peppers

■ **20" x 30" sheets of tissue paper:**
  6 white
  8 red, yellow, or green
  1 green (for stems)
■ **2 ounces papier-mâché art paste (powder form)**
■ **Twenty-four 2" brass eye pins**
■ **Acrylic gloss varnish**

You'll also need:
11" x 18" (or larger) clear vinyl; disposable pint container with lid; measuring cup; measuring spoons; scissors; 1" and 1½" foam brushes; ½" flat bristle brush; small pliers; wire cutter; wire coat hangers; large corrugated carton; large plastic trash bag; and newsprint.

mini-piñatas or party favors. Before applying the varnish, cut a short slit into the outer skin and slip in small gifts such as brass charms, hard candies, jewelry, beads, coins—anything that will fit. If you need a bigger cavity, remove some of the chili's inner tissue with tweezers. After the gift is inserted, varnish the body area only, leaving the stem uncoated so that it can be pulled out later to reveal the hidden gift.

Kathryn Phelan is a craft designer living in Tuscon, Arizona.

INSTRUCTIONS

1. *Prepare paste.* Place 1½ cups cold water in pint container. Slowly add 1½ tablespoons art paste, stirring thoroughly for 2 minutes. Cover and let stand 15 minutes.

2. *Set up work area.* Line work surface with newsprint; top with clear vinyl. Tuck flaps of corrugated cardboard carton to inside and line with plastic trash bag. Unbend several wire coat hangers. To make drying line, cut four or five lengths of wire and lay them across box opening.

3. *Cut tissue paper.* Referring to cutting diagrams (next page), cut each white tissue sheet into eight pieces and each colored sheet into twelve pieces. For stems, cut six of the green rectangles into four equal-size strips each.

4. *Shape chili forms.* Loosely crumple one white tissue rectangle lengthwise. Twist once at middle. Using pliers, wind plain end of eye pin once or twice around twisted section, keeping eye pin stem as

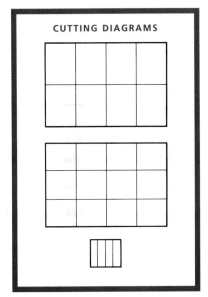

CUTTING DIAGRAMS

Making the Peppers

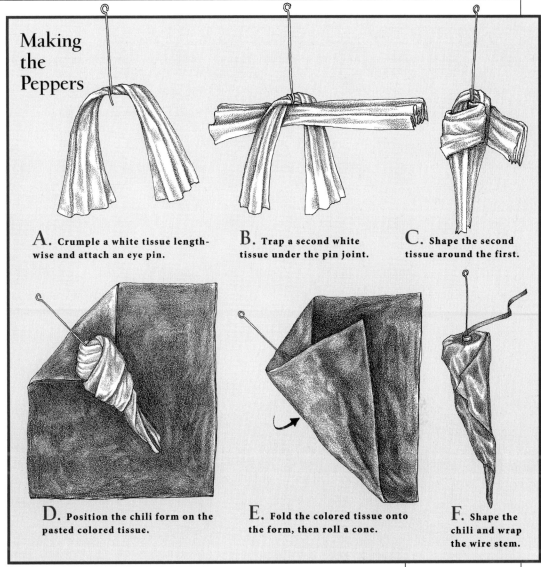

A. Crumple a white tissue length-wise and attach an eye pin.

B. Trap a second white tissue under the pin joint.

C. Shape the second tissue around the first.

D. Position the chili form on the pasted colored tissue.

E. Fold the colored tissue onto the form, then roll a cone.

F. Shape the chili and wrap the wire stem.

long as possible. Bend both tissue arms down, away from pin (*see illustration A, right*). Crumple second white rectangle lengthwise. Lodge one end between tissue arms directly under pin (illustration B). Loosely wrap second tissue around first to form shoulders of chili (illustration C). Continue wrapping both tissues downward to form tapered tip. Repeat process to make 24 chili forms total.

5. *Layer and paste colored tissue.* Lay one colored tissue rectangle flat on vinyl. Using 1½" foam brush, apply very thin coat of paste to top surface. Make sure all areas are moistened; if tissue tears, use less moisture. Place second tissue (same color) on top, and apply paste. Repeat process to paste together four tissue layers. Apply paste to top tissue.

6. *Roll chili cone shape.* Fold down top left corner of pasted tissue layers. Place chili form on it at angle, wire stem extending beyond fold (illustration D). Bring lower left corner up and around white tissue form (illustration E). To wrap remaining tissue, roll form toward right. Allow white tissue inside form to remain loose and crumpled. Paste down loose edges, and tuck in excess tissue at bottom. Crimp tissue at crown and press in at center to form stem dimple. Press fingertips into chili skin to create realistic dimpling and hollows.

7. *Add stem.* Using 1" foam brush, apply paste to one green tissue strip. Fold lengthwise, apply more paste, and fold again. Starting at crown, press strip around base of stem, then wrap strip up wire towards eye (illustration F). Eye may be covered or left exposed. Bend stem into hook shape and hang on coat wire to dry. Repeat steps 5 through 7 to make each chili. Wipe vinyl occasionally with paper towel to remove excess paste. Let chilies dry at least 24 hours. Use flat brush to apply clear gloss sealer. Hang to dry. ◆

JALEPEÑO JELLY

MATERIALS
Makes 5 cups jalepeño jelly

- 8 jalepeño chilies
- 2 medium bell peppers
- 1⅛ cups distilled white vinegar
- 4½ cups sugar
- ¼ cup lemon juice
- 3 ounces liquid pectin
- 8 drops green food coloring (optional)
- Five ½-pint canning jars with lids

You'll also need:
blender; 8-quart pot; measuring cups; large Pyrex cup with spout; large spoon or ladle; oven mitts; sharp knife; and timer.

Note: About an hour ahead, wash jars and lids in normal dishwasher cycle so they are clean and hot for step 2.

1. COOK PUREE. Remove stems from chilies and discard; slice remainder into ¼"-thick coins. Core bell peppers and cut into 1" pieces. Transfer chilies, peppers, and vinegar to blender, and puree. Transfer puree to pot. Bring to boil, then lower heat to medium and boil 10 minutes, stirring occasionally.

2. COMPLETE AND CAN JELLY*. Remove pot from heat. Stir in sugar and lemon juice.

Return pot to heat, stirring to dissolve sugar. Add pectin and food coloring. Cook at rolling boil for 1 minute. Skim off foam and remove from heat. Transfer mixture in batches to large Pyrex cup with spout. Pour mixture into clean, hot jars to within ⅛" of rim. Screw on tops, then turn jars upside down for 5 to 10 minutes. Turn right side up. Jar lid will pop within 1 to 2 hours, indicating seal.

*Option: refrigerate in covered container for up to two weeks.

Windowsill Greenhouse

The secret: Frame a fish tank with basswood strips to build this elegant miniature conservatory.

≈ BY MICHIO RYAN

You can use your greenhouse for a kitchen herb garden or for starting seedlings in the spring.

THIS ELEGANT BOTANICAL ENVIronment will coddle delicate plants by providing the perfect combination of sunlight and condensation. A plain inexpensive glass fish tank provides the basic structure. The peaked roof consists of four pieces of single-pane glass bonded together with silicone caulk. The ornamental Victorian look is created by gluing basswood strips along the exterior of the tank and topping off both ends of the roof with painted finials.

Almost any type of fish tank is suitable for this project as long as it has an inset flange in the top rim into which you can fit the roof glass. These inserts, commonly ¼" wide all around, are designed to hold a screen or lighted hood. Choose a tank with neatly fitted, narrow plastic or metal edging that will blend nicely with the wood trim. You can easily adapt materials and measurements to larger fish tanks.

For the roof glass, consider having a hardware store or picture framer cut the glass to size. If you want to do this yourself, refer to "Mosaic Tile Candle Shades," Winter 1998, for tips on using a glass cutter.

MATERIALS
Makes one 6" x 12" x 12½"-high greenhouse

- 6" x 12" x 8"-high glass tank (with 5½" x 11⅝" rim recess)
- Single-pane glass:
  Two 3¾" x 11½" rectangles
  One 3¾" square, cut diagonally
- 24"-long basswood sticks:
  Two ½" x ½" L-bars with ⅛"-thick legs (a)
  Two ½" x ⅜" (b)
  One ⅜" x 1/16" (c)
  Five ¼" x ⅛" (d)
  Three ⅛" x ⅛" (e)
  Four ⅛" x 1/16" (f)
- Two 1½" lamp finials
- 9" x 12" x ⅛" black craft foam
- 2 ounces white acrylic craft paint
- 1 ounce DecoArt Ultra Gloss white acrylic enamel (for primer)
- Elmer's clear Squeez-N-Caulk
- 5-minute epoxy

You'll also need:
small piece of sea sponge; small miter box; X-Acto knife with saw blade; utility knife; single-edged razor blade; 180-grit sandpaper; 100-grit wet/dry emery paper; small wood block; 1" foam brush; ruler; rag; newsprint; index card; glass spray cleaner; paper towels; and wax paper or foil.

INSTRUCTIONS

1. *Prepare glass panes for gluing.* Line work surface with newsprint. Clean roof glass panes, front and back, using glass spray and paper towels. Place the two rectangles side by side on newsprint, long edges ⅛" apart. Join rectangles temporarily with short strips of tape. Fold one end of each tape onto itself for easy removal later (*see* illustration A, next page).

2. *Glue glass roof.* Turn both rectangles taped side down. Apply generous bead of Elmer's clear caulk along peak edges (⅛" gap). Next, apply caulk to the two short edges of one glass triangle. Stand one rectangle upright at right angle to work surface. To form L-shaped peak, glue glass triangle into position at one end, recessing it 1/16". Repeat for second triangle (illustration B). Using damp rag, wipe oozing caulk from outside edges only. Let dry 24 hours; remove tape. Wrap 100-grit wet/dry emery paper around small wood block. Sand sharp glass edges using rotating oval motion and wetting emery as needed.

3. *Cut wood trim.* Using X-Acto saw blade and miter box, cut 51 lengths of basswood per cutting chart (page 25). To cut same-length strips accurately, bind sticks with tape and cut them together.

4. *Prime wood pieces.* Line work surface with wax paper or foil. Lay same size wood strips side by side. Using small sea sponge, swab white acrylic paint over entire facing surface. Turn pieces over and repeat until all wood has one coat. Stack pieces randomly, pickup-stick style, for maximum air exposure. Rotate after 10 minutes. Let dry 30 minutes. Sand lightly to remove any burrs.

5. *Glue wood trim to lid.* Test-fit wood trim pieces on lid before gluing; sand ends if necessary to ease fit. To glue trim, apply thin bead of clear caulk to wrong side of

⅜" square. Stand piece on end, set utility knife blade across end diagonally, and press down firmly to split in half. Using wood glue, join cut edges to roof peak to form flat pedestal. Repeat to make two pedestals. Glue finial to each pedestal with epoxy, following manufacturer's directions (illustration C).

6. *Prepare and prime tank.* Wash tank in warm, soapy water; dry thoroughly. Using 180-grit sandpaper wrapped around small wood block, sand upper and lower plastic rims of tank lightly to provide some tooth for painting. Mask glass at top inside of tank just below plastic rim on outside of tank (illustration D). Using foam brush, apply DecoArt Ultra Gloss white acrylic enamel to top and bottom plastic rims and top inside glass (to tape edge). To avoid coating glass on outside, slip edge of index card under edge of plastic. Use same foam brush to prime the finials. Let dry one hour.

7. *Glue wood trim to tank.* Using caulk and following same process as in

step 5, glue wood pieces to tank in following order: Around lower plastic rim, glue four (d) and four (b) pieces. Around upper rim, glue four (e) pieces. To glass walls, glue an L-shaped (a) to each corner, three (d) spines evenly spaced to each large side, and one (d) spine centered to each short side (illustration E). Let dry one hour. Curved arches will be added after final painting.

8. *Work finishing details.* Wrap 180-grit sandpaper around small wood block. Sand off protruding ends of roof spines and gable supports so roof fits snugly into tank's recessed rim. Remove roof from tank. Using sea sponge, apply white craft paint to all exposed wood and plastic surfaces and finials. Let paint dry 10 minutes; use single-edged razor blade to scrape excess paint from glass. Sand wood lightly. Repeat process to apply second coat. Let dry 30 minutes. To install arches, apply dot of craft glue to both ends of (f) piece. Bend (f) and slip into position between vertical spines. Repeat process to install 12 pieces total, reversing every other one to form Gothic arches. Line floor with craft foam cut to size. Set roof into rim (illustration F). ◆

STRIP CUTTING CHART

From this size: of 24"-long sticks	Cut these lengths for tank:	Cut these lengths for roof:
(a) ½" x ½" L-bar	four 6⅝"	one 11⅝"
(b) ½" x ⅜"	two 13", two 6⅛"	two ¾"
(c) ⅜" x 1⁄16"		two 4", two 3⅝"
(d) ¼" x ⅛"	two 12½", two 6⅛", eight 6⅝"	four 3⅝"
(e) ⅛" x ⅛"	two 12½", two 6⅛"	six 3⅝"
(f) ⅛" x 1⁄16"	twelve 7½"	

wood trim, and press trim into place on glass. Wipe any oozing caulk immediately with damp rag. Glue pieces in following order: To peak, glue 11⅝" L-shaped (a), letting it extend evenly at each end. To each gable, glue two (c) pieces. To each roof piece, glue (d) at each end and three (e) pieces, evenly spaced, in between. Trim each (b) piece lengthwise so end measures

Making the Windowsill Greenhouse

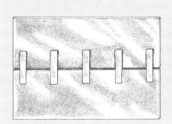

A. Join two glass panes temporarily with tape.

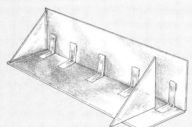

B. Bond all four panes permanently using silicone caulk.

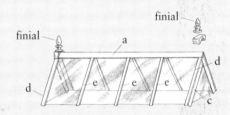

C. Trim roof with wood strips and add finials for a Victorian touch.

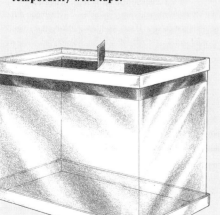

D. Define the rim edge with tape before priming and painting.

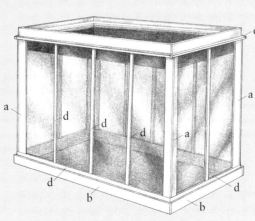

E. Glue wood trims to the tank, and complete the final painting.

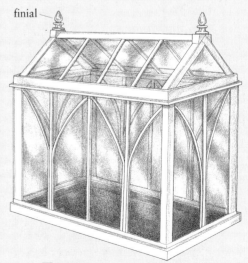

F. Add slim sticks, bending them to form Gothic arches.

Striped Floor Runner

Recycle cotton bath rugs into a lush decorator floor covering.

&❧ BY ELIZABETH CAMERON

Making the Runner

A. Draft your runner design to scale on graph paper.

B. Mark the stripes for each color on the rug backing.

C. Cut out the stripes, arrange them in order, and whip the seams.

D. On the right side, fluff the yarn at each join.

INSTRUCTIONS

1. *Draft your design.* Determine required length for finished runner (e.g., 17" wide x 42" long). Draft rectangle to scale on graph paper. Select stripe design for rug (e.g., even stripes, thick-and-thin stripes, or random stripes), and mark diagram (*see* illustration A, above). Indicate stripe colors, and number stripes from left to right if desired. Tally widths of same color stripes to determine how many mats are needed.

2. *Mark and cut rugs.* Turn rugs face down. Mark stripes for each color on appropriate rug. Note that curved corners must be used for ends of runner only and cannot be used for interior stripes (illustration B).

3. *Cut and rejoin rugs.* Using scissors, cut on each line through rubbery backing; guide scissor blades between yarns whenever possible. Discard waste. Lay segments flat, wrong side up, in desired order. Thread embroidery needle with 18" strand of upholstery thread. To join two segments, butt cut edges (do not overlap them) and whip together (illustration C). Repeat process to join all segments. Turn runner right side up. Rub each seam lightly to shed loose tufts of yarn and disguise join (illustration D). ◆

MATERIALS

Makes one striped runner up to 60" long

- **Two or three contrasting 17" x 24" bath mats**
- **Neutral carpet thread**

You'll also need:
large quilter's acrylic grid ruler; pencil; graph paper; sharp scissors; and embroidery needle.

COLOR PHOTOGRAPHY:
Carl Tremblay

ILLUSTRATION:
Mary Newell DePalma

STYLING:
Ritch Holben

Snip and stitch: Cut apart inexpensive bath rugs and sew them back together to create a bright and stylish runner for your bathroom.

AFTER RESTYLING MY BATH-room, I wanted to replace my bath rug. This, however, turned out to be much more difficult than I'd imagined. The few attractive rugs I saw seemed overpriced, and the only affordable ones were boring—small and monochromatic. But as I stood considering their colors, their value suddenly became apparent to me—these inexpensive and unnoteworthy bath rugs could be cut and spliced together to create a stylish striped runner that would match my new decor, fit my space requirements, and liven up the room.

This runner requires two or more single-color bath rugs with rubbery nonskid backings. Instead of using new rugs, you could salvage the useable parts of existing rugs, or even combine new and recycled ones.

Each rug is cut crosswise into strips according to either a predetermined plan or a random configuration. The pieces are then reassembled and hand-sewn together with carpet thread. The bound edges of the rugs become the bound edges of the runner, eliminating the need for any further finishing. If you have leftover strips, turn them into a smaller companion rug.

Keepsake Easter Eggs

Accent traditionally dyed eggs with medallions made from sealing wax, brass charms, and ribbon.

🐦 BY DAWN ANDERSON

COLOR PHOTOGRAPHY:
Carl Tremblay

ILLUSTRATION:
Michael Gellatly

STYLING:
Ritch Holben

THIS FAST DECORATING METHOD is a beautiful variation on the tradition of personalized letter seals. There are really only two simple steps after dyeing the eggs. To "seal" the egg, wrap a ribbon around the middle and glue the medallion on top.

There are several ways in which this technique can be varied to create unique designs. One way is to experiment with the colors of the eggs, the ribbons, and the sealing wax so they match or contrast. You can also create unusual medallions using old jewelry, including bracelet charms, small pendants, or earrings.

Dawn Anderson is a writer and designer living in Redmond, Washington.

INSTRUCTIONS

1. *Prepare eggs for dyeing.* Use egg blowing tool to pierce egg at each end and remove contents; rinse shell well. Repeat process to blow 12 eggs total. Cut twelve 7" lengths of 18-gauge stem wire. Pierce each stem through cover of closed empty egg carton, one over each compartment, to make drying stand.

2. *Mix dyes.* Boil four cups water in teakettle. Set four mugs on thick layer of newsprint. Add 1 teaspoon white vinegar to each mug. Using a separate mug for each dye color, squeeze 20 drops blue food color for blue dye, 20 drops yellow food color for yellow dye, 18 drops yellow and 5 drops red for orange dye, and 30 drops yellow and 5 drops blue for lime-green dye. Add ⅔ cup boiling water to each mug and stir with teaspoon.

3. *Color eggs.* Put on latex gloves. Insert wire from egg carton into hole at narrow end of eggshell. Lower eggshell into dye with spoon, then use wire to keep it submerged for several minutes, or until desired color saturation is reached (*see illustration A, below*). Lift eggshell from

dye, and drain excess liquid back into mug. Stand wire upright in egg carton and let shell air-dry. Repeat process to color 12 eggs total.

4. *Make medallions.* Using wire cutters, clip top loop from brass charm; file down sharp edges. Melt sealing wax onto paper label on side of can to create dime-sized spot with curved back (to hug egg surface later). Using tweezers, immediately position charm on hot, soft wax, and press in place. Let cool 1 to 2 minutes. Peel wax seal from paper label. Repeat process to make 12 medallions total.

5. *Glue ribbon and medallions.* To complete each egg, glue ribbon once around widest part of egg with glue stick; trim off excess (illustration B). Affix seal to egg with white craft glue, concealing ribbon ends (illustration C). ◆

This new use for sealing wax turns dyed eggs into holiday treasures.

MATERIALS
Makes 12 decorated eggs

- 12 white eggs
- 12 assorted brass charms (rabbits, chicks, flowers)
- Assorted ⅜"-wide lavender ribbons, 2 yards total
- Blue and lavender sealing wax sticks
- Liquid food colors (red, yellow, blue)
- White vinegar
- Glue stick
- White craft glue

You'll also need:
empty egg carton; egg-blowing tool; wire cutters; jeweler's file; tweezers; scissors; six 18" stems 18-gauge floral stem wire; ruler; teakettle; Pyrex measuring cup; 4 mugs; 4 teaspoons; latex gloves; newsprint; can with paper label; and matches.

Decorating the Egg

A. Dye each eggshell using ordinary food colors.

B. Glue ribbon around the mid-section.

C. Conceal the ribbon ends with a wax seal.

Folk Art Lamb

Use wool pompons and selective cutting to create traditional soft sculpture.

🐑 BY DAWN ANDERSON

Make one of these lambs with twenty-one pompons and nine chenille stems; finishing accents include glass eyes, leather ears, and a brass bell.

PATTERNS
See page 45 for pattern.

COLOR PHOTOGRAPHY:
Carl Tremblay

ILLUSTRATION:
Michael Gellatly

STYLING:
Ritch Holben

THESE FOLK ART LAMBS HAVE THE same appealing wooly coats and spindly legs as real lambs. Though they may look hard to make, you need only very simple techniques. The lamb's head and body consist of wool pompons clipped into shape with scissors and tied to a simple frame made from chenille stems (also known as pipe cleaners). The lamb's coat depends on the type of wool yarn you use. If you want a fluffy lamb, choose a soft yarn. Generally, machine-washable wool yarns are the softest, but a hand-washable merino yarn would also make a fluffy lamb. If you want a nubby look or a coarser feel, use a textured or virgin wool.

Making the pompons involves three steps: winding yarn around a piece of cardboard, tying the yarn in two places, and cutting it from the cardboard. The ties become the center of each pompon. To ensure neat, fluffy pompons, I recommend winding the yarn in neat rows (approximately 10 to 15 wraps across), alternating directions as you go.

Sculpting the pompons seems difficult if you believe that you have to trim out the specific contours of the lamb, but it is much simpler than that. Think of each part of the lamb as a familiar shape—circle, cone, pear, and so on. Then trim the pompons until the basic shapes emerge.

MATERIALS
Makes 6"-high lamb

- **5 ounces ivory* worsted wool yarn**
- **1 skein black Persian wool**
- **Nine 12" x 6mm white chenille stems**
- **Two 6mm glass animal eyes on wire**
- **Scrap of ivory leather**
- **6mm brass bell**
- **½ yard seam binding**
- **Polyester kite string**
- **Cosmetic blush**

***For black sheep, use charcoal gray yarn, black chenille stems, and black leather.**

You'll also need:
ear pattern (*see* page 45); corrugated cardboard scraps; X-Acto knife; grid ruler; self-healing cutting mat; wire cutter; scissors; darning needle; and cotton swab.

The finishing touches will really bring your lamb to life. Glass eyes are more realistic looking than plastic, so if you can't find glass animal eyes, substitute small round glass shank buttons. Once you have assembled all the parts, give your lamb a final trim to refine its body contours—pay special attention to the pear-shaped tufts at the top of its legs.

Dawn Anderson is a writer and designer living in Redmond, Washington.

INSTRUCTIONS
Making the Basic Pieces
1. *Make pompons.* Using X-Acto knife, grid ruler, and mat, cut one 2" square from corrugated cardboard. Wind ivory yarn neatly and tautly around cardboard square, making 100 complete wraps; clip off excess. Thread darning needle with 24" length of kite string. Slip needle between yarn and cardboard and draw through; repeat once more to loop string around yarn at midsection. Adjust string so ends are even, pull snug, and tie square knot; do not cut string ends. Tie yarn on other side of cardboard square in same way. Using scissors, clip yarn even with edges of cardboard to yield two small pompons (*see* illustration A, next page). Referring to guide, next page, repeat process to make small, medium, and large pompons. For tail pompon, tie one side

only and cut along middle of opposite side. Group pompons by size; set aside those that are not needed.

2. *Make legs.* Hold two 12" chenille stems together. Fold stems in half, then unfold them. For hoof, bind stems

together at middle with black yarn, making eight to ten tight consecutive wraps (about 1"); wrap yarn back over same section. Refold stems at middle, and trim yarn ends to 2". Starting at hoof, wrap ivory yarn around chenille stems for 3"; lock starting end and black ends under first few wraps and clip off excess (illustration B). Wrap leg twice more, down to hoof and back up; trim yarn, leaving 24" end. Repeat to make four legs total.

3. *Join legs in pairs.* On each leg, twist four chenille stems together tightly for ½", then clip off two stems. Place two legs end to end, forming straight line with hoof at each end. Twist remaining stem ends together in middle in tight spiral, then trim off excess. Wrap exposed section once with ivory yarn ends (to lessen bulk, do not triple-wrap). To finish, thread yarn ends into darning needle and take a few stitches through yarn wrapping.

Making the Lamb Head

1. *Sculpt head and muzzle.* Trim large pompon to make 2½" dome. Trim small pompon to make rounded cone 1¼" long (illustration C). To make nose, thread darning needle with black yarn. Insert needle into tip of cone, draw it out at kite string knot, reinsert needle at knot, and draw it back out at cone tip. Trim black yarn even with ivory cone yarn. Tie cone and dome together to make head and muzzle (illustration D). Trim head further to about 2" diameter.

2. *Make ears.* Cut two ears from ivory leather; pierce holes near base with darning needle. Thread chenille stem through one hole from back and second hole from front. Fold ear and pull stem snug to hold pleat. Join other ear to same stem so ears are about 1" apart. Twist stem ends together between ears, then clip off excess. Wind ivory yarn around stem between ears, securing starting end with first few wraps; end off as for legs. Use cotton swab to apply blush inside pleat.

3. *Attach ears to head.* Tie 24" length of kite string to middle of ear stem; thread string ends onto darning needle. Insert

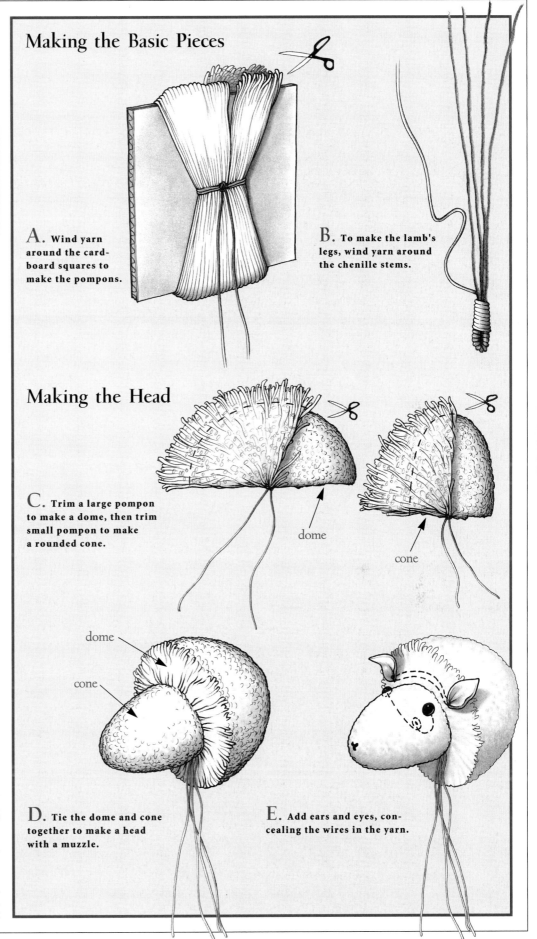

Making the Basic Pieces

A. Wind yarn around the cardboard squares to make the pompons.

B. To make the lamb's legs, wind yarn around the chenille stems.

Making the Head

C. Trim a large pompon to make a dome, then trim small pompon to make a rounded cone.

dome

cone

dome

cone

D. Tie the dome and cone together to make a head with a muzzle.

E. Add ears and eyes, concealing the wires in the yarn.

needle at center of head, ¼" behind muzzle, and draw it down toward neck, concealing ear stem within yarn of head pompon. Tie string ends to other head strings. Fluff yarn around ears (illustration E). Trim head further to refine appearance, but leave wisps of yarn in front of ears.

4. *Attach eyes to head.* Spiral eye wires together so eyes are 2½" to 3" apart. Lay wire across muzzle ¼" below head, part yarn, and push wire between fibers. Bend wire down on each side of muzzle and twist ends together under muzzle. Bend each end up on opposite side and position eyes in front of ears. Adjust so wire is concealed (illustration E). If wire is too long or too short, remove and start again.

Assembling the Lamb Body
1. *Sculpt body.* Tie eight medium pompons into 4 pairs. Bend one 12" chenille stem in half. Tie one pair to stem at bend, then spiral stem ends together loosely

(illustration F). Tie second pair to spiraled stem as close as possible to first pair (about ½" apart). Tie on two remaining pairs in same way for body. Bend remaining stem up for neck. Using scissors, clip yarn ends to form oval-shaped body. Do not clip strings (illustration G).

2. *Add neck and head.* Tie one small pompon to spiraled stem ½" above body pompons. Tie another small pompon to stem as close to lamb's shoulder area as possible. Using wire cutter, clip stem ½" above neck pompon; curl down ends. Fit head against neck portion of body, and tie head strings to curled stem (illustration H). Tie head and neck strings together. Trim small pompons to blend into lamb chest and back. Trim head to blend into neck area.

3. *Join legs to body.* Lay one leg pair across front underside of body, perpendicular to body stem. Part yarn at this spot and press middle of leg piece in

between fibers until it lodges against body stem. Bend each leg up around body stem and down opposite side. Repeat process to attach rear legs (illustration I). Trim remaining small pompons into pear shape with flat back. Tie two pieces to each upper leg, widest part of pear toward top, to create inner and outer thigh. Trim yarn to blend into body near top and to taper into leg at bottom. Tie thigh strings to body strings (illustration J).

4. *Attach tail.* Trim tail pompon into oval shape with flat back. Tie to body stem at rump. Tie tail and body strings together. Trim top of tail even with lamb's back. Shape remainder to create raised area at sides and back (illustration J).

5. *Complete lamb.* Trim all kite string ends close to knots. Trim entire lamb as needed to smooth out body contours and achieve a realistic profile. Thread bell onto ribbon, then tie ribbon in bow around lamb's neck. ◆

Assembling the Lamb

F. To build the body, start by tying a pair of medium pompons to a chenille stem.

G. Complete the shape by tying on three more pairs. Use scissors to sculpt an oval body.

H. Tie on the neck pompons and the head. Continue the scissor sculpting.

I. Secure each leg piece around the body stem.

J. Pad each thigh. Add a tail to the rump.

Making the Journal

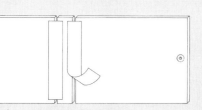

A. Hinge the chipboard covers to the spine.

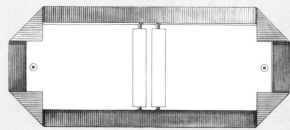

B. Glue on the green paper cover.

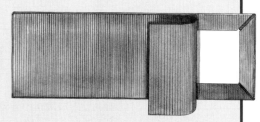

C. Glue on the matching green lining.

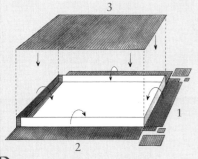

D. Glue green paper to the box.

velcro placement   side view

E. Attach the notepad and box to the binder with Velcro tabs.

F. Thread ribbons through two eyelets for the side closure.

On each chipboard cover, measure ½" in from middle of short edge and mark dot. Using awl, pierce scant ¼"-diameter hole at dot; trim off excess paper pulp with small, sharp scissors. Test-fit eyelet in each hole. Apply loose-leaf reinforcements to both sides of both holes.

3. *Hinge chipboard pieces.* Lay chipboard spine flat and align cover on each side, hole toward outside edge; leave ⅛" gap between pieces. Cut seam binding into four 6¾" lengths. Spread glue on one length and center it lengthwise along gap, glue side down; rub firmly to adhere. Hinge second gap in same way (*see* illustration A, above). Turn pieces over and glue remaining two hinges to opposite side. Carefully bend binder at hinges. To prevent buckling along inside of hinges, tuck excess seam binding into gap with fingernail.

4. *Glue green paper cover to binder.* Lay green cover wrong side up on newsprint. Center hinged binder on top, and trace outline lightly with pencil. Remove binder. Brush thin, even coat of Yes glue on green paper, stopping just beyond pencil outline. Position binder on paper, turn binder and paper over, and using your palm, rub gently in a circular motion from center out to edges to remove air bubbles and ensure good adhesion. Brush glue onto paper margin all around. Fold corners diagonally onto binder and press firmly to adhere (illustra-

tion B). Fold and glue down 4 edges. Carefully bend binder to "set" hinges, then unbend and lay flat.

5. *Glue liner to binder.* Test-fit green liner on binder, and trim if necessary (illustration C). Brush glue on wrong side of liner, going out beyond edges. Glue liner to binder, rubbing in circular motion as for cover. Bend each hinge 90 degrees. Tuck excess lining toward gap as before. Open binder and lay flat, cover side up. Glue ivory "Herbs" label to its celery backing, then glue entire label, centered, to front cover. Weight entire binder with books, and let dry one hour. Relocate each hole and pierce with awl. Install eyelets following manufacturer's instructions.

6. *Glue green paper to box.* Lay green paper box cover wrong side up. Glue box, centered, to paper, following same procedure as for cover in step 4 (illustration D). Fold short edges up around box and down to inside, trimming out corners to reduce bulk. Glue down shorter edges (1), then longer edges (2). Test-fit lining, trim if necessary, and glue to box floor (3).

7. *Glue green paper to notepad.* Slip two thick rubber bands around notepad pages to keep them aligned (leave top cover loose). To remove spiral wire, straighten both ends with needle-nose pliers. Grip one end, and twist it gently and continuously out of holes. Remove cover. Glue green paper notepad cover to it, as in step 4; use X-Acto and cutting guide to trim paper margins even with cover edge.

Glue ivory notepad label to its celery backing, then glue entire label to notepad cover. Weight with book and let dry 30 minutes. Reposition cover on notepad, and using pliers, twist spiral binding back into place. Rebend wire ends to lock binding in place.

8. *Attach box and notepad.* Cut two 18" lengths ribbon. Using sewing machine, zigzag one ribbon to each end of elastic strip. Place supplies in box and place lid on top. Tie ribbon around box horizontally, with bow on top and elastic concealed underneath (illustration E). Turn notepad and box face down. Apply four self-stick Velcro loop dots to back of notepad and six dots to box bottom (detail). Attach Velcro hook dot to each loop dot. Open binder. Position box on inside back cover, flush with spine; press to adhere. Align notepad face down on top, so spiral rings overhang box (side view detail). Close front cover and press to adhere.

9. *Attach ribbons.* Cut two 13" lengths of ribbon. For each, knot one end and trim the other end diagonally. Seal knot and cut end with fray preventer, and let dry overnight. Trim tail from knot. Thread pointed end of ribbon through eyelet from inside of binder (illustration F). Close binder and tie ribbon ends together in bow. ◆

Appliqué Story Quilt

Tell a nursery story using character-motif appliqués and fine cotton prints.

🙚 BY DAWN ANDERSON

COLOR PHOTOGRAPHY:
Carl Tremblay

ILLUSTRATION:
Mary Newell DePalma: E, F, G

Judy Love: A, B, C, D, H

SILHOUETTE PHOTOGRAPHY:
Daniel van Ackere

STYLING:
Ritch Holben

Use bold graphics as a background for the little characters on this charming and colorful baby quilt.

I MADE MY FIRST STORY QUILT USING a handful of appliqués cut from a juvenile print fabric. I chose circles to resemble large and small beads strung along a cord. The bead sequence suggests the flow of a story.

To begin, choose a fabric that offers an interesting range of characters and images—my fabric contained bears, ducks, and sailboats. You'll need enough of the print-motif fabric to yield 10 appliqués—probably ½ to 1 yard. Once you have selected the motifs, use the colors from these images as a guide for selecting two coordinating fabrics for the top and back of the quilt. For the softest quilt, use 100% cotton, and be sure to machine-wash, machine-dry, and press the fabrics flat before sewing.

To place your picture appliqués, first swirl the bias tape into a curving design that follows the outside border of the quilt top, and play with the arrangement of appliqués until you are pleased with the design. You may want to lightly chalk outlines of the appliqués to indicate their final position before you remove them to sew on the bias tape.

Once the cord and appliqués are sewn to the top of the quilt, remove the excess fabric and bias tape from behind them. This will keep the quilt smooth and pliable.

The final assembly requires only four

MATERIALS
Makes one 42" x 51" quilt

- **45"-wide juvenile print-motif cotton fabric** (for ten appliqués)
- **1³⁄₈ yard 45"-wide print cotton fabric** (for quilt top)
- **1⁷⁄₈ yard 60"-wide striped cotton fabric** (for backing and border)
- **5½ yards double-fold bias tape** (for "cord")
- **5½ yards extra-wide double-fold bias tape** (for binding)
- **45" x 60" low-loft bonded polyester batting**
- **Two 20" x 36" sheets Totally Stable iron-on tear-away stabilizer**
- **Pearl cotton to match fabrics**
- **Sewing threads to match fabrics**
- **Monofilament nylon thread**

You'll also need:
sewing machine; iron; rotary cutter; quilter's acryli grid ruler; self-healing cutting mat; sewing shears; embroidery scissors; embroidery needle; hand sewing needle; quilter's straight pins; large safety pins; fabric glue stick; fabric marker; cotton blankets; cotton sheet; compass; and pencil.

more steps—sewing the border strips to the quilt top, basting the layers together, tufting the quilt, and binding the edges. If your quilt will be washed frequently, I recommend spacing the tufts 3" to 4" apart.

Dawn Anderson is a writer and designer living in Redmond, Washington.

INSTRUCTIONS
Prepare and Cut Fabrics
1. *Cut quilt top and borders.* Machine-wash fabrics in cold water, tumble-dry, and press well. Using rotary cutter, grid ruler, and mat, cut one 37½" x 46½" rectangle from print fabric for quilt top. Cut two 2⅝" x 37½" and two 2⅝" x 50¾" strips across width of striped fabric for quilt borders. Set remaining striped fabric aside for quilt back. To stabilize quilt top, cut 7"-wide strips of iron-on stabilizer. Following manufacturer's instructions, fuse strips to wrong side of quilt top about 2" from each edge all around.

2. *Prepare circles for appliqué.* From print motif fabric, pick six large motifs (3" to 4" across) and four small motifs (about 2" across). Set compass point at center of each motif, touch down pencil point ½" to ¾" beyond outermost edge of motif, and draft circle around it (up to

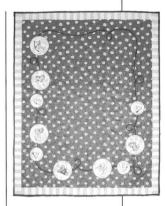

5½" in diameter). Cut piece of iron-on stabilizer slightly larger than each circle; fuse to wrong side. Cut out each circle on marked line.

3. *Prepare bias tape for appliqué.* Open double-fold bias tape. Trim off narrower side about ⅛" beyond center fold. Refold remaining tape and press well.

Sew Quilt Top

1. *Appliqué bias tape to quilt top.* Pad large work surface with cotton blankets and cotton sheet. Lay quilt top face up on sheet. From upper left corner of quilt top, measure 10" down and 7" to right; mark with pin. Starting at pin, lay bias tape on quilt top, swirling and looping it in a freeform design following quilt edge. At same time, position large and small appliqués on top of tape to suggest beads on a loose string. Then press tape only with warm iron to set loops and curves. Pin tape to quilt top; overlap tape ends at starting point and trim off excess. Topstitch around both tape edges (*see* illustration A, right).

2. *Appliqué circles to quilt top.* Cut square of stabilizer slightly larger than circle; fuse to wrong side of quilt top at bead location. Affix circle to right side using fabric glue stick. Set machine for narrow zigzag stitch and sew around circle edges. Set machine for satin stitch (wide, closely spaced zigzag), and stitch around circle again. When you reach starting point, overlap stitching for ¼", and make a few short straight stitches to lock threads (illustration B). Repeat to appliqué ten circles total. Trim thread ends.

3. *Trim out excess bulk.* Lay quilt top wrong side up; tear away stabilizer. Pull circle appliqué and quilt top fabric apart with fingers, then use sharp embroidery scissors to carefully slash quilt top/bias tape fabric only (illustration C). To reduce bulk, trim away the quilt top fabric a scant ⅛" inside the stitched circle (illustration D). Repeat process for each circle appliqué.

4. *Add border strips.* Pin shorter striped border strips to top and bottom edges of quilt top, right sides together. Machine-stitch ¼" from edges, easing to fit. Press seam allowances toward border. Stitch longer border strips to side edges in same way.

Assemble Quilt

Note: Refer to illustration H to arrange the appliqués, add the border strips, and tuft the quilt.

1. *Baste quilt layers.* Tape backing fabric wrong side up to smooth, flat work surface. Center batting on backing. Center quilt top on batting. Tack all three layers together at center using safety pin. Continue safety-pinning layers every 6", working from center out to edges in all directions. Hand-baste ⅜" from outer edge all around.

2. *Tuft and bind quilt.* Using fabric marker, make dot at each corner of quilt 1" in from basting stitches. On each short edge, measure and mark three more dots evenly spaced (about 9" apart); on each long edge, mark four dots. Use these border dots to plot 12 more dots on interior area. Thread embroidery needle with 18" length of pearl cotton. Insert needle into quilt top at dot. Draw needle down through all layers, then back up and out a scant ¼" away; draw through, leaving 3" tail (illustration E). Make second stitch along same path, and pull thread through (illustration F). Clip, leaving 3" tail.

Repeat process for all 30 dots. Tie tails together in square knot and trim to ½" (illustration G).

3. *Bind edges.* Untape quilt back. Cut length of wide bias tape to fit top edge of quilt. Unfold narrow side of tape and pin to quilt top, right sides together, and fold line along basting stitches. Machine-stitch on fold line through all layers. Trim batting and backing even with quilt top and binding. Fold binding over raw edges to quilt back, concealing stitching; pin from right side. Using monofilament thread, stitch in the ditch. Bind bottom and side edges in same way. For sides, cut tape 1" longer, fold in excess at each end, and slipstitch.◆

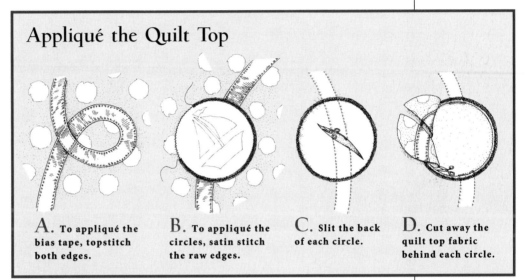

Appliqué the Quilt Top

A. To appliqué the bias tape, topstitch both edges.

B. To appliqué the circles, satin stitch the raw edges.

C. Slit the back of each circle.

D. Cut away the quilt top fabric behind each circle.

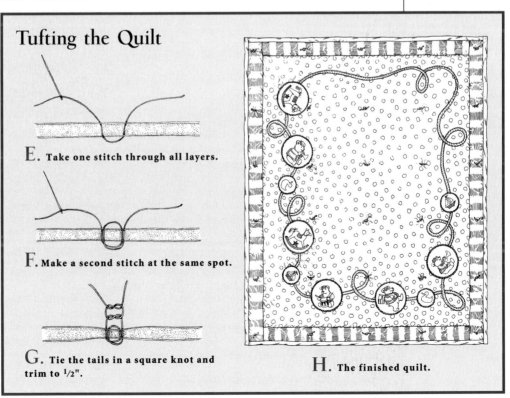

Tufting the Quilt

E. Take one stitch through all layers.

F. Make a second stitch at the same spot.

G. Tie the tails in a square knot and trim to ½".

H. The finished quilt.

Custom "Printed" Director's Chair

Create the look of screened prints using a transfer medium and photocopied art.

BY NANCY OVERTON

By transferring elegant illustrations onto a fabric chair, you can turn simple deck furniture into conversation pieces.

AN ORDINARY DIRECTOR'S chair can be transformed into designer seating by transferring an elegant print to a custom-made backrest. Since this photo-transfer technology is well-suited to finely detailed artwork, I decided to transfer black and white engravings to my chairs. The technique is simple: The image you select is photocopied onto a sheet of photo-transfer paper, and then transferred to fabric with the heat of an iron.

I found these floral and ship engravings at the library. The shelves were full of collections of copyright-free engravings that are perfect for a project like this. You can use any color or black and white image; however, even for a black and white print, you must use a color laser copier to transfer the image to the transfer paper successfully.

My chair's original backrest was too coarse to produce a clear print and too heavy for my sewing machine. But I found I could easily create a new backrest—using the original one as a pattern—out of a muslin blend and cotton duck. The muslin let me achieve a clear, sharp print. Fusing the muslin to the

MATERIALS

- **Director's chair (off-white canvas)**
- **1/3 yard 45"-wide cotton/ polyester muslin**
- **1/4 yard 29"-wide off-white cotton chair duck**
- **Fusible web**
- **Heavy-duty sewing thread**

You'll also need:
artwork for transfer (see step 1); photo transfer paper; access to laser color copier; sewing machine with size 110/18 heavy-duty needle; Teflon-covered ironing board; iron; seam ripper; old, clean 100% cotton pillowcase; X-Acto knife; self-healing cutting mat; tracing paper; scissors; and pencil.

duck adds durability and strength. The duck I used was a medium, 20-oz. weight made especially for deck chairs at 29" wide. It was easy to sew on a home machine using a size 110/18 heavy-duty needle, sometimes called a "denim" needle, and heavy-duty thread.

Nancy Overton of Oakland, California, has designed and written about crafts for more than twenty years.

INSTRUCTIONS

1. *Prepare pattern and select image.* Remove canvas backrest from deck chair. Pick out stitching with seam ripper, and lay canvas flat (*see* illustration A, next page). Iron out folds. Place canvas on tracing paper and trace around edges with pencil. Cut on marked line with scissors to make backrest pattern. To select image for backrest, look for copyright-free artwork (e.g., drawing, print, engraving) with a horizontal orientation and a length about two times the width. Size is not critical, since image can be enlarged on photocopier.

2. *Photocopy image onto transfer paper.* Read transfer paper instructions provided by manufacturer. Take instructions, transfer paper, artwork, and backrest pattern to copier center. Have artwork enlarged as necessary to fill tracing pattern; ask for a sample print on plain paper and lay tracing over it to see how image will appear. Once size is determined, have mirror image of artwork printed on transfer paper. Note that transfer paper prints on one side only and must be inserted correctly in the paper tray.

3. *Transfer image to muslin.* From muslin, cut rectangle about 2" larger all around than tracing pattern. Using X-Acto knife and cutting mat, trim transfer paper image close to outline. To prepare iron, drain all water from it, preheat on hottest (linen) setting for 8 minutes, then gently shake back and forth horizontally to release remaining water droplets or steam. Turn steam feature off. Lay pillowcase on Teflon-covered ironing board, and smooth out wrinkles. Lay muslin rectangle on top. Press muslin with hot iron. Immediately, while muslin is still hot, center transfer facedown on it. Press lightly with iron for 20 seconds to initiate bond, then with heavy, even pressure move iron slowly back and forth across transfer for 1 minute. Make sure iron sole plate covers all parts of transfer, including edges. To remove transfer paper, rotate iron to reheat entire surface, then immediately peel up paper from one corner; if peeling is difficult, reheat and try peeling from a different corner.

4. *Fuse and sew backrest.* Lay backrest pattern on top of printed muslin with transferred image centered. Using fabric-marking pencil, trace pattern outline (illustration B). Cut out muslin backrest on marked line. Also mark and cut one backrest from canvas and one from fusible webbing. Following manufacturer's instructions, fuse muslin and canvas backrests together (illustration C). Fold long edges to back side; fuse in place with thin strips of webbing or stitch down edges with machine. Fold in sides and stitch down to form channels for deck- chair stiles (illustration D). ◆

Creating the Chair Back

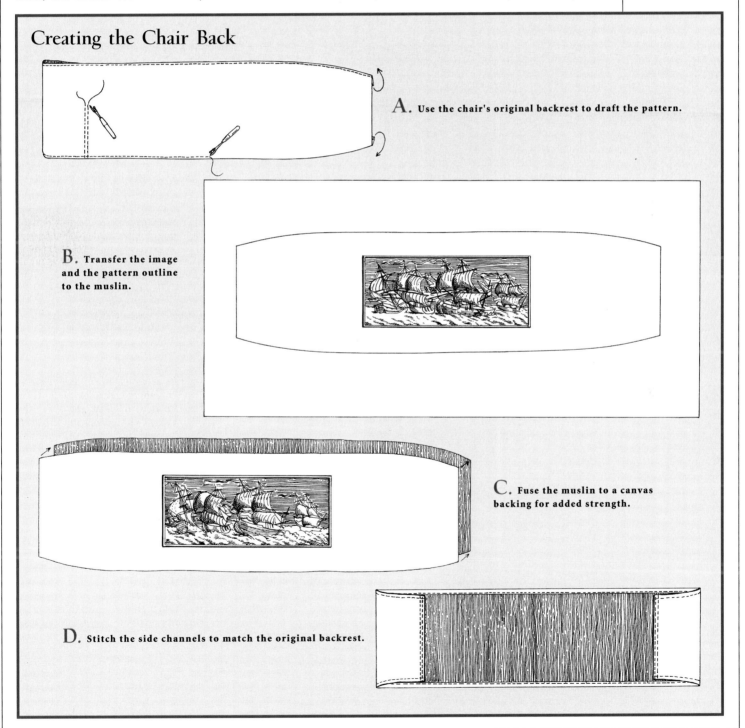

A. Use the chair's original backrest to draft the pattern.

B. Transfer the image and the pattern outline to the muslin.

C. Fuse the muslin to a canvas backing for added strength.

D. Stitch the side channels to match the original backrest.

Sheer Bedroom Canopy

The simplest way to evoke a *plein aire* bedroom: a quilting hoop and sheer fabric.

❧ BY CHIPPY IRVINE

The French term "plein aire" means outdoors or in the fresh air—the effect created by this canopy.

COLOR PHOTOGRAPHY:
Carl Tremblay

ILLUSTRATION:
Judy Love

STYLING:
Ritch Holben

CONJURE UP SOFT TROPICAL breezes no matter where you live with this sheer hoop canopy. The airy fabric cascades down from a large wooden embroidery hoop, which is suspended above the bed. The fabric is gathered and crimped between the hoop rings.

To evoke the mosquito netting used in the tropics, select a light, sheer fabric. Possibilities include fine cotton batiste, nylon or polyester curtain fabrics, and bridal tulle. The fabric width is not critical, since the thinner weights gather readily and can be eased to fit the embroidery hoop circumference. The design shown here features three panels, each 45" wide and 9 feet long. For a more enclosed canopy, consider buying 4 yards of 118"-wide lightweight curtain fabric, and gather and mount the selvage edge. Fabrics for either style can be purchased for around $30.

For other dramatic looks, wrap the panels of the canopy over or through an open headboard, or tie a loose overhand knot in the lower third of each panel and rest the knots against the outside corners of the bed.

Chippy Irvine is a crafts designer living in Patterson, New York.

MATERIALS

- 18" wooden embroidery hoop
- 10¼ yards 45"- to 60"-wide sheer fabric
- 3½ yards white seam binding
- White sewing thread
- 2 yards x ¾" white self-adhesive Velcro
- 2½ yards white cord
- 1" wooden bead (³/₈" hole)
- ¾" metal pot hook
- ½" double-sided tape

You'll also need:
sewing machine; scissors; sewing shears; tape measure; fabric marker; safety pins; and iron.

INSTRUCTIONS

1. *Cut fabric.* From sheer fabric, cut three 108"-long panels. For frill, cut two 7½"-wide strips from width of fabric. Set 18"embroidery hoop on remaining fabric as template. Using fabric marker, draw circle 1" beyond hoop edge all around. Cut out 20" circle on marked line.

2. *Join sheer circle to inner hoop.* Zigzag raw edge of sheer circle to prevent raveling. Remove outer ring from hoop and set it aside. Apply double-sided tape around inner ring. Grip sheer circle by opposite edges and center it over ring, stretch gently until taut, then press edges down onto taped rim. Rotate hoop ¼ turn and repeat. Stretch and secure remaining sections. Trim even with lower edge of rim. Mark outside rim into quarters. Cut four 20" lengths of cord; knot each end. Pin one cord at each mark so knot falls just below lower edge (*see* illustration A, next page). Apply double-sided tape to rim all around.

3. *Join and gather panels.* Fold and press lower edge of each panel ½" to wrong side twice, then topstitch. Press hemmed edges; press out creases. Place two panels right sides together with selvages matching. Beginning at raw edge, stitch selvages together for 1½" only, making ¼" seam. Repeat to join third panel, then join first and third panels. Measure and divide continuous raw edge into quarters using four safety pins placed 1" from raw edge. Machine-gather entire raw edge to 56½", or to fit around inner hoop. Adjust gathers to align four safety pins to four cords. To hold gathers, stitch seam binding to gathered edge on right side.

4. *Join panels to hoop.* Arrange gathered edge of panels evenly around inner hoop, aligning safety pins with cords. Make sure cords extend freely. Once position is confirmed, press gathered section against double-sided tape to secure. Add outer ring to hoop, securing gathered panels and cord within, and tighten screw (illustration B).

5. *Make and attach frill.* Stitch two frill strips together at selvages to make continuous loop. Double-hem lower raw edge, same as panels in step 3. Machine-gather top edge to about 63", or large enough to fit around hoop, including screw mechanism. To secure gathers, sew seam binding to gathered edge on right side, same as panels in step 3. Cut Velcro strip to fit once around hoop, including screw mechanism. Separate into hook and loop tapes. Remove backing from hook tape and adhere to hoop. Adhere loop tape to right side of frill, concealing seam binding (illustration C). Fold Velcro edge of frill to inside and press against hoop Velcro all around (illustration D).

6. *Suspend canopy.* Thread the four hoop cords through wooden bead; knot ends. Cut one 9" cord, and knot ends. Fold cord in half, then push folded end into bead hole from bottom and pull through (illustration E). Screw pot hook into ceiling above bed, securing into beam. Hang canopy from hook, and drape panels around bed. Shorten cord if necessary (illustration F). ◆

Making the Canopy

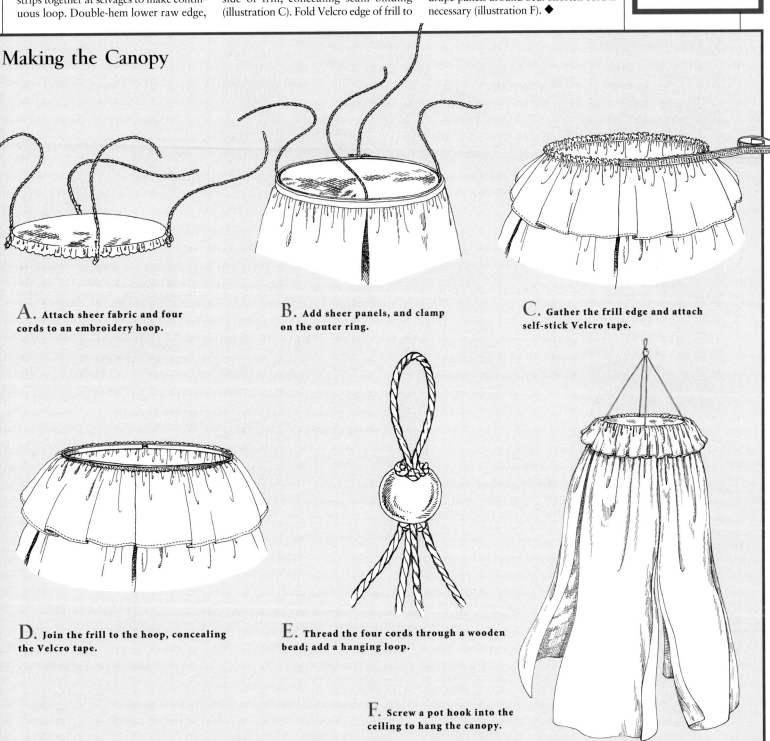

A. Attach sheer fabric and four cords to an embroidery hoop.

B. Add sheer panels, and clamp on the outer ring.

C. Gather the frill edge and attach self-stick Velcro tape.

D. Join the frill to the hoop, concealing the Velcro tape.

E. Thread the four cords through a wooden bead; add a hanging loop.

F. Screw a pot hook into the ceiling to hang the canopy.

Custom-Designed Flatware

Transform mismatched utensils into elegant picnicware using rubber stamps and enamel paint.

❧ BY DAWN ANDERSON

A rubber-stamped design unifies these three sets. The result: colorful bistroware for informal dining.

MATERIALS

- **Flatware with colored plastic handles**
- **Delta CeramDecor Perm Enamel products: paint (in contrasting colors), conditioner, and clear gloss glaze**

You'll also need: rubber stamp with ¼" image; ⅛"-thick craft foam; ⅜" flat brush; styrofoam block(s); newsprint; and paper towels.

WANT TO ADD FLAIR TO your spring entertaining without spending a lot of money? This fast and easy technique can be used to accent everyday flatware. All you do is rubber-stamp a design with enamel paint on the front and back of plastic-handled utensils and coat them with glaze for protection.

You can use this technique to create a wide range of flatware styles. For a more elegant setting, you could stamp traditional designs in gold paint to white-handled pieces or geometric designs in white to black-handled pieces. For a fresh spring look, you could stamp a lime-green leaf pattern onto white-handled pieces. You may want to pair custom-designed flatware with coordinating table linens to create a shower gift.

Dawn Anderson, a writer and designer, lives in Redmond, Washington.

INSTRUCTIONS

1. *Prepare handles for stamping.* Wash flatware with soap and water; rinse and dry. Following manufacturer's instructions, brush plastic handles with Perm Enamel conditioner. Let dry 10 minutes.

Stamping the Flatware

A. To load the stamp, use a thin foam pad brushed with paint.

B. Stamp the image on the flatware handle.

C. Glaze each handle, and stand the piece vertically to dry.

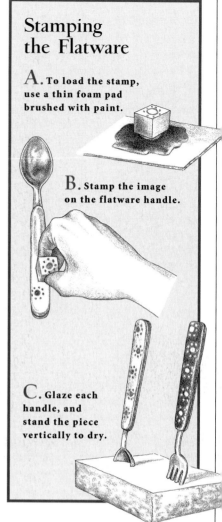

2. *Stamp handles.* Protect work surface with newsprint. Shake paint container well. Using brush, transfer small amount of paint to craft foam, and brush in two directions until paint forms smooth, thin, even layer. To load stamp, tap it lightly on foam several times (*see* illustration A, above). Press stamp onto handle of flatware and immediately lift off; do not rock stamp from side to side. Repeat process to stamp several images (illustration B). If an image is blurred or imperfect, wipe it off immediately, while paint is still wet, using paper towel moistened with conditioner. To prevent paint buildup, clean stamp every three or four images. Repeat process to stamp each utensil. Let paint dry 20 minutes. Turn flatware over and stamp back of handles in same way. Let dry one hour.

3. *Seal handles.* Brush clear gloss glaze over front and back of handle. Poke metal end into foam block so utensil dries in vertical position. Repeat process for each utensil (illustration C). Let dry one hour. Apply second glaze coat in same way. Let paint cure 10 days before using or washing utensils.◆

Vintage Canisters

Recreate the look of 50's keepers using spray paint, brightly colored knobs, and labels made from self-adhesive film.

❧ BY MICHIO RYAN

COLOR PHOTOGRAPHY:
Carl Tremblay

ILLUSTRATION:
Mary Newell DePalma

STYLING:
Ritch Holben

REMEMBER OLD-FASHIONED enamelware? These sturdy kitchen accessories are now reappearing at flea markets and antique shops as pricey collectibles. You can easily replicate this look by spray painting an assortment of tinware containers, adding custom labels to each one, and topping them with matching knobs.

All sorts of tinwear can be used for this project. I used a nesting set of three tins from IKEA which cost $7.95. Raw stamped steel containers are also readily available and can be painted with a minimum of preparation. Discarded toffee boxes, biscuit tins, and tea tins can also be recycled as long as they are rust- and dent-free. Even though the containers you find may be different sizes and shapes, a unifying paint color and style will create a matching set.

INSTRUCTIONS

1. *Prepare canisters for painting.* Wash canisters in warm, soapy water to remove residual oils; dry thoroughly. Place lids on canisters. Rub 220-grit sandpaper over all surfaces except bottom. Wipe dust with tack cloth. Remove lids. Locate and mark center of each lid. To punch hole for knob, prop lid top-side down on wood block, set nail at mark, and tap with hammer. Smooth jagged edges by tapping dowel against hole.

2. *Paint canisters green.* Mask outside rim of each canister with tape (*see* illustration A, below). Seat lid on top, but don't press it down all the way. Set up ventilated area for painting and line work surface with newspaper. Elevate canister on wood slats. Using light, even strokes, spray thin coat of paint over entire surface, including lid. Let dry 20 minutes. Spray second thin coat; let dry. If needed, spray third very light coat. Let dry in place 1 hour.

Create spatterware by dripping or flecking paint over a white base coat.

3. *Paint rim band black.* Remove lid but not tape from canister. Apply second band of tape ¼" below rim, leaving rim unmasked. Turn canister face down. Tape paper around sides and base to protect from overspray. Spray light coat of black paint onto area between bands of tape. Let dry 20 minutes. Repeat once.

4. *Paint knobs red.* Drive screw partway into each knob. Sink screw head into piece of modeling compound to hold knob upright for painting and drying. For primer, mix equal amounts wood putty powder and rust-red acrylic craft paint in disposable plastic lid. Brush evenly over knobs. Let dry 10 minutes, then sand smooth using 400-grit emery paper. Brush fast-drying red enamel on each knob in thin coat; let dry 20 minutes. Repeat for four coats total. Let dry 24 hours before handling.

5. *Add labels and knobs.* Photocopy desired type (page 47) onto clear, self-adhesive film, or print your own from a computer. (I used Glaser SteD font at 48 pts.) Using X-Acto knife, grid ruler, and cutting mat, cut film into individual labels. Peel off backing and adhere to canister (illustration B). Rub firmly to eliminate frosted appearance. Place lid on canister. Following manufacturer's instructions, spray very light coat acrylic sealer on canister and lid. Let dry 10 minutes. Repeat process to apply three sealer coats total. Screw knobs onto canisters, using washers against lid underside (illustration C). ◆

MATERIALS
Makes set of three canisters

- 6"-, 6½"-, and 7½"-diameter metal canisters
- 1¼"-, 1½"-, and 2"-diameter unfinished wood-ball knobs
- Three large washers with ⅛" holes
- 8½" x 11" clear matte self-adhesive film
- 12 ounces Krylon Jade Green (#2003) enamel spray paint
- Black enamel spray paint
- 2 ounces Odds 'n' Ends Insignia Red (#B13) fast-drying enamel paint
- 2 ounces rust-red acrylic craft paint
- Matte acrylic spray sealer
- Wood putty (powder form)

You'll also need:
type (see page 47); access to photocopier; X-Acto knife; quilter's acrylic grid ruler; self-healing cutting mat; hammer; screwdriver; 8d nail; 220- and 400-grit sandpaper; ⅜" x 4" wooden dowel; wood block; wood slats; tack cloth; ½"-wide flat, soft-bristled brush; newspaper; masking tape; permanent marker; modeling compound, and disposable plastic lid.

SUGAR

LABELS
See page 47 for labels and enlargement instructions.

Make a Retro Canister

A. **Prepare the lid and can for spray painting.**

B. **After the paint dries, add a clear self-stick label.**

C. **Screw in the ball knob from the lid underside.**

Tiered Scenic Card

Cut textured paper and fold it into an accordian-style southwestern landscape.

⅋ BY ELIZABETH CAMERON

Use this tiered style to create smaller two-fold versions that can serve as placecards or party invitations.

PATTERNS

See page 46 for pattern and enlargement instructions.

COLOR PHOTOGRAPHY:
Carl Tremblay

ILLUSTRATION:
Mary Newell DePalma

SILHOUETTE PHOTOGRAPHY:
Daniel van Ackere

STYLING:
Ritch Holben

DIMENSION ADDS CHARACTER to a greeting card. You can easily create this desert landscape card by joining corrugated cardboard to colored paper, and cutting a pattern that ascends from one side of a long rectangle to the other. The card is then folded, accordian style, to form increasingly distant vistas. Adapt this accordian-style design by creating different foregrounds or backgrounds, using your favorite vacation spots for inspiration. Simple graphic shapes, such as palm trees or skyscrapers, which are easy to cut and don't rely on color for definition, will work best.

INSTRUCTIONS

Note: Follow the instructions below for each card.

1. *Cut papers.* Using X-Acto knife, grid ruler, and cutting mat, cut one 7" x 19" rectangle from green paper and a matching rectangle from ribbed paper, ribs parallel to 7" edges. Cut one 4⅝" x 6⅝" rectangle from red-orange paper. Using compass, draft 3⅛" diameter circle on yellow paper. To cut out circle, hold X-Acto knife blade stationary on marked outline and rotate yellow paper.

2. *Mark design.* Using scissors, cut out 19" desert landscape pattern on marked lines to make silhouette. Lay green rectangle flat; align landscape pattern on top, bottom, and one side edge. Using pencil, lightly trace grass, cactus, and mountain silhouette. Spray back side of green rectangle lightly with adhesive, following manufacturer's instructions, and affix to same-size corrugated rectangle (*see* illustration A, next page).

3. *Cut design.* Lay rectangle green side up on cutting mat. Using X-Acto knife, cut on all marked lines through all layers; to cut straight lines, run blade along edge of ruler. For inside points (e.g., between blades of grass), cut in from both directions. When all cuts are made, turn piece over and trim off snags from corrugated side.

4. *Fold card.* Lay card flat, green side up. Referring to pattern and using ribs as guide, fold card accordian-style: First, fold mountain silhouette onto plain area, ribbed side up (illustration B). Next, fold cactus silhouette onto mountains, green side up (illustration C). To end, fold grass silhouette onto cactus, ribbed side up (illustration D). Reattach papers with glue stick if needed.

5. *Add sky and sun.* Open card to inside, green side up. Test-fit red-orange rectangle on plain green background, leaving border on any two sides. Add yellow circle for sun (illustration E). Close card to double-check positions (illustration F). Glue the sky and sun inserts in place. ◆

Designing the Card

DESIGNER'S TIP

Use the leftover red-orange, green, or yellow papers to make coordinating envelopes. See "Five-Minute Envelope Liners," Fall 1997.

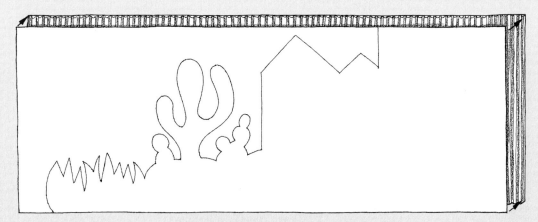

A. Mark the green paper and glue it to the ribbed paper.

B. Cut out the desert silhouette, and make the first fold.

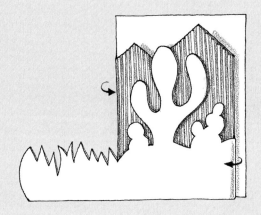

C. Make the second fold accordian-style.

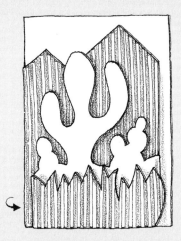

D. Make the final fold.

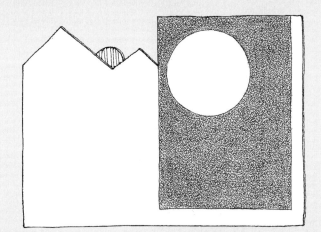

E. Position the red-orange sky and yellow sun inserts.

F. Close the card to confirm their placement, then glue in place.

Natural Floral China

Arrange fresh flowers between glass plates for unique china patterns.

🌺 BY RITCH HOLBEN

Delicate, fragile flowers look lovely pressed under glass. Try snapdragon, pansy, freesia, geranium, phlox, sweet pea, and morning glory. For a green accent, use ferns, ornamental grasses, or herbs.

Decorating the Plate

A. Peel back one petal to reveal the inner blossom.

B. Arrange individual blossoms, petals, and leaves on a glass plate.

C. Set a second plate on top to press and hold the arrangement.

MATERIALS
Makes one floral cake platter

- **Two clear glass plates**
- **Assorted fresh flowers and greens**

You'll also need: small floral shears.

COLOR PHOTOGRAPHY:
Carl Tremblay

ILLUSTRATION:
Michael Gellatly

STYLING:
Ritch Holben

BRING THE VIVID PALETTE OF nature to your table with your own floral china patterns. Start by arranging fresh flowers on a glass plate, and then stack a second clear glass plate on top to hold the flowers in place. You can tailor the colors and textures of the flowers to your table linens, match them to your centerpiece, or coordinate them with other florals around your home. You can use small glass plates to create serving dishes for appetizers or desserts.

The flowers that flatten best have thin plant matter and light, delicate blossoms. Examples include pansies, violets, and morning glories. If you want to use denser flowers, such as chrysanthemums or roses, pull off individual petals and arrange them in a radiating pattern or scatter them for a confetti effect.

Ritch Holben is a designer and photo stylist living in Nahant, Massachusetts.

INSTRUCTIONS
1. *Begin arranging flowers.* Select four to eight large flowers. If flowers are cup-shaped, peel back one petal to reveal inner blossom (*see* illustration A, above). Snip across base to remove stem and eliminate bulk. Arrange flowers around rim of one glass plate, clustering several together or spacing them evenly like numerals on a clock face. Flatten each blossom slightly with fingertip.

2. *Fill out design.* Select 10 to 12 smaller blossoms, and trim as in step 1. Arrange these on plate rim, filling in spaces between larger blossoms. You can also add individual petals. Place leaves last, snipping off thick portion of stem at base and slipping cut edge under a flower to conceal it. Leaf tips can extend beyond rim (illustration B).

3. *Add second plate.* Once arrangement is set, hold second plate directly over first plate and lower it into position. Work slowly to press flowers flat without dislodging (illustration C). ◆

Spring 1998 Patterns

Fifties-Style Apron and Mitts
(*see* article, page 14)

NOTE: PHOTOCOPY OVEN MITT PATTERN AT 200%.

CUT OUT PATTERN ON OUTLINE.

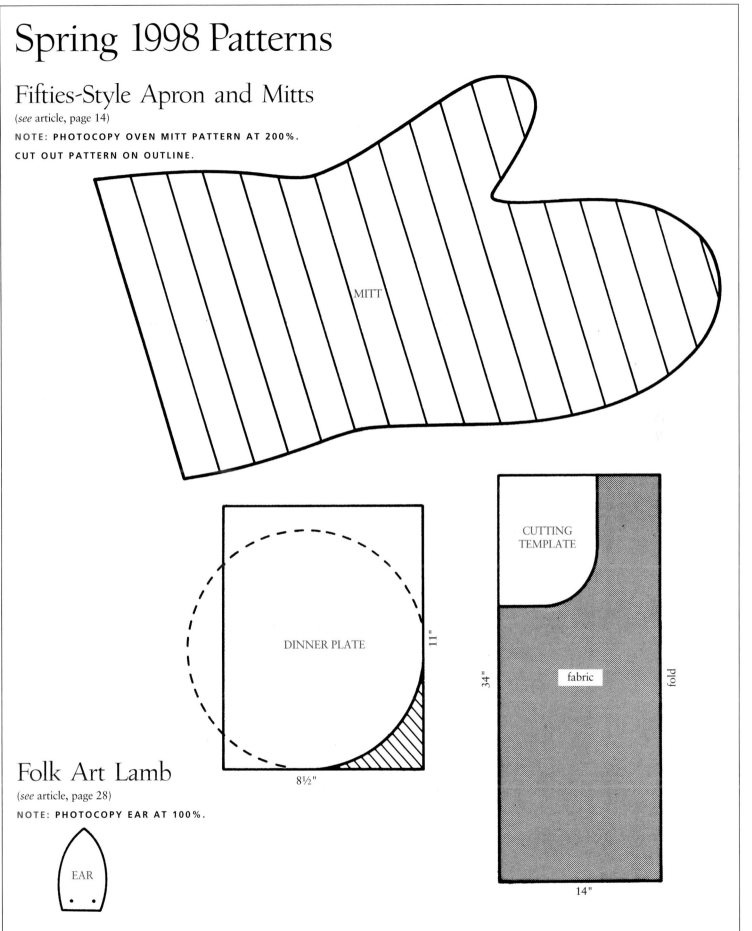

MITT

DINNER PLATE

11"

8½"

CUTTING
TEMPLATE

fabric

34"

fold

14"

Folk Art Lamb
(*see* article, page 28)

NOTE: PHOTOCOPY EAR AT 100%.

EAR

Apple Silhouette Wall Border

(*see* article, page 31)

NOTE: PHOTOCOPY AT 200%.

Tiered Scenic Card

(*see* article, page 42)

**NOTE: PHOTOCOPY AT 200% ON TWO SEPARATE SHEETS.
TAPE SHEETS TOGETHER TO MAKE 18¹/₈" LONG PATTERN.**

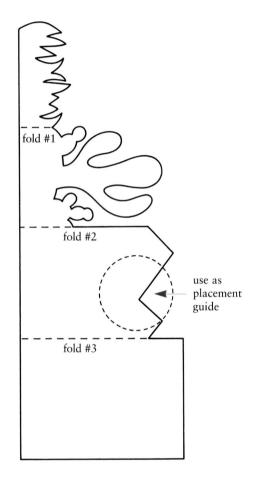

fold #1

fold #2

use as
placement
guide

fold #3

SUN

Mariner's Stool
(*see* article, page 20)

NOTE: PHOTOCOPY COMPASS PATTERN AT 200% TO FIT A 12¹/₂" DIAMETER STOOL SEAT.

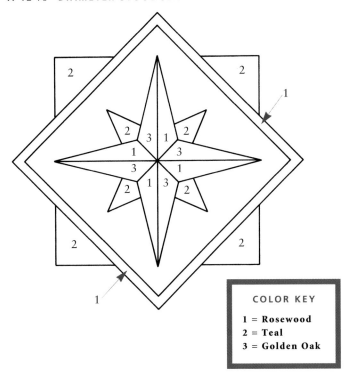

COLOR KEY

1 = Rosewood
2 = Teal
3 = Golden Oak

Vintage Canisters
(*see* article, page 41)

NOTE: PHOTOCOPY ALL PIECES AT 200%.

SUGAR

FLOUR

TEA

COFFEE

BISCUITS

COOKIES

Easter Party Favor
(*see* article, page 8)

NOTE: PHOTOCOPY THE PARTY FAVOR PATTERN TWICE AT 200%. CUT THE EGG FROM ONE COPY AND THE RABBIT FROM THE OTHER COPY.

Sources & Resources

Specific sources are listed below for harder-to-find project items.

Most of the materials used in this issue are available at your local craft supply store, florist, fabric shop, hardware store, or bead and jewelry supply. Generic craft supplies can be ordered from catalogs such as **Dick Blick Art Materials, Craft King, Pearl Paint Company, or Sunshine Discount Crafts**. The following are specific sources for harder-to-find items, arranged by article. The suggested retail prices listed here were current at press time. Contact the suppliers directly to confirm prices and availability.

Quick Home Accents, *page 6*
Daisy trim appliqué (1 inch) for $1.05 from Pacific Fabrics & Crafts. Daisy trim appliqué (1½ inch) for $5 per yard from North End Fabrics. Liqui-fuse webbing for $5.19 per 4-ounce-bottle from Alpine Imports.

Perfect Gift, *page 7*
Linen place mat with hemstitched edges starting at $6 from Crate & Barrel.

Floral Letter Seals, *page 12*
Clear stationery seals (600 for under $20) available through Maco.

Fifties-Style Apron and Mitts, *page 14*
Cotton cording for 50 cents per yard from Nancy's Sewing Basket. Teflon batting for $8.99 per yard from Hartsdale Fabrics. Lime green, cotton piqué fabric for $13.79 per yard from G Street Fabrics.

Miniature Memory Album, *page 16*
Mulberry paper for $1.99 per 22"x 30" sheet from The Paper Zone. Striped vellum for 20 cents per sheet, self-adhesive photo corners for $4.75 per pack, and gold baby shoe charm for 50 cents, all from Impress.

Flowerpots, *page 18*
Three-inch pots (64-605) for $9 and five-inch pots (64-625) for $21 from Earthmade Products.

Mariner's Stool, *page 20*
Craft woodburning tool (#22038) for $14.99 from The Woodworker's Store.

Graphite transfer paper for $8.99 per roll from Charrette.

Papier-Mâché Peppers, *page 22*
Art paste starting at $3.75 for 2-ounce package (#310-0641) from Sax Arts & Crafts.

Windowsill Greenhouse, *page 24*
Basswood strips (in varying dimensions) starting at 25 cents from Pearl Paint. Lamp finials starting at $1 available through True Value Hardware.

Keepsake Easter Eggs, *page 27*
Egg blower starting at $5 from Ukrainian Gift Shop. Sealing wax for $5 per stick from Impress. Ribbons starting at 25 cents from Nancy's Sewing Basket. Charms starting at 25 cents each from Creative Beginnings.

Folk Art Lamb, *page 28*
Glass animal eyes for $1.70 per pair from Carver's Eye Company. Ivory worsted wool starting at $5.25 per skein from Halcyon Yarn.

Apple Silhouette Wall Border, *page 31*
Stencil cutting pen (#1741200) for $19.99 from Dick Blick.

Garden Journal, *page 32*
Lime-green ribbed paper for $2.25 per 20"x30" roll from Impress. Foam-core ³⁄₁₆" board for $1.97 per 20"x 30" board from Pearl Paint.

Director's Chair, *page 36*
Director's chair starting at $49 from the Door Store.

Sheer Bedroom Canopy, *page 38*
Hoop (18 inch) for $17.70 and sheer fabric (54"-wide) starting at $3 per yard from North End Fabrics.

Custom-Designed Flatware, *page 40*
Rubber stamps starting at $2 from Impress.

Vintage Canisters, *page 41*
Acrylic sealer for $4.79 from Craft King.

Tiered Scenic Card, *page 42*
Sheets of drawing paper for 98 cents and corrugated sheets for $1.74 from Pearl Paint.

Mini-Chest, *Backcover*
Six-drawer chest (#95716309) for $19 from IKEA.

❧ ❧ ❧ ❧ ❧

The following companies are mentioned in the listing above. Contact each individually for a price list or catalog.

ALPINE IMPORTS
7104 N. Alpine Road, Rockford, IL 61111; 800-654-6114

CARVER'S EYE CO.
P.O. Box 1118, Gresham, OR 97030; 503-666-5680

CHARRETTE
P.O. Box 4010, Woburn, MA 01888-4010; 800-367-3729

CRAFT KING
P.O. Box 90637, Lakeland, FL 33804; 800-769-9494

CRATE & BARREL
Call 800-323-5461 to find the location nearest you.

CREATIVE BEGINNINGS
P.O. Box 1330, Morro Bay, CA 93443; 800-367-1739

DICK BLICK ART MATERIALS
P.O. Box 1267, Galesburg, IL 61402-1267; 800-447-8192

DOOR STORE
940 Massachusetts Avenue, Cambridge, MA 02139; 617-547-8937

EARTHMADE PRODUCTS
P.O. Box 609, Jasper, IN 47547-0609; 800-843-1819

G STREET FABRICS
12240 Wilkins Avenue, Rockville, MD 20852; 800-333-9191

HALYCON YARN
12 School Street, Bath, ME 04530; 800-341-0282

HARTSDALE FABRICS
275 South Central Avenue, Hartsdale, NY 10530; 914-428-7780

IKEA
Catalog Department, 185 Discovery Drive, Colmar, PA 18915; 800-434-4532

IMPRESS
120 Andover Park E., Tukwila, WA 98188; 206-901-9101

MACO
Call 800-221-9983 for a store in your area.

NANCY'S SEWING BASKET
2221 Queen Anne Avenue N., Seattle, WA 98109; 206-282-9112

NORTH END FABRICS
31 Harrison Avenue, Boston, MA 02111; 617-542-2763

PACIFIC FABRICS AND CRAFTS
1645 140th Avenue N.E., Bellevue, WA 98009; 206-747-3551

THE PAPER ZONE
3828 148th Avenue N.E., Redmond, WA 98052; 425-883-0273

PEARL PAINT COMPANY, INC.
308 Canal Street, New York, NY 10013-2572; 800-451-7327 (catalog) or 800-221-6845 x2297 (main store)

SAX ARTS & CRAFTS
P.O. Box 510710, New Berlin, WI 53151; 800-558-6696

SUNSHINE DISCOUNT CRAFTS
P.O. Box 301, Largo, FL 33779-0301; 800-729-2878

TRUE VALUE HARDWARE
Call 800-642-7392 for the nearest location.

UKRAINIAN GIFT SHOP
2512 39th Avenue N.E., St. Anthony, MN 55421; 612-788-2545

THE WOODWORKER'S STORE
4365 Willow Drive, Medina, MN 55340; 800-279-4441

Quick Projects

Create classic guest towels using scissors and lace.

These towels, left to right, are edged with filigree lace, looped lace, and cutout lace.

LACE-INSET TOWELS

The laces that border these crisp, white hand towels may look fragile and delicate, but in fact, are quite easy to sew. Start by purchasing white piqué, available in many weights and fabric variations. You can use just about any lace motif you want for the trimming, but be sure to select washable lace. You can make three towels from ¾ yard of 45"-wide piqué, or four towels from ¾ yard of 60"-wide fabric.

To prepare, establish the straight grain across the fabric by pulling a thread from the selvage. Cut the fabric into pieces measuring 15" x 27". If you apply trim at one end only, finish the other end with a simple topstitched hem.

■ **Filigree lace-edged towel:** Measure width of lace border to match width of towel. Determine right side of lace, then center lace across towel. Press ¼" single hem towards right side at one end. Sew lace to right side of piqué, covering pressed hem as you go. Topstitch to stabilize lace and hem. Repeat at other end of towel if desired. Press ¼" double-fold hem on each side of towel. Topstitch side hems, trapping lace as you stitch.

■ **Looped lace-edged towel:** Press ¼" double-fold hem to wrong side all around piqué towel. Topstitch hem. Pin lace in place along one edge of piqué towel. Stitch using straight line (if lace permits) and covering as much of hem as possible. Do not stretch lace.

■ **Cutout lace-edged towel:** Establish best side of lace. From piqué, measure and cut off 4" x 15" strip. Sew lace to piqué strip, right sides facing, using ¼" seams. Fold piqué lengthwise with right sides facing, trapping lace. Sew ¼" seam following previous seam stitches to form tube with lace trapped inside. Trim off corners at either end. Use large safety pin to turn tube right side out and press. Poke in ½" seams at both ends and press. Topstitch ¼" across piqué seam to hold lace firm and flat. Lay free side of lace on raw end of towel body, right sides together. Sew lace edge to towel using ¼" seams. Press seam away from lace. Topstitch ¼" on piqué to hold lace flat and to cover raw edge of piqué. Finish side hems as above. ◆

COLOR PHOTOGRAPHY:
Carl Tremblay

DESIGN:
Chippy Irvine

STYLING:
Ritch Holben

Painted Mini-Chest

Squirrel away your valuables in the drawers of this retro-style mini-chest. The retro-look is created by using acrylic paints, graphic rubber stamps, and collectible buttons. Start with a small, unfinished wooden chest. Even out imperfections in the surface with wood filler and, after it dries, sand the chest lightly with 100-grit sandpaper. If you need to add knobs to the chest, draw diagonal lines across each drawer and drill a hole in the center, where the lines intersect. Paint the chest, alternating colors on the sides and the drawer fronts. When dry, lightly sand the surface with 220-grit sandpaper, and remove any dust with a lightly misted paper towel. Repeat this process, adding two more layers of paint. Paint the knobs in the same fashion.

Use rubber stamps to add designs to the drawer fronts. Place a small pool of paint on craft foam and spread it over the surface using a brush. Stamp impressions on three of the drawers.

Apply clear acrylic sealer to the chest, drawer fronts, and knobs, following manufacturer's instructions. Allow to dry. Trim the shanks from the back of the decorative buttons using a wire cutter. Glue the buttons to the faces of the lightly sanded knobs with 5-minute epoxy. When dry, screw the knobs into the drawers.

COLOR PHOTOGRAPHY: **Carl Tremblay**   STYLING: **Ritch Holben**   DESIGN: **Dawn Anderson**

NUMBER TWENTY-ONE

FALL 1998

Handcraft
ILLUSTRATED

Fall Decorating

everlasting florals
easy silk pillows
scented candles
cozy throws

Thanksgiving Floral Turkey
Plant Dried Flowers in a Foam Ball

Jeweled Partridge Ornament
Encrust an Artificial Bird with Rhinestones

Natural Lip Balms
Customize a 2-Minute Recipe to Suit Your Skin

Traveling Blanket
Quick-Sew Colorful Boiled Wool Rectangles

Pop-Up Jester
Replicate an Antique Movable Toy

Lacelike Windows
Cut Patterns from Film to Create Window Designs

ALSO
Scarves · Candles · Frames
Sachets · Cards
Packaging · Ornaments

Get a Head Start on Holiday Gifts!

Contents

**Scented Modular
Candles, page 12**

**Pop-Up Jester,
page 30**

**Reversible Silk
Velvet Scarf,
page 34**

COVER PHOTOGRAPH:
Carl Tremblay

STYLING:
Ritch Holben

Melt natural oils and wax to make a moisturizing lip balm. See page 8.

Handcraft
ILLUSTRATED

EDITOR
Carol Endler Sterbenz

SENIOR EDITOR
Mary Ann Hall

CREATIVE PROJECT DIRECTOR
Michio Ryan

RESEARCH AND TESTING EDITOR
Candie Frankel

CONTRIBUTING EDITOR
Elizabeth Cameron

EDITORIAL ASSISTANT
Livia McRee

❧

ART DIRECTOR
Amy Klee

CORPORATE MANAGING EDITOR
Barbara Bourassa

COPY EDITOR
Carol Parikh

❧

PUBLISHER AND FOUNDER
Christopher Kimball

MARKETING DIRECTOR
Adrienne Kimball

CIRCULATION DIRECTOR
David Mack

FULFILLMENT MANAGER
Larisa Greiner

CIRCULATION MANAGER
Darcy Beach

MARKETING ASSISTANT
Connie Forbes

PRODUCTS MANAGER
Steven Browall

❧

VICE PRESIDENT OF PRODUCTION AND TECHNOLOGY
James McCormack

EDITORIAL PRODUCTION MANAGER
Sheila Datz

DESKTOP PUBLISHING MANAGER
Kevin Moeller

PRODUCTION ARTIST
Robert Parsons

PRODUCTION ASSISTANT
Daniel Frey

❧

CONTROLLER
Lisa A. Carullo

SENIOR ACCOUNTANT
Mandy Shito

Handcraft Illustrated (ISSN 1072-0529) is published quarterly by Boston Common Press Limited Partners, 17 Station Street, Brookline, MA 02146. Copyright 1998 Boston Common Press Limited Partners. Second-class postage paid at Boston, MA, and additional mailing offices, USPS #011-895. For list rental information, please contact List Services Corporation, 6 Trowbridge Drive, P.O. Box 516, Bethel, CT 06801; (203) 743-2600; Fax (203) 778-4299. Editorial office: 17 Station Street, Brookline, MA 02146; (617) 232-1000, FAX (617) 232-1572, e-mail: hnd-cftill@aol.com. Editorial contributions should be sent or e-mailed to: Editor, *Handcraft Illustrated*. We cannot assume responsibility for manuscripts submitted to us. Submissions will be returned only if accompanied by a large, self-addressed stamped envelope. Subscription rates: $24.95 for one year; $45 for two years; $65 for three years. (Canada: add $6 per year; all other countries add $12 per year.) To order subscriptions call (800) 526-8447. Postmaster: Send all new orders, subscription inquiries, and change of address notices to *Handcraft Illustrated*, P.O. Box 7450, Red Oak, IA 51591-0450. Single copies: $4 in U.S.; $4.95 in Canada and other countries. Back issues available for $5 each. PRINTED IN THE U.S.A.

Rather than put ™ in every occurrence of trademarked names, we state that we are using the names only in an editorial fashion and to the benefit of the trademark owner, with no intention of infringement of the trademark.

Note to Readers: Every effort has been made to present the information in this publication in a clear, complete, and accurate manner. It is important that all instructions are followed carefully, as failure to do so could result in injury. Boston Common Press Limited Partners, the editors, and the authors disclaim any and all liability resulting therefrom.

From the Editor

andmade. To me, the word conjures up the image of an object made by human hands, a unique manifestation of human touch. I see muscular hands gripping forging tools, slender fingers holding knitting needles, cupped hands steadying a tower of clay on a potter's wheel, pudgy young hands flattening a gob of Play-Doh on a kitchen table. And whether the hand itself is the tool, or the hand wields a brush, hammer, needle, pick, or some other implement, the spirit of the maker will infuse the object and affect its form and its visible surfaces. A handmade object shows us the fingerprints of a life in a series of strokes, or stitches, or strikes.

It is interesting to me that we persist in making things by hand in spite of the fact that our super-automated society can supply us with objects to meet our every need. Many of these mass-produced items are constructed by machines to look "handmade," and yet we leave them on store shelves and retreat in goodly numbers to work spaces tucked in attic eaves, to kitchen tables cleared of the evening meal, or to professional studios. Why are we so intent on creating something new?

We might say that our drive to make something by hand is practical, that things made by our hands are less expensive than things we can buy. To some extent, this is true. However, if the old adage "time is money" is also true, we are spending a fortune cutting up fabric to sew it back together again to construct a quilt, or looping wool over skinny metal rods to knit sweaters that can be bought easily from a street vendor, or stringing miles and miles of tiny beads on fine wire to make lampshades that would be much less costly to buy. There is more than practicality in our search to find enough time to make something by hand.

Making something by hand makes us part of a community of kindred spirits who speak the same tactile language. Sitting with friends as we sew or craft gives us the sweet pleasure of belonging. We love getting together with those of like mind, whether quilter, cross-stitcher, potter, or silversmith. The camaraderie of sharing is certainly part of our motivation. But there

Making something by hand is one way in which we become known to ourselves and witness our own presence here on earth.

is more. Transforming raw materials into objects of aesthetic and functional value, objects that fully express our personal style, brings us pleasure and satisfaction. We take pride in our accomplishments and want to share the fruits of our labors. We present our crafts as gifts; we install them at fairs and maybe even in museums after boards have filtered and edited them.

And we affix them to our refrigerator doors, veritable art galleries with no jury except the heart. Although cultural monitors would most certainly evaluate each expression differently, who among us would argue a mother's claim that her child's handmade project carries greater personal value than an item produced by someone to whom she has no connection at all. I believe it is this that is at the heart of all our efforts.

Connection. It is a word that means handmade. It is the most powerful motivator of all our efforts to make something of our own. On one level, we use our hands to establish and solidify the connection we have to ourselves, for every handmade object begins as an abstract idea and has the power to make our inner world visible. Making something by hand is one way in which we become known to ourselves and witness our own presence here on earth. But it is also a way we forge our connection to humanity, because our handmade objects embody our ideas and perpetuate them—for a moment or for all eternity.

When archaeologists unearth clay artifacts, it is not uncommon for them to find fingerprints on the sides and bottoms of vessels, each mark giving testimony to the potters who lived centuries ago and have been given immortality by the find. Although we may differ greatly in our training, backgrounds, attitudes, and personalities, our touch forges dynamic links that vitally connect us to each other. These are not epiphanies, just simple reminders that a complete world dwells within each object shaped by our hands, and that each object reveals a human life.

Carol Endler Sterbenz

Notes from Readers

Find out the best paint for pillowcases, make your own mosaic tiles, learn how to protect yourself from fumes, and create your own terrarium.

🙠 COMPILED BY LIVIA McREE

The Best Fabric Paint for Pillows

Is there a good fabric paint to use on pillowcases, one which will sink in and not be scratchy to the touch?

LAURA EPPERSON
MILTON, MA

We tested eight brands of fabric paint on typical 50% cotton, 50% polyester pillowcases. The directions for use varied widely; some paints needed to be heat-set with an iron while others didn't, and some could be washed after three days while others couldn't be washed for a week. We found that the paints that required ironing to heat-set the color produced a softer hand than those that didn't.

The brands resulting in the softest finish were Accent Elegance Fabric Dye, Jacquard Textile Color, and Deka's Nature's Design fabric paint. If you have trouble finding these brands, try any paint that requires heat-setting, because we found that all our ironed samples were comparably soft to the touch. You might also try thinning the paint, which creates a pleasing watercolor effect and helps maintain a soft finish on the fabric. Heat-setting and diluting the paint result in a smoother surface because they help the paint bond to the fabric's fibers.

Preserving Fall Leaves

I'd like to use autumn leaves for craft projects. What's the best way to preserve them? Is there anything I can do to keep them from getting too brittle?

JACQUELINE CONNERS
CHARLOTTESVILLE, NC

To preserve autumn leaves, try using silica gel, which works much faster than air drying or pressing the leaves. Silica gel is a desiccant, a granular substance that absorbs moisture. It is commonly used by floral artists because it helps retain the color of the material being preserved and is reusable.

To preserve leaves using this method, coat the bottom of an airtight glass, plastic, or metal container (such as a cookie tin or Tupperware container) with about one inch of silica gel, lay the leaves on top, and cover them gently with another one-inch layer of silica gel. Make sure the leaves are flat and that they don't touch each other. It should take three to four days for the foliage to dry, depending on the thickness of the plant materials you are preserving. Air drying or pressing can take between one and two weeks. You should check your leaves after two days to see how they are progressing. As soon as the leaves are firm to the touch, they are dry. Avoid over-drying, which will make the leaves brittle.

After the leaves are dry, they can be coated with satin acrylic varnish or cooking oil to make them more supple and give them a fresher look. Apply oil with a cotton ball or swab; remove the excess with a clean cotton ball. Silica gel can be found at many craft stores and can be mail-ordered from Craft King, 800-769-9494. One quart is $6.29; one gallon is $13.19.

Make Mosaic Tiles Yourself

I love the look of mosaics, and I've used glass, ceramic tiles, broken plates, and shells in my projects. I'd like to know if there is an easy way to make my own tiles.

HELENA SCORER
TAOS, NM

We recently tested a line of products from Plaid called "Make-It Mosaics." Using their Faster Plaster and reusable plastic molds, you can make your own round, triangular or square tiles as well as your own "broken plate" pieces. You can also buy trivet, coaster, frame, box, and stepping-stone templates, or use the plaster with any kind of flexible plastic container you have around the house, such as ice cube trays or clear disposable food containers. After Faster Plaster firms up, which takes 1 to 1½ hours, it can be thoroughly dried in a microwave oven in about three minutes (air drying would take 24 to 36 hours).

To color the plaster or the grout, Plaid offers liquid tints in terra cotta, emerald green, dark gray, sapphire blue, and wine. Colored plaster takes about three times as long to firm up before it can be dried in a microwave. We thought the terra-cotta coloring looked quite realistic.

The products in this line cost from $2 to $10, and are available at most craft stores nationwide. They can also be mail-ordered from Craft King, 800-769-9494.

Color Coordinating Made Easy

I think I have a clear idea of the colors I use in my home, but many times when I buy something that seems right in the store, it ends up not matching once I get it home. Do you have any suggestions?

NATHALIE MORRIS
LOS ANGELES, CA

One of our designers, Elizabeth Cameron, has come up with a solution to this common problem. Inspired by a Pantone color selector she saw in an art-supply store, Elizabeth devised a way to create a similar collection of colors for free. (Consisting of perforated color chips in gradients for every color you can think of, Pantone books usually cost $60 to $80, and are used by graphic designers to select colors that printers can match.) She went to her local hardware store and asked the manager if she could have one of every sample color swatch in one line of paint (such as Behr or Dutch Boy). Then she punched holes in the swatches and put them on a metal ring from an office supply store; you could also use a large key ring, cord, or ribbon to hold your color samples together. Mark the samples that match the colors in your home and take the "swatch book" whenever you go shopping.

Resilvering Mirrors

I have an antique mirror that I absolutely love. The trouble is, there are so many spots on it where the silver is damaged that I don't really want to display it. Is there any way to fix this myself or will that make the mirror less valuable?

AMANDA NIESWAND
PORTLAND, ME

Glassmaking and resilvering technology, like everything else, has changed through the years. As a result, mirrors from different time periods don't look the same and if you have your mirror resilvered, it will have to be completely stripped. The backing used on many early mirrors was a mix of tinfoil and mercury, which was then either painted black or covered with red lead. Today silver nitrate and specially formulated black paint are applied by computerized machines using a form of electroplating.

Jacquelyn Peake, in her book *How to Recognize & Refinish Antiques for Pleasure & Profit* (Globe Pequot Press, 1992), says you really can't resilver a mirror yourself. She does, however, suggest two alternatives. If the original glass is plain, flat, and not of any particular value, simply get new glass cut to fit the frame. If the glass is beveled, thick, and of real quality, she suggests having the backing stripped off and getting a new mirror specially cut and installed behind the original glass. This way the glass is preserved, but you have a perfect, fully functional mirror. Stripping the mirror yourself involves using a harsh chemical called nitric acid, but is relatively simple (see her book for details). You might also consider just displaying the mirror with all its imperfections; the uneven finish can produce a beautiful patina that suggests age and integrity. For a free catalog of home-improvement and how-to books, write to Globe Pequot Press, P.O. Box 833, Old Saybrook, CT 06475.

Protect Yourself from Fumes

I've recently started using glass-etching cream. Should I be wearing a mask to protect myself from the fumes?

SHERYL ASHBY
ROCK SPRINGS, WY

When doing any kind of craft project in which you will be exposing yourself to fumes, paint mist, dust, or particles of any kind, you should wear the proper protective gear and work in a well-ventilated space, especially if you plan to work over an extended period of time.

We asked a representative at U.S. Safety (a manufacturer of protective gear) about respirators. These protective masks, used in many industries, protect the wearer from fumes as well as particles. (Dust masks protect the wearer only from particles and can actually concentrate fumes.) We learned that the home crafter should wear a half mask called an organic vapor/N95 (or OV/N95) respirator, which covers the nose and mouth. It has two parts: a cartridge that eliminates fumes and a particle filter. The cartridge needs to be replaced when you can smell fumes, and the filter needs to be replaced when it becomes difficult to draw air. This type of respirator filters out the contaminants that crafters come across: paint mist, sawdust, and fumes from etching creams or varnishes. The respirators offered by U.S. Safety will filter out 99% of fumes and particles, and the industry standard is 90%.

Respirators cost from $13 to $30, and replacement fume cartridges and particle filters are sold in varying quantities; you can purchase a pack of two cartridges and two filters for the OV/N95 for $11.50 from the manufacturer. You can call U.S. Safety customer service at 800-821-5218, extension 229, with specific questions. If you tell them what sort of work you do, they will recommend the best respirator. They accept credit card orders or will let you know of a retailer close to you.

Homemade Papier-Mâché

I want to make Halloween masks with my children, but I don't want to go shopping for lots of supplies. Can you recommend a good recipe for papier-mâché and an easy method for mask-making?

KATHERINE CREWE
CAPE GIRARDEAU, MO

A simple papier-mâché recipe combines one tablespoon of any all-purpose glue to one cup of warm water, then mixes flour in thoroughly by the tablespoon until the mixture is the consistency of heavy cream (about four tablespoons). This will make enough paste for two masks.

You can use almost any kind of paper to make the mask, as long as it's not too thick or glossy. Newspaper is a convenient choice. Whatever paper you use, tear rather than cut the strips; the torn edges adhere better and will be less visible in the finished product. The strips should be torn with the grain of the paper, and should be about 1 inch by 2 or 3 inches. Longer pieces will crease on a rounded surface.

Next, inflate a balloon to roughly the head size of the anticipated mask-wearer. Mark the approximate size of the mask on the balloon, and place it on a bowl so it won't roll around when you start placing the strips. You can create a nose using cardboard; I used part of a paper towel tube to make a pig's snout. Tape or glue the nose to the balloon and cover it completely with plastic wrap.

Dip the paper strips in the paste, squeeze off the excess with your fingers, and coat the balloon with at least three layers of paper. It will take several hours for the mask to dry. After it is dry, pop the balloon to remove it, and trim the mask with scissors to the appropriate size. To get a better fit, lightly mist the inside of the mask with a spray bottle and mold it to a comfortable position.

You can make ears out of cardboard and glue them to the dried mask. I used part of a torn paper towel roll to make curled pig's ears. Finally, mark eye, nose, and mouth holes and cut them out using an X-Acto knife, scissor blade, or other small, sharp knife; then make holes in the sides for ribbon or elastic to hold the mask on. Paint and decorate it, and it's ready to wear!

Terrarium Basics

I loved the "Windowsill Greenhouse" project in your Spring 1998 issue. I'd like to install real plants and create a terrarium. What do I need to know?

NINA CAMBELL
COLORADO SPRINGS, CO

Making a terrarium is easy and satisfying. Terrariums can be open or closed, self-sustaining or in need of daily tending. The first step is to select small, slow-growing plants that do well indoors, so that you don't have to remove overgrown plants too often. Consider the amount of sun the terrarium will get and choose plants that have roughly the same needs; for example, you wouldn't put a cactus in the same container as ivy. Good choices for your first terrarium are ferns, miniature palms, and other tropical foliage plants that are sold as house plants at gardening stores. These plants thrive in humid, low-light conditions.

In addition to plants and soil, you will need horticultural charcoal to absorb odors, and washed pebbles, gravel, shells, or broken pot pieces for drainage. Horticultural charcoal is available at gardening stores; you can also use the charcoal sold for fish-tank filtration systems. A "soil separator" between the charcoal and the soil will help keep the soil from settling into the bottom layers. An old nylon stocking works well; it is porous enough to allow water through but fine enough to hold back the soil, and because it's synthetic, it won't decompose.

Once you've gathered your materials, you need to determine how much of everything should be put in the container. The windowsill greenhouse in our Spring 1998 issue is 8-inches high; a terrarium of this height should have at least 1 inch of gravel, ½ inch of charcoal, and 2 inches of soil. First add the gravel, then the charcoal, then the soil separator cut to fit the dimensions of the terrarium, then half the soil you plan to use; arrange your plants and then build up the remaining soil around their roots. Leave plenty of space between the plants; they will grow fast and fill the aquarium very quickly. Finally, add decorative accents such as shells, stones, or twigs to finish your miniature environment. You can also landscape your terrarium by building up a slope, or covering the soil with moss, sand, or bark chips.

After the terrarium is completed, water it thoroughly by misting it with a spray bottle; this will keep soil from splashing onto the glass sides and prevent over-watering. If you notice that the drainage level is filled with water, let it evaporate before you close the terrarium or your plants may rot. If too much condensation builds up once it's closed, leave it open for a while; eventually you should be able to balance the moisture level so that you can keep it closed all the time. You should, however, air it out every week or so for about 15 minutes to prevent mold or mildew.

Children Make Handcraft Projects in School

We recently received the following letter from Marta Brakke, a schoolteacher who adapted the "Easter Party Favor" project in the Spring 1998 issue of Handcraft Illustrated *for her students:*

I am a Montessori teacher and am always looking for an idea to adapt for the children to do by themselves. When I saw the Easter party -favor bags, I knew that was a possibility. We photocopied the bunny and the egg patterns onto white paper and the children colored, cut, and pasted their own little Easter sacks. Every bunny and egg was individual and each child was thrilled.

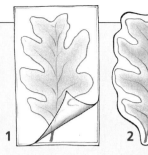

Quick Tips

AUTUMN LEAF KEEPSAKES

If you can't resist saving a few of nature's leaves each autumn, go one step further and laminate them, suggests Jackie Jank of Laguna Beach, California. They make perfect bookmarks and gift tags. (For tips on preserving the fall colors, *see* Notes from Readers, page 2.)

1. **Seal a pressed leaf between two sheets of clear self-adhesive film.**

2. **Cut around the edges, leaving a margin.**

NATURAL ROOM SCENT

Joan Y. Grace of Bath, Maine, shares a Halloween tip: Carve a jack-o-lantern as usual, then sprinkle the inside lid with ground cinnamon. When you light the candle inside, the aroma will be of pumpkin pie.

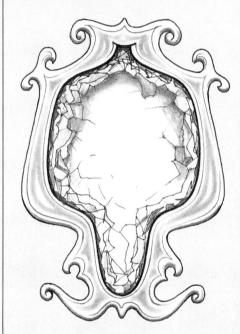

MIRROR GUARD

Use tinfoil to shield a mirror when you're painting or refinishing the frame, writes Joyce Hathaway of Alexandria, Virginia. Just fold or crumple the foil to conform to the frame's inner edge. It is easier than taping the glass, particularly if the contours are irregular.

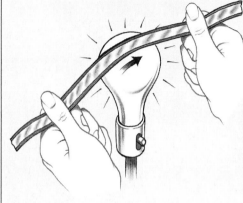

WRINKLE-FREE RIBBONS

To "iron" a wrinkled ribbon, run it over a hot light bulb a few times. Thanks to Patricia Cesario of New City, New York, for this handy tip.

SCENTED GREETING CARDS

Use the perfume samples bound in fashion magazines to scent handmade or purchased greeting cards. Cut out the scented paper and attach it to the card in an unobtrusive spot. This suggestion is from Lisa Koide of San Diego, California.

ATTENTION READERS

CALLING ALL CRAFTERS

Do you have a craft, sewing, or decorating technique that saves time or money? Send it our way! We'll give you a one-year complimentary subscription for each Quick Tip that we publish. Send your tip to:

QUICK TIPS
Handcraft Illustrated
17 Station Street
Brookline, MA 02146

Please include your name, address, and daytime phone number with all correspondence.

ILLUSTRATIONS:
Michael Gellatly

TREE BRANCH CURTAIN ROD

Use a sturdy tree branch in place of a purchased rod to hang stationary curtains and valances, writes Sarah Selelky of Ontario, Canada. Peel off the bark, saw the ends evenly, and clip back any shoots that might snag the fabric.

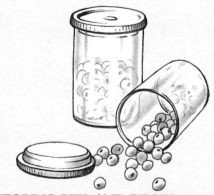

STORING BITS AND PIECES

Use clear 35mm film canisters to store beads, sequins, rhinestones, and other small findings, writes Kimberly Kiniry of Bristol, Connecticut. Tight-fitting caps make these plastic canisters perfect for paints, too. Ask for extra canisters at a film developing store. Janice Low of Vancouver, Canada, sent a similar tip.

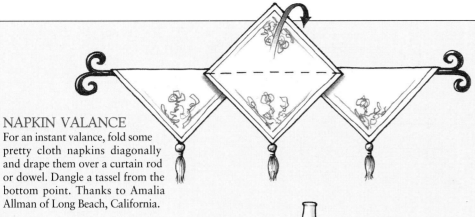

NAPKIN VALANCE

For an instant valance, fold some pretty cloth napkins diagonally and drape them over a curtain rod or dowel. Dangle a tassel from the bottom point. Thanks to Amalia Allman of Long Beach, California.

COLOR LABELS

Paint the flip tops of your acrylic paints the color in the bottle for quick and easy identification. This will allow you to store the bottles upright in a drawer or tote box. Thanks to Linda Trialonas of Port Matilda, Pennsylvania.

WREATH STORAGE

Jan Rodrian of Grafton, Wisconsin, saves large covered deli platters to store wreaths and other fragile decorations. She writes that the platters are designed for stacking, and the clear plastic lets her make selections without having to unpack everything.

ONE WREATH, MANY SEASONS

Use Velcro to affix decorations to wreaths and remove them easily. You can use one wreath base year-round and change the look with seasonal decorations. Thanks to Margaret Gilbert of Princeton, Illinois.

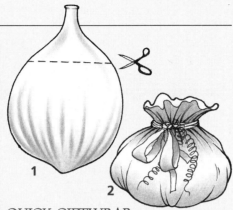

QUICK GIFTWRAP

Use mylar balloons as giftwrap bags, writes Teresa Mirabile of Pleasantville, New York. Either side can face out.

1. Trim off the neck to make a wide opening.

2. Place the gift inside and tie with a ribbon.

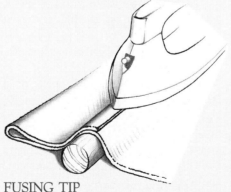

FUSING TIP

To avoid crushing nubby or napped fabric when fusing a straight edge (such as a hem), slip a wooden dowel under the section to be fused. Now you can press down on this area with the iron without marring the rest of the fabric. Thanks to Alicia Quain of Santa Clara, California.

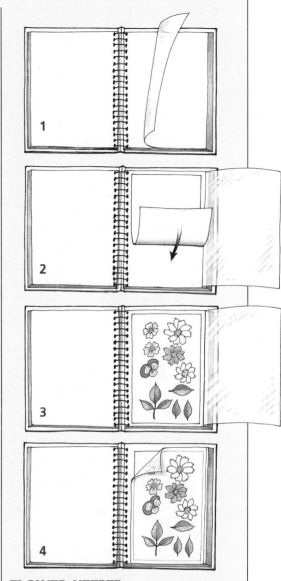

FLOWER KEEPER

Store pressed flowers in a magnetic photo album until you're ready to use them, writes Julie Sewnarine of Central Islip, New York.

1. Lift the clear film to expose the sticky album page.

2. Lay down a sheet of white paper, leaving a margin all around to "seal" later.

3. Place the dry pressed flowers on the white sheet.

4. Fold the film back onto the page and "seal" the edges.

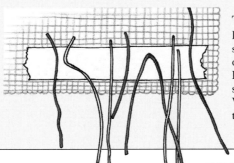

THREAD CATCHER

Each time you begin work on an embroidery or sewing project, stick a length of double-sided tape onto a corner of the fabric, writes Lyn Slade of Bolton, Massachusetts. Now you have a place to stick all those loose threads that you clip off. When you're through, peel off the tape and throw the whole thing away.

Quick Home Accents

Dress up any window using patterns cut from self-adhesive film.

FLEUR-DE-LIS WINDOW DESIGN

COLOR PHOTOGRAPHY:
Carl Tremblay

DESIGN:
**Carol Endler
Sterbenz**

STYLING:
Ritch Holben

For a beautiful window decoration, cut self-adhesive film into pretty shapes and apply them directly to your window glass. Use translucent vinyl or contact paper, both of which come with a peel-off paper backing.

There are several ways to create the pattern for your window design. One way is to trace a pattern onto a sheet of paper from a sheer lace curtain. This method creates a window design that echoes the patterns in your curtains. Another way to make a pattern is to draw or trace an image from a book. Look for curving floral or feathery motifs. You can use just one pattern, or a few patterns that work together. To create the design on the featured window, we used one pattern that was 6" high and 5" wide.

Use a self-healing cutting mat and an X-Acto knife to cut the film, following your patterns.

To create the window design, peel off the paper backings and position the motifs on the windowpanes. Covering the entire surface of the glass with a lacy design will add privacy. Don't worry about placing the motifs within the wood frames perfectly; you can trim them at the edges, or place leftovers on the adjacent glass. To create a more open design, consider placing the designs around the edges of the glass, or alternately, in a smaller central pattern that flares out toward the edges. When desired, remove the motifs and throw them away. ◆

The Perfect Gift

Personalize a gift pouch with iron-on appliqués.

MONOGRAMMED CACHE

This small pouch with its drawstring collar is an attractive, easy-to-make alternative to a standard gift box. Designed to hold small holiday gifts, such as cosmetic brushes, scarves, or candles, this pretty cache will be kept and used for other purposes. A cylindrical chipboard sleeve sits inside the velvet pouch to protect the gift contents, and iron-on appliqués form a monogram that personalizes the gift.

All you need to make the cache is an 11" x 14" piece of decorator fabric; almost any type will work. I used an iridescent stretch rayon velvet that has both visual and tactile appeal and drapes nicely at the cinched closure. You will also need a paper tube or piece of single-ply chipboard, ¾ yard of ribbon, two beads, and iron-on monograms.

To make the inner tube, cut the chipboard and roll it on a flat surface to make a tube 2"-3" diameter and 6"-7" high; use tape or glue to secure the edges. If you wish, you can quickly line the tube with any decorative material at hand (I used a pink grosgrain). Just cut a piece of the fabric large enough to wrap around the tube once, and long enough to extend past the top and bottom edges by 2". Roll the fabric tightly and insert it into the tube, allowing it to unfurl. Spread it around the inside of the tube, then fold over and hot-glue the top edge. Repeat for the bottom end of the tube.

It is easiest to apply the appliqué monograms while the fabric is flat. The script-style monograms I used have an iron-on adhesive backing and come in white or navy and in two heights, so that a tall 1½" one can be used in the center with the two small ¾" ones on each side. To attach the appliqués, use a medium setting on your iron and an ironing cloth to prevent sticking or scorching. I used fairly heavy pressure and in about 10 seconds embedded the thin appliqués neatly into the fabric.

To sew the cache, fold the fabric in half, lengthwise, right sides in; machine-stitch along its entire height to form a tube (*see* diagram, page 47). Fold the bottom edge ¾" to the wrong side and sew a ½" channel. Run a plain cord through and tie it as tightly as possible to close the bottom of the tube. Knot

and clip the cord, turning the ends toward the inside to conceal them.

Fold the top edge down by 2". Stitch 1¼" and 1¾" from the fold, making a ½" channel, or one wide enough to accommodate a thin gauzy ribbon; if you use a heavier ribbon, adjust the channel width as needed.

Thread your ribbon through the channel, picking out a few stitches in the outside seam to gain access. Then tuck each ribbon end into a bead. I used acrylic beads with a bit of sparkle

but you can use any bead that will accommodate your ribbon. To get the ribbon through the bead, fold the ribbon end in fourths and run a needle with a short knotted thread through the folds. Push the needle through the bead and pull in the ribbon. Trim off the thread and set the ribbon with hot-glue. If the bead hole is too large for a tight fit, push the ribbon in with a toothpick, which can be used as a shim; break off any of the toothpick that extends from the bead. ◆

PATTERNS

See page 47 for sewing diagram.

COLOR PHOTOGRAPHY:
Carl Tremblay

DESIGN:
Michio Ryan

STYLING:
Ritch Holben

How to Make Lip Balm

This recipe allows you to formulate a custom blend.

✤ BY MARY ANN HALL

The paints used on these tins are heat-set in an oven and become permanent. You can paint with the tip of the tube to create a relief pattern.

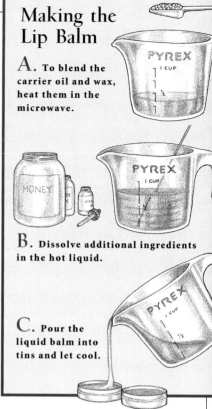

Making the Lip Balm

A. To blend the carrier oil and wax, heat them in the microwave.

B. Dissolve additional ingredients in the hot liquid.

C. Pour the liquid balm into tins and let cool.

MATERIALS
Makes 6 ounces of lip balm

- ¼ cup + 2 table-spoons carrier oil
- 4 tablespoons wax pearls/pastilles OR 2 tablespoons + 2 teaspoons granulated wax
- 1 teaspoon honey
- ½ teaspoon vitamin E oil
- ½ teaspoon cocoa butter or shea butter (optional)
- 15cc to 45cc powdered color pigment (optional)
- 2 to 3 drops fragrance oil (optional)
- Twelve ½-ounce tins

You'll also need:
1-cup Pyrex measuring cup; measuring spoons; chopstick (for stirring); teaspoon; and microwave oven.

COLOR PHOTOGRAPHY:
Carl Tremblay

ILLUSTRATION:
Mary Newell DePalma

STYLING:
Ritch Holben

FORMULATING RECIPES FOR YOUR own cosmetics is a creative and earth-friendly alternative to buying commercial products; lip balms, in particular, are easy and fun to make. After lots of reading, testing, and chatting with enthusiastic experts, I came up with a master lip balm recipe that you can use as a starting point.

Lip balm has two primary components: wax and carrier oil. Essentially, all you do is melt them together in a microwave. From there, you can add or omit optional ingredients to come up with a blend that is perfect for your skin, your senses, and your tastes.

I tested beeswax in three different forms: pearls, granulated, and pastilles. I also tested granulated candelilla wax, which is derived from the candelilla plant found in Mexico and the Southwestern United States. All the forms of these waxes work extremely well and eliminate the added labor of grating or chopping up wax chunks.

I also tested five types of carrier oils: sweet almond oil, avocado oil, hempseed oil, olive oil, and castor oil. The first three were my personal favorites. I found the olive flavor of virgin olive oil too strong and would recommend using a lighter, nonvirgin oil. Castor oil added a nice texture and would be a good choice if you prefer the minty, herbal, medicinal types of lip balms.

Secondary components, such as vitamin E oil, honey, cocoa or shea butter, fragrance oils, and colorants, can be added or omitted as you choose. Cocoa butter and shea butter have natural emulsifying properties, as does Vitamin E oil, which is also a preservative. If you want to make a scented lip balm, cocoa butter will add a chocolate note. Many people flavor lip balm with the kind of flavoring oils used in candy and bakery products. I prefer fragrance oils that have been specifically designed for use on the lips because they are much more subtle. You sense them more than you taste them. The only natural flavoring I recommend is honey, which adds just the slightest hint of sweetness and masks any oily or waxy flavor.

Another option for personalizing your lip balm is to add coloring. The powdered pigments that I used, which are also used to color commercial lipsticks, come with a small 15cc scoop. One 15cc scoop of pigment will add a subtle tint to the pot, but not your lips, while adding additional scoops will eventually create a deeply colored sheer gloss that may tint your lips slightly. In order to get the pigment to dissolve completely, mix it with a little carrier oil first and allow it to set while you mix the rest of the ingredients.

INSTRUCTIONS

1. *Prepare tins.* Wash tins in warm soapy water and dry thoroughly. Paint tins, if desired (*see* Decorating the Tins, next page).

2. *Combine base ingredients.* Place car-

Design Ideas for Lids

A. For simple swirls, draw the letter S forward and backward.

B. For snail spirals, draw a small C and keep coiling.

C. Add a large spiral over a swirled background.

D. Add dots at random or space them round the rim.

E. Use rim dots to plot V-shaped wedges.

rier oil and wax in Pyrex cup (*see* Selecting Your Ingredients, below). Microwave on high about two minutes (or place in double boiler) until wax is melted (*see* illustration A, page 8). Immediately add honey to hot liquid and stir with chopstick to dissolve. Stir in vitamin E oil (illustration B).

3. *Add optional ingredients.* Add any remaining ingredients one by one, stirring after each addition. To add color, dissolve pigment in a few drops of oil, then add colored oil to balm and stir. Let mixture cool slightly before adding fragrance.

4. *Fill tins.* Dip teaspoon into balm to coat tip. Let balm harden on spoon for a few seconds, then apply some to your lips. Adjust as follows until mixture has desired texture: if balm feels too soft or oily, stir in melted wax 1 teaspoon at a time; if too hard or waxy, add more oil in same fashion. Pour balm into individual tins (illustration C, page 8). Let cool and harden 20 minutes, then replace lids.

Decorating the Tins

These tins are decorated with newly developed, permanent water-based coloring formulas that can be set in an ordinary oven. I have used two products for these easy relief designs—a paint, which I applied with a fine brush, and two cloisonné outliners, which have a thicker consistency than paint and are applied through special pointed tips that come with the tubes.

INSTRUCTIONS

1. *Paint designs on lids.* Clean residual oils and fingerprints from tin lids using cotton ball and alcohol. Apply Pébéo Porcelaine color to top and rim of lids with fine-tipped brush or directly from outliner tube. Use a light touch to make fine designs. Try the design ideas to the left singly or in combination, using one or more colors. Let each color dry three minutes before layering over it. Rinse brush in water and dry with cotton ball after each use.

Curled shapes. Paint S-shaped swirls or snail-shaped spirals in a random all-over pattern (*see* illustrations A and B, left). This type of design can stand alone or serve as the background for another design. For a large single snail, start at the center of the lid and coil outward (illustration C).

Dots. Touch tip of cloisonné outliner to surface, lightly squeeze, and lift up. On lid top, apply dots at random over a swirled background. To space dots evenly around rim, visualize a clock face and fill in the hours (illustration D).

Wedges. Paint six or seven dots around rim; let dry. Paint straight line from one dot toward center, then go back up to next dot, forming a V. Repeat all around (illustration E). Fill in wedges with oscillating S curves or other shapes.

2. *Bake on finish.* Let painted lids dry 24 hours in dust-free area. Preheat oven to 300 degrees. Place lids on cookie sheet and bake 35 minutes. Remove from oven, set sheet on rack, and cool 20 minutes or until cool enough to handle. Baked-on finish is permanent and washable. ◆

MATERIALS
Makes 12 decorated tins

- **Twelve ½-ounce tins**
- **1.5 ounces ivory Pébéo Porcelaine**
- **Pébéo Porcelaine cloisonné outliner: Vermeil 08 Copper 09**

You'll also need: round, fine-tipped sable brush; cookie sheet; cooling rack; cotton rag; cotton balls; and rubbing alcohol.

DESIGNER'S TIP

If you don't have vitamin E oil, you can squeeze the amount needed from vitamin E capsules.

SELECTING YOUR INGREDIENTS

CARRIER OILS

- **Sweet almond oil: very pale yellow; moisturizing and nourishing for all skin types; rich in protein.**

- **Avocado oil: dark green; heals dry, mature, or dehydrated skin; contains vitamins A, D, E, and protein.**

- **Hempseed oil: greenish gold; obtained from the seeds of a tall Asiatic herb; a balanced moisturizing oil; smoothes and softens skin.**

- **Castor oil: colorless to pale yellow; obtained from the beans of a tropical plant; soothing to skin; strong aroma is suitable for minty, herbal, or medicinal balms.**

- **Olive oil: light green to yellow; soothes and moisturizes by penetrating skin with proteins, vitamins, and minerals; for less pronounced flavor, use a light pure olive oil instead of virgin.**

WAXES

- **Beeswax: a soft substance secreted by honeybees to build honeycombs; ranges in color from off-white to caramel-yellow depending on how much it is filtered; available in three forms for easy measuring: granulated, pearls, and pastilles.**

- **Candelilla wax: a hard vegetable wax derived from the scales of the candelilla plant, which grows in dry, rugged climates; available in granulated form; preferred by vegans.**

OTHER INGREDIENTS

- **Cocoa butter: a vegetable fat extracted from the beans of the tropical cacao tree in the process of making chocolate; softens skin; thickens balms.**

- **Shea butter (also called Karite butter): a thick white fat extracted from the seeds of an African tree; softens skin.**

- **Vitamin E oil: promotes elasticity and acts as a preservative for other oils.**

- **Flavoring oils: Some of our favorites are creamy vanilla, apricot, blueberry, floriental, natural tangerine, and coconut.**

- **Colorants: FDA-approved cosmetic-grade colorants with names like D&C Red #6 are available in small packets of fine powder with half-pea-size 15cc measuring spoons.**

Diorama Greeting Card

Use a rubber stamp to create this dreamy landscape.

🐾 BY CAROL ENDLER STERBENZ

Unlike most cards that end up in drawers, this card has a decorative use: The panels fold into a tree-lined window diorama.

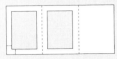

PATTERNS

See page 46 for cutting diagram.

COLOR PHOTOGRAPHY:
Carl Tremblay

ILLUSTRATION:
Mary Newell DePalma

STYLING:
Ritch Holben

MATERIALS
Makes 5⅛" x 6¾" greeting card (folded)

- 18" x 24" watercolor paper
- 9" x 12" tracing vellum
- Light-colored organdy fabric scraps
- Blue embossing powder
- Yes Stikflat glue

You'll also need:
window card cutting diagram (*see* page 46); 2" x 3½" spruce tree rubber stamp; stamp pad with blue fabric ink; toaster (or substitute heat source); grid ruler; quilter's acrylic grid ruler; X-Acto knife; self-healing cutting mat; small soft-bristled brush; scissors; pencil; heavy book; and newsprint.

INSTRUCTIONS:

1. *Cut papers and organdy.* Use ruler, pencil, and diagram (*see* page 46) to draft card on watercolor paper. Using X-Acto knife, quilter's acrylic grid ruler, and mat, cut out card and two window openings as marked; score foldlines lightly. Repeat to mark and cut two single 5" x 6¾" window panels for liners (use first window panel on diagram as reference). From vellum, cut one 4¾" x 6¼" rectangle for window insert. Cut two matching inserts from organdy.

2. *Stamp window inserts.* Lay vellum insert horizontally on newsprint. Using blue ink, stamp one tree in middle. Quickly re-ink and stamp second tree to left of center tree, overlapping branches slightly. Re-ink and stamp third tree to right of center (illustration A, below). Sprinkle embossing powder on images while ink is wet. Shake off excess powder. Dust off lingering particles with soft brush. Hold stamped image over toaster for 20 seconds to activate and melt embossing powder. Let cool three minutes. Stamp three trees on each organdy insert, but do not emboss.

3. *Glue window inserts.* Lay card scored side down with solid panel at right. Position vellum insert over window in panel at far left, embossed side up and treetops pointing right. Glue edges of vellum to card. Lay organdy insert on top, offsetting trees to create shadow effect; glue organdy edges to vellum. Glue remaining organdy insert over middle panel, treetops pointing left (illustration B). Glue liner to each window panel to conceal insert edges (illustration C). Fold card and weight with book for one hour. To display card, prop upright, using solid panel as base. ◆

T HIS THREE-PANELED GREETING card, which fits into a standard card-size envelope when folded, is created from watercolor paper, sheer fabric, vellum, and a rubber stamp. When sitting in its triangular display position, the sheer windows shimmer in the surrounding light and reveal a lovely three-dimensional landscape.

The two standing panels have cut-out windows and act as a frame for the sheer organdy and vellum inserts that are printed with rubber stamps and glued at the edges. The stamped patterns are slightly offset to create the illu-sion that you are looking into a pine forest and can see the shadows of distant trees. The fabric edges are concealed by adding two liner panels. The solid third panel allows you space for writing and acts as a base when the card is displayed.

Making the Diorama Card

A. Stamp each window insert.

B. Glue the inserts to the card over the window cutouts.

C. Glue down liners to conceal the insert edges.

Jeweled Tumblers

Transform your everyday tumblers by bonding jewels to the glass.

BY DAWN ANDERSON

COLOR PHOTOGRAPHY:
Carl Tremblay

ILLUSTRATION:
Michael Gellatly

STYLING:
Ritch Holben

THIS SIMPLE TECHNIQUE WILL TURN a set of ordinary glass tumblers into festive party glasses. There are only three steps: apply etching cream to create an exterior matte finish, daub a gold enamel circle on the center of the glass, and add a cabochon.

Handling these glasses during the first step is a little tricky since the bottoms are frosted, too. I found it easiest to stick one gloved fist inside the glass and brush on the etching cream with the other hand. I held the glass in this position for the three to five minutes it takes the etching cream to work. If you want to avoid the fumes, rest the glass on the rim while the etching cream works. To achieve an evenly frosted coat, be sure to follow the manufacturer's tips from the label of your etching cream precisely. For example, if you work in a room where the temperature is lower than 70 degrees or higher than 80 degrees, the etching may be uneven, streaked, or blotchy.

After painting and sealing the circle, let the glass dry for 10 days before adding the cabochon. This ensures that the painted parts are fully hand washable.

Dawn Anderson is a writer and designer living in Redmond, Washington.

INSTRUCTIONS

1. *Frost glass tumblers.* Read etching cream manufacturer's instructions. Work in well-ventilated area and wear long sleeves. Lay newspaper on counter next to sink; top with single layer of newsprint. Clean each glass with spray cleaner and paper towels. Mask inside rim with tape. Put on rubber gloves and goggles. Stick one fist inside glass and hold it up off work surface. Using foam brush, apply ⅛"-thick layer of cream to outside surface, including bottom and rim. Let cream work 3 to 5 minutes. Rinse thoroughly with water to reveal etching. Remove tape. Wash glass in warm soapy water and let dry. Repeat to frost each glass (*see* illustration A, below).

2. *Paint gold circle.* Measure glass tumbler vertically to find middle. Stick piece of masking tape on glass from ¾" below middle to bottom. Dip index finger in gold enamel and rub gently to make 1¼"-diameter circle above tape (illustration B). Remove tape. Let dry 15 minutes. Paint second gold coat. Repeat for each glass; let dry 1 hour. Using ⅜" flat brush, seal each circle with clear gloss glaze; let dry 1 hour. Apply second coat. Let dry 10 days.

3. *Add cabochons.* Mix 5-minute epoxy on scrap cardboard; let set 1 to 2 minutes. Apply epoxy to back of cabochon with craft stick, affix stone to center of gold circle, and tape down. Repeat for each glass. Let dry 30 minutes before removing tape (illustration C). ◆

Shiny glass gems stand out on the matte finish of these frosted tumblers. Choose any size tumbler you wish; these stand 4½" tall.

DESIGNER'S TIP

See "Protect Yourself from Fumes," page 3.

MATERIALS

Makes four tumblers

- 4 green glass tumblers
- 4 iridescent green glass cabochons
- Delta CeramDecor 2-ounce gold Perm Enamel
- Delta CeramDecor 2-ounce clear gloss glaze
- Armour Etch glass etching cream
- 5-minute epoxy

You'll also need: rubber gloves; goggles; foam brush; ⅜" flat paintbrush; ruler; glass spray cleaner; masking tape; newspaper; newsprint; and paper towels.

Making the Tumblers

A. Use etching cream to frost the outer glass.

B. Paint a gold circle with your fingertip at the tape marker.

C. Glue a cabochon to each circle.

Scented Modular Candles

You can still use milk cartons to make candles: Just start with the perfect wax recipe and finish with stylish packaging.

❧ BY MICHIO RYAN

MATERIALS
Makes one 4" candle

- **1 pound paraffin**
- **¹/₃ pound bleached, filtered beeswax**
- **1¹/₂ teaspoons Vybar #103**
- **#2 square-braided wicking**
- **1 tablespoon liquid candle scent (see chart, page 13)**
- **Reddig-Glo color chip(s) (see chart, page 13)**

You'll also need:
label patterns (*see* page 44), 1-quart waxed milk carton; wax or candy thermometer; double boiler; frying pan; 2-cup Pyrex measuring cup; skewer; paring knife; metal spoon; plate; nylon stocking; mineral spirits; X-Acto knife; scissors; masking tape; duct tape; ruler; and pencil.

For other fragrance combinations, try using florals such as water lily, violet, and freesia, or zingy citrus and herbal scents like lemon verbena, lavender, green tea, and tomato leaf.

PATTERNS
See page 44 for label patterns and gift box diagram.

COLOR PHOTOGRAPHY:
Carl Tremblay

ILLUSTRATION:
Mary Newell DePalma

STYLING:
Ritch Holben

A BOXED SET OF SCENTED CANDLES is surprisingly easy to make, using milk cartons as molds and a photocopier for custom labels. For the gift box, a paper-covered sheet of chipboard folds up around the candles; the sides are secured with a ribbon.

A few simple tricks will ensure that your hand-cast candle burns well and doesn't sag in the middle. We've come up with an excellent wax recipe and an easy way to make one or several molded candles in any size. You won't need fancy equipment like molds, or special materials like mold

release or finishing polish. Aside from Vybar, a hardener, and beeswax, everything you need is a common kitchen tool or can be found in a grocery or craft store.

We used three different kinds of natural scents to make up the boxed set: Tuberose Deluxe, a luxurious floral; Sandalwood Vanilla, a woody scent layered with sweet vanilla; and Plum Spice, a rich fruity scent with piquant accents.

We colored the wax to match the scent—for example, our plum-scented candle is lavender. (See the chart for the scents and colors we used.) Take advan-

tage of the sheer opalescence of the wax and use dye or pigment very sparingly. It's impossible to tell what the final color will look like when the wax in the melting pot is hot (the sage green looks blackish gray, for example), so before pouring the hot wax into the mold, spoon a few drops onto a sheet of white paper to test the color of the cooled wax.

For a perfectly smooth finish, buff the candle with a nylon stocking. If you have trouble smoothing the corners, try mineral spirits, which will level deep defects very quickly. It actually dissolves the wax so use it sparingly. It's also great for cleaning up any spilled wax; just follow it with soap and water.

INSTRUCTIONS
Making a Candle
1. *Prepare mold.* Wash milk carton and dry thoroughly. Using X-Acto knife, cut off peaked section (*see* illustration A, next page). Slit each corner edge, stopping 4¼" from bottom, and fold down flaps (illustration B). Secure flaps with masking tape.

2. *Add wick.* Cut small X in center of carton base. Poke end of wick through opening from outside, draw it up inside carton for 8", and wind it around pencil in a half-hitch. Notch two opposite edges of carton (illustration C). Pull down on wick from underside until pencil rests in notches and wick is taut; secure wick to underside of carton with duct tape, pressing duct tape up onto sides of carton to create tight seal. Cut off excess wick with scissors.

3. *Melt wax.* Break paraffin into small (1" to 2") chunks. Melt paraffin, beeswax, and Vybar in double boiler on low to medium heat, attending it the entire time. Monitor temperature of melted wax with candy or wax thermometer; do not let it exceed 180 degrees. When wax is thoroughly melted, stir in color chips (see chart) with metal spoon until thoroughly blended. Add scent last (see chart) and stir briefly. For easier handling, transfer hot liquid wax to Pyrex measuring cup. Double-check temperature, and let cool to 180 degrees, if necessary.

4. *Mold candle.* Place mold on plate. Tilt mold slightly and slowly pour in hot melted wax, funneling it down a crevice to prevent air bubbles. When mold is half full, stand it upright. Continue filling to within ¼" of top edge, but reserve some wax for refilling (illustration D). Let wax cool 30 minutes. To fill sunken area around wick, push skewer vertically into soft wax in two or three places. Remelt reserved wax to 200 degrees and pour some into cavity, taking care not to overflow original wax walls. Set aside entire plate (do not try to move mold alone). Check wax around wick every hour or so for further sinking and refill as needed. Let cool and harden overnight.

5. *Unmold candle.* Tear off and discard waxed paper carton. Stand candle upright. If bottom is wobbly, rub it gently around inside of frying pan over low heat until it melts flat. (If you are making several candles, use this method to even up their heights.) Use paring knife to shape and round off edges and corners. Rub nylon stocking in circular motion to buff down seams and polish entire candle surface.

MATERIALS
Makes gift packaging for three candles

- **Matte gold metallic paper**
- **Swirl-print tissue giftwrap**
- **Buff parchment paper**
- **Cream paper**
- **9" x 13" 3-ply chipboard**
- **1¾ yards 1½"-wide sheer ribbon**
- **Yes Stikflat glue**

You'll also need:
gift box diagram (*see* page 44); colored pencils, markers, or watercolors; X-Acto knife; quilter's acrylic grid ruler; stiff brush; cutting mat; and pencil.

Making the Gift Box

1. *Cut out box.* Using grid ruler and pencil, draft gift box diagram (page 44) on 3-ply chipboard. Using X-Acto knife, grid ruler, and cutting mat, score or cut lines as indicated. Fold up flaps on score lines.

2. *Add paper and lining to box.* Using chipboard box as template, cut same shape from cream paper for lining; set lining aside. Lay gold paper wrong side up on cutting mat. Lay box on top, scored side down. Using X-Acto knife, cut paper

¾" beyond box edges; cut to inside corners and trim outside corners diagonally (illustration E). Fold gold paper onto chipboard, corners first and then flaps. Glue in place; fold up box sides before glue dries. Trim ¼" from cream lining all around. Test-fit lining on inside of box and glue down (illustration F).

3. *Wrap and label candles.* For each candle, cut one 3½" x 12" piece of printed tissue. Wrap evenly around candle, overlapping ½" at back, and secure with glue. Photocopy labels (page 44) onto buff-colored parchment paper, or design your own 2" x 2⅜" labels using a computer and laser printer. Tint the botanical images using watercolors, markers, or colored pencils; color the borders metallic gold. Cut out each label ⅛" beyond border and glue to wrapped candle front (illustration G). Place three wrapped candles side by side in box. Tie ribbon around box to hold up flaps (illustration H). ◆

SCENT	COLOR
1 T Plum Spice	1 chip lavender + ⅛ chip orchid
1 T Sandalwood Vanilla	¼ chip butterscotch
1 T Tuberose Deluxe	1 chip sage green + ¼ chip butterscotch

Making the Candle

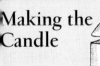

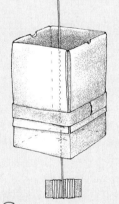

A. Slice off the top of the milk carton.

B. Slit the sides and fold down the flaps.

C. Thread the wicking up through the bottom of the carton.

D. Pour the hot liquid wax into the mold.

Making the Gift Box

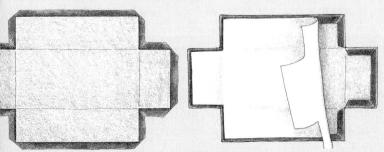

E. Cover the outside of the box with gold paper.

F. Line the inside with cream paper.

G. Wrap tissue around each candle and add a label.

H. Package three candles in the gift box.

Frosted Almonds

Create this delicious mixture of roasted, sugared, and chocolate-drizzled almonds in less than an hour.

BY EMILY GRIMES

Make festive almond-filled gift packages with a rubber stamp, a white box, and long silky ribbon.

MATERIALS
Makes 6 to 7 cups of nuts

- **6 cups whole blanched almonds**
- **1 cup water**
- **1 cup sugar**
- **Dash of salt**
- **2 ounces semisweet bar chocolate**

You'll also need:
2 baking sheets with 1" sides; 12" skillet; wet and dry measuring cups; wooden spoon; 3 medium-size bowls; heavy-duty 1-quart zip-close freezer bag; wax paper; and scissors.

COLOR PHOTOGRAPHY:
Carl Tremblay

ILLUSTRATION:
Michael Gellatly

PACKAGING DESIGN:
Elizabeth Cameron

STYLING:
Ritch Holben

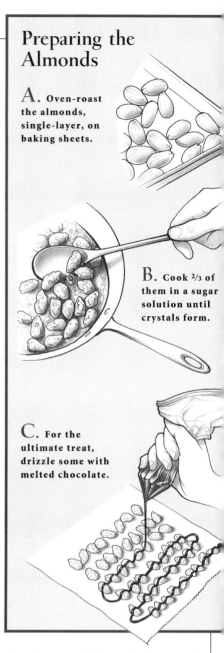

Preparing the Almonds

A. Oven-roast the almonds, single-layer, on baking sheets.

B. Cook ⅔ of them in a sugar solution until crystals form.

C. For the ultimate treat, drizzle some with melted chocolate.

THESE THREE DIFFERENT TYPES OF almonds—plain roasted, sugar-frosted, and drizzled with chocolate—look like three different recipes when packed together in a gift box. In reality, you make them in succession and the entire procedure takes about one hour. All the almonds are roasted, two-thirds of them receive a sugar coating, and then half of those are drizzled with chocolate.

The first step, roasting the almonds, takes just a few minutes in the oven, and improves the flavor and the texture. In the second step, which is almost equally simple, the almonds are cooked in a skillet in a mixture of sugar, water, and salt; when the water boils away, sugar crystals form on the almonds. (You will notice some extra sugar crystals left in the bottom of the pan. This is to be expected and the recipe includes enough sugar to compensate for it.)

It is important to use bar chocolate or baking squares for melting. Avoid using chips because they contain more lecithin, an ingredient that inhibits smooth melting.

If you want to present your almonds as gifts, try this fast and beautiful packaging idea: Add an embossed rubber stamp design to the top of a gift box. Cut small slits above and below the image and weave a ribbon through them. Fold a rectangle of white Bristol board into a simple compartment separator, and wrap the almonds with tulle netting. Tie the box closed with a satin ribbon.

Emily Grimes is a culinary instructor and recipe designer living in Raleigh, North Carolina.

INSTRUCTIONS
Making the Almonds

1. *Roast almonds.* Preheat oven to 350 degrees F. Spread almonds on baking sheets in single layer (*see* illustration A, above). Set on oven racks and roast 10 minutes, or until slightly browned and fragrant. Remove from oven; let cool 5 minutes. Set aside 2 cups almonds.

2. *Frost almonds.* Combine water, sugar, and salt in 12" skillet. Cook over medium heat, stirring with wooden spoon until sugar is dissolved. Stir in 4 cups roasted almonds. Continue stirring and cooking at medium heat 10 to 15 minutes, or until water evaporates and sugar crystals form on almonds (illustration B). Transfer sugar-frosted almonds to baking sheets and spread in single layer (some sugar will remain in pan). Let cool 30 minutes to 1 hour. Divide almonds in half; set one half aside.

3. *Drizzle chocolate.* Spread remaining half of frosted almonds on wax paper. Break 2 ounces chocolate into individual squares and place in one lower corner of heavy-duty freezer bag. Microwave unsealed bag 1½ minutes at medium power. Squeeze outside of bag gently to see if chocolate is melted. If necessary, continue microwaving in 30-second increments at medium power; do not overheat. Using scissors, snip lower corner of bag diagonally to make tiny opening. Drizzle fine line of chocolate through opening, going back and forth over almonds (illustration C). Let almonds rest undisturbed overnight, or until chocolate cools and hardens. To recycle any leftover chocolate, let it cool and harden in the bag.

MATERIALS
Makes one gift box for 3 cups of nuts

- **White 1-pound candy box (7" x 3¼" x 1⅞")**
- **White Bristol board**
- **Three 9" white flocked tulle circles**
- **1 yard ⅝" satin ribbon**
- **Gold detail embossing powder**

You'll also need:
3½" cherub rubber stamp; stamp pad; toaster (or other heat source); X-Acto knife; self-healing cutting mat; quilter's acrylic grid ruler; gluestick; scissors; pencil; and white paper.

Making the Package
Note: Stamp the cherub image on scrap paper and plan the ribbon placement before you decorate the lid.

1. *Emboss cover.* Lay unassembled box flat on paper, lid face up. Stamp cherub image on lid, then sprinkle embossing powder on stamped image while ink is still wet. Shake off excess powder and reserve for future use. Hold stamped image over toaster for 20 seconds, or enough to activate and melt embossing powder. Let cool 3 minutes.

2. *Weave ribbon through cover.* Lay box flat on cutting mat, lid face up. Using X-Acto knife and grid ruler, cut two ¾" slits on each side of cherub, parallel to front flap. Thread ribbon through slits (*see* illustration A, below).

3. *Make inside divider.* Using X-Acto knife, grid ruler, and mat, cut 3¼" x 14⅝" rectangle from Bristol board. Using pencil, lightly mark each long edge into three 2⅜" and four 1⅞" segments. Make six accordion-style folds at marks to create two peaks (illustration B). Glue peaked sections together back to back. Fold and assemble box; test-fit divider inside box, trimming ends to fit. Glue divider to box floor, making three compartments (illustration C).

4. *Package nuts.* Lay three tulle circles flat. Place one cup plain roasted nuts on first circle. Draw edges of circle up around mound of almonds and set in one compartment. Repeat for sugared and chocolate-coated nuts (illustration D). Tuck in excess tulle and close cover. Wrap ribbon around box and tie in bow. ◆

DESIGNER'S TIP

Use white chocolate instead of dark, or use dark and white together. Drizzle the new chocolate at a different angle for the best effect.

Gift-Wrapping the Almonds

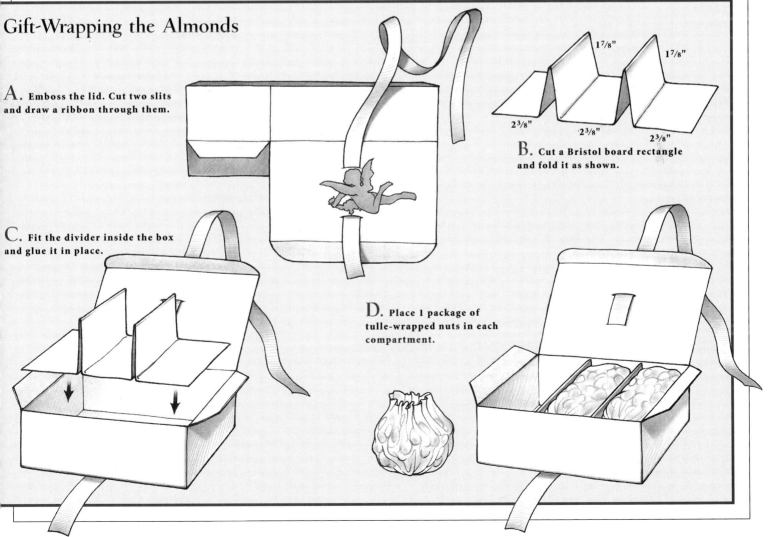

A. Emboss the lid. Cut two slits and draw a ribbon through them.

C. Fit the divider inside the box and glue it in place.

1⅞" 1⅞"
2⅜" 2⅜" 2⅜"

B. Cut a Bristol board rectangle and fold it as shown.

D. Place 1 package of tulle-wrapped nuts in each compartment.

Harvest Wheat Bouquet

Lash together four bundles of wheat with ribbon to create a simple and elegant autumn door decoration.

❧ BY CAROL ENDLER STERBENZ

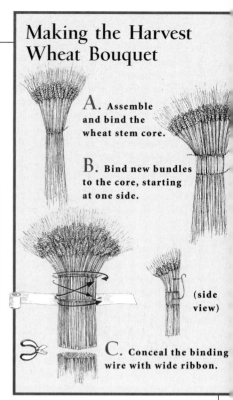

Making the Harvest Wheat Bouquet

A. Assemble and bind the wheat stem core.

B. Bind new bundles to the core, starting at one side.

(side view)

C. Conceal the binding wire with wide ribbon.

The design can be customized by changing the accents: Use differently colored ribbons, gold leaves, or flowers rather than grapes.

COLOR PHOTOGRAPHY:
Carl Tremblay

ILLUSTRATION:
Mary Newell DePalma

STYLING:
Ritch Holben

THE DESIGN OF THIS WHEAT BOUquet is visually straightforward, with clean lines, monochromatic color, and strong textural interest. It is the very simplicity of this wheat design, inspired by the golden stacks of wheat in the painting "Wheat Harvest" by Pieter Brueghel the Elder, that makes it successful and appealing.

The construction technique is also simple—you create four bouquets of ripened honey-colored wheat and lash them together into one large bouquet. To maximize the natural volume of the wheat heads, lay the stalks in slightly descending rows. The bound bouquets are tied with ribbon and accented with a few sprigs of seasonal berries.

There are a few tips to keep in mind when you are working with wheat stalks. Since wheat has a natural tendency to twist slightly as it is bundled into a central core, it is important to hold the stems securely in one hand while you are building the layers of the bouquet with the other.

Second, trim a few heads from the back of the arrangement so that the bouquet lies flat against the door or display surface. If you prefer to stand up the bouquet, you needn't trim the wheat heads. Instead, to balance the bouquet and make it stable, trim the stems to lower the center of gravity.

INSTRUCTIONS

1. *Make core.* Sort wheat stalks into four equal piles. To make core, take stalks one by one from first pile and hold them together so grain ears are even (stalk ends will be uneven). Continue until entire pile is used. Bind tightly about 6" below ears with florist wire (*see* illustration A, above).

2. *Complete bundle.* Take stalks one by one from second pile and hold them against left side of core. Make grain ears even with core at back of bundle but let them slope down away from core at front and side edges. Bind tightly over previous binding and again 2" to 3" below it (illustration B). Repeat process to bind third pile of stalks to right side of core. Adjust stalks so side that will face door or wall is as flat as possible. Add stalks from fourth pile to fill out front area as well as any gaps. Let ears in foreground fall forward so they are slightly lower than those in rear. Bind securely. Trim stems even across bottom with pruning shears.

3. *Add hanger and trims.* Run 18" length of stiff wire through middle of bundle from side to side. Twist together at back, leaving one tail long. Add a second wire just below ears in same way. Twist the two longer tails together and bend them into hanging loop. Test hanger on door or wall and adjust as necessary so bundle lies flat (see side view detail). Bind middle section with green ribbon, crisscrossing it to conceal wire binding; tie in back (illustration C). Tuck leaf and berry sprigs into ribbon folds. ◆

Bracelet-Style Napkin Ring

Use a delicate jewelry clasp to accent this beaded napkin ring.

🐚 BY DAWN ANDERSON

COLOR PHOTOGRAPHY:
Carl Tremblay

ILLUSTRATION:
Michael Gellatly

STYLING:
Ritch Holben

THIS NAPKIN RING, which resembles a grapevine, wraps around a napkin like a bracelet. The construction is easy: two of the five strands are made by stringing seed beads along a single length of wire. The other three have accent beads that twist off the central strand. To finish off, strands are attached to a jewelry clasp.

Before purchasing beads, make sure the holes are big enough to accommodate two strands of wire. I recommend using Japanese seed beads—they are generally uniform in size and have larger holes than other types.

Modify your beads and findings to create the look you want. To use a clasp that contains a mismatched bead, remove the "wrong" bead and glue on a coordinating one.

Dawn Anderson is a writer and designer living in Redmond, Washington.

INSTRUCTIONS

1. *String two 2-color strands.* Cut 12" length of wire. Using round-nose pliers, make ⅛" loop 2" from end. Twist wire to form tight spiral at base of loop. Clip off shorter wire. Crimp spiral to prevent unwinding. String lime beads on wire for

Wrapping a fifth bead strand around the other four creates the rambling grapevine effect. The circumference of this napkin ring is 5½".

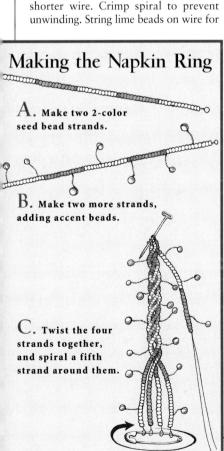

Making the Napkin Ring

A. **Make two 2-color seed bead strands.**

B. **Make two more strands, adding accent beads.**

C. **Twist the four strands together, and spiral a fifth strand around them.**

about 1" and slide to loop. String amethyst beads for 1". Repeat for 5" total. End off with ⅛" loop. Repeat to make second strand (*see* illustration A, left).

2. *String two accent bead strands.* Cut 30" length of wire; make ⅛" loop at center. Hold both ends of wires together and string on several lime beads. Slide accent bead onto one wire only, stopping about ½" from last bead. To secure bead, bend wire back on itself and twist in tight spiral. Resume bead stringing in 1" color increments; add an accent bead every ¾" to longer wire. At 4½", clip one wire. Continue stringing to 5"; end off with loop. Repeat to string second strand (illustration B). Begin a third strand, stopping

after first accent bead.

3. *Spiral strands together.* Join four completed strands at one end with safety pin. Link other ends with T-pin, add strand in progress, and anchor to foam brick. Twist safety pin to spiral the four strands. Resume stringing third accent bead strand, as in step 2. For less abrupt color changes, alternate individual bead colors for ½" before changing completely to new color (illustration C). As strand grows, spiral it around other four strands. Loop end; add to safety pin.

4. *Assemble napkin ring.* Using jump rings, join loops from T-pin to one side of clasp; join safety pin loops to other side. Attach grape cluster. Crimp all joins. ◆

MATERIALS
Makes one napkin ring

- Size 11 Japanese seed beads:
  15" lime string
  10" amethyst string
- 3mm to 6mm accent beads:
  10 lime
  10 amethyst
- 1½" grape cluster bead
- Decorative jewelry clasp
- 28-gauge wire
- 4mm jump rings

You'll also need:
chain-nose jewelry pliers; round-nose pliers; wire cutter; ruler; T-pin; safety pin; and florist foam brick (wrap with plastic).

Boiled Wool Traveling Blanket

This soft wool throw will become your faithful companion for fall car trips, football games, and country picnics.

BY DAWN ANDERSON

MATERIALS

- Tube-knitted boiled wool (width varies from 27" to 29") 34" length of pen blue 34" length of light peacock 23" length of alpine green
- 70 yards dark red wool yarn
- 20-meter roll ³⁄₈"-wide black iron-on tape
- 10 yards ³⁄₈"-wide iron-on adhesive

You'll also need:
rotary cutter; quilter's acrylic grid ruler; self-healing cutting mat; iron; scissors; size 18 chenille needle; masking tape; and pencil.

Pen blue, light peacock, and alpine green wool were used in this blanket. If you want to vary the color scheme, you have many options—boiled wool comes in over 30 colors.

COLOR PHOTOGRAPHY:
Daniel van Ackere

ILLUSTRATION:
Mary Newell DePalma

T HIS SOFT, LUXURIOUS TRAVELING blanket is made of boiled knitted wool. "Felting," "fulling," or "boiling" wool refer to a process in which heat, moisture, and mechanical agitation cause the fibers of knitted wool to shrink, interlock, and mat together. The resulting fabric is dense, warm, windproof, lightweight, and very soft. While it is possible to cook up your outgrown sweaters or wait for thrift-store finds in the colors you like, boiled wool can also be purchased. Though somewhat expensive, the ready-made fabric can be cut and sewn into cov-

erlets and throws that wear like iron.

The boiled wool used in this project is knitted and sold in the form of a tube. To obtain a single layer of fabric, you must cut along the fold on one side of the tube and open the fabric flat. These cut pieces are rarely perfectly square, so always purchase a little more fabric than you actually need. The wool is sold by length, and costs about $1 per linear inch. Because the shrinkage cannot be precisely controlled, tube widths will vary from about 27 to 29 inches.

The nubbier (purl) side of the fabric is

considered the right side. If you look closely, you may be able to detect the stockinette stitch on the wrong side. There is no noticeable grain, so the fabric can be run in either a lengthwise or cross-wise direction. Additionally, because of the boiling, the cut edges do not ravel.

To make a blanket, you cut and join rectangles of boiled wool with fusible tape. The seams are then stitched with decorative embroidery. Use a worsted weight yarn. You will need approximately 70 yards, which can be obtained from one or two large skeins. Tapestry yarn is also suitable for this type of embroidery, but the skeins are much smaller (8 meters per skein) and more expensive. To preserve the wool embroidery and prevent shrinkage, I recommend dry cleaning for the long-term care of your blanket.

Dawn Anderson is a writer and designer living in Redmond, Washington.

INSTRUCTIONS

1. *Cut four wool rectangles.* Lay one boiled wool tube flat. Using scissors, cut along one folded edge. Open piece and lay it flat. Repeat to cut remaining two tubes. Using rotary cutter and mat, cut four wool blocks: 16" x 34" and 13" x 23" pen blue, 23" x 29" alpine green, and 26" x 34" light peacock (*see* Cutting Guide, next page). Note: Dimensions may be adjusted as needed to accommodate your fabric widths.

2. *Join wool rectangles.* Lay green block right (or nubbier) side up. Following manufacturer's instructions, fuse ³⁄₈" adhesive to one 23" edge. Let cool and peel off backing. Lap 23" edge of pen blue block over adhesive edge by ³⁄₈", both blocks facing right side up (*see* illustration A, next page). Fuse to join. [Ed. note: For a tip on fusing, *see* Quick Tips, page 4].

3. *Make stitching guide.* Lay piece right side up, with seam horizontal and pen blue block at top. Cut 23" length of masking tape and affix to grid ruler. Using pencil, mark edge of tape every ³⁄₈" for stitching guide. Apply tape to alpine green block along seam, so marked edge butts pen blue fabric.

4. *Embroider pen blue/alpine green seam.* Thread chenille needle with 40" length of dark red yarn. To anchor yarn, pull seam apart at left edge for ¾" and take a few shallow backstitches in exposed pen blue fabric, without letting needle or yarn show through on other side. Close seam and draw needle out slightly to left of ¾" mark. Insert needle at (a) through single thickness of pen blue fabric and draw it out at ¾" mark (b), with yarn under needle (illustration B). Reinsert needle at (a) and draw out at next ⅜" mark (c), with yarn under needle (illustration C). Repeat these two stitches from left to right across seam for closed buttonhole stitch; stitches will form triangle pattern on right side, zigzag on reverse (illustration D). To end off, peel seam apart and take a few backstitches in exposed pen blue fabric. Start new strand in same way. End off ⅜" from right edge. Re-fuse areas where fabrics were peeled apart. Remove and save tape guide.

5. *Complete remaining seams.* Follow step 2 to fuse remaining pen blue and light peacock blocks along 34" edge. Follow steps 3 and 4 to embroider seam, starting ⅜" from left edge and ending off ¾" from right edge (illustration E). Repeat steps 2, 3, and 4 once more to join all four blocks in 42" vertical seam; begin and end embroidery ¾" from edges (illustration F).

6. *Hem edges.* Lay throw flat, wrong side up. Fuse ⅜" black tape to the two shorter sides, along raw edges. Apply iron-on adhesive over tape, let cool, and peel off backing. Fold edge ⅜" to wrong side and fuse in place. Repeat to hem two remaining edges (illustration G).

7. *Embroider hemmed edge.* Lay throw flat, right side up. Place tape guide around perimeter, ½" in from edge. Anchor yarn within seam allowance and draw needle out on fold. Embroider closed buttonhole stitch along edge, working from left to right so point (a) corresponds to tape marks. Stitching will enclose hemmed edge and be reversible (i.e., appear the same from both sides).

To turn corner, work four stitches at (a) instead of two (illustration H). Continue all around until you reach starting point (illustration I). Re-fuse areas where you peeled fabric apart. ◆

Cutting Guide

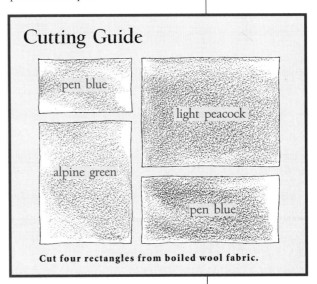

Cut four rectangles from boiled wool fabric.

Joining the Blocks

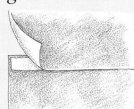

A. **Overlap and fuse two block edges.**

B. **Use a masking-tape guide to locate the first stitch.**

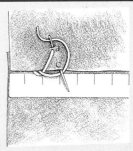

C. **Take a second stitch at a ⅜" interval.**

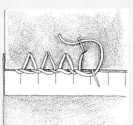

D. **Embroider the closed buttonhole stitch along the seam.**

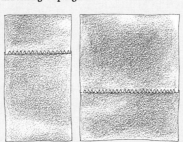

E. **Fuse the other two blocks and embroider that seam.**

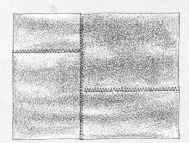

F. **Fuse and embroider the vertical seam.**

Finishing the Edge

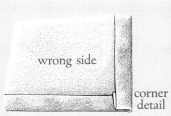

G. **Fold and fuse each raw edge to the wrong side.**

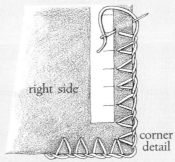

H. **Embroider the hemmed edge, taking four stitches to turn the corner.**

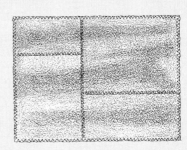

I. **Continue the closed buttonhole stitch around the entire edge.**

Thanksgiving Floral Turkey

The secret: Your favorite dried flowers on a Styrofoam base.

BY CAROL ENDLER STERBENZ

MATERIALS
Makes 24"-high x 30"-wide turkey

- **14"-diameter foam ball**
- **120 long-stemmed cattails**
- **40 stems orange-dyed statice**
- **30 stems golden yarrow**
- **25 stems green-dyed thistle**
- **25 yellow chrysanthemums**
- **12 medium yellow roses**
- **24 small yellow roses**
- **2 bunches artificial red grapes**
- **1 bunch artificial white grapes**
- **50 lemon leaves**
- **Four 7"-long dark green ferns**
- **4 or 5 oak leaves**
- **Florist pins**
- **Stiff paper-wrapped wire (for head support)**
- **Florist wire**

You'll also need:
small pruning shears; long serrated knife; wire cutters; hot-glue gun; tape measure; and bold-tip permanent marker.

You can easily combine natural finds with purchased florals. Just remember to choose dried materials with sturdy stems and flower heads and an autumn color palette.

COLOR PHOTOGRAPHY:
Carl Tremblay

ILLUSTRATION:
Mary Newell DePalma

STYLING:
Ritch Holben

THERE IS LITTLE THAT CAN RIVAL the majesty and appeal of this floral Thanksgiving turkey, a deceivingly simple centerpiece to make, regardless of your skill level. Requiring commonly found dried flowers and foliage, this grand bird would be just as beautiful made from dried herbs, grasses, and weeds found on a country walk as from the purchased roses, yarrow, and cattails featured here.

The construction principle is easy: Insert the stems of dried flowers into a Styrofoam base, altering the height of each of the materials according to the feature and feather pattern of a live turkey. Build several tall rows for the tail using cattails, statice, and thistle; lay a lower tail border of open yellow tea roses; and finish the shoulders and back with a low layer of chrysanthemums and golden yarrow, using smaller yellow roses to fill in gaps.

For a crowning touch, add bunches of grapes to a hook-shaped wire to form the head and throat. Insert a few stems of fern at an angle to form a generous wing span, exploiting the natural feathery shape of this ground cover. Conceal the remaining foam by pinning leaves in overlapping tiers, beginning at the border of flowers and moving to the base of the bird.

Do not be concerned if your turkey grows in size or develops a different shape than you planned. The fun of this project is that you can build a bird of exquisite color and proportion and achieve a beautiful decoration. Now you know that as complicated as this turkey may appear, it can be made in an hour or two of planting stems.

INSTRUCTIONS

1. *Make foam base.* Using serrated knife, slice foam ball straight across and slightly off center to make dome about 8" high. Slice off each end by 2" to yield piece about 10" across (*see* illustration A, right). Stand foam upright on flat side (illustration B). Shave corners and edges to make ovoid dome resembling a turtle shell (illustration C). Sketch rough guidelines on dome with marker (illustration D).

2. *Create turkey tail feathers.* Clip cattail stems to measure between 20" and 24". Insert stems into back of base (a) to form a 180-degree fan measuring 30" across. Insert orange statice in front of cattails (b), also in a fanlike arrangement. Push statice stems in so cattails rise above and behind them. Push green thistle stems into (b) area as accents (illustration E).

3. *Make turkey body.* Insert yellow roses and chrysanthemums into base (c), using longer-stemmed pieces at back, adjacent to statice, and shorter pieces at front, to suggest body mass that slopes up toward tail feathers. Fill in gaps with smaller yellow roses. Push 15 stems of

Preparing the Base

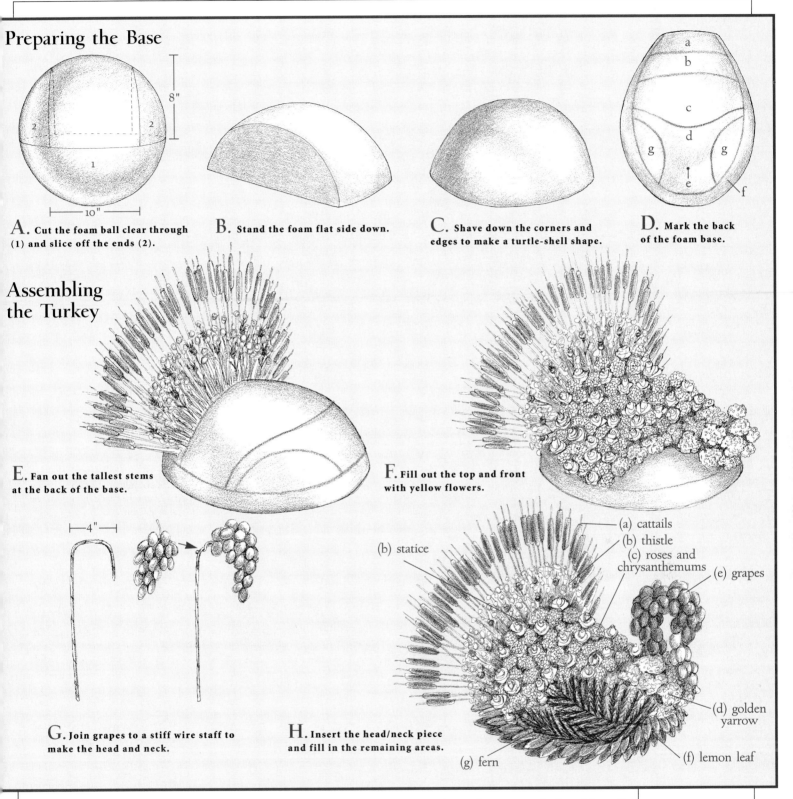

A. Cut the foam ball clear through (1) and slice off the ends (2).

B. Stand the foam flat side down.

C. Shave down the corners and edges to make a turtle-shell shape.

D. Mark the back of the foam base.

Assembling the Turkey

E. Fan out the tallest stems at the back of the base.

F. Fill out the top and front with yellow flowers.

G. Join grapes to a stiff wire staff to make the head and neck.

H. Insert the head/neck piece and fill in the remaining areas.

(a) cattails
(b) thistle
(b) statice
(c) roses and chrysanthemums
(e) grapes
(d) golden yarrow
(f) lemon leaf
(g) fern

golden yarrow into base (d), letting flower heads "float" to give appearance of full breast (illustration F). Save remaining yarrow for step 5.

4. *Add head and neck.* Cut 20" length of stiff paper-wrapped wire; shape into staff with 4" crook. Using florist wire, bind one bunch of red grapes to crook and second bunch to staff so they appear

as continuous growth (illustration G). Insert straight end into yarrow-covered area at point (e) for turkey neck and head. Tilt head back to give neck a slight S-shaped curve. Wire bunch of white grapes to lower neck, letting them drape onto breast for wattle.

5. *Complete base and wings.* Using hot-glue gun and/or florist pins, attach

lemon leaves around edge of base (f). Glue or pin two dark green ferns to each wing location (g), overlapping each pair to suggest feathers. Tuck red maple leaves into base and around wings for extra color at random locations. Examine turkey for gaps and fill in. Conceal foam behind tail feathers with remaining yarrow (illustration H). ◆

Gift Card Ideas

Use a few simple techniques to create miniature gift cards for any occasion.

✒ BY DAWN ANDERSON

COLOR PHOTOGRAPHY:
Carl Tremblay

ILLUSTRATION:
Mary Newell DePalma

STYLING:
Ritch Holben

For a different look, substitute other rubber stamps or vary the color of the ink pads and card stock.

E ACH OF THESE FOUR GIFT CARDS, made from simple stationery supplies and brass charms, is designed around a central theme that can be easily adapted for various occasions. If you want to make the cards in multiples, complete one card from start to finish to understand the construction, then make additional cards assembly-line style.

The teapot invitation shown here has the look of a die-cut card. The design trick is to take advantage of a rubber stamp image to create the outline of the card. The easiest way to cut around an irregular shape like this teapot is to hold your X-Acto knife still against a glass surface while you rotate the paper against the blade. The invitation lines are created and printed on a computer, cut into strips, and inserted into a small slit in the card.

The monogrammed key envelope also uses a rubber stamp but further enhances the design with detail-embossing powder. While conventional embossing powders tend to blur fine lines, this formulation accentuates their detail. A tiny brass key complements the ornamental design and creates a hint of mystery and expectation. This gift envelope is perfect for presenting a set of keys to house guests.

The trick to the third gift card is to use two thematically related images—in this case an acorn and an oak leaf—to link the envelope and the hand-cut card that fits inside. To take this idea one step further, you could also thematically link the gift card to the gift—for example, if you are giving a pot of daisies, you might stamp a sun on the envelope and a watering can on the card.

The final card gives you the opportunity to send special messages by placing an engraved brass charm inside the tiny envelope on the front cover. A piece of gold cord threaded through the spine lets you "bind" extra pages, gift certificates, or photographs.

Dawn Anderson is a writer and designer living in Redmond, Washington.

MATERIALS
Makes one card of each design

Teapot Invitation
- **White card stock**
- **12" length 1"-wide voile ribbon**

You'll also need:
3¼" x 4" teapot rubber stamp; sky blue dye ink pad; computer, printer, paper; X-Acto knife with new blade; glass pane (mask edges with tape); self-healing cutting mat; quilter's acrylic grid ruler; hot-glue gun; scissors; and book (for weight).

Monogrammed Key Envelope
- **1¾" x 2¾" white envelope**
- **Gold detail-embossing powder**
- **Brass key charm**
- **8" fine gold cording**

You'll also need:
1¼"-square monogram rubber stamp; gold pigment ink pad; ⅛" holepunch; toaster (or substitute heat source); small, soft paintbrush; and white paper.

Oak and Acorn Gift Enclosure
- **2⅜" x 3⅜" white envelope**
- **Gold detail-embossing powder**

You'll also need:
1½" x 2¼" oak leaf rubber stamp; ½" x ⅞" acorn rubber stamp; gold pigment ink; X-Acto knife; quilter's acrylic grid ruler; self-healing cutting mat; toaster (or substitute heat source); small, soft paintbrush; and white paper.

Envelope Gift Card
- **White card stock**
- **Blue card stock**
- **1"-square white envelope**
- **½ yard fine gold cording**
- **Engraved flat brass charm**
- **Gluestick**

You'll also need:
X-Acto knife; quilter's acrylic grid ruler; self-healing cutting mat; ⅛" holepunch; bone folder; and scissors.

Teapot Invitation

A. Cut out the teapot following the stamped outline.

B. Cut a slit along the teapot lid.

C. Slip the invitation into the slit. Glue on a sheer bow.

Monogrammed Key Envelope

D. Emboss a monogram at the bottom of the envelope.

E. Add a key charm and hanging cord at the top.

Oak and Acorn Gift Enclosure

F. Emboss an oak leaf on the card's front cover.

G. Emboss an acorn on the face of the envelope.

Envelope Gift Card

H. Lightly score the spine and punch a hole at each end.

I. Glue a blue panel and tiny envelope to the front cover.

J. Thread a gold cord through the holes.

INSTRUCTIONS

Teapot Invitation

1. *Make teapot.* Using sky blue ink pad, stamp teapot image on white card stock. Let dry 3 minutes. Place card stock right side up on glass. Cut along teapot outline with X-Acto knife; to cut tight curves accurately, hold knife steady and rotate paper (*see* illustration A, above). Also cut out area inside handle. Cut 1" slit in interior following edge of teapot lid (illustration B).

2. *Add invitation slip.* Use computer to type invitation on single line, e.g., "You're invited to tea at Anna's — Tues. Aug. 4 at 4 p.m." Select point size and font using computer software. (I used 12-point Village, italic, small caps.) If making several invitations, run test print first, then print multiples. Using X-Acto knife, grid ruler, and mat, cut printed invitation to make narrow strip similar to a Chinese cookie fortune. Insert slip into teapot slit (illustration C).

3. *Add bow.* Tie ribbon into bow; trim ends diagonally with scissors. Apply dot of hot-glue to teapot handle, set bow on glue, and weight with book 1 to 2 minutes, or until dry and cool (illustration C).

Monogrammed Key Envelope

1. *Emboss envelope.* Lay envelope flat, seam face down, on white paper. Using gold ink, stamp monogram on lower half of envelope, allowing ¼" margin at sides and bottom. Sprinkle embossing powder on stamped image while ink is still wet. Shake off excess powder and reserve for future use. Dust off lingering particles with small paintbrush. Hold stamped image over toaster for 20 seconds to activate and melt embossing powder. Let cool 3 minutes (illustration D).

2. *Add cord and key.* Fold envelope flap into closed position. Punch hole in center top ⅛" from upper edge. Fold gold cord in half and tie ends together. Insert looped end through hole from back, slip key charm on cord at front, then draw cord ends through loop (illustration E).

Oak and Acorn Gift Enclosure

1. *Make card.* Using X-Acto knife, grid ruler, and mat, cut one 3" x 4½" rectangle from card stock. Lay rectangle shiny side up. Measure 2¼" from short edge and lightly score line for card spine.

2. *Emboss card.* Lay card flat, shiny side up, on white paper. Using gold ink, stamp oak leaf to right of score line, for card front. Sprinkle embossing powder on stamped image while ink is still wet. Shake off excess powder and reserve for future use. Dust off lingering particles with small paintbrush. Hold stamped image over toaster for 20 seconds to activate and melt embossing powder. Let cool 3 minutes (see illustration F). Fold card on score line.

3. *Emboss envelope.* Lay envelope on copier paper, seams face down and flap at top. Stamp acorn in lower left corner. Proceed as in step 2 to emboss acorn motif (illustration G).

Envelope Gift Card

1. *Make card.* Using X-Acto knife, grid ruler, and mat, cut one 3½" x 5½" rectangle from white card stock. Measure 2¾" from short edge and lightly score line for card spine. Punch hole on spine ¼" in from each edge (illustration H). Fold card on score line, then unfold.

2. *Decorate card front.* Cut 2¼" x 3" rectangle from blue card stock. Glue blue panel, centered, to card front. Glue tiny envelope, seam side up, to center of panel. Slip brass charm into envelope (illustration I).

3. *Add gold cord.* Thread gold cord through holes, and draw to outside. Fold card in half. Tie cord in bow at middle of spine. Knot ends to prevent raveling (illustration J). ◆

Studded Velvet Frames

Learn how to laminate any frame with fabric, using upholstery tacks as accents.

❧ BY MARY ANN HALL

MATERIALS
Makes one frame

- **Nylon or rayon velvet fabric remnant**
- **Upholstery tacks**
- **Flat wooden picture frame**
- **Spray adhesive**

You'll also need:
iron; velvet board (*see Designer's Tip on page 42*); rotary cutter; quilter's acrylic grid ruler; self-healing cutting mat; small, sharp scissors; hammer; screwdriver; 2 dozen ⅜" shirt buttons; fabric-marking pencil; and newsprint.

DESIGN IDEAS

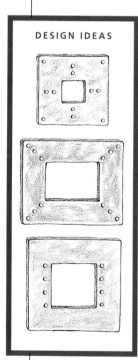

COLOR PHOTOGRAPHY:
Carl Tremblay

ILLUSTRATION:
Mary Newell DePalma

STYLING:
Ritch Holben

Select velvet colors and a tack arrangement that complement the photograph or artwork that you plan to frame.

U SE SCRAPS OF VELVET AND A FEW upholstery tacks to revitalize a plain wooden frame. This simple technique is adaptable to a frame of any size, as long as the opening rim is no deeper than ¼". If it is deeper, the velvet won't adequately cover the inside corners.

If the frame has a paint or finish on it, sand it lightly with 200-grit sandpaper before you begin. If the frame is unfinished, no preparation is needed. You will need a remnant of velvet fabric that is 2" larger all around than the frame you are planning to cover. To cover the frame, lightly coat the back of the velvet with spray adhesive and lay the frame in the center. Cut out a rectangle at each corner and fold the edges around to the back of the frame, then run a rotary cutter diagonally through the overlap and remove the excess fabric to prevent the corners from bulking up.

Use upholstery tacks to complete the design. Though hardware stores generally stock a sufficient range of tack styles to choose from, you will likely find more variety at a fabric store specializing in upholstery supplies.

Plan the tack arrangement before you tap them in; make sure to position them far enough from the inner opening to clear the lip that holds the glass.

INSTRUCTIONS

1. *Cut velvet rectangle.* Lay velvet face down on velvet board and press with cool iron to remove wrinkles. Measure frame, e.g., 7" x 9". Using rotary cutter and mat, cut rectangle from velvet 2" larger all around, e.g., 9" x 11".

2. *Adhere velvet to frame.* Lay velvet rectangle face down on newsprint and spray wrong side with adhesive, following manufacturer's instructions. Center frame face down on velvet and press to adhere. Fold one velvet edge up onto side of frame (do not fold onto back of frame). Using scissors, trim out corner rectangle at each end and discard (*see illustration A, below*). Fold remainder onto back of frame and press to adhere. Repeat process on opposite edge of frame. Fold two remaining edges onto side and back of frame (illustration B). Use rotary cutter to cut diagonally from inside to outside corner (illustration C). To reduce bulk, remove two triangles. Butt edges to make miter join.

3. *Make picture opening.* Lay frame face down on cutting mat. Using rotary cutter, cut fabric in frame opening diagonally, from corner to corner. Repeat from opposite corners to make X-shaped cut. Use scissors to complete cuts into corners. Fold one triangular flap up onto rabbet edge and press to adhere. Run rotary cutter along inside edge to trim off excess. Repeat process for three remaining edges.

4. *Plan upholstery tack pattern.* Lay frame right side up on flat, hard surface. Use buttons to plot upholstery tack design, experimenting with different arrangements until you create a look you like. Remove buttons, marking dot at each location. Check placement with grid ruler to ensure symmetry. Use hammer to tap upholstery tack into frame at each dot. ◆

Covering the Corners

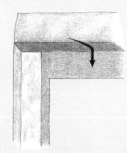

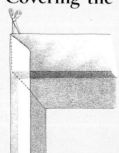

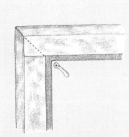

A. **Fold two opposite edges onto frame, and trim out the corners.**

B. **Fold the two remaining edges, overlapping the corners.**

C. **Miter-cut the overlapped sections and remove the surplus triangles.**

Jewel-Tone Spiral Pillow

Learn the easiest way to embroider using a sewing machine and metallic mesh trim.

❧ BY DAWN ANDERSON

THIS PILLOW DESIGN JUXTAPOSES A vivid diagonal division of color with soft, swirling curves of metallic trim. The spiral appliqué is created by machine stitching a fine zigzag over a piece of metallic mesh trim that is positioned in a swirl.

To achieve inconspicuous stitching, practice sewing the trim onto scrap fabric. Adjust your machine settings to determine the proper width of the zigzag stitch needed to clear the trim on each side; you don't want the needle to actually pierce the trim. If the mesh trim spreads or flattens while you are stitching, pull gently on the trim to ease the threads back together.

Though I used cranberry and green dupioni silk, you could adapt the colors to your home; just choose two colors with a similar tone or saturation.

Dawn Anderson is a writer and designer living in Redmond, Washington.

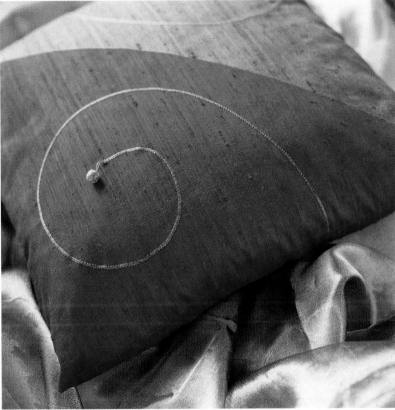

The brilliant jewel colors and the sophisticated simplicity of this design make this pillow a lively addition to any decorating scheme.

Making the Spiral Pillow

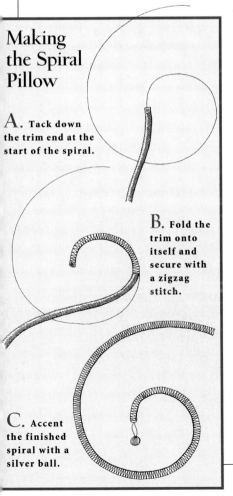

A. Tack down the trim end at the start of the spiral.

B. Fold the trim onto itself and secure with a zigzag stitch.

C. Accent the finished spiral with a silver ball.

MATERIALS
Makes one 16"-square pillow

- **45"-wide silk dupioni:**
  ¹/₂ yard cranberry
  ¹/₂ yard green
- **1⁵/₈ yards ¹/₈"-wide silver mesh trim**
- **Two ³/₈" silver mesh balls**
- **Thread to match fabrics and trim**
- **Nylon monofilament thread**
- **16"-square pillow form**
- **Clear nail polish**

You'll also need:
spiral pattern (*see* page 45); transfer paper; sewing machine; iron; rotary cutter; quilter's acrylic cutting guide; self-healing cutting mat; tear-away stabilizer; hand-sewing needle; pins; scissors; and pencil.

DESIGNER'S TIP

To get the most fabric mileage, make two pillows. Back one pillow with green silk and the other with cranberry. For a luxurious feel, use down-and feather-pillow forms.

INSTRUCTIONS

1. *Prepare pillow front.* From either silk, cut one 16¾" square for pillow back. From both, cut one 17½" square, then cut square in half diagonally. Pin two contrasting triangles right sides together and edges matching. (The two remaining triangles are not used, but could be saved for a second pillow.) Stitch diagonal edge, making ½" seam. Press seam open. Lay piece flat, right side up. Position spiral pattern on one triangle, aligning corners and seamline. Slip transfer paper between layers, and trace design with pencil to mark fabric. Repeat process to mark remaining triangle. Back each design with tear-away stabilizer, inserting pins from the right side.

2. *Sew mesh spirals.* Cut silver mesh trim in half. Seal one end of each length with clear nail polish for ½". Let dry 5 minutes, then trim off ³/₈". Hold sealed end against spiral's innermost point, so trim faces away from spiral. Using mono-filament thread, machine-tack trim to fabric ¹/₈" from trim end (*see* illustration A, left). Stop with needle in down position in fabric only. Fold trim back on itself to conceal stitching. Using short zigzag (26 stitches per inch), stitch down trim following marked spiral design (illustration B). Cut off excess trim even with fabric edge. Repeat process to stitch second spiral. Gently tear away stabilizer from wrong side. You do not need to remove paper caught under the stitches.

3. *Assemble pillow.* Place pillow front and back right sides together on cutting mat. Align pattern on one corner, and cut along taper lines with rotary cutter. Repeat at each corner (tapering this way prevents the pillow corners from flaring). Machine-stitch ½" from edges all around, leaving 12" opening on one side for turning. Clip corners diagonally. Turn right side out. Tack silver ball to each inner spiral. Insert pillow form, and slipstitch opening closed. ◆

PATTERNS
See page 45 for pattern pieces and enlargement instructions.

COLOR PHOTOGRAPHY:
Carl Tremblay

ILLUSTRATION:
Judy Love

STYLING:
Ritch Holben

Rhinestone Partridge & Pear

Pave artificial forms with clay and glittering stones.

🕊 BY DAWN ANDERSON

A springy gold clip allows the partridge to perch on a tree branch; the same style clip serves as the stem of the accompanying pear.

COLOR PHOTOGRAPHY:
Carl Tremblay

ILLUSTRATION:
Mary Newell DePalma

STYLING:
Ritch Holben

RADIANT SOPHISTICATION CHARACterizes this pair of keepsake tree ornaments. Fully encrusted with a colorful mix of rhinestones, this sparkling partridge and pear will surely be treasured as family heirlooms.

The ornaments are easy to make. The forms are first covered with a layer of clay and lightly sanded and painted to create a color guide; then matching rhinestones in corresponding colors are glued to each area. The tail feathers and crest of the partridge are made from short lengths of wire planted into the form and strung with beads.

The ornaments shown here were made from glass rhinestones, which will cost ap-

proximately $20 to $30 for each ornament. I thought this was reasonable, considering what one could spend for comparable glass or decorator ornaments at department stores. A less expensive alternative is to use acrylic rhinestones, which are about half the price; although the weight and feel of the ornament will be different, they will look practically the same on the tree. You can also substitute less expensive glass seed beads for the Austrian diamond-shaped crystal beads that are used on the crest and tail feathers.

Dawn Anderson is a writer and designer living in Redmond, Washington.

MATERIALS
Makes one partridge and pear ornament set

- 3"-long artificial bird
- 2½"-high plastic pear
- 6mm flat-backed rhinestones: approximately 300 topaz, 100 sapphire, 75 emerald, 15 ruby, 3 clear
- 4½ mm rhinestones: approximately 300 topaz, 100 sapphire, 75 emerald, 15 ruby, 15 clear
- 2¾ mm Austrian diamond-shaped crystal beads: 53 sapphire, 41 topaz
- Two 4mm red glass bird eyes
- Two gold bird leg clips
- Five 3" head pins
- Two 2" head pins
- 28-gauge brass craft wire
- 16-gauge brass craft wire
- One 2" velvet leaf
- Scrap of green cotton fabric
- 8 ounces Creative Paperclay
- 2 ounce Folk Art acrylic paints: Pure Metallic Gold, Blue Sapphire, Engine Red, Garnet Red, Shamrock, Emerald Green, Pearl White, Black
- White high-tack glue

You'll also need:
jewelry pliers; round-nose pliers; wire cutter; awl; mini screwdriver; tweezers; 240-grit sandpaper; plastic paint palette; ½" flat paintbrush; ¼" round paintbrush; foam brick; spray mister; paper towels; scissors; and pencil.

INSTRUCTIONS
Making the Partridge
1. *Make wire holder.* Remove feathers and legs/feet, if any, from artificial bird. Cut 10" length of 16-gauge wire. Bend 2"-long portion into hairpin shape. Use awl to pierce two holes in bird's back and one in underbelly. Insert wire through holes so hairpin shape lodges in body. Stand wire stem in foam brick to hold bird upright while you work.

2. *Add head pins.* Pierce one hole at top center of head and two holes ¼" away on each side. Insert 2" head pin through each side hole and out top hole, and twist together once at top of head. Bend wires forward slightly. In same way, pierce 5 evenly spaced holes across base of tail feathers, about ¼" from edge. Pierce 5 corresponding holes along edge rim. Thread 3" head pin through each base hole and out of rim hole. Pull wires snug and bend up slightly (*see* illustration A, next page).

3. *Coat bird with clay.* Press and mold Creative Paperclay over entire bird body, making ³⁄₁₆" layer. Smooth with wet fingers; if air bubbles develop, break them open and resmooth. Let dry overnight.

Sand to achieve extra-smooth finish. Wipe off dust with lightly misted paper towel (illustration B).

4. *Paint bird.* Paint bird body metallic gold; let dry 20 minutes. Using pencil, sketch in lines to denote different color areas of bird's body. Paint wings green, back and chest blue, and throat white as indicated. Apply additional coats as needed for full, even coverage. Paint beak black (illustration C).

5. *Glue rhinestones to bird.* Clip wire that joins glass eyes, leaving each eye with ⅛" stem. Push each stem into gold area of head and glue in place. Glue small topaz rhinestones around each eye by applying dot of glue to bird and positioning rhinestone. Use tweezers to butt rhinestones together so gaps are as small as possible. Continue gluing stones until gold area of head is fully encrusted (illustration D).

In same way, glue clear rhinestones to throat, sapphire stones to back and breast, emerald stones to wings, and gold stones to underbelly, matching rhinestone color to painted color. Intersperse large and small stones to fill in each color area without gaps.

6. *Add beaded plumage.* Separate head wires so one falls slightly forward. Thread 7 topaz and 2 sapphire crystal beads on front wire. Bend excess wire at 90-degree angle and clip, leaving ½" tail. Use round-nose pliers to coil tail into loop. Repeat process for second head wire, using 9 topaz and 2 sapphire beads. Treat tail wires in similar way: Starting with end wire, thread on 9 sapphire and 5 topaz beads. Bend up excess wire 90 degrees and coil in flat spiral. Continue in this fashion, using 10 sapphire beads on next wire and 11 sapphire beads on middle wire. Bead remaining wires in mirror image so sapphire color flares out at middle (illustration D).

7. *Attach clip.* Using mini screwdriver, pry up prongs on top half of clip to release curved spring-clip mechanism. Set aside bottom half of clip. Slip coiled spring from clip onto wire stem and slide it snug against bird's underbelly. Cut wire ⅞" beyond end of spring and bend it onto clip. To rejoin the two halves, set curved mechanism back in position. Reclamp prongs, securing wire stem underneath (illustration E).

Making the Pear

1. *Make wire holder.* Remove pear stem and leaf, if any. Attach wire as described in partridge, step 1, making sure the long wire emerges from the stem hole.

2. *Coat pear with clay.* Use same technique as described in partridge, step 3 (illustration F).

3. *Paint pear.* Paint pear metallic gold;

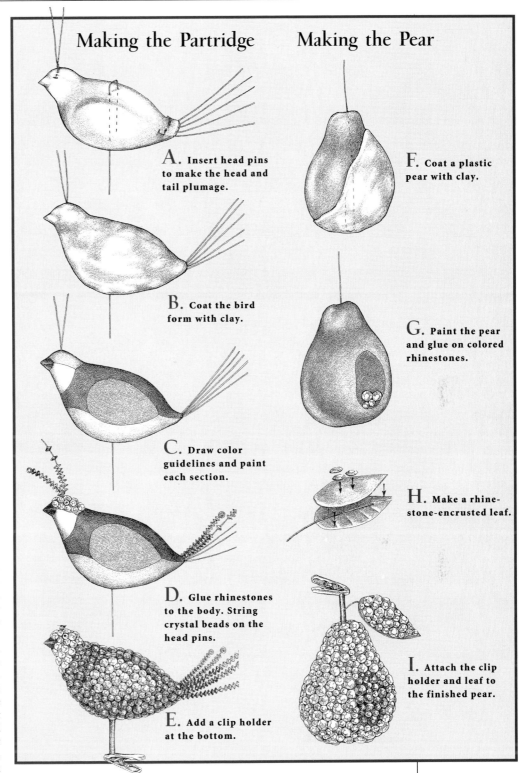

Making the Partridge   Making the Pear

A. Insert head pins to make the head and tail plumage.

B. Coat the bird form with clay.

C. Draw color guidelines and paint each section.

D. Glue rhinestones to the body. String crystal beads on the head pins.

E. Add a clip holder at the bottom.

F. Coat a plastic pear with clay.

G. Paint the pear and glue on colored rhinestones.

H. Make a rhinestone-encrusted leaf.

I. Attach the clip holder and leaf to the finished pear.

let dry 20 minutes. Mix 1 part Garnet Red and 1 part Engine Red to paint red oval blush on pear surface. Apply additional coats as needed for even coverage.

4. *Glue rhinestones to pear.* Glue topaz and ruby rhinestones to pear, using technique described in partridge, step 5 (illustration G).

5. *Make leaf.* Remove stem from velvet leaf. Use leaf as template to cut same shape from green cotton fabric. Cut 9"

length of 28-gauge wire. Glue leaves back to back, sandwiching wire in between for a stem. Glue emerald rhinestones to one side of leaf (illustration H). Let dry 30 minutes. Glue rhinestones to other side.

6. *Attach clip and leaf.* Attach clip to pear at stem location, using same technique as for partridge, step 7. Coil wire leaf stem neatly around spring and clip off excess (illustration I). ◆

Little Red Schoolhouse Clock

Drop a timepiece into a balsawood core and disguise it with model-making trim.

🐌 BY MICHIO RYAN

The bell tower is merely a right-angle corner cut from a scrap of balsa. Cut about 1/8" outside the desired edge, then rub it over sandpaper on a flat table top as you would Parmesan on a cheese grater.

PATTERNS
See page 45 for pattern pieces.

COLOR PHOTOGRAPHY:
Carl Tremblay

ILLUSTRATION:
Mary Newell DePalma

STYLING:
Ritch Holben

A LTHOUGH THIS SCHOOLHOUSE desk clock might look like a time-consuming woodworking project, it is very simple to make. Pop-in quartz clock movements are usually inserted into a predrilled hole on a commemorative plaque, but in this project, the clock rests in a three-dimensional schoolhouse that looks finished from all sides.

The core is made from three blocks of model-making balsa, which is as easy to cut and shape as Styrofoam. Instead of a saw, X-Acto blades are used to cut the thin basswood siding

that is glued over the core.

The hole for the clock is drilled through just one of the core blocks and then trimmed out of the front surface sheet with an X-Acto blade. Although this edge should be neat enough to make a snug fit for the clock movement, it doesn't need to be perfectly cut because it is ultimately hidden by the bezel of the clock.

The steeple is a right-angle corner cut from a scrap of balsa and trimmed at a 45-degree angle. A bell and the four sticks upon which the bell tower will rest are

MATERIALS
Makes 5½"-tall clock

- 1⁷⁄₁₆" quartz clock insert (Klockit #15209)
- 3" x 24" x ¾" balsawood
- 3" x 24" basswood ¼" clapboard siding
- 3½" x 24" basswood ½" beaded siding
- ⅛" x 24" L-shaped corner beading
- ⅛"-square craft sticks
- ½" brass bell
- Green self-stick padding
- 2-ply chipboard scrap
- Fine-gauge wire
- 2-ounce acrylic paints: Green, Gray, Red
- Shellac
- Wood glue
- Contact cement

You'll also need:
schoolhouse clock cutting diagrams (*see* page 45); drill with 1⅜" bit; needle-nose pliers with wire cutter; X-Acto knife with craft and saw blades; self-healing cutting mat; cork-backed steel ruler (for cutting); grid ruler (for drafting); 180-grit sandpaper; ½" disposable bristle brush; soft-bristled paintbrushes; plastic paint palette; painter's tape; denatured alcohol; metal skewer; wooden spoon; and pencil.

easily pushed into holes in the bottom of the balsa. The posts are then glued to the peaked roof, and the outside is colored with acrylic paint.

INSTRUCTIONS

1. *Cut balsa pieces.* Using grid ruler and pencil, draft three schoolhouse shapes and one bell tower shape (*see* page 45) on ¾"-thick balsa. Drill 1⅜" hole in one schoolhouse shape as marked on diagram. Use sandpaper wrapped around handle of wooden spoon to sand inside wall of hole. Cut out the four pieces by sawing on marked lines.

2. *Rough-cut clapboard siding.* Using X-Acto knife, steel ruler, and cutting mat, rough-cut four 3¾"-wide pieces from clapboard siding. Lay one piece smooth side up. To mark hole, use balsa schoolhouse as a template: Lay it flat on top, bottom edges aligned (confirm clapboard direction on right side) and excess extending evenly at each side. (Gable will be added later.) Trace hole outline onto siding. Carefully cut out hole with X-Acto knife, making first cuts with the grain to avoid splintering. (You can refine the cut edge later by sanding.)

3. *Assemble schoolhouse core.* Apply wood glue to face of two solid balsa schoolhouses and glue together. Glue on balsa piece with hole to complete core (*see* illustration A, next page). Wrap core with tape and dry 1 hour. Remove tape. To

Constructing the Schoolhouse Clock

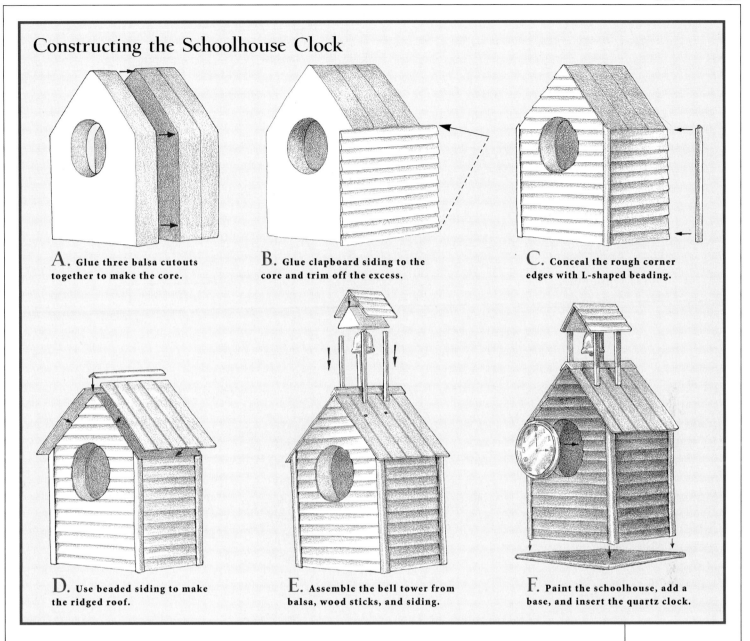

A. Glue three balsa cutouts together to make the core.

B. Glue clapboard siding to the core and trim off the excess.

C. Conceal the rough corner edges with L-shaped beading.

D. Use beaded siding to make the ridged roof.

E. Assemble the bell tower from balsa, wood sticks, and siding.

F. Paint the schoolhouse, add a base, and insert the quartz clock.

smooth uneven areas, lay sandpaper flat and rub core against it, one plane surface at a time. Sand bell tower in same way to smooth sawed edges. Press wooden spoon handle into underside of bell tower to make dimple for bell. Seal core and bell tower with 2 coats shellac applied with ½" brush. Let dry 5 minutes between coats, 15 minutes after second coat. Clean brush with denatured alcohol.

4. *Glue clapboard siding to core.* Brush contact cement on one side wall of core and the back of one clapboard piece. Let cement set up 1 minute or so, until tacky. Stand clapboard siding upright on work surface, sidle bottom edge against core, and press into place (illustration B). To trim off excess, lay core on cutting mat, clapboard side down, and cut as close to core edge as possible with X-Acto knife. Sand down any areas that still

protrude. Repeat process on remaining walls of core, aligning hole cutouts on front wall. Fill in front and back gables with a smaller piece of clapboard, glue in place, and trim off excess. Cut L-shaped beading to conceal corner edges, and attach with wood glue. Sand beading even with angled roof line after glue is dry (illustration C).

5. *Glue on roof.* From beaded siding, cut two 2" x 2⅝" roof panels, beading parallel to shorter edges. (Use beading as a cutting guide.) Glue both panels to roof, overlapping edges at peak. Conceal peak join with L-shaped beading (illustration D).

6. *Assemble and attach bell tower.* Slip bell onto 1" length of wire, twist ends together in tight spiral, and clip ⅜" from bell. Push ends of wire into dimple at underside of tower. Cut four 1¾" lengths from ⅛"-square stick. Using skewer,

pierce four holes in underside of bell tower, one at each corner. Insert one stick into each hole. Hold bell tower in position on roof, about ¾" back from front wall, and make corresponding marks on roof with pencil. Pierce roof at pencil marks. Test-fit bell tower, making sure bell clears roof peak. Secure all joins with wood glue. Cut two 1" x 1⅛" pieces from clapboard siding and glue to bell tower for roof (illustration E).

7. *Add base and clock.* From 2-ply chipboard, cut one 2¾" x 3" rectangle for base. Using soft-bristled brush, paint base green, roofs gray, and walls and bell tower red. Cut one 2⅝" x 2⅞" rectangle from green padding. Peel off backing and apply to underside of base. Glue schoolhouse to top of base with contact cement. Push clock insert into opening, concealing rough edges (illustration F). ◆

Pop-Up Jester

Make this collectible toy with a movable stem that conceals or reveals a smiling jester.

❧ BY DAWN ANDERSON

Display the jester by resting the stem in a 6"-high stand made from a tassel topper and two blocks of wood.

T HIS POP-UP JESTER IS A MODERN replica of an old-fashioned toy. The jester's head is glued to the top of a dowel that slides in and out of a small cone. To work the toy, you hold the cone with one hand, and with the other, you push the dowel up to pop the jester out or pull it down to hide her. The jester rests in a wooden stand in the pop-up position.

The jester's garment is made from silk dupioni and requires only minimal sewing. The face is purchased ready-made and is glued to the sewn fabric head. The cone, made from rolled chip-board, is coated with fabric glue and covered with silk. The lower edge of the jester's garment is glued around the top of the cone, with the raw edges disguised by braided trim.

I assembled the stand for the jester out of a tassle topper and two wood blocks, but you could substitute other wood pieces. Just be sure that the stand has a broad base for stability and is wide enough at the top to accommodate the ¼" jester dowel.

Dawn Anderson is a writer and designer living in Redmond, Washington.

MATERIALS
Makes one pop-up jester and stand

- Amaco 1½" "Grace" face
- 45"-wide silk dupioni:
  ¼ yard turquoise
  ¼ yard red
  ¼ yard lime green
- Thread to match fabrics
- ½ yard 26"-wide fusible knit interfacing
- ⅓ yard 1½"-wide red sheer ribbon
- ⅜ yard ⅜"-wide braid trim
- Red pearl cotton
- Five ¼" gold jingle bells
- Fiberfill
- 4¼" wood tassel topper
- ½" wood candle cup
- ¾" x 3" x 3" wood block
- ½" x 2" x 2" wood block
- ¾" wood dowel (scrap)
- ¼" wood dowel
- 12"-square 2-ply chipboard
- Double-sided tape
- Masking tape
- Delta Ceramcoat 2-ounce acrylic paints: Azure Blue, Cardinal Red, Leaf Green, Light Ivory, Lime Green
- Delta Ceramcoat satin varnish
- Clear nail polish
- Wood glue
- Goop glue
- Tacky glue
- Fabric glue

You'll also need:
tracing patterns for cone, garment, front head (2), and back head (see page 47); drill with ⁹⁄₃₂" bit; large and small C-clamps; small handsaw; 100-, 180-, and 240-grit sandpaper; wood block; ⅜" flat paintbrush; liner brush; plastic paint palette; spray mister; paper towels; cotton swabs; pencil; sewing machine; iron; rotary cutter; quilter's acrylic grid ruler; self-healing cutting mat; small, sharp scissors; point turner; hand-sewing needle; and pins.

INSTRUCTIONS
Making the Wood Stand and Handle

1. *Assemble stand.* Plug entire hole of tassel topper with ¾" dowel sawn to size; glue in place. Let dry 30 minutes. Sand base smooth. Clamp tassel topper to work surface. Using ⁹⁄₃₂" bit, drill into top end 1½" to make smaller opening for ¼" dowel. Glue 2" block, centered, to 3" block. Glue base of tassel topper to 2" block (see illustration A, next page). Clamp entire assembly and let dry overnight.

2. *Prepare jester handle.* Lay candle cup on side and clamp to work surface. Using ⁹⁄₃₂" bit, drill hole through base at center. Cut 16" length of ¼" dowel. Sand lightly, then wipe off dust with lightly misted paper towel. Test-fit dowel through candle-cup hole. It should slide easily.

3. *Paint wood pieces.* Apply all paints with flat brush, let dry 20 minutes, and sand lightly with 180-grit sandpaper. Apply second and third coats as needed for even coverage. Apply final coat with minimal brush strokes for a smooth finish. First paint dowel and lower tier of base azure blue. Then mix together equal parts lime and leaf green and use to paint candle cup, smaller tier of base, and adjacent end of tassel topper. Paint remainder of tassel topper ivory. Using liner brush, paint six blue dots around belly of tassel topper, just above widest section. (Hint: To space dots evenly, view tassel topper from drilled end.) Sketch undulating line between and below dots around belly. Apply red paint from this line down to green paint (illustration A for stand components, illustration F for candle cup and dowel). Seal all wood pieces with two coats of satin varnish.

Making the Jester

1. *Make cone.* Use pattern (page 47) to cut one cone from chipboard. Apply double-sided tape to one edge, then roll into cone shape with small hole at bottom and overlap taped edge. Secure seam further with masking tape. Lay red silk on interfacing (do not fuse) and use pattern to cut cone from both layers. Trim one straight edge of interfacing cone by ½". Fuse pieces together. Press ½" silk allowance to wrong side. Lay red silk cone flat with interfacing side up. Brush thin coat of washable fabric glue on outside of chipboard cone, then set taped edge of cone along raw edge of fabric and press to adhere. Roll cone onto fabric toward folded edge, pressing as you go. Reglue fabric overlap if needed. Set cone aside.

2. *Cut and fuse remaining fabrics.* Using rotary cutter and accessories, cut one 7" and two 4" squares from lime silk, the same set from turquoise silk, and two sets from fusible knit interfacing. Fuse interfacing to wrong side of silk squares.

3. *Sew garment.* Place 7" lime and 7" turquoise squares right sides together. Pin garment pattern to both layers. Machine stitch along stitching lines. Cut on solid

outline. Remove pattern tissue and discard. Press seams open.

4. *Sew jester head.* Place two 3" turquoise squares right sides together. Pin front head tracing pattern to both layers. Using short stitch length, machine-stitch between dots along curved stitching line. Stitch again over previous stitching. Using small, sharp scissors, cut top layer only along solid center front line. Remove and discard pattern. Turn piece over. Align back head tracing pattern on stitching and pin. Cut remaining layer on solid center back line. Remove and save pattern. Trim excess fabric close to stitching, clip inside curves, and turn right side out (illustration B). Repeat process with lime green squares, reversing patterns to make same piece in mirror image. Join both head halves by stitching along center front and center back seams. Turn entire head right side out. Stuff fiberfill into curved points (illustration C).

5. *Glue face to head.* Cut 1¼" square from chipboard. Bend square, insert it into head through neck opening, and open flat. Spread Goop glue on back of sculpted face and press face on front head, centering over seam. Cover face with thick felt or fleece, lay wood block on top, and clamp to work surface. Let dry 24 hours. Remove chipboard and stuff cavity with fiberfill (illustration D).

6. *Attach garment to head.* Pull garment, wrong side out, over head and match neck edges. Align garment seams with front and back head seams so colors reverse (see color photograph). Hand-sew once around neck edge, and end off. Hand-baste once around, leaving thread ends for gathering. Apply Goop glue to tip of dowel for 1½" and insert into head at neck opening. Pull loose thread ends snug, wrap around neck, and tie knot (illustration E). Glue loose neck fabric to dowel. Turn garment right side out and let hang down.

7. *Add collar and bells.* Seal ends of red sheer ribbon with clear nail polish. Lay red pearl cotton along middle of ribbon and zigzag over it, backstitching at each end. Pull pearl cotton ends to gather ribbon into ruffled collar. Tie collar around neck, knot ends, and trim off thread tails. Secure with tacky glue. Tack one jingle bell to each hat point and three to center front seam of garment.

8. *Attach cone.* Insert dowel into cone and draw it out small opening at bottom. Lap lower edge of garment over upper edge of cone by ¼". Pin all around, then adhere with tacky glue. Conceal raw edges by gluing ⅜" trim all around. Apply tacky glue to red silk at tip of cone. Thread candle cup up dowel and nestle glued area of cone tip into it (illustration F). Insert other end of dowel into stand. Let dry 24 hours. ◆

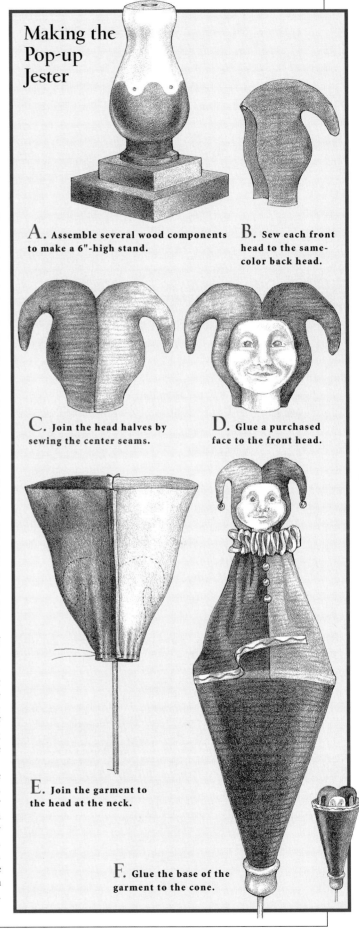

Making the Pop-up Jester

A. Assemble several wood components to make a 6"-high stand.

B. Sew each front head to the same-color back head.

C. Join the head halves by sewing the center seams.

D. Glue a purchased face to the front head.

E. Join the garment to the head at the neck.

F. Glue the base of the garment to the cone.

Stained-Glass Cookies

Bake crushed hard candy into cut-out cookie windows
to make vividly colored glass-like centers.

🐦 BY ELIZABETH CAMERON

MATERIALS

Makes thirty 3"-round cookies

- 1 cup butter
- 1 cup sugar
- 1 egg
- ½ cup milk
- 1 teaspoon vanilla
- 3½ cups flour
- 1 teaspoon baking powder
- 10 Jolly Rancher hard candies
- Assorted ribbon/cord for hanging

You'll also need:
3" round cookie cutter; 1" to 1½" cookie cutters (assorted novelty shapes); electric mixer; flour sifter; mixing bowls; wet and dry measuring cups; measuring spoons; rolling pin; cookie sheets; cooling racks; baby's spoon; X-Acto knife; drinking straw; small, soft-bristled brush; hammer; baking parchment paper; small zip-close freezer bags; wax paper; and plastic wrap.

COLOR PHOTOGRAPHY:
Carl Tremblay

ILLUSTRATION:
Mary Newell DePalma

STYLING:
Ritch Holben

Though a round shape was used to make the cookies shown here, you can use cookie cutters in any shape for the inside or the outside; just make sure that the inside shape has a cookie border of at least ½".

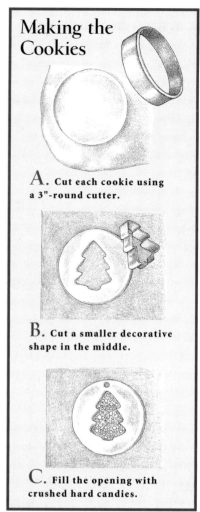

Making the Cookies

A. Cut each cookie using a 3"-round cutter.

B. Cut a smaller decorative shape in the middle.

C. Fill the opening with crushed hard candies.

THESE DELICIOUS COOKIES ALSO look beautiful hung on a Christmas tree or attached to gift packages. The recipe is easy to follow and lots of fun for children.

All you need to do is make the dough and roll it out. Then use a round cookie cutter to form the outside of the cookie and a smaller cookie cutter to cut a design into the center of the dough. You'll need Jolly Rancher candies to fill and color the center cutout. Though I tested other hard candies, I found Jolly Ranchers to have the clearest, brightest colors—they actually glowed when light was shining through them. You can buy them in small packs (like Life Savers) or by the bag. The small 1.6-ounce pack contains 10 wrapped candies and is enough for one batch of 30 cookies.

To prepare the candies, you must crush them. Divide them by color into freezer bags, place them on a hard surface, and then tap the bags with a hammer to break the pieces into small crystals. Spoon the crushed candy into the center hole in each cookie. After the cookies are baked and cooled, you can string them on colorful ribbons to make tree ornaments or package decorations.

INSTRUCTIONS

1. *Make cookie dough.* Using electric mixer, cream butter and sugar together. Beat in egg, milk, and vanilla until well blended. Sift together flour and baking powder; add to butter mixture in 1 cup increments, beating in thoroughly after each addition. Shape dough into round ball, flatten slightly, and wrap in plastic. Chill ½ hour.

2. *Roll and cut cookies.* Unwrap dough and place on baking parchment. Lay sheet of plastic wrap on top to prevent sticking, then roll out dough to scant ¼" thickness. Remove plastic wrap. Cut 3" round cookies 1½" apart (*see* illustration A, above). Remove excess dough. Transfer entire baking parchment to cookie sheet. Using smaller cookie cutter(s), cut novelty shape in middle of each cookie (illustration B). Remove excess dough and clean up cut edges with X-Acto knife. Use drinking straw to cut small round hole at top of cookie, ⅜" in from outer edge.

3. *Add crushed candies and bake.* Unwrap Jolly Rancher hard candies. Separate candies by color into individual freezer bags. Tap each bag with hammer to crush candies into small crystals resembling rock salt. Use small measuring spoon to sprinkle candy crystals into cut-out section of each cookie, ½ to ¾ full (illustration C). Do not overfill; one candy will fill 3 cookies. Brush any stray crystals back into well. Bake at 350 degrees for 8 minutes, or until candy melts and edges of cookie just start to brown. Transfer entire parchment sheet to rack for cooling. Remove cookies from parchment when candy filling is hardened. Thread ribbon or cord through holes for hanging. ◆

Decorative Memo Blocks

Turn those dull but essential note cubes into unique desk accents using rubber stamps and coordinated paper.

🐌 BY GEORGIA MORROW

COLOR PHOTOGRAPHY:
Carl Tremblay

ILLUSTRATION:
Mary Newell DePalma

STYLING:
Ritch Holben

I DON'T KNOW ABOUT YOU BUT I CAN no longer live without note pads. And I have them everywhere. Fortunately, my note-making now enhances more than my memory—it makes my desk and my kitchen counter look brighter and more welcoming. I simply covered a pencil and the spine of my pad with decorative paper and rubber stamped the edges of the paper. I made my memo cubes even more convenient by drilling a hole through the pad to hold a pencil.

Though you might not think so, you can drill through paper. All you need to do is stabilize the cube between wooden slats. Position the hole in the upper left corner so that when the pencil is lifted, the point is at the location where you will begin writing. If you don't have much experience drilling, you can use a drill bit guide, a small attachment available at hardware stores, to ensure that you are drilling straight down. Once you have drilled about halfway through the cube, reduce the drill speed and slowly draw the bit out of the hole to spin off accumulated paper shreds. Reinsert the drill in the hole and continue clear through to the bottom slat. The paper that covers the spine of the cube will fold underneath to cover the hole.

To decorate the memo cube, cover the spine and a pencil with decorative paper. Then add rubber-stamped patterns to the paper edges.

Georgia Morrow is a writer and designer living in Washington, D.C.

INSTRUCTIONS

1. *Drill pencil hole.* Stand memo cube on wood slat, aligning spine with slat edge. Place second slat on top in same position, and clamp entire sandwich together. Elevate assembly on bricks to avoid drilling into underlying work surface. Measure ¾" in and down from top left corner of cube and mark location on top wood slat. Put on goggles. Using ⅜" bit, drill hole at mark clear through cube (*see* illustration A, right).

2. *Glue paper to spine.* Measure cube spine height and width. Add 1½" to height, e.g., 4½" x 3½", and using X-Acto knife, grid ruler, and mat, cut rectangle from matte paper. Lay rectangle face down on newsprint and apply spray

Create a decorated note pad to keep near every phone; you can coordinate the color and pattern with each room's decor.

MATERIALS
Makes one 3½" memo block

- 3½" memo cube
- Decorative matte paper(s)
- Unfinished wood lead pencil
- Wood glue
- Spray adhesive

You'll also need: rubber stamp; stamp pad; drill with ⅜" bit and guide; 5" C-clamp; two ½"-thick wood slats; two bricks or wood blocks; wooden clothespins; safety goggles; X-Acto knife; self-healing cutting mat; quilter's acrylic grid ruler; pencil; and newsprint.

adhesive to wrong side. Apply paper to cube spine, folding the 1½" allowance onto base of pad to cover pencil hole. Smooth with fingers (illustration B).

3. *Stamp paper edges.* Stand cube on one side and hold pages together firmly with your fingers (or use clamp arrangement from step 1). Use rubber stamp to decorate paper edges on three sides. Overlap some impressions and let others fall off the edge for a free-form design (illustration C).

4. *Make coordinating pencil.* Measure wooden pencil barrel. From matte paper, cut rectangle this length x 1¼", e.g., 6¾" x 1¼". Lay rectangle face down on newsprint and brush wood glue over back surface in thin, even coat, going out beyond edges. Move rectangle to clean area of newsprint. Position pencil on rectangle about ⅜" in from long edge. Fold this allowance up onto pencil barrel, and press to adhere. Spread your fingers across barrel and roll pencil onto

remaining rectangle, pressing as you go (illustration D). Clamp with clothespins and let dry overnight. ◆

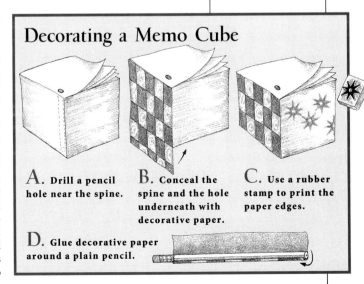

Decorating a Memo Cube

A. Drill a pencil hole near the spine.

B. Conceal the spine and the hole underneath with decorative paper.

C. Use a rubber stamp to print the paper edges.

D. Glue decorative paper around a plain pencil.

Reversible Silk Velvet Scarf

Learn how to make custom-colored silk velvet scarves using cold-water dyes.

❧ BY RODNEY T. STERBENZ

For a variation on the dot design, try other shapes. Cosmetic sponges can be cut with scissors into stars, diamonds, triangles, and other simple silhouettes.

MATERIALS
Makes 8" x 44" reversible scarf

- ⅝ yard 45"-wide light-colored silk velvet
- Two 3.5-ounce bottles Tinfix silk fabric dye (see chart, next page, for color suggestions)
- Sewing thread to match dye colors

You'll also need:
⅛ cup (about 1 ounce) soda ash; envelope moistener with round foam applicator; three 5-quart bowls or basins; rubber gloves; measuring cup; measuring spoons; large plastic spoon; wide, flat paintbrush; large sponge; sewing machine; iron; rotary cutter; quilter's acrylic cutting guide; self-healing cutting mat; hand-sewing needle; pins; clean white fabric (such as an old sheet); and large plastic trash bags.

foam pad on an envelope sealer (sold in stationery stores) to stamp the polka dots. Because the bottle didn't release an even amount of dye into the sponge, I ended up emptying the bottle and dipping the sponge directly into the dye bath, blotting it a few times before making each dot.

To complete the dyeing process, set the dyes with an iron and give the fabric a final cool rinse to remove any soda ash residue. Once the velvet is completely clean and dry, all you do is sew the two halves together. If you desire, fringe can be added to the ends. Or, for a variation, replace one half of the scarf with a silk or satin liner, so that only one side is dyed velvet.

Rodney T. Sterbenz is a prop and model maker living in New York City.

INSTRUCTIONS
Note: Do not reuse dye containers, utensils, or sponge for food preparation or cleanup.

1. *Cut velvet.* Using rotary cutter, grid ruler, and cutting mat, cut two 9"-wide strips across width of velvet (*see illustration A, next page*). From remaining velvet, cut several 4" squares for test swatches.

2. *Prepare work area.* Locate a large flat work surface that you don't mind getting wet and that you can reserve in 48-

DESIGNER'S TIP

To darken a polka dot that appears too faint, dip a cotton swab in the dye and dab the center of the dot. The dye will spread and fill the area.

COLOR PHOTOGRAPHY:
Carl Tremblay

ILLUSTRATION:
Judy Love

STYLING:
Ritch Holben

NOW YOU CAN CREATE THE SHIMmering shifts of color associated with expensive velvet using cold water dyes and a simple dyeing technique. All you need is your choice of dyes in different colors and a narrow band of silk velvet. Begin by selecting a light-colored silk velvet. Silk velvet is not actually pure silk, but 18% silk and 84% rayon. The fabric backing is silk and the pile is rayon, creating a soft, pliable blend with a fluid-like drape.

Next, choose two contrasting dye colors. (Tinfix design dyes come in over 100 colors.) If you want to add a pattern, such as the polka dots, choose a light color dye for one side of the scarf, and a medium to dark color for the polka dots and the reverse side. These fabric dyes are highly concentrated pigments and need to be diluted before using. As the directions explain, you should test smaller swatches of the velvet in your dye baths and adjust the dilution to achieve the color you want.

To make a polka dot design, always dye the lighter background color first. Be sure to lay the wet dyed pieces flat on large plastic garbage bags to let them dry. If you hang the fabric, the color will migrate, resulting in a stronger color intensity at the lower edge. Once the fabric has dried completely, you can print a simple pattern. I used the round

Making the Scarf

hour blocks. A garage floor is ideal since you can open the doors for ventilation. Cover surface with several plastic trash bags to accommodate velvet strips which must dry flat. Set up a separate area for each strip to prevent colors from running together. Set equipment nearby.

3. *Presoak silk velvet.* Put on rubber gloves. Fill one bowl with 2 quarts warm water, add ⅛ cup soda ash, and stir with large plastic spoon. Wait several minutes, then restir until fully dissolved. Immerse both velvet strips in solution until fibers become fully saturated and no air pockets remain (illustration B). Add test swatches to solution. Let all the fabric soak 10 minutes.

4. *Mix 2 dye baths.* Use separate bowl for each dye color. Referring to dye recipe chart, measure appropriate amount of water into each bowl. Measure and add liquid dye to each bowl, stirring to dissolve. Dunk test swatches in each solution to test the color saturation. For richer, deeper color, add more dye; to lighten color, add more water. Retest with new swatches until desired two colors are achieved. Keep in mind that color will look darker when wet. Lay test swatches on plastic to dry.

5. *Dye velvet strips.* Wearing rubber gloves, lift one velvet strip from soda ash solution, wring gently, and transfer to first dye solution. Swirl fabric through dye for several minutes, rearranging folds to expose every surface (illustration C). Lift dyed strip gently by one edge, and allow water to drain off (do not wring or twist); lay flat on plastic. Using wide, flat paintbrush, smooth out creases and folds, working from middle out to edges. Try to eliminate as many tiny pockets as possible, since dye will pool in them and dry to a darker color (illustration D). Brush back over edges to erase any fingerprints made during transfer. Repeat process to dye second strip in second color. Periodically sop up excess water around strip edges with sponge. If printing polka dots, reserve darker dye, otherwise wash dyebaths down drain. Let strips dry flat overnight, or until damp-dry. Transfer velvet to fresh plastic, and let rest until bone-dry (up to 48 hours). Do not line-dry, since colors will migrate.

6. *Print polka dots (optional).* Lay lighter dyed strip right side up on fresh, dry plastic. Slip several paper towels under strip to serve as blotters. Dip round foam applicator pad of envelope moistener in reserved darker dye. Blot pad to shed excess liquid. To print dot, touch pad lightly to velvet, press gently, and lift. Repeat process to print dots at random over surface of velvet strip. To prevent running, always use paper towel blotter underneath area being printed; change to fresh towels as needed (illustration E).

Transfer velvet to fresh plastic, and let rest until bone-dry (up to 48 hours).

7. *Dry and cure velvet.* Protect ironing board with white fabric; place velvet on top, wrong side up. To set colors, heat steam iron to hottest (linen) setting. Holding iron so it hovers just above surface of fabric, let steam penetrate fibers. Do not let weight of iron press down on velvet at any time. Let cool. Rinse velvet in basin of cool water to remove any lingering soda ash residue and dye. Squeeze gently under water until no more color is released. Dry flat on plastic 24 to 28 hours.

8. *Sew scarf.* Place two velvet strips right sides together and edges matching; pin edges. Machine-stitch ½" from edge

all around, leaving 5" opening for turning on one long edge (illustration F). Clip corners diagonally. Turn right side out. Slipstitch opening closed. ◆

A. Cut two strips of light-colored silk velvet.

B. To help the dyes set, presoak the strips in a soda ash solution.

C. Dye each strip a separate color.

D. Lay each dyed strip on plastic and brush out the wrinkles.

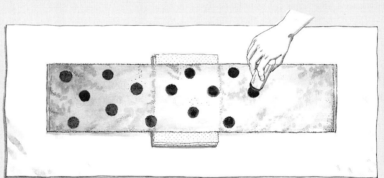

E. When the strip is bone-dry, you can print the polka dots.

F. Sew strips together to make a reversible scarf.

TINFIX DYE RECIPES
(for Pictured Scarves)

SOLID SCARF
- Side 1: 5 teaspoons #64 Mineral Green, 2 cups water
- Side 2: 5 teaspoons #83 Helios Brown, 2 cups water

POLKA DOT SCARF
- Side 1: 5 teaspoons #43 Indian Purple, 3 cups water
- Side 2: 5 teaspoons #65 Pine Green, 2 cups water

Bedpost Sachet

A new use for sachets: to induce a relaxing and peaceful sleep.

BY DAWN ANDERSON

MATERIALS
Makes one sachet

- 1¹/₂ cups dried chamomile flowers
- 1¹/₂ cups dried lavender flowers
- ¹/₄ yard 45"-wide:
  royal lilac silk dupioni
  mustard silk dupioni
  purple metallic organza
  gold metallic organza
- ³/₈ yard cotton batting
- ³/₈ yard gold metallic cord
- Amethyst bee button
- ⁵/₈" gold filigree bead
- 220-yard spools thread:
  light gold rayon
  medium gold rayon
  gold metallic
- Thread to match fabrics

You'll also need:
diamond pattern (*see* page 46); sewing machine; iron; sewing shears; tapestry needle; embroidery needle; hand-sewing needle; pins; point turner; masking tape; 5"-square corrugated cardboard; and small box or bag.

Fabric diamonds are sewn together patchwork style to make this hanging sachet pillow.

S HEER ORGANZA LAYERED OVER silk dupioni creates the shimmering opalescence of this sachet. Designed with a cord that can slip over a bedpost or a doorknob, the sachet is more than just a beautiful room accent. The filling is lavender and chamomile, herbs that offer a variety of natural benefits and may just coax you to sleep.

Lavender's soothing scent is sweet, flowery, balsamy, and light. Historically, it has been used to ease headaches, drive away nightmares, and lift spirits. Chamomile is sweet also, and its fragrance has spicy-green and slightly fruity notes. It, too, has multiple healing properties, and has been used to relieve insom-

nia, reduce stress and anxiety, and soothe muscular aches and pains.

Because silk and organza are slippery, I found it easier to make accurate cuts with sewing shears than with a rotary cutter. I also recommend that you hand-baste the seams before machine stitching.

Dawn Anderson is a writer and designer living in Redmond, Washington.

INSTRUCTIONS
Making the Tassel
1. *Wind tassel.* Tape thread ends from three gold spools to 5"-square cardboard. Contain spools in small box or bag, then hold three threads together and wind

them around cardboard 300 times. Tape free ends and clip from spools. Thread tapestry needle with six 14" strands of the gold thread. Slip needle between cardboard and wrapped threads at middle and pull strands through halfway. Repeat to make double wrap at middle of square. Pull ends snug, and tie square knot (*see* illustration A, next page). On reverse side, clip across threads at middle to release hank from cardboard.

2. *Bind tassel neck.* Hold three gold threads together; do not clip from spools. Make small loop 7" from end and press against top of hank. Begin winding spool thread around hank, trapping loop as you go (illustration B). Continue winding snugly for ¹/₄". To end off, clip threads from spools and draw loose ends through loop. Pull gently but firmly at both ends until loop disappears down into neck of tassel. Press using cool, dry iron (rayon setting). Trim tassel threads evenly across bottom (illustration C).

Making the Sachet
1. *Cut diamonds.* Using pattern (*see* page 46), cut four diamonds each from lilac silk, mustard silk, purple organza, and gold organza. Place an organza diamond on similar-colored silk diamond; hand-baste ¹/₄" from raw edges all around. Repeat to make eight layered diamonds.

2. *Sew harlequin diamonds.* Place one purple and one gold diamond right sides together, matching one edge and offsetting others. Machine-stitch ³/₈" from matched edge (illustration D). Open this pair and finger-press seam (illustration E). Repeat to sew a second pair. To join two pairs, lay one pair flat, right side up. Lay

COLOR PHOTOGRAPHY:
Carl Tremblay

ILLUSTRATION:
Judy Love

STYLING:
Ritch Holben

Making the Tassel

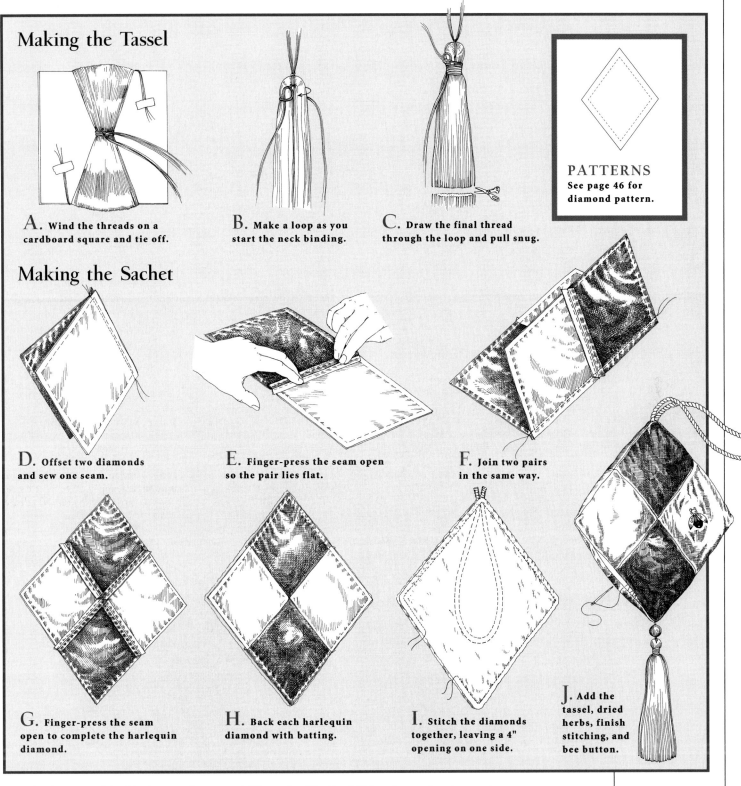

A. Wind the threads on a cardboard square and tie off.

B. Make a loop as you start the neck binding.

C. Draw the final thread through the loop and pull snug.

PATTERNS
See page 46 for diamond pattern.

Making the Sachet

D. Offset two diamonds and sew one seam.

E. Finger-press the seam open so the pair lies flat.

F. Join two pairs in the same way.

G. Finger-press the seam open to complete the harlequin diamond.

H. Back each harlequin diamond with batting.

I. Stitch the diamonds together, leaving a 4" opening on one side.

J. Add the tassel, dried herbs, finish stitching, and bee button.

second pair on top, right side down, and match edges so purple fabric is visible at each end and seams align; stitch ⅜" from edge (illustration F). Finger-press long seam open (illustration G). Repeat process to make second diamond.

3. *Assemble pillow.* Using harlequin diamond as template, cut two diamonds from cotton batting. Line each harlequin diamond with batting and baste all around (illustration H) . Cut 14" length of gold cord. Flatten cord ends, and baste to upper point of harlequin diamond. Stack harlequin diamonds right sides together, matching edges and seams and sandwiching cord inside. Machine-stitch ⅜" from edge all around, leaving 4" opening on one side (illustration I). Trim seam allowances to ⅛" (do not trim opening); clip corners. Turn right side out, and push out points.

4. *Complete assembly.* Using embroidery needle, draw three tassel head threads through filigree bead and into lower point of harlequin diamond. Repeat with remaining three threads. Knot ends together on inside of sachet. Fill cavity with dried chamomile and lavender. Slipstitch opening closed. Sew bee button to gold diamond (illustration J). ◆

Gilt Scallop Shell Tray

Re-create the style of opulent porcelain salt cellars by transforming a simple shell into a decorative tray.

COLOR PHOTOGRAPHY:
Carl Tremblay

ILLUSTRATION:
Michael Gellatly

STYLING:
Ritch Holben

BY MICHIO RYAN

THIS MINIATURE TRAY CAN BE USED as a ring holder on a dresser, as a soap or sachet holder in a powder room, or as a salt cellar on a holiday table. The smooth, lustrous gold interior surface contrasts with the textured silver of the rough underside. Three oversized faceted pearls serve as feet.

The gold-colored leaf, actually composed of brass, will tarnish or turn green if exposed directly to acidic items like soap, but a protective finish of epoxy applied under and over the gold leaf prevents direct contact. The inner surface of the shell can be directly leafed, but I found that applying epoxy as a base under the leaf yielded a liquid gold surface that resembled mercury.

Epoxy is a two-part compound that yields a thick, resinous finish with just one coat. Make sure to spread the epoxy over the outer edge to provide a complete seal. Though the epoxy finish is nontoxic after it dries, the shell should not be used to hold hot foods.

Though many types of shells can be used for this project, a scallop is the most suitable since it is flat and wide. If you don't already have one, scallop shells, also called pectens, can be purchased for as little as $1 or $2 apiece. If you want to make a salt cellar, a mussel might also be used; its elongated shape would complement a resting salt spoon.

INSTRUCTIONS

1. *Prepare shell surface.* Rub both sides of shell with moist 220-grit emery paper to smooth gritty areas. Sand down thin, sharp rim until blunt.

2. *Attach pearl feet.* Tape three pearls to outer shell—two near front edge and one near hinge. Test balance; shell should not touch table top and dish should be level. Adjust or substitute pearls as needed (I used a smaller pearl near the hinge). Mix 5-minute epoxy on scrap cardboard with toothpick; let set until no longer runny. Affix two front pearls first, then rear pearl (*see illustration A, right*). Stand upright and let dry 15 minutes.

3. *Seal shell surface.* Following manufacturer's instructions, mix one teaspoon epoxy sealer in disposable cup. Brush light coat onto inner shell and rim (illustration B). Blow gently across surface to dissipate tiny bubbles. Set in well-ventilated place, and cover with overturned bowl to keep off dust. Let cure 24 hours, or until hard. Remove specks and lint using moistened 600-grit emery or your fingertip.

4. *Apply gold and silver leaf.* Lay newsprint on work surface. Brush thin coat of size on inner shell and rim; tilt shell to prevent pooling. Clean brush with mineral spirits. When size reaches tack (1 to 3 hours), transfer gold leaf sheet to copy paper. Tear into irregular 1" pieces. Apply leaf to shell surface and tamp down with brush to gild entire inner shell and rim (illustration C). Let dry 24 hours. Buff lightly with cotton ball. Remove fingerprints using cotton ball moistened with rubbing alcohol. Seal gilded area, as in step 3. After seal dries, coat outer shell with silver leaf, avoiding legs and rim; do not seal. ◆

This glowing scallop shell can hold a variety of items, from jewelry to dinner mints. Instead of pearl feet, try substituting jade, quartz, glass, or Chinese cloisonné beads.

MATERIALS
Makes one shell tray

- 5" to 6" scallop shell
- Several large baroque pearls in various sizes (you will use three)
- Gold composition leaf
- Silver composition leaf
- Gold size
- Epoxy sealer
- 5-minute epoxy

You'll also need:
220- and 600-grit wet/dry emery paper; 2 disposable ¾" bristle brushes; ¼" masking tape; mineral spirits (to clean size from brush); rubbing alcohol; medium-size bowl; butter knife; cotton balls; toothpicks or small craft sticks; small disposable plastic cup; 1 sheet white paper; newsprint; and scrap cardboard.

DESIGNER'S TIP

If you harvest your own shells, soak them in several changes of fresh tap water to remove the salt. Let the shells dry one or two days before leafing.

Making a Scallop Shell Tray

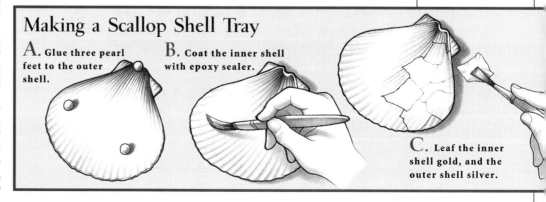

A. Glue three pearl feet to the outer shell.

B. Coat the inner shell with epoxy sealer.

C. Leaf the inner shell gold, and the outer shell silver.

Drawer-Liner Sachets

Use these delicately scented rice paper envelopes to freshen your drawers.

☙ BY ELIZABETH CAMERON

COLOR PHOTOGRAPHY:
Carl Tremblay

ILLUSTRATION:
Michael Gellatly

STYLING:
Ritch Holben

THERE IS SOMETHING INDESCRIBABLY luxurious about being greeted by the scent of lavender or freesia every time you open a drawer. These sachets are essentially rice paper envelopes of potpourri that lie flat along the bottom surface of your drawer.

Take your drawer measurements along when you go to the art supply store to select your sheets of rice paper. Choose lightweight rice papers that will allow the scent to circulate; you will need to buy two sheets for each drawer. Cut the rice paper with a rotary cutter or sewing shears as you would a fabric. The fibers that make up rice paper are longer and tougher than those in wood pulp papers so using an X-Acto knife may tear through them rather than produce a clean cut. Once cut to size, glue two sheets together on three edges to create a pouch, then fill it with any combination of dried flowers or potpourri.

It's not necessary to decorate your sachet, since the shapes of the petals and leaves will show through the diaphanous papers and can be quite pretty on their own, but I decided to add gold accents to dress up the sachets for gift giving. To create corner accents I used fan-shaped jewelry findings snipped in half to yield quarter-circles. I also added a monogram with gold letters. Small triangles of Velcro on the underside of each corner hold the sachet secure at the bottom of the drawer.

These sachets are so fast to assemble that you could line your entire dresser in an afternoon.

MATERIALS
Makes one custom-size liner

- **1 to 2 sheets rice paper**
- **Dried flowers or herbs (e.g., rose petals, freesia, lavender)**
- **Two 1½" gold filigree fans**
- **1" to 2" gold foil letters (for monogram)**
- **1" x 2" strip white self-adhesive Velcro**
- **Yes Stikflat glue**

You'll also need: rotary cutter; quilter's acrylic grid ruler; self-healing cutting mat; tape measure; scissors; tin snips; and flat, stiff 1" brush.

DESIGNER'S TIP

Drawer liner sachets make distinctive shower gifts. Choose a rice paper with a lacy pattern and embellish it with the bride's new monogram.

INSTRUCTIONS

1. *Make rice paper envelope.* Measure inside drawer bottom, e.g., 15" x 30". Using rotary cutter, grid ruler, and mat, cut two rectangles of rice paper ⅛" larger than bottom of drawer. Brush ½" strip of glue around three edges of one sheet. Place second sheet on top, align edges, and press to adhere (*see* illustration A, right). Let dry 10 minutes. Use cutting tools to trim uneven edges and to square corners. Test-fit in drawer, and retrim if necessary.

2. *Decorate sleeve.* Center monogram letters on sleeve front, glue, and press to adhere. Using tin snips, cut each gold filigree fan in half to yield two quarter circles. Glue one quarter circle to each corner (illustration B).

3. *Fill sleeve.* Insert dried petals or herbs in sleeve, allowing approximately ⅛ cup for every 25-square-inch area (5" x 5"). Distribute dried material evenly, adding or removing material as needed so sleeve lies

flat. Glue opening closed (illustration C).

4. *Add Velcro.* Using scissors, cut Velcro into two 1" squares, then cut each square in half diagonally. Separate each triangle into hook and loop pieces. Affix

hook triangles to back of sleeve at each corner (top left corner of illustration C). Affix loop triangles to drawer floor at corners. Set liner in drawer and press down on corners to adhere. ◆

Making the Drawer Liner

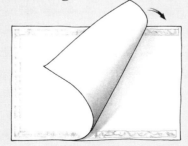

A. Glue two pieces of rice paper together on three sides.

B. Add a gold foil monogram and corner trim.

C. Fill the sachet and glue the fourth side closed. Affix Velcro to sachet and drawer corners.

Satin and Ribbon Tissue Wrap

Conceal a stack of tissues with a reversible Hollywood-style slipcase.

BY ELIZABETH CAMERON

As your stack of tissues diminishes, fold or crimp the fabric panels back and redo the ties.

COLOR PHOTOGRAPHY:
Carl Tremblay

ILLUSTRATION:
Mary Newell DePalma

DESIGN:
Chippy Irvine

STYLING:
Ritch Holben

MATERIALS
Makes one tissue slipcase

- ¼ yard 45"-wide fabric (for outside)
- ¼ yard 45"-wide fabric (for lining)
- 1¾ yards ribbon (for outside trim)
- 1⅔ yards ribbon (for outside ties)
- 1⅔ yards ribbon (for inside ties)
- Thread to match fabrics and trim ribbon
- Box of tissues

You'll also need:
sewing machine; iron; rotary cutter; self-healing cutting mat; quilter's acrylic cutting guide; and pins.

THIS PROJECT REVIVES THE decorated tissue box — but without the box! Made with a combination of satin remnants and colorful, contrasting ribbons, this reversible slipcase, designed to hold a stack of self-dispensing tissues, makes a beautiful accessory for your bathroom.

The featured slipcase is made from satin, but you could also use silk, cotton, or linen. For an interesting variation, consider recycling vintage napkins, placemats, or upholstery fabric. Plaids, prints, stripes, embroidered fabrics, or florals might be used to underline the spirit of a season.

Once you have selected the fabrics, choose coordinating ribbons. I recommend a stiff-bodied ribbon, such as grosgrain or embroidered cotton, for the trim. One exception is twill tape, which coordinates well with a striped ticking or denim. The ribbons that tie the tissue in place can be softer. Rayon, silk, flat metallic, and wire-edged ribbons are suitable.

INSTRUCTIONS

1. *Cut fabric and ribbon.* Using rotary cutter, cutting guide, and mat, cut one 5½" x 20½" rectangle and two 5½" x 10½" rectangles from each fabric. Cut trim ribbon into six 10½" lengths. Cut remaining ribbon to yield four 15" outside ties and four 15" inside ties.

2. *Sew two side panels.* Place two small contrasting rectangles right sides together and edges matching. Using ¼" seam allowance, stitch one long edge (*see* illustration A, next page). Open flat and press seam open (illustration B). On right side, place trim ribbon perpendicular to seam at each end, concealing raw edge. Topstitch inner ribbon edge (illustration C). Fold entire piece in half, right side in. Stitch remaining long edge, securing ribbon ends in seam (illustration D). Turn piece right side out and press. Stitch each short end closed through both ribbon layers (illustration E). Repeat process to sew second side panel.

3. *Sew slipcase base.* Lay large lining rectangle flat, right side up. For ribbon tie placement, measure 7½" in from each corner and mark long edge with pin. Secure one inside tie and one outside tie at each pin, outside tie on top (illustration F). Place remaining fabric rectangle on top, right sides together and edges matching. Sew one long edge, trapping ties in seam where pinned. Proceed as in step 2 to press seam open, add ribbon trim at sides, sew remaining edge, and topstitch ribbon at each end (illustration G).

4. *Assemble slipcase.* Lay base flat, lining face up. On one long edge, fold inside ties onto lining but let outside ties extend off fabric. Lay side panel on top, lining face down, so base extends evenly at each side. Stitch side panel to base along long edge through all layers. Repeat process to join remaining side panel (illustration H).

5. *Enclose tissues in slipcase* (illustrations I through M). ◆

Making the Slipcase

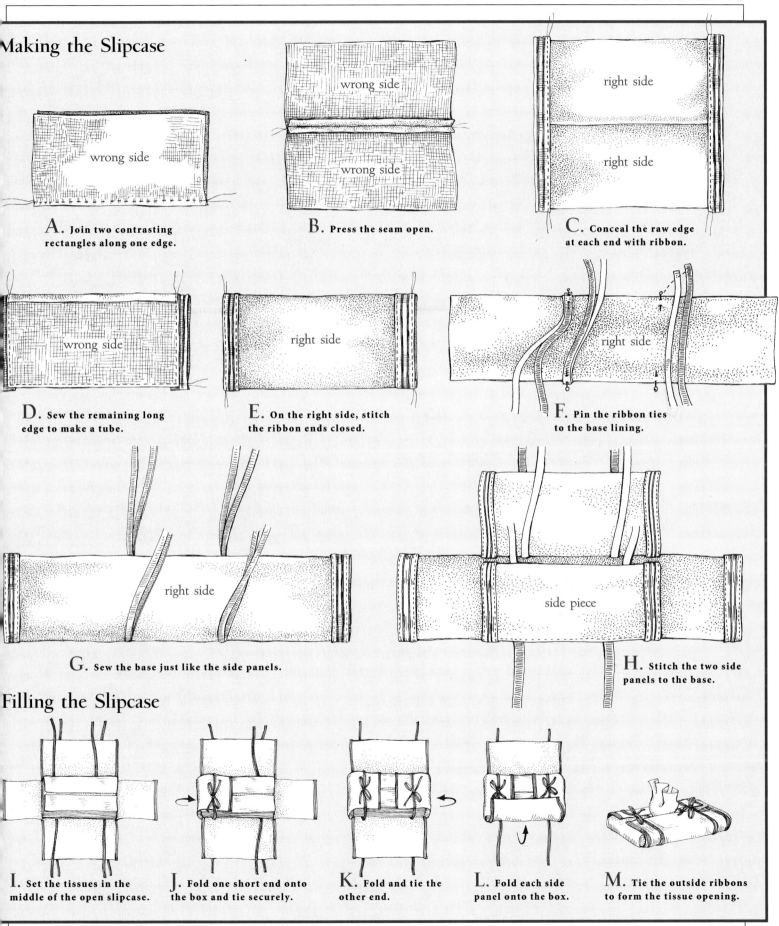

A. Join two contrasting rectangles along one edge.

B. Press the seam open.

C. Conceal the raw edge at each end with ribbon.

D. Sew the remaining long edge to make a tube.

E. On the right side, stitch the ribbon ends closed.

F. Pin the ribbon ties to the base lining.

G. Sew the base just like the side panels.

H. Stitch the two side panels to the base.

Filling the Slipcase

I. Set the tissues in the middle of the open slipcase.

J. Fold one short end onto the box and tie securely.

K. Fold and tie the other end.

L. Fold each side panel onto the box.

M. Tie the outside ribbons to form the tissue opening.

Patchwork Velvet Floor Cloth

Create a luxurious patchwork floor cloth out of multicolored upholstery-weight velvet.

❧ BY CHIPPY IRVINE

This floor cloth measures 48" x 64" and is made from seven colors of velvet. The rich color scheme is inspired by Amish quilting designs.

MATERIALS
Makes 48" x 64" floor cloth

- **60"-wide upholstery-weight velvet:**
  1¾ yards teal (for border)
  ⅜ yard maroon
  ¼ yard each of black, royal blue, olive, honey, and yellow
- **2 yards 60"-wide natural linen (for backing)**
- **Matching sewing thread**

You'll also need:
sewing machine with walking foot; iron; velvet board; rotary cutter; quilter's acrylic grid ruler; self-healing cutting mat; scissors; light and dark fabric-marking pencils; hand-sewing needle; and pins.

give firm footing and a neat finish. Any firm fabric can be used, as it will not show. We used a natural heavy linen, which is the traditional backing, but it would also be fine to use firmly woven plain or printed cloth. Unusual backings are often seen on vintage floor cloths. The floor cloth is softest underfoot when laid over wall to wall carpeting, an area rug, or a nonskid rug padding.

Chippy Irvine is a crafts designer living in Patterson, New York.

INSTRUCTIONS

1. *Cut velvet pieces.* Using rotary cutter, grid ruler, and mat, cut the following: From teal velvet, cut two 5" x 57" strips on lengthwise grain (parallel to selvage) and two 5" x 41" strips on crosswise grain (perpendicular to selvage). From all seven fabrics, cut five 9" squares each. From leftover maroon fabric, cut four 5" squares. Mark arrow on back of each piece to note nap direction.

2. *Lay out design.* Work on the floor or other ample flat surface. Referring to illustration A, arrange 9" squares in a grid of 7 rows and 5 columns. Lay teal strips around edges and 5" maroon squares in four outer corners. (Edges will match once seams are sewn.) Arrange all pieces so nap runs in same direction.

3. *Sew patchwork grid.* Start with right-hand column. Turn top square facedown on square directly below it, edges matching. Pin top edges together to prevent slipping, then machine-stitch through both layers, making ½" seam. Repeat process to join second square to third

DESIGNER'S TIP

A velvet board is a shallow bed made up of thousands of tiny vertical needles. When velvet fabric is pressed (always from the wrong side), the needles hold the pile up off the surface and prevent the weight, heat, and steam of the iron from crushing or matting the fibers.

COLOR PHOTOGRAPHY:
Carl Tremblay

ILLUSTRATION:
Judy Love

DESIGN:
Michio Ryan

STYLING:
Ritch Holben

STEP OUT OF BED ONTO THIS LUSH and welcoming floor cloth. Made of differently colored patches of furnishing-weight velvet, this floor cloth can stand up to a surprising amount of hard wear.

When selecting velvet for this project, choose colors that enhance—or establish—the color scheme of your bedroom. The patchwork floor cloth depicted in the photograph has a border of teal velvet anchored at each corner by four squares of maroon. To suit your particular bedroom, you may prefer to make a three-color floor cloth. For instance, make the patchwork in a simple checkerboard arrangement of light and dark colors, and the border in a third, medium shade.

The direction of the nap is important in this project. On the vertical grain, parallel to the selvages, velvets stroke smooth in one direction and rough in the other, giving an amazing variance in the richness of the color. The variance is less pronounced across the grain. Be sure all the pieces in this project have their nap running in the same direction. A good idea is to mark or notch each piece as you cut it to indicate nap direction. This way, if the cut pieces get mixed up, you can easily re-sort them.

The floor cloth should be backed to

Making the Patchwork Velvet Floor Cloth

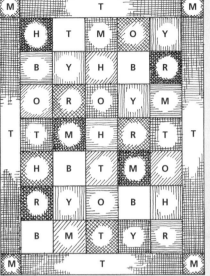

B = Black
R = Royal Blue
T = Teal
M= Maroon
O = Olive
H = Honey
Y = Yellow

A. Cut and arrange the velvet pieces.

B. Sew the velvet squares together in a patchwork grid.

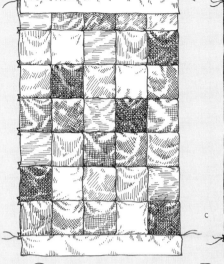

C. Sew the shorter border strips to the patchwork.

D. Add the border corner squares to the longer strips.

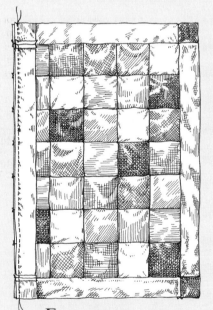

E. Join the longer strips to the patchwork.

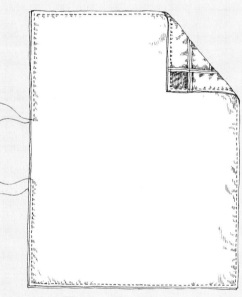

F. Sew a linen lining to the patchwork piece.

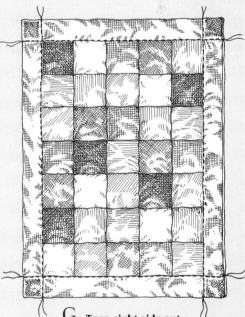

G. Turn right side out and stitch in the "ditch."

square, third to fourth, and so on until entire column is joined. Press seams open, using velvet board to prevent flattening. Assemble remaining columns in same way, then sew columns together to complete patchwork grid (illustration B).

4. *Sew borders.* Pin shorter border strip to corresponding edge of grid, right sides together. Stitch ½" from edges. Press seam open. Repeat on opposite edge (illustration C). Sew 5" maroon squares to ends of remaining border strips (illustration D). Sew these strips to the two remaining sides, matching seams (illustration E). Press seams open.

5. *Line floor cloth.* Lay linen fabric flat, right side up, and smooth out wrinkles. Lay patchwork face down on top. Pin all around through both layers. Trim off excess linen even with patchwork. Sew ½" from edge all around, leaving 14" opening on one edge for turning (illustration F). Press seam allowance toward linen all around. Along opening, press back linen edge ½". Trim seams to ¼", and trim corners diagonally. Turn right side out, and slipstitch opening closed. Press edge all around so linen rolls toward underside and is not visible from top.

6. *Stabilize lining.* Lay floor cloth flat. Pin patchwork layer to lining along border seams all around. Using teal upper thread and natural-colored bobbin thread, stitch in the border seam "ditch" all around. The stitching will sink into seam and be invisible from right side (illustration G). ◆

Fall 1998 Patterns

Scented Modular Candles

(*see* article, page 12)

NOTE: PHOTOCOPY AT 100%.

CUTTING DIAGRAM

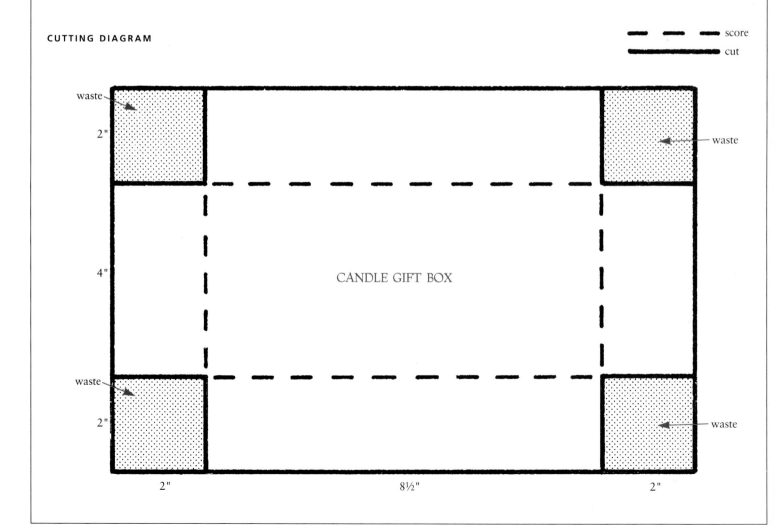

Little Red Schoolhouse Clock

(*see* article, page 28)

NOTE: PHOTOCOPY AT 100%.

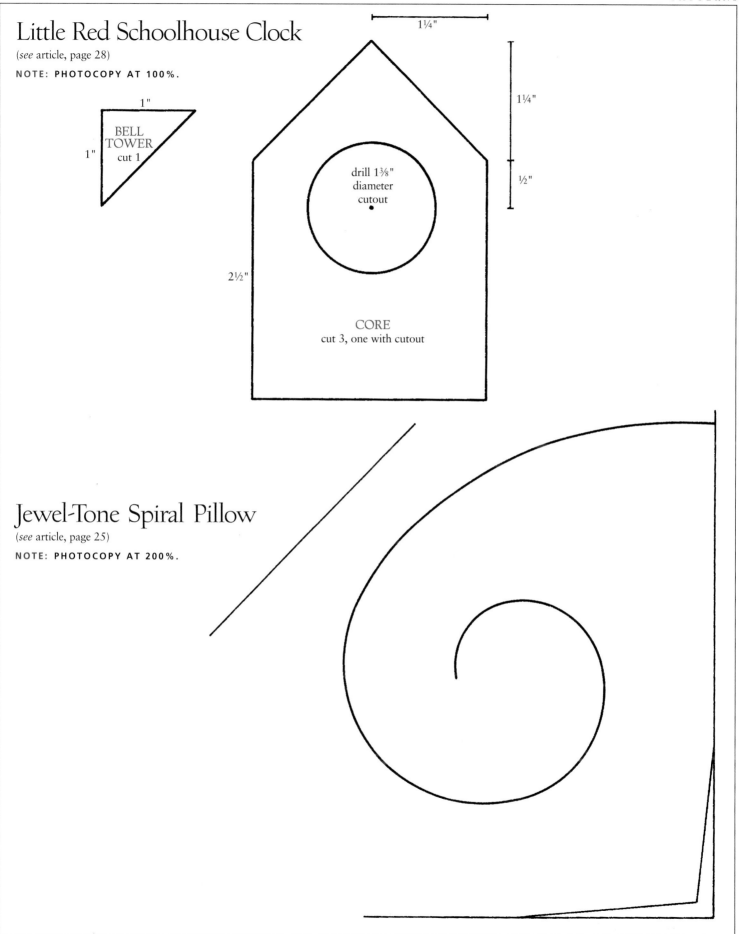

1"

BELL
TOWER
cut 1

1"

1¼"

1¼"

½"

drill 1⅜"
diameter
cutout

2½"

CORE
cut 3, one with cutout

Jewel-Tone Spiral Pillow

(*see* article, page 25)

NOTE: PHOTOCOPY AT 200%.

Bedpost Sachet

(*see* article, page 36)

NOTE: PHOTOCOPY AT 100%.

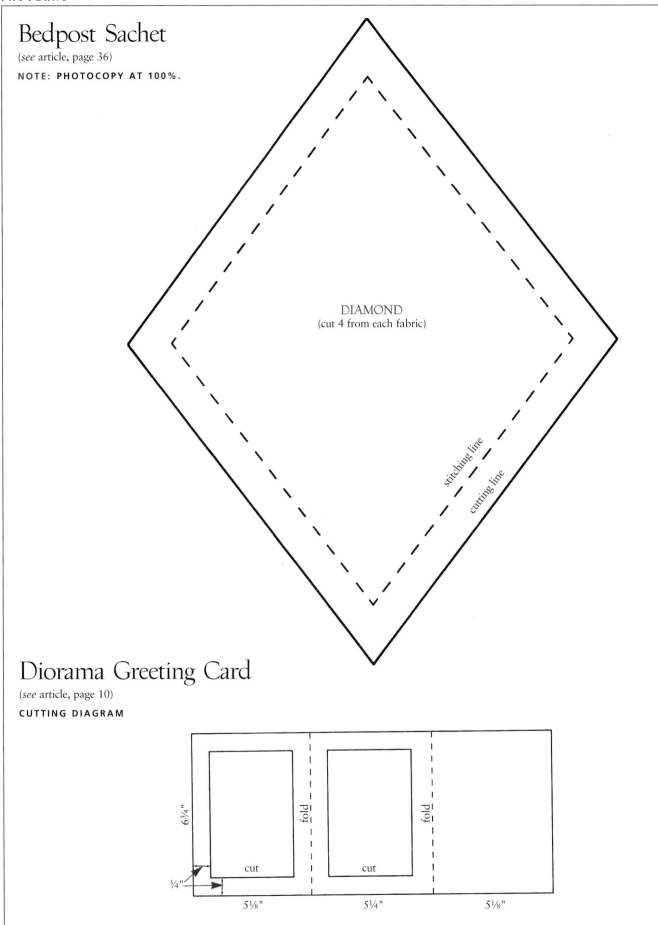

DIAMOND
(cut 4 from each fabric)

stitching line

cutting line

Diorama Greeting Card

(*see* article, page 10)

CUTTING DIAGRAM

6¾"

fold

fold

cut

cut

¾"

5⅛"

5¼"

5⅛"

Pop-Up Jester

(*see* article, page 30)

NOTE: PHOTOCOPY AT 200%.

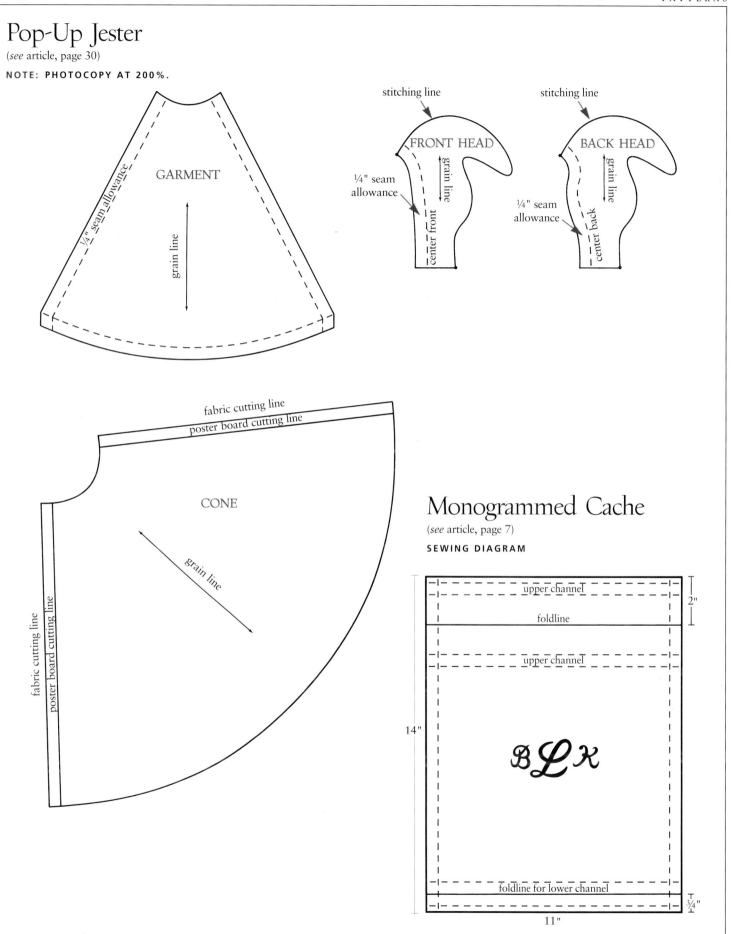

GARMENT

¼" seam allowance

grain line

stitching line

FRONT HEAD

¼" seam allowance

grain line

center front

stitching line

BACK HEAD

¼" seam allowance

grain line

center back

fabric cutting line

poster board cutting line

CONE

grain line

fabric cutting line

poster board cutting line

Monogrammed Cache

(*see* article, page 7)

SEWING DIAGRAM

upper channel

2"

foldline

upper channel

14"

𝓑𝓛𝓚

foldline for lower channel

¾"

11"

Sources & Resources

The following are specific mail-order sources for particular items, arranged by article.

Most of the materials used in this issue are available at your local craft supply store, florist, fabric shop, hardware store, or bead and jewelry supply store. Generic craft supplies can be ordered from catalogs such as Craft King, Pearl Paint Company, or Sunshine Discount Crafts. The following are specific sources for harder-to-find items, arranged by article. The suggested retail prices listed here were current at press time. Contact the suppliers directly to confirm prices and availability.

The Perfect Gift, *page 7*
Iron-on monograms ranging from 79 cents to $2, made by Joy Insignia.

How To Make Lip Balm, *page 8*
Waxes starting at $1.50 for 1 oz., carrier oils starting at $1.50 for 4 oz., and tins for 35 cents each (#LTIN), all available from Lavender Lane. Fragrances, $3-$4 for 1 oz., from Sweet Cakes Soapmaking Supplies. Pigments starting at $8 for a 2 oz. jar available from Simple Pleasures. Pébéo products available through Pearl Paint, starting at $2.97.

Scented Modular Candles, *page 12*
Beeswax for $9/lb.; parafin $6.60 for 5.5 lbs.; Vybar #103, $5.67 for 8 oz.; color chips for 89 cents each; and #2 square braided wicks, 3 yards for 68 cents, all available from Pourette. Fragrances, $3-$4 for 1 oz., from Sweet Cakes Soapmaking Supplies.

Frosted Almonds, *page 14*
Candy boxes $4.55 for a pack of 10 from Sweet Celebrations; tulle circles, $1.99 for 25 from Sunshine Discount Crafts.

Harvest Wheat Bouquet, *page 16*
Wheat stems available in ½ lb. bunches for $8 from J & T Imports Dried Flowers.

Bracelet-Style Napkin Ring, *page 17*
Japanese seed beads starting at $1.90 for 40 grams and accent beads starting at $2.45 for 10 from Fire Mountain Gems; 1½" grape cluster bead for 30 cents from Hands of the Hills.

Boiled Wool Traveling Blanket, *page 18*
Knitted boiled wool $30 per yard and black iron-on tape for $10 a roll available from Karen's Kreations.

Thanksgiving Floral Turkey, *page 20*
Cattails available during the Fall, 100 stems for $12 from J & T Imports Dried Flowers.

Gift Card Ideas, *page 22*
Brass charms $3.99 for an assorted package of 12+ from Craft Catalog. Staffordshire teapot stamp for $12 from Make an Impression. White envelopes and glassine envelopes available in packages of 20 (assorted sizes) for $3; monogram stamps starting at $4.25 all from Impress. Embossing powder available from Craft King, starting at $1.99 for ½ ounce.

Jewel-Tone Spiral Pillow, *page 25*
Silk dupioni for $9.95 per yard from Super Silk.

Rhinestone Partridge, *page 26*
Bird (item # FPHK212) for $1.60 from Craft Catalog. Red glass bird eyes, 4mm, 12 pairs for $11.35 from Carver's Eye. One-leg clips $3 for a package of 3 from D. Blumchen & Company. Flat back Austrian crystal rhinestones starting at $6.75 for ½ gram from Rings & Things.

Little Red Schoolhouse Clock, *page 28*
Wood for 59 cents to $3 from Pearl Paint (order from New York store). Bells starting at 59 cents for 2 from Craft King. Clock movement (item # 15209) $7.25 from Klockit.

Pop-Up Jester, *page 30*
Silk dupioni for $9.95 per yard from Super Silk; Amaco face for $2 from Pearl Paint (order from Massachusetts store).

Decorative Memo Blocks, *page 33*
Memo blocks for $5.25 from Impress.

Reversible Silk Velvet Scarf, *page 34*
Tinfix silk dye $7.50 for 3.5 fl. oz. from Pearl Paint.

Bedpost Sachet, *page 36*
Silk dupioni for $9.95 per yard from Super Silk. Bee button $1.50 each from On the Button. Dried chamomile and lavender from San Francisco Herb Co.

Gilt Scallop Shell Tray, *page 38*
Epoxy $7.39 for 1 pint from Craft King. Composition leaf starting at $4.20 for 1 book from Pearl Paint.

Drawer-Liner Sachets, *page 39*
Filigree fans (#MC1406) $6 for 12 from Craft Catalog.

Quick Projects, *page 49*
Mylar foil bag (silver or gold) for 60 cents each and paint cans for $1.50 each, available from Impress.

❧   ❧   ❧   ❧   ❧

The following companies are mentioned in the listing above. Contact each individually for a price list or catalog.

CARVER'S EYE COMPANY
P.O. Box 1118, Gresham, OR 97030; 503-666-5680

CRAFT CATALOG
800-777-1442

CRAFT KING
800-769-9494

D. BLUMCHEN & COMPANY
P.O. Box 1210, Ridgewood, NJ 07451-1210; 201-652-5595

FIRE MOUNTAIN GEMS
800-423-2319

HANDS OF THE HILLS
3016 78th Avenue SE, Mercer Island, WA 98040; 206-232-8121

IMPRESS
120 Andover Park East, Tukwila, WA 98188; 206-901-9101

J & T IMPORTS DRIED FLOWERS
P.O. Box 642, Solana Beach, CA 92075; 619-481-9781; www.driedflowers.com

JOY INSIGNIA COMPANY
888-CALL JOY for the retailer nearest you.

KAREN'S KREATIONS
6542 125th Ave. S.E., Bellevue, WA 98006; 425-643-9809

KLOCKIT
P.O. Box 636, Lake Geneva, WI 53147 800-KLOCKIT

LAVENDER LANE
7337 #1 Roseville Rd., Sacramento, CA 95842; 916-334-4400

MAKE AN IMPRESSION
Gilman Village, 317 NW Gilman Blvd. #16, Issaquah, WA 98027; 425-557-9247

ON THE BUTTON
800-473-0470

PEARL PAINT COMPANY
800-451-PEARL (fine arts catalog) or 800-221-6845 x2297 (NY store); 617-547-6600 (MA store)

POURETTE
PO Box 15220, Seattle, WA 98115; 206-789-3188; www.pourette.com

RINGS & THINGS
800-366-2156; www.Rings-Things.com

SAN FRANCISCO HERB COMPANY
800-227-4530; www.sfherb.com

SIMPLE PLEASURES
P.O. Box 194, Old Saybrook, CT 06475; 860-395-0085; http://members.aol.com/pigmntlady/

SUNSHINE DISCOUNT CRAFTS
800-729-2878; www.sunshinecrafts.com

SUPER SILK
P.O. Box 527596, Flushing, NY 11352; 800-432-SILK

SWEET CAKES SOAPMAKING SUPPLIES
249 North Road, Kinnelon, NJ 07405; 973-492-7406; www.sweetcakes.com

SWEET CELEBRATIONS
P.O. Box 39426, Edine, MN 55439; 800-328-6722

Quick Projects

Transform ordinary containers into stylish gift boxes using trims, ribbons, and decorative paper.

FUN PACKAGING IDEAS

By adding colorful accents and gift tags, you can remove these containers from their familiar contexts and convert them into festive gift packages. We started with a Chinese food container, a small paint can, a foil bag, and a round tin with a wire handle. You can fill the containers with candy, tea, or baked goods to make hostess gifts.

■ **Candy bag:** Draw and then cut a circle on center front of bag about 2½" from lower edge. Tape square of acetate sheeting inside of bag to back circle window. Fold down top of bag and punch three holes. Run cord through gift card and punched holes to secure top of bag.

■ **Paint can:** Measure and cut a strip of giftwrap to fit around can. Secure paper to can using double stick tape. To make label, use gold ink to stamp a leaf motif onto a small square of colored paper and apply gold embossing powder. Adhere label to front of paint can.

■ **Chinese food container:** Tie a piece of rayon tape in a contrasting color around container. Insert gift tag onto ribbon. Tie ribbon into bow, and trim ribbon tails at an angle.

■ **Round tin with wire handle:** Remove wire handle. Cut a strip of giftwrap paper to fit around tin. Tape one short end of giftwrap to center back of tin, using double-stick tape. Wrap paper around can, marking and cutting nickel-size holes to accommodate handle holders; adhere with double-stick tape as you go. Reattach handle and remove lid of can. Position a wide ribbon across tin between handles; replace lid. Tie ribbon in bow around lid, and trim ribbon tails at an angle. ◆

COLOR PHOTOGRAPHY:
Carl Tremblay

DESIGN:
Dawn Anderson

STYLING:
Ritch Holben

Speckled Leaves

Savor the ephemeral colors of fall by creating realistic leaves from watercolor paper, light green 18-gauge cloth-covered wire, and paint. Wet the watercolor paper and wash two or three colors of watercolor paint over the surface, allowing the colors to bleed into one another. To add a stippled effect over the wash, use your thumb to spatter burnt sienna paint from the bristles of a toothbrush. Use the same techniques to color the other side of the paper and the cloth-covered wire. Let dry.

Cut out leaf shapes from the painted paper and add tiny veins using colored pencils. Snip the wire into 2- to 3-inch stems. Separate the layers of paper with an X-Acto knife and slide the wire stems into the leaves. Secure them with a small drop of glue. Seal the leaves with two light coats of spray matte finish.

Curl the leaf corners around a pencil before scattering them over a table, piling them in a basket, or adding them to dried arrangements.

COLOR PHOTOGRAPHY: **Carl Tremblay**   STYLING: **Ritch Holben**   DESIGN: **Gabrielle N. Sterbenz and Elizabeth Cameron**

NUMBER TWENTY-TWO

HOLIDAY 1998

Handcraft

ILLUSTRATED

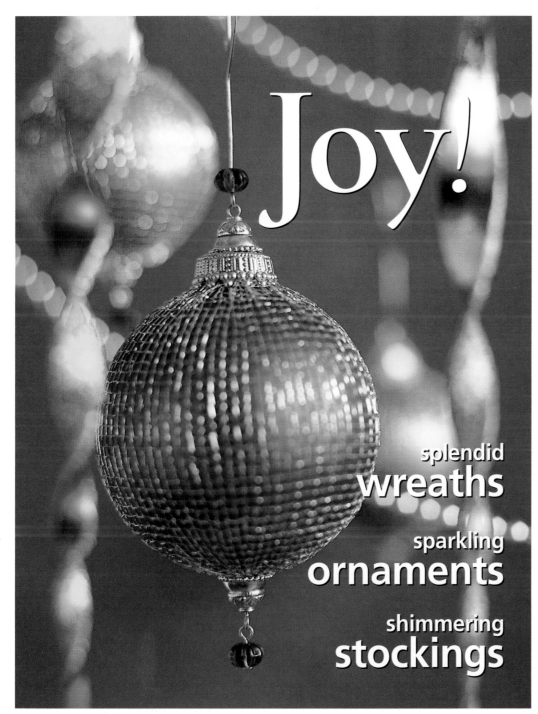

Joy!

splendid
wreaths

sparkling
ornaments

shimmering
stockings

Sugarplum Wreath
Accent a Vine Wreath with
Lustrous Fruit

Holiday Bouquet Garland
Bind Fresh Herbs into
a Mantel Swag

Christmas Tree Vases
Add Fresh Flowers to Your Tree

Frosted Holiday Coasters
Etch Your Own Festive Greeting

Heirloom Giving Box
Use Illuminated Artwork to Create
a Tzedakah Box

ALSO
Icicle Ornaments
Rhinestone Dragonfly
Victorian Paper Angels
Candle Lantern Card
Marzipan Star Candies

$4.00 U.S./$4.95 CANADA

85>

0 71486 02716 4

Contents

Marzipan Star Candies, page 7

Checked Stockings, page 8

Mosaic Seed Globes, page 10

COVER PHOTOGRAPH:
Carl Tremblay

STYLING:
Ritch Holben

Make a sparkling sugarplum wreath. See page 18.

Handcraft
ILLUSTRATED

From the Editor

EDITOR
Carol Endler Sterbenz

SENIOR EDITOR
Mary Ann Hall

CREATIVE PROJECT DIRECTOR
Michio Ryan

RESEARCH AND TESTING EDITOR
Candie Frankel

CONTRIBUTING EDITOR
Elizabeth Cameron

EDITORIAL ASSISTANT
Livia McRee

ART DIRECTOR
Amy Klee

DESIGNER
Elaine Hackney

CORPORATE MANAGING EDITOR
Barbara Bourassa

COPY EDITOR
Carol Parikh

PUBLISHER AND FOUNDER
Christopher Kimball

MARKETING DIRECTOR
Adrienne Kimball

CIRCULATION DIRECTOR
David Mack

FULFILLMENT MANAGER
Larisa Greiner

CIRCULATION MANAGER
Darcy Beach

MARKETING ASSISTANT
Connie Forbes

PRODUCTS MANAGER
Steven Browall

VICE PRESIDENT OF PRODUCTION AND TECHNOLOGY
James McCormack

EDITORIAL PRODUCTION MANAGER
Sheila Datz

DESKTOP PUBLISHING MANAGER
Kevin Moeller

PRODUCTION ARTIST
Daniel Frey

SENIOR ACCOUNTANT
Mandy Shito

Handcraft Illustrated (ISSN 1072-0529) is published quarterly by Boston Common Press Limited Partners, 17 Station Street, Brookline, MA 02146. Copyright 1998 Boston Common Press Limited Partners. Second-class postage paid at Boston, MA, and additional mailing offices, USPS #011-895. For list rental information, please contact List Services Corporation, 6 Trowbridge Drive, P.O. Box 516, Bethel, CT 06801; (203) 743-2600; Fax (203) 743-0589. Editorial office: 17 Station Street, Brookline, MA 02445; (617) 232-1000, FAX (617) 232-1572, e-mail: handcraftillustrated@bcpress.com. Editorial contributions should be sent or e-mailed to: Editor, *Handcraft Illustrated*. We cannot assume responsibility for manuscripts submitted to us. Submissions will be returned only if accompanied by a large, self-addressed stamped envelope. Subscription rates: $24.95 for one year; $45 for two years; $65 for three years. (Canada: add $6 per year; all other countries add $12 per year.) Postmaster: Send all new orders, subscription inquiries, and change of address notices to *Handcraft Illustrated*, P.O. Box 7450, Red Oak, IA 51591-0450. Single copies: $4 in U.S.; $4.95 in Canada and other countries. Back issues available for $5 each. PRINTED IN THE U.S.A.

We recognize the value of handmade gifts and save them along with our most precious things, but there are other gifts, intangible and sacred, that are saved in the family canon of shared memory. Such is the nature of this story of a Christmas ice storm many years ago.

The ice storm began innocently enough as light snow flurries, encouraging us to go ahead with our plans to spend Christmas in Vermont at a house loaned by friends. It was Christmas Eve and we had packed our car with everything we felt we needed for our usual Christmas—turkey with all the trimmings, wrapped gifts, and even our little goldfish. But as we moved north, the snow began to fall more heavily, and by the time we left the main highway for the state road, heavy downpours of frozen rain slowed us down to a creep.

When at last we reached our final turn, the car slid sideways, as if in slow motion, until it stopped on the low grass that bordered the edge of a frozen lake, its inky black surface revealed in eerie cone shapes illuminated by the car's headlights. We decided it was safer to leave the car where it was and walk to the house, perhaps a quarter of a mile away. We abandoned everything except the goldfish, which we transferred to a plastic bag, and slowly inched our way up the hill in a bizarre conga line, with one or another of our feet flying out from under us with every few steps we gained. We finally reached the house, fingers and toes painfully cold and our clothes drenched. We hurried inside, longing for heat and light and finding neither. We built a fire in the stone fireplace, settled down like corn in a crib, and waited for Christmas morning.

By daylight the land was muffled in several feet of ice-encrusted snow that glittered and flared in the pale early sun. Rather than risk the dangers of a walk back to the car for all our food and gifts, we decided to celebrate Christmas day using whatever we could find in the house. We pushed the dining table near the fireplace and slowly shed our flannel shirts and oversized coats. A deep drawer in a hallway dresser held a

> To me, the day of the ice storm that reduced our celebration to simple essentials was a most holy Christmas.

hodgepodge of games, stationery supplies, and spools of curly ribbon, and we made little paper rings and stapled them into the most languorous garlands. We draped them everywhere, as long as it didn't require our leaving the warm umbra of the fire. We unscrewed the lights from the little chandelier and Genevieve put a tall white candle in each little socket. I pulled lengths of ribbon across the blade of a pair of junky scissors and Gabrielle hung the colorful ringlets from the armatures.

Rodney braved a trek outside to saw off a small pine branch arched with the frozen snow, and John placed it in a silver ice bucket. I made Christmas breakfast (Swedish pancakes poured in the shapes of stars and trees, together with warm applesauce and fruits canned by our friends), while the kids cut and pinched shiny silver foil into calling birds. We laid an embroidered linen bed sheet on the table, icy smooth and white, with pristine folds that partitioned the table into large squares. We placed the potted pine branch in the middle, hung foil birds on each narrow sprig, and lit the candles. When we sat down for our Christmas feast, we devoured the golden pancakes, now running warm with syrup tapped from nearby maples the previous fall. Afterwards we played games and read, but early dark sent us closer to the fire, where we fell asleep.

John and the children don't tell the story of the ice storm in exactly the same way I do, but they love to tell it. Sometimes we start with one story and continue on, each of us adding more—not just for the fun of retelling the tale, but for the feeling of connection it brings, of being connected to something larger than ourselves. To me, the day of the ice storm that reduced our celebration to simple essentials and the sweet company of family was a most holy Christmas, a priceless gift.

All of us at *Handcraft Illustrated* wish you a holiday filled with warm times with your family and loved ones.

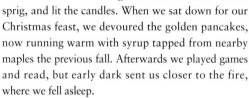

Notes from Readers

Discover the differences in glass paints, create custom holiday postcards, learn about wax for candle making, and find a source for affordable gemstone beads.

🐚 COMPILED BY LIVIA McREE

Working With Glass Paint

I recently started painting glassware and I'm having trouble getting the effects I want—I end up with visible brush strokes and areas of streakiness. Can you suggest a good paint or technique to minimize this?

ANGELINA SCALFANI
BROOKLYN, NY

Different glass paints have different characteristics, which can be advantageous or not, depending on the effect you are trying to create. We considered the opacity, viscosity, and coverage of the paints we tested, and the results varied greatly.

Pébéo Porcelaine 150 paints are available in translucent, semi-translucent, and opaque colors. This brand is the least viscous of the paints we tested—a quality that helps to eliminate brush strokes when a thick coat is applied, but one that also results in a tendency for the paint to drip and/or run over a curved surface. We found that the Pébéo translucent colors created the illusion of stained rather than painted glass. Though Pébéo paints don't show brush strokes, some areas can dry lighter than others when the paint is not applied evenly. It is a "thermohardening" water-based paint and needs to be baked for 35 minutes at 325 degrees after drying for 24 hours; otherwise it remains soft and prone to fingerprints, and can be peeled off easily.

Delta CeramDecor Permenamel is an opaque, air-drying paint that looks similar to nail polish when dry. It can be mixed with clear Permenamel for a translucent effect, but we think the Pébéo is more convincing if you are aiming for a stained-glass look. Permenamel, however, is a little more viscous than Pébéo, so it does not drip or run on a curved surface to the same extent; it also covers evenly when a heavy coat is applied. The clear Permenamel can be used as a top and base coat for increased durability or can be baked to make an item dishwasher-safe.

DecoArt Ultra Gloss is also an opaque, air-drying enamel paint, but it is similar to craft acrylics in appearance. Since it is very thick, it does not drip, but it does hold brush strokes, which gives the result a textured, hand-painted look. We found that using a soft, natural hairbrush and a light touch minimized, but did not eliminate, the brush strokes. We suggest applying two coats of paint to minimize streaking, especially if painting a large area. This paint does not need to be baked, but it can be baked for durability.

To prevent cracks when baking glass, start by placing items into a cool oven. To finish, turn off the oven, open the door, and let them cool before removing.

We recommend practicing on a piece of scrap glass with whichever paint you decide to use so that you become familiar with its properties and effects before starting your project. All the paints mentioned are available in a wide range of colors and can be obtained through mail-order suppliers such as Pearl Paint and Craft King (*see* Sources & Resources, page 48, for contact information).

Hang Holiday Decorations Easily

Do you have any suggestions on how to hang wreaths so that they don't fall or ruin your walls? In the past, some of my heavier decorations have made a mess of my plaster walls. And Christmas lights are always a pain!

MAUREEN McLEOD
NEWCASTLE, WY

We tested a new product from 3M: plastic hooks and small clips with replaceable, nontoxic "command adhesive" strips, which enable you to hang temporary decorations such as wreaths and light strings securely without making holes in your walls. The clips—suggested for hanging light strings—are available in one size, and the hooks are available in five sizes, ranging from mini, which will support a few ounces, to jumbo, which will safely support 7.5 pounds. All items are available in gray, white, and clear. You can also purchase replacement strips without having to buy new hooks or clips.

This product can be used on most flat surfaces, including wood, wallpaper, paint, glass, mirror, tile, hollow drywall, and plaster, and the strips can be removed without damage or residue. This simplifies holiday decorating and opens up new decorating possibilities, like hanging wreaths directly on windows or mirrors. Though simple to use, it is important to follow the directions carefully to prevent damage.

The products in this line are available at hardware stores nationwide; call 800-934-7355 for more information.

Christmas (Post)cards

Greeting cards are necessary during the holidays, but frankly, I'm rather bored with them. Can you give me any suggestions on making this process more interesting?

REBECCA MORRISON
MODESTO, CA

As a creative alternative to sending commercial greeting cards, try sending holiday postcards. Blank, pre-stamped postcards are available at the post office, or you can make them yourself using card stock or other heavyweight paper; just keep in mind that the minimum dimensions for a 20-cent postcard are 3½" by 5", and the maximum dimensions are 4¼" by 6". It will cost 32 cents to mail a larger piece up to 6⅛" by 11½". (Any design exceeding these specifications should be brought to your local post office for pricing and approval.) You can also use appropriately sized unlined index cards, which come in a variety of colors. When decorating your postcards, keep the bottom ⅝" on the side to be addressed free of all printing, marks, or colored borders because the bar code will be printed there.

Set aside an afternoon for postcard-making and involve the whole family. Produce your cards in assembly-line fashion to speed up the process. In addition to decorating your cards with holiday-themed rubber stamps, photocopied calligraphy, stickers, or with the art from last year's cards, you can add a personal touch—a small drawing, a picture from a magazine, a photo, or a sentiment—and the baby can add his or her fingerprint.

Decorating Outdoor Trees

We have some beautiful evergreen trees in our front yard which we try to decorate every Christmas. Lights look great, but they can be a lot of trouble. Do you have any other decorating ideas?

DOROTHY HEALY
POTSDAM, NY

How about decorating outdoor trees with edible ornaments for your neighborhood bird population? Winter is the time of year when their natural food sources are limited, so feeding them is a lovely gesture in the spirit of the holiday; and children will have lots of fun making the ornaments and then watching them being enjoyed.

The natural diet of most wild birds consists mainly of berries and insects, so try stringing colorful berry garlands or "icicles." For ornaments, you can purchase ready-to-hang honey and seed clusters in bell and other shapes at your local pet or grocery store, or make your own using wooden curtain rings or wooden turnings in holiday shapes (which are available from general craft supply stores and mail-order suppliers). Slather them with peanut butter and coat them with the seed and grain mixtures available at pet stores. Some mixtures are formulated to attract certain species, and can be rather colorful. To hang them, use a loop of cord rather than metal hooks or wire, which will rust.

Be careful not to use anything toxic or harmful to animals in your ornaments. It is best to use food prepared for birds, and if you have any doubts, consult a pet store worker or a local veterinarian.

Don't miss the upcoming Spring 99 issue, which will feature an article on edible birdhouses.

Mail-Order Glass Ornaments

I try to make holiday gifts for my friends every year, but I have trouble finding the time to do it. This year, I'd like to make ornaments for them. Do you have any quick and beautiful ideas?

LOTTIE-DEAN WILLIAMS
CHATTANOOGA, TN

Why not create heirlooms by making etched-glass ornaments? Glass-etching is a simple, fast technique that yields elegant results. (*See* "Frosted Holiday Coasters" in this issue for etching instructions, page 28.) A great selection of flat, beveled glass, plain glass, and mirror ornaments is available by mail-order from Eastern Art Glass. Several shapes are available and each ornament comes with a pre-drilled hole for hanging. Prices range from $1.75 to $5.95 each. Also available is an extensive line of stencils that make decorating and personalizing your ornaments easy. In addition to etching, you can also paint or engrave these ornaments. For a complete catalog, write or call Eastern Art Glass, P.O. Box 9, Wyckoff, NJ 07481; 201-847-0001.

Inexpensive Gemstone Beads

I make necklaces and would like to use gemstone beads more often, but they cost so much. Do you know of any sources that sell at a discount, but don't require bulk purchase?

MARIKA KONSTANTINIDES
WATERTOWN, MA

A fellow jewelry maker on our staff recommends a mail-order supplier called Fire Mountain Gems. They offer a vast array of semiprecious and precious gemstone beads, including jade, pearl, amethyst, emerald, turquoise, and amber. Their low prices make it affordable to create beautiful, expensive-looking jewelry that would retail for a much higher cost. They also carry a variety of cabochons, faceted gems and settings, silver, gold, and glass beads, as well as jewelry-making supplies, books, and findings. For a catalog, write or call Fire Mountain Gems, 28195 Redwood Highway, Cave Junction, OR 97523-9304; 800-423-2319.

Combine and Condition Wax for Candles

I'd like to try my hand at candle making. I know there are different kinds of wax I could use. Do you have any recommendations?

GINNY SHAEFER
COLFAX, WA

Paraffin—a byproduct of petroleum distillation—and beeswax are the main waxes used in candle making, and both are available in sheet, pellet, and bar form. We recommend using a combination of the two to get the advantages of both. (*See* the "Scented Modular Candles" project on page 12 in our Fall 1998 issue for an easy wax recipe.)

Beeswax is more expensive than paraffin so a combination is less costly than pure beeswax. Beeswax also burns longer and does not shrink as much as paraffin, so using them in combination helps to prevent a well from forming in the center of a molded candle as it cools. Beeswax, however, is very soft, so the addition of paraffin produces a harder candle, and the harder the wax, the brighter your candle is likely to burn. A combination of waxes will also be resistant to cracking as the candle cools, which is a possibility with pure paraffin, which is extremely hard. In addition, beeswax tempers the plastic look of paraffin. Rather than blending your waxes yourself, you can purchase pre-formulated wax specially made for different types of candle making from suppliers like the one listed below.

Hardeners such as stearin, a common additive derived from either animal or vegetable fat, and Vybar, a polymer (a substance that reacts on a chemical level and is used to achieve certain effects) are available to condition wax. In addition to making the candle harder and therefore longer-burning, they help wax burn off more completely, resulting in tapers that drip less and molded candles that burn down evenly. They also help distribute dyes and lend opacity to the candle (a side effect which you may or may not want). *Handcraft's* creative project director Michio Ryan prefers using Vybar. It helps to bind scented oil and wax; binds up any stray water molecules that may cause sputtering; eliminates mottled coloring; and yields a creamier surface finish and consistency to the candle than stearin does. Also, because it is used at a lower ratio than stearin, it is less expensive to use, even though, ounce per ounce, Vybar is more expensive.

To ensure success, it's best if your waxes and other additives, like scents, are prepared or formulated specifically for candle making. For example, perfume oils typically do not blend well with candle wax and will cause sputtering. For a complete line of candle making products, write or call Pourette, P.O. Box 17056, Seattle, WA 98107; 206-789-3188; www.pourette.com.

Use Kitchen Items As Craft Tools

As a beginning general crafter, I find that I am often held back because I have few or none of the tools and supplies I would need for a project. Can you suggest some substitutions that might save me money?

MARGUERITE SALTHAM BLANC
CHICAGO, IL

Our research and testing editor, Candie Frankel, suggests raiding your kitchen for tools. Instead of storing or throwing away old or worn appliances, utensils, and other kitchen items, give them new life as craft tools.

Knives, forks, spoons, and other gadgets make great modeling tools for clay and papier-mâché (a meat mallet can create texture, and a garlic press can be used to make clay or dough "hair"); rubber spatulas can be used to mix or spread paint, plaster, papier-mâché, gesso, or glue. Serrated knives, especially the curved ones used for grapefruits, are excellent for cutting and shaping Styrofoam. Ceramic or glass plates can become paint palettes or a work surface for clay, and if you don't have a rolling pin, use a jar to roll out clay. Your old measuring cups and spoons are perfect for making potpourri, soap, or candles (but they should not be reused for food). Wooden chopsticks can be used as stirrers, and wooden skewers can be both a tool and a craft material.

Various plastic items, like the disposable containers with lids used for margarine and yogurt (which can be made airtight when lined or covered with plastic wrap) or old Tupperware, can be used to store loose materials or to hold clay, paints, glazes, and diluted glue. Ice cube trays can hold sorted beads, sequins, buttons, or can be used as a paint palette; and condiment squeeze bottles and salad dressing bottles are great for mixing and dispensing paint or glue mixtures.

Electric appliances can also be adapted to craft uses. A toaster can be used as a heat source for embossing. Hand-held mixers can be used to stir paint, and blenders can be used to create slurry for paper making. When you are ready to buy a new iron, save your old one for velvet embossing or photo transfer projects. A mug tree is perfect for hanging painted ornaments to dry; cooling racks can be used to elevate painted items and to dry all sorts of other painted or glued projects. Salt shakers and store-bought spice containers with shaker tops can be used to store and dispense glitter bought in bulk.

You might also try making your own "creative kitchen" or "idea factory." Start collecting anything and everything that catches your fancy and put it all in one box or in your work area: scraps of fabric, pictures from magazines, ribbons from items you've purchased, leftover wrapping paper, old jewelry, glass and wooden objects that might be thrown out—anything that catches your fancy or that you think could be recycled into something new. This way, the next time you start a project, you might already have what you need or be able to find substitutes. Your collection can also be inspiring; seeing things that wouldn't normally be together might give you great ideas for projects.

Quick Tips

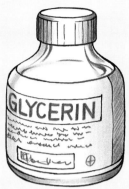

HOMEMADE EMBOSSING LIQUID

Make your own liquid for rubber stamp embossing. Just mix equal amounts of water and glycerin, available at pharmacies. Use with embossing powder as you would a purchased product. Thanks to Trish Klus, of Cobble Hill, British Columbia, Canada.

WRITE WHITE

To write or draw on colored paper, use a white correction pen, also from Trish Klus, of Cobble Hill, British Columbia, Canada. This look is perfect for handmade holiday cards and gift tags.

ATTENTION READERS

Calling All Crafters

Do you have a unique craft, sewing, or decorating technique that saves time or money? Send it our way! We'll give you a one-year complimentary subscription for each Quick Tip that we publish. Send your tip to:

Quick Tips

Handcraft Illustrated
17 Station Street
Brookline, MA 02445

Please include your name, address, and daytime phone number with all correspondence.

ILLUSTRATIONS:
Michael Gellatly

EASY EMBOSSING

You can do rubber stamp embossing without a heat gun or a toaster, writes Lucinda Poel, of Grand Rapids, Michigan. Warm a clean cookie sheet or cake pan over a low stove top flame. Place the project paper face up on the hot metal and hold it down with toothpicks until the embossing powder melts.

BEAD-STRINGING TIP

Here's how Sheila Castelbaum, of Oswego, New York, coaxes cord or elastic through a narrow bead hole.

1. **Fold a 5" length of beading wire in half.**

2. **Lock the tip of the cord in the "V" and pull through.**

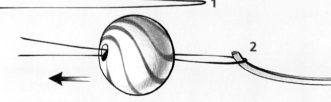

PERFECT SPACING

Use continuous-feed computer paper as a handy guide to make evenly spaced blanket stitches, writes Donna Roche, of Chicago, Illinois. When you're finished, just tear the paper away. A similar tip was also sent by Lois Watts, of Veradale, Washington.

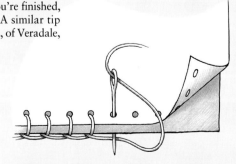

ROTARY BLADE REVIVAL

When your rotary cutter starts losing its cutting edge, try flipping the blade over, suggests Lillian Turner, of Winter Park, Florida. Use caution when handling the loose blade.

EASY CLEANUP

For glue oozes, stencil leaks, and similar "rescues," baby wipes are indispensable, writes Sue Heron, of Largo, Florida.

SURPRISE SUGAR BOWL

Sprinkle colored sugar crystals leftover from holiday baking in your sugar bowl to jazz it up for company. Thanks to Sandra Rabena, of Phoenixville, Pennsylvania, for this fun tip.

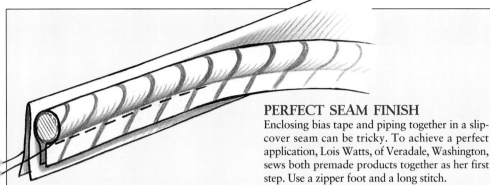

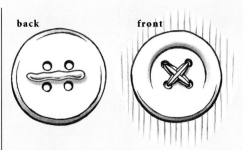
back   front

PERFECT SEAM FINISH

Enclosing bias tape and piping together in a slip-cover seam can be tricky. To achieve a perfect application, Lois Watts, of Veradale, Washington, sews both premade products together as her first step. Use a zipper foot and a long stitch.

BUTTON PLACEMENT

A dab of white fabric glue on the back of a button will hold it in position while you sew it on. Robin Jaslow, of Westfield, New Jersey, sent this tip.

PAINTING TOOL

Kristine Minami, of Astoria, New York, achieves sophisticated painted effects using a large hair comb. Just drizzle or drip paint from the comb's teeth onto paper or fabric.

COPPER-FOIL STORAGE

Remove the paper and plastic packaging from an extra compact disc case and you have the perfect dispenser for the copper foil used in stained glass work. Thanks to Kim Ensminger, Johnston Island, APO AP.

CORD PROTECTOR

Painting or decoupaging a lamp base? To protect the cord from splatters, wind it up, put it in a zip-close bag, and zip the seal as tightly as possible. This tip was sent by Sue Heron, of Largo, Florida.

MARKER LONGEVITY

Prevent marking pens and paints you use only occasionally from drying out prematurely, writes Martha Bowen, of Warrenton, Missouri. Just cap them tightly and store them in a canning jar with a rubber seal.

STAMP ORGANIZER

Losing track of your rubber stamp collection? To organize hers, Rosemary Schenden, of Farmington Hills, Michigan, keeps a sample image of each stamp in a file folder so she can assess her collection without making endless test runs. Planning multiple image designs is easier, too.

HOMEMADE ENVELOPE GLUE

If you make your own envelopes, you'll appreciate this recipe sent by Lucinda Poel, of Grand Rapids, Michigan.

1. Stir together 1 tablespoon white nontoxic glue, 1 teaspoon white vinegar, and 1 drop peppermint extract.

2. Brush the mixture on the envelope flap and let dry. Lick at any time to reactivate.

Quick Home Accents

Transform your house plants into a spectacular holiday display.

HOLIDAY ASSEMBLAGE

COLOR PHOTOGRAPHY:
Carl Tremblay

DESIGN:
Carol Endler Sterbenz

STYLING:
Ritch Holben

To create a unique centerpiece, bring together some simple items from your home, then add Christmas lights and balls for sparkle. You will need a few potted plants, some candles, a decorative garden pot or vessel, tree lights, tree ornaments, a few fresh flowers, and some moss.

To create a backdrop, I arranged two tall ivy topiaries and two round myrtle topiaries in a semicircle. In the right foreground, I positioned a miniature rose bush for color, and, to the left, a terra cotta pot tipped on its side. I filled the pot with moss and let it spill out in front of the display. Next, I arranged an assortment of silver ball ornaments and garlands in the mouth of the pot and over the layer of moss. Between the garden pots, I interspersed a few white lilies.

As you are creating your own assemblage, use three tiers to integrate the arrangement and create a balanced visual field. Start with taller potted plants to create a statuesque backdrop. For the middle tier, create a colorful focal area in front using smaller ornamental plants and fresh flowers. The lowest level will ground the arrangement. Use an overturned pot as a nest for spreading moss and ornaments.

For visual drama, especially at night, I wrapped white tree lights around the tallest ivy topiary and surrounded my composition with ivory pillar candles. The lights and flames will also serve to draw the eye around the composition. ◆

The Perfect Gift

Make these stellar holiday candies using a star-shaped cookie cutter on layers of marzipan and chocolate.

MARZIPAN STAR CANDIES

It may look like these layered star candies require professional expertise to make, but, in fact, they are deceivingly simple. The trick is to start with purchased ingredients. To make two dozen candies, you'll need one 24-ounce package of chocolate fondant, four 4-ounce cans of marzipan paste, red food coloring for the roses, and a yard of ¼"-wide gold ribbon. You'll also need a 3" star-shaped cookie cutter, a rolling pin, two wooden skewers, wax paper, a watercolor brush, a spoon, a toothpick, and scissors.

■ **Rolling the layers:** Divide the chocolate fondant into three equal pieces. Knead and flatten one section into a disc. Place the disc between two sheets of wax paper and roll out to a ³⁄₁₆" thickness, using skewers to support the rolling pin on each side and to keep it level. Repeat for the remaining sections. Roll the marzipan in the same way, combining two cans at a time and reserving one tablespoon from each can to make roses.

■ **Stacking the colors:** To create the horizontal striping, alternate layers of chocolate fondant and marzipan, beginning and ending with fondant. Place stacked layers on cookie sheet and chill in refrigerator for 10 minutes.

■ **Cutting the candies:** Press the star-shaped cookie cutter down through all five layers and lift straight up. Carefully nudge candy star out of cutter and place on wax paper. Smooth any cracked fondant with a clean watercolor paintbrush dipped in a drop of water. Repeat to cut two dozen stars.

■ **Making the roses:** Add ¼ drop of red food coloring to remaining marzipan.

Mash with spoon to color pink.

To form the bud of a rose, roll a pinch of pink marzipan into a 1" x ¼" tube and set aside. To form one petal, pinch off a small amount of marzipan from remainder, roll it into a ball, and press it into a flat heart shape; curl up the edges to resemble a rose petal. Press the base of the petal onto one end of the bud. Continue making petals and pressing them around the bud until the rose takes on the desired shape. Repeat to make a rose for each star.

■ **Decorating the candies:** Snip ribbon into 1½" segments, cutting on the diagonal. Twist segment once to form V-shape. Set point of V at middle of star and press in with toothpick. Top with marzipan rose. Store in airtight containers until served. ◆

COLOR PHOTOGRAPHY:
Carl Tremblay

DESIGN:
Genevieve A. Sterbenz

STYLING:
Ritch Holben

Check Your Stockings

Jazz up your mantel with stockings sewn from unconventional patterns and fabrics.

❧ BY DAWN ANDERSON

Use brass chains and glass beads to add sparkle to these checked stockings.

PATTERNS

See page 43 for pattern pieces and enlargement instructions.

COLOR PHOTOGRAPHY:
Carl Tremblay

ILLUSTRATION:
Judy Love

STYLING:
Ritch Holben

MATERIALS
Makes three 12" stockings

- 45"-wide silk dupioni
  1 yard multicolor check (body)
  7/8 yard oasis (lining + one cuff)
  1/3 yard crimson (cuff)
  1/3 yard turquoise (cuff)
- 2/3 yard 60"-wide fusible tricot interfacing
- Thread to match fabrics
- Assorted glass beads
  Three 16mm to 34mm
  Two 12mm to 16mm
  Five 9mm
  Fourteen 3mm
- 28" brass jewelry chain
- Three 3/8" brass rings
- Head pins
- Eye pins

You'll also need:
stocking pattern (*see* page 43); sewing machine; iron; round-nose jewelry pliers; chain-nose jewelry pliers; wire cutter; sewing shears; hand-sewing needle; pins; and pencil.

THIS YEAR, MAKE STOCKINGS with unexpected style and flair. Start by selecting a fabric with a striking multicolor check such as the vibrant silk dupioni featured here. Checks, while often traditional or country in style, can be quite contemporary when woven in bold, zesty colors. In silk, they can also be elegant.

To coordinate a set of checked stockings, make each cuff from a different solid-colored fabric that matches one of the check colors.

For a final touch, make unique cuff accents out of brass chains and glass beads. You can make swag-style accents by tacking the beaded decoration to both side seams, or you can make fringe-style embellishments that hang from just one side of the cuff.

Dawn Anderson is a writer and designer living in Bothell, Washington.

INSTRUCTIONS

1. *Cut fabrics.* From checked silk, cut six stockings, reversing three (*see* Designer's Tip). From oasis (lime green) silk, cut six stockings for lining (reverse three). Cut one 9½" x 14¾" cuff each from oasis, crimson, and turquoise silk, short edge parallel to selvage. From tricot interfacing, cut six stockings (reverse three) and three cuffs. Fuse interfacing to wrong side of checked stockings and solid cuffs, following manufacturer's instructions.

2. *Sew stockings and linings.* Pin each checked stocking pair right sides together. Stitch curved edge, making ½" seam. Trim seam allowance to a scant ¼". Stitch each oasis lining pair in same way, increasing seam allowance to ¾" around foot and leaving a 4" opening on back seam for turning, as per pattern (*see* illustration A). Turn checked stockings right side out and press well. Trim but do not turn linings.

3. *Sew cuffs.* Fold each cuff in half lengthwise, wrong side in, and press to set fold. Unfold, pin short edges right sides together, and stitch ½" from edge. Trim seam allowance and press seam open. Refold along previous fold and baste raw edges together (illustration B). Pin cuff to upper edge of each checked stocking, matching raw edges and back seam. Baste ⅜" from edge all around.

4. *Assemble stockings.* Slip checked stocking inside lining stocking, right sides together (illustration C). Match top edges and pin. Machine-stitch ½" from edge all around through all layers (illustration D). Trim seam allowance. Turn lining right side out by pulling checked stocking through opening. Slipstitch opening closed (illustration E). Push lining down inside stocking, and press upper cuff edge.

Hand-tack one brass ring to back of cuff for hanging.

5. *Add beaded chains.* Try the embellishment ideas below or create your own designs. To make a beaded drop (*see* how-to illustration, below), thread the bead(s) onto a head or eye pin; bend the pin wire down 90 degrees and clip to leave a ⅜" tail. Use round-nose pliers to shape this tail into a loop. Pry the loop open with chain-nose pliers to attach the drop to a chain link or another drop.

Oasis cuff: Make two drops, each with a 3mm bead and a large accent bead. Attach a drop to each end of a 12" chain. Hand-tack chain to inside top cuff so beads dangle down sides of stocking.

Turquoise cuff: Hand-tack 8" chain to inside cuff so chain drapes across cuff front. Make five drops by threading 9mm bead on eye pin. Attach drops across chain. Make nine drops by threading 3mm bead on head pin. Attach five to existing drops, and attach remaining four to chain in between (illustration F).

Crimson cuff: Make three drops, each with a 3mm bead and a large accent bead on head pin. Attach drops to 3", 2⅝", and 2⅜" chains. Tack all three chains to inside cuff on right side. ◆

Making the Checked Stocking

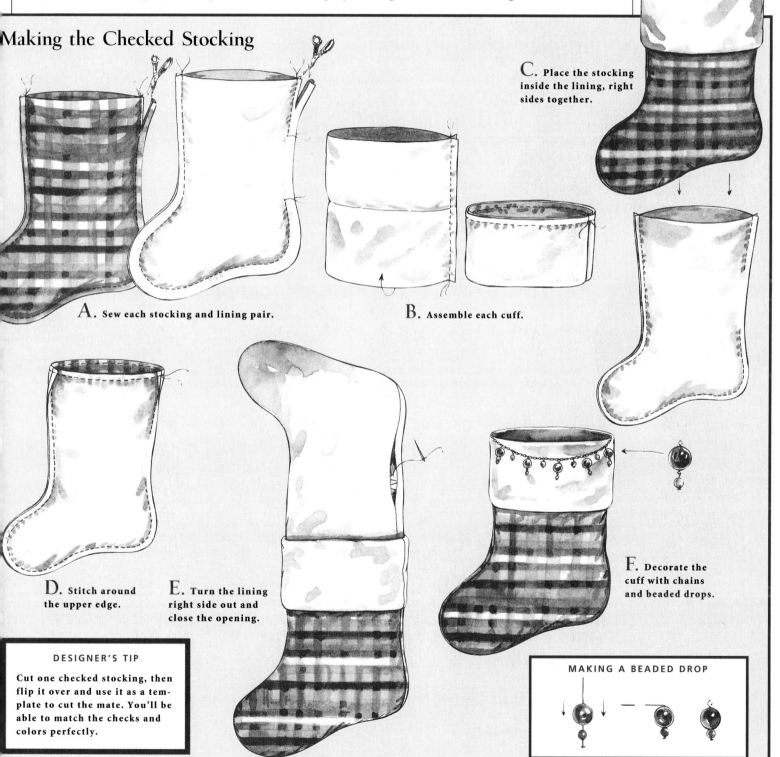

A. Sew each stocking and lining pair.

B. Assemble each cuff.

C. Place the stocking inside the lining, right sides together.

D. Stitch around the upper edge.

E. Turn the lining right side out and close the opening.

F. Decorate the cuff with chains and beaded drops.

DESIGNER'S TIP

Cut one checked stocking, then flip it over and use it as a template to cut the mate. You'll be able to match the checks and colors perfectly.

MAKING A BEADED DROP

Mosaic Seed Globes

Coat foam balls with moist clay and pave them with dried beans or corn to make your own natural bibelots.

≈ BY ELIZABETH CAMERON

Featured here are large red kidney beans, small red adzuki beans, green mung beans, white navy beans, black beans, and yellow corn kernels.

COLOR PHOTOGRAPHY:
Carl Tremblay

STYLING:
Ritch Holben

MATERIALS
Makes one 2½" to 3½" ball

- **2" to 3" Styrofoam ball**
- **¼ to ¾ cup dried beans or corn**
- **1 pound nonhardening modeling clay (to match bean color)**

You'll also need:
butter knife; and dinner plate.

I N THIS PROJECT, THE HUMBLE charm of colorful dried beans and corn produces a spectacular effect. The technique is simple enough for anyone to do and requires only two steps: coating a foam ball with clay, and layering the clay with beans or corn in a mosaic pattern.

You will need a nonhardening plastic clay (like Plastalina) that can be found in craft departments nationwide. This type of clay, designed to stay moist indefinitely, will hold the beans and kernels snug for many seasons. Though it comes in a wide range of very bright, almost neon colors, you will want to use the quiet earth tones for your seed globes. Colors such as gray, tan, yellow, ochre, dull orange, and sage green are an easy match to the different dried beans you might choose—like mung beans, soybeans, pinto beans, navy beans, kidney beans, or red beans. Corn kernels offer other possibilities. You can use yellow kernels, white kernels (which are very pale and appear almost translucent), or even Indian corn kernels leftover from a fall decoration.

Keep in mind that you will need a slightly thicker layer of clay to accommodate larger beans. If the beans start to come loose or fall out, it means that the layer of clay is too shallow and that you will need to increase the depth of the paving surface by adding more clay.

Experiment with different ways of setting the beans into the clay. For example, to create a cobblestone effect, try fitting each bean into the niche created by the two beans above it. You could also try standing corn kernels on their pointed ends to create a knobby surface.

Once you've completed a few seed globes, your decorating options will abound. Consider nestling an assortment on a serving platter or in a glass bowl to create a centerpiece bursting with rich color and robust textures. To make ornaments, wrap a ribbon around each globe pomander-style and secure it with straight pins. You could also tie a cluster of globes from a door, chandelier, or plant hook.

INSTRUCTIONS

1. *Create paving surface.* Use dinner plate as work surface. If using 3" Styrofoam ball, cut off 4 ounces of clay; for 2" ball, start with 2 ounces. Work clay with your fingers until soft, warm, and malleable. Roll clay into ball, then flatten ball into pancake ⅛" to ¼" thick. Wrap pancake around Styrofoam ball, covering one hemisphere. Repeat process with fresh clay to cover remaining area. Pinch off excess clay, and smooth seams with your fingertips. Work out any air bubbles. Strive for consistent clay depth around entire ball.

2. *Add beans.* Press one bean into clay surface so it is one-half to three-fourths submerged. Insert new beans, one at a time, around first bean, allowing thin line of clay to show between them. Continue pressing beans into clay until entire surface is covered. ◆

'50s-Style Tree Topper

Use a simple scoring technique to mold mat board cutouts into a multidimensional star.

COLOR PHOTOGRAPHY:
Carl Tremblay

ILLUSTRATION:
Judy Love

STYLING:
Ritch Holben

BY GENEVIEVE A. STERBENZ

THIS GLOWING ANTIQUE-STYLE tree topper is the perfect highlight for any Christmas tree. The star is constructed from two pieces of mat board, each cut in the shape of a 5-point star. By scoring lines on both sides of the cardboard, you can easily mold the facets of the star. The two faceted stars are glued edge to edge to form the final shape.

The stylizing consists, first, of a layer of gold leaf. Antique highlights are then added using dark paint. Paint the highlights with a small sponge so you're sure to get into the crevices of the star. You can use a small piece of cellulose sponge or a sea sponge. Small sea sponges called elephant's ears, which are sold for pottery making, are another option.

Genevieve A. Sterbenz is an author and designer living in New York City.

INSTRUCTIONS

1. *Make stars.* Lay star pattern on mat board. To mark board, use T-pin to pierce center point and each inner and outer star point (11 pinholes total). Connect 10 pinholes dot-to-dot to draft star outline. Using utility knife, steel ruler, and mat, cut out star as marked. On right side, score 5 lines from center point to each outer point. On reverse side, score 5 lines from center point to each inner point. Fold on score lines to make dimensional star. Repeat process to make second star.

2. *Make stand.* Cut 3½" square from corrugated cardboard. Roll into tube, overlap edges ½", and hot-glue together. Flatten one end. Using scissors, cut semi-

Postwar imports brought affordable luxury to families everywhere by transforming inexpensive materials into realistic and beautiful reproductions.

circle through both layers (*see* illustration A, *left*).

3. *Glue stars together.* Test-fit stars back to back. To join, put generous dab of hot-glue on wrong side of one outer point. Fit both stars together and hold while glue sets. Repeat process at each inner and outer point, proceeding around star until halves are fully joined. Cup curved end of stand around one inner point and secure with hot-glue (illustration B).

4. *Gild star.* Gild one side at a time. Brush size across surface and let come to tack (check after 10 minutes). Tear gold

leaf in 1" to 2" pieces. Transfer pieces one at a time to star and tamp down. Repeat to leaf entire surface. Gild other side in same way. Let dry overnight. Burnish with cotton ball to remove skewings and bring up shine.

5. *Add paint and trims.* On plate, place 3 drops burnt sienna to every 1 drop black. Dip a damp-dry sponge in both paints, blot off excess, and dab onto star. Repeat process to mottle entire gilded surface. Let dry 15 minutes. Working one section at a time, hot-glue gold cord along each raised ridge. Glue double strand of gold cord around star's outer edge. ◆

MATERIALS
Makes one 11" treetop star

- **20" x 32" mat board**
- **Gold composition leaf**
- **Gold size**
- **4 yards gold twisted cord**
- **Scrap of corrugated cardboard**
- **2 ounces black acrylic paint**
- **2 ounces burnt sienna acrylic paint**

You'll also need:
star pattern (*see* page 42); hot-glue gun; utility knife; self-healing cutting mat; steel ruler; scissors; ½" flat brush; small sea sponge; old plate (for palette); pencil; T-pin; and cotton balls.

PATTERNS
See page 42.

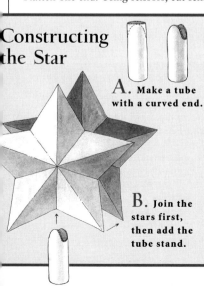

Constructing the Star

A. Make a tube with a curved end.

B. Join the stars first, then add the tube stand.

Boxwood Welcome Tree

Use live greens to make this front door topiary that looks like it was just cut from the forest.

❧ BY DAWN ANDERSON

Select a ribbon that complements the color and design of the container.

PATTERNS

See page 43 for pattern pieces and enlargement instructions.

COLOR PHOTOGRAPHY:
Carl Tremblay

ILLUSTRATION:
Judy Love

STYLING:
Ritch Holben

MATERIALS
Makes one 30" door decoration

- 3 to 4 bunches fresh boxwood
- 10" x 10" x 4"-deep flush-mount container
- Sheet moss
- 4 yards 2"-wide pink plaid wire-edged ribbon
- 2" x 12" x 36" foam sheet
- 18-gauge 18" florist wire stems
- 20-gauge 18" florist wire stems
- 30-gauge wire
- Florist pins
- Two 6" florist picks
- ¾" wood dowel
- Hold the Foam glue
- Hot-Glue Help Mate

You'll also need:
tree form pattern (*see* page 43); hot-glue gun; wire cutter; small handsaw; serrated knife; pruning shears; tape measure; scissors; and spray mister.

G REET YOUR HOLIDAY VISITORS with this fresh tree-shaped topiary, designed to lay flush against any door or wall. Its only ornamentation consists of a piece of wire-edged ribbon looped into a bow at the top, with tails that cascade down the sides.

The featured topiary is made with boxwood, but you can substitute other fresh evergreens. Purchase your greenery from a florist, or better yet, gather cuttings from your garden or a nearby woods, or use the extra branches trimmed from your Christmas tree.

To make the base, glue the foam sheets together with Hot-Glue Help Mate, which holds even in cold temperatures. For additional weatherproofing, choose a colorfast, water-repellent ribbon that will stand up to the elements.

Dawn Anderson is a writer and designer living in Bothell, Washington.

INSTRUCTIONS

1. *Make tree form.* Lay pattern on Styrofoam sheet. Run serrated knife along pattern outline to score foam, then cut clear through. Repeat to cut second piece. Reserve excess foam. Following manufacturer's directions, use Hot-Glue Help Mate and hot-glue to join pieces together to make one 4"-thick piece (*see* illustration A, right). [Editor's note: Hot-glue cools and holds immediately, while Hot-Glue Help Mate requires overnight drying time. You may proceed with project while Help Mate is drying, but keep in mind that wet glue will ooze.] Using knife, shave off edges to create half-cone shape that is 4" thick at bottom center and tapers to 1½" thickness at peak (illustration B).

2. *Cover form with sheet moss.* Lightly spray-mist sheet moss for easier handling. Open misted sheets, mist again, and set aside so moisture can seep in. Cut a dozen or so 3" to 6" lengths of 20-gauge wire. Using pliers, bend each wire into a hairpin shape and crinkle the ends. Push hairpins into foam form according to depth to help secure layers together. Layer sheet moss over form and secure with hot-glue and hairpin wires. Continue until entire form, including flat back, is covered.

3. *Add wire hanger.* Bend 18-gauge wire stem at middle, twist to make 2" loop, then bend loop up 90 degrees. Insert free ends of wire into flat back of tree 5" below peak (illustration C). Push through until loop rests flush against moss. On front, twist ends together and bend up.

4. *Fit dowel stem.* Cut excess foam to fit into flush-mount container. Pack tightly, and secure with extra-long handmade hairpins. Saw 14" length from ¾" dowel. Center dowel above container and push straight down into foam. To join tree, lay container and tree flat on work surface, center end of stem against base of tree, and push both pieces together until tree and container are flush (illustration D). Remove dowel from both pieces. Use Hold the Foam glue to secure dowel in container hole only.

5. *Attach boxwood sprigs to tree.* Using pruning shears, cut boxwood into 6" to

Making the Topiary

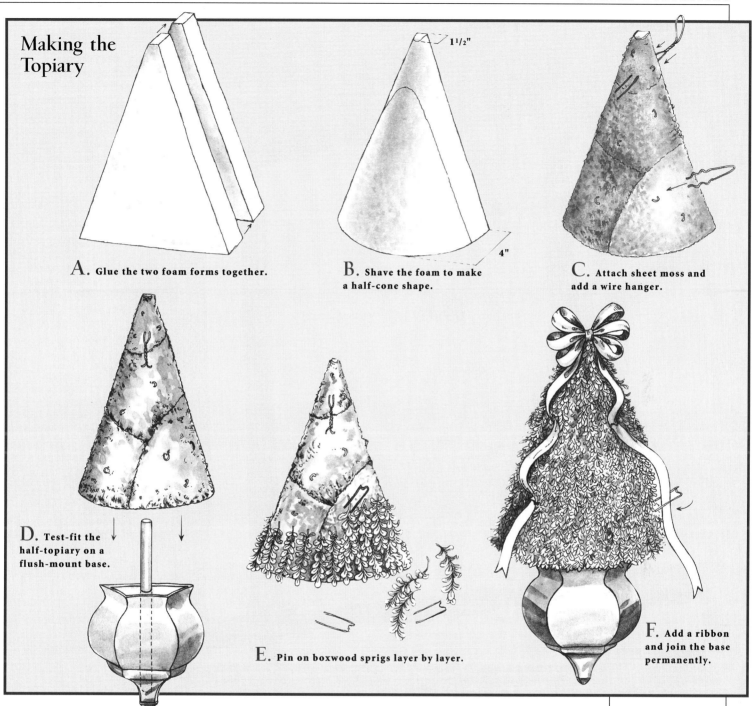

A. Glue the two foam forms together.

1¹⁄₂"

4"

B. Shave the foam to make a half-cone shape.

C. Attach sheet moss and add a wire hanger.

D. Test-fit the half-topiary on a flush-mount base.

E. Pin on boxwood sprigs layer by layer.

F. Add a ribbon and join the base permanently.

8" sprigs. Place one sprig at base of tree, leaves "growing" down and extending 1" to 1½" beyond lower edge. Secure with florist pins. Repeat process to conceal entire lower edge. Add second row of sprigs in same way, overlapping first row to conceal pins (illustration E). Strive for lush, full appearance rather than rigidly spaced rows. Continue until you reach top (pins will be concealed by bow). Also pin sprigs to underside of base, radiating out from center hole.

6. *Add bow with streamers.* Refer to "Making a Six-Loop Bow," right. Fold ribbon in half to locate middle. Observing midpoint, fold ribbon accordion-style to

make six 8" loops. Crimp loops at middle, bind with 30-gauge wire, and clip off excess wire. To hide wire, wrap one ribbon streamer once around middle. Secure bow to top of tree by inserting wire ends through Styrofoam, twisting together at back, and clipping off excess. Fluff out bow loops, and trim ends of streamers with inverted V. Arrange streamers down each side of tree, securing cascades with florist pins. Insert two 6" florist picks halfway into base foam on each side of dowel. Apply Hold the Foam glue to exposed dowel. Insert dowel in tree, pushing firmly. Picks will lend stability. Let dry 24 hours. ◆

MAKING A SIX-LOOP BOW

Beaded Window Icicles

Use an easy double-back technique to turn crystal beads into a wintry window accent.

❧ BY ELIZABETH CAMERON

The featured window icicles use light blue, clear, and opalescent crystal-cut beads to achieve their frosty effect.

COLOR PHOTOGRAPHY:
Carl Tremblay

ILLUSTRATION:
Judy Love

STYLING:
Ritch Holben

MATERIALS

Fits window 24" to 30" wide

- **250 to 350 assorted crystal beads**
- **32-gauge silver wire**
- **1/2" x 3/8" x 30" basswood strip**
- **Putty adhesive (such as FunTak)**
- **Paint to match window frame**

You'll also need:
staple gun with 5/16" staples; round-nose pliers; flat-nose pliers; wire cutters; small saw; sandpaper; small, flat brush; and tape measure.

INSTRUCTIONS

1. *Cut wire.* Cut basswood strip to fit window frame. Measure down from mounting location to determine longest icicle drop and cut one wire double this length. Determine length of shortest icicle drop and cut one wire double this length. Snip various lengths in between these two until you have one wire for every inch of basswood strip.

2. *String bottom bead.* Select one pre-cut wire strand. Insert wire into bead with wire extending 2". Bring end of wire around bead and reinsert it through same hole. Pull wire ends tight, trapping bead in loop. Bend short end 90 degrees and clip, leaving 3/8" tail (*see* illustration A, below). Use round-nose pliers to shape tail into loop.

3. *String succeeding beads.* Slide new bead onto wire, stopping 1/4" to 1" above bottom bead. Draw working end of wire around bead and through hole from bottom to top. Pull snug, trapping bead in loop (illustration B). Repeat stringing and trapping motion to string beads to desired length. Repeat steps 2 and 3 for each pre-cut strand.

4. *Mount beaded strands.* Paint basswood strip to match window frame; let dry. Lay strip flat with 1/2"-wide surface face up. Arrange beaded strands in desired order. Using pliers, crimp excess wire at top of each strand into zigzag no wider than strip. Clip off any excess. Staple each zigzag section to strip, spacing strands at 1" intervals. To mount, apply putty adhesive to back of strip at 6" intervals and press onto window frame. ◆

T HESE CASCADING STREAMS OF crystal beads conjure up images of icicles dripping in the sunlight. They even twinkle in the glow of evening lights.

The construction technique is so simple that no beading experience is necessary. Simply run a wire through a bead as if you were stringing a necklace, and then, before you string the next bead, double back, looping the wire around the outside of the first bead and back through it again, trapping it in place.

Create your beaded strands in various lengths to imitate the uneven formation of real icicles. To suggest the shapes of melting icicles, you can string smaller beads at the bottom of the strand and increasingly larger beads as you work your way up.

Once the strands are complete, staple them to a lightweight basswood strip, then attach the strip to the window with a putty adhesive. The length of the basswood strip and the length of the icicles are very adaptable. For instance, if draperies hide part of your window, you can string beads to fill the space between them. When spring arrives, you can easily peel away your winter decorations.

Stringing the Beads

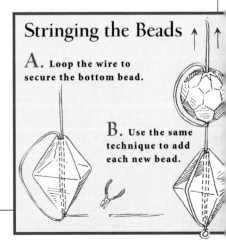

A. Loop the wire to secure the bottom bead.

B. Use the same technique to add each new bead.

Gold Mesh Ornament

Envelop a simple glass ornament with gold mesh ribbon.

❧ BY DAWN ANDERSON

COLOR PHOTOGRAPHY:
Carl Tremblay

ILLUSTRATION:
Mary Newell DePalma

STYLING:
Ritch Holben

TRANSFORM ANY GLASS BALL ornament with a simple corset of gold mesh ribbon. The ribbon is sewn into a narrow sleeve that slips over the ball and is cinched at each pole. Both cinched ends are covered with delicate, decorative bead caps.

The featured ornament uses a glass ball with a satin finish, but you can substitute ornaments with a shiny or satin-thread finish. In fact, you can even use your much-loved faded or paint-worn glass ornaments; this gold mesh finish will disguise their tiny flaws.

Dawn Anderson is a writer and designer living in Bothell, Washington.

INSTRUCTIONS

1. *Make mesh sleeve.* Wrap mesh ribbon once around ball, allowing ½" overlap. Cut off excess. Remove wire, if any, from ribbon edges. Fold ribbon in half, cut edges matching. Using invisible thread, backstitch ¼" from cut edges (or sew by machine). Finger-press seam allowance to one side. Turn right side out.

2. *Cover ball with mesh.* Ease sleeve onto 3" ball ornament with open ends at top and bottom. Remove ornament cap. Using invisible thread, hand-baste 1" from top edge once around. Pull thread ends to gather mesh around top of ball and tie off. Gently poke excess mesh into opening with eraser end of pencil (*see* illustration A, below). Twist opposite end until mesh hugs ball, bind twisted section with thread, and tie off. Trim close to knot. Using invisible thread, backstitch around ornament neck to take up slack.

3. *Assemble cap.* Remove wire from ornament cap and discard. Cut 4" length of brass wire. Using chain-nose pliers, make 90-degree bend at middle and again ⅜" away. Grip middle section with round-nose pliers, then bend each arm down to shape loop. Insert wire ends through bead

cap and ornament cap. On underside, press wires against inside of bead cap. Cross wires at top, then bend at right angles to follow cap contours. Reattach cap to ornament (illustration B).

4. *Add wire hanger.* Cut 3½" length of brass wire. Using chain-nose pliers, make 90-degree bend ⅜" from one end. Using round-nose pliers, shape this short section into loop. Slip bead onto wire, then loop other end in same way. To shape hook, make 135-degree bend 1" above lower loop. Roll section above bend around dowel to shape hook. Open lower loop, slip through ornament cap loop, and close.

5. *Cap bottom.* Slide remaining bead onto head pin. Bend pin wire down 90 degrees, clip ⅜" from bend, and shape loop. Slip eye pin through bead cap, and clip and loop end. Join bead and bead cap. Glue bead cap over knot at bottom of ornament; secure top cap with glue if needed (illustration C). ◆

The original ornament cap is enhanced with glass beads, gold bead caps, and a hand-shaped brass hanger.

MATERIALS
Makes one 3" ornament

- 3" ball ornament with gold cap
- Two matching 8mm glass beads
- 12" x 5½"-wide gold mesh ribbon
- Two ½" gold bead caps
- 20-gauge brass wire
- 2" head pin
- 2" eye pin
- Invisible nylon sewing thread
- Sewing thread
- Tacky glue

You'll also need:
sewing machine (optional); round-nose pliers; chain-nose jewelry pliers; wire cutter; ½" dowel; scissors; ruler; hand-sewing needle; and pencil with eraser tip.

Making the Ornament

A. Sheathe a glass ball ornament with gold mesh.

B. Bend wire to fit the ornamental caps.

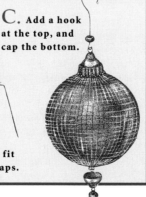

C. Add a hook at the top, and cap the bottom.

Candle Lantern Card

Use a rubber-stamped vellum window and a gilded interior to create a card that opens into a votive candle screen.

BY CAROL ENDLER STERBENZ

For an alternative color scheme, try combining powder blue cardstock with a silver leaf interior. Candlelight will make your picture glow.

COLOR PHOTOGRAPHY:
Carl Tremblay

ILLUSTRATION:
Mary Newell DePalma

STYLING:
Ritch Holben

I F YOU'RE LOOKING FOR A SMALL gift for someone special, tuck this miniature card under a napkin on your holiday table or attach it to the ribbon of a gift box. Made from cardstock and a scrap of vellum, the folded card opens into a small box-style lantern, perfectly sized to house a standard votive candle. The recipient peels up a star sticker found on an inside flap and uses it to secure the screen in its display position. The gilded interior reflects the candle's glowing light, a process made simple by using spray adhesive to adhere the leaf.

You will need to cut a window in one panel of the card to accommodate the vellum through which the candlelight shines. The fun part of this project is choosing the silhouette image to fit this space. I used a rubber stamp depicting a cozy house, but there are numerous other possibilities. You could use small graphic images like stars, pine cones, or holly leaves, or, to personalize the card, you could use initials to create a lighted monogram or spell out a longer greeting like JOY or PEACE. The stamped image is enhanced with embossing powder, which adds a textural accent and shines even when the candle isn't lit.

MATERIALS
Makes two cards with envelopes

- 11" x 17" red cardstock
- Scrap of vellum
- Composition gold leaf
- Four ½" self-adhesive gold stars
- Gold embossing powder
- Yellow stamp pad ink
- Invisible tape
- Yes Stikflat glue
- Spray adhesive

You'll also need:
envelope pattern (page 17); gold metallic pen; holiday theme rubber stamp, image not to exceed 1½" x 2"; toaster (or other heat source); X-Acto knife; quilter's acrylic grid ruler; self-healing cutting mat; thin craft foam; small flat brush; butter knife; heavy book; pencil; newsprint; cotton balls; and T-pin.

INSTRUCTIONS
Note: Complete each step twice to make two cards with envelopes.

Making the Card
1. *Cut and fold card.* Using X-Acto knife, grid ruler, and mat, cut 3" x 11" rectangle from red cardstock. Fold in one end about ½" and crease well to make flap. Bring folded edge to opposite cut edge, crease at middle, and open (*see* illustration A). Bring cut edge almost to middle crease, crease well, and open. Repeat from folded edge. Side facing up is inside of card.

2. *Cut window opening.* Cut 2½" x 3" panel from red cardstock. Draft lines ½" in from each edge. Cut on marked lines to make 1½" x 2" window opening. Counting from flap, position panel on second card panel. Trace window opening on card and cut out (illustration B).

3. *Gild card and window panel.* Transfer two sheets of gold leaf to newsprint, placing them end to end. Lay card flat, inside face up, on separate newsprint. Apply spray adhesive, following manufacturer's instructions. As soon as card surface is tacky with no wet spots (15 seconds or less), press card, adhesive side down, on gold leaf and rub gently to adhere. Turn card over and press gently with cotton ball. Use leaf remnants to gild remaining bare spots. Gild separate

Making the Candle Lantern Card

A. **Start by making two folds.**

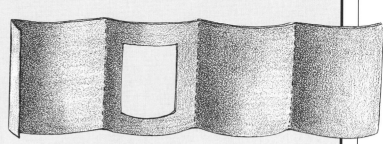

B. **Fold four panels total, then cut a window opening.**

C. **Gild the inside, and add a vellum insert and gold star.**

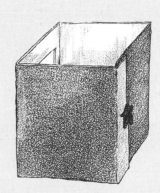

D. **Close the flap with the self-stick star.**

window panel with leaf remnants in same way. Let dry 30 minutes to 1 hour. Buff edges with cotton ball to remove skewings.

4. *Create window insert.* Brush yellow ink on craft foam. Load rubber stamp with ink, and stamp image on vellum. Immediately, while ink is still wet, sprinkle with embossing powder. Shake off and reserve excess. To activate embossing powder, hold vellum a few inches above toaster and heat for 20 seconds, or until powder melts. Let cool 5 minutes.

DESIGNER'S TIP

See **page 4 for an easy recipe for making your own embossing liquid and an alternative method for activating embossing powder.**

---

5. *Assemble card.* Lay card flat, gilded side up, with flap at left. Center embossed image facedown within window opening. Trim away excess vellum, allowing ¼" margin all around. Using Yes Stikflat glue, affix vellum to win-

dow frame, then glue on window panel, gilded side up, sandwiching vellum in between. Fold flap in, and apply short piece of invisible tape to lower end. Press one gold star on tape (illustration C). Weight under heavy book overnight. Write your own greeting on red surface of card with gold metallic pen. To use card, open into box shape, and seal flap with star. Set over votive candle placed in a glass holder (illustration D).

Making the Envelope

1. *Cut cardstock.* Lay enlarged envelope pattern on red cardstock. Using T-pin, pierce each inner and outer point of perimeter (12 pinholes total). Connect pinholes dot-to-dot to draft envelope outline. Cut on marked lines.

2. *Assemble envelope.* Fold in four flaps in order indicated on pattern. Open flat. Brush Yes Stikflat glue on outer edges of bottom triangle. Fold in side flaps, fold up bottom flap, and press to adhere. Weight under heavy book overnight. Insert folded card, and seal top flap closed with self-adhesive star. Write name or greeting on face of envelope with gold metallic pen. ◆

ENVELOPE CUTTING DIAGRAM

NOTE: PHOTOCOPY AT 200%.

top flap

fold 4

fold 1

envelope

fold 2

fold 3

Sugarplum Wreath

The secret: Use road sign reflective beads to add sparkle to the fruits.

❧ BY MICHIO RYAN

To attain the airy and delicate style of this wreath, create a slender framework of grapevines and position the fruit and tendrils loosely around it.

COLOR PHOTOGRAPHY:
Carl Tremblay

ILLUSTRATION:
**Mary Newell
DePalma**

STYLING:
Ritch Holben

MATERIALS
Makes one sugarplum wreath

- **12 assorted 2" to 4" artificial fruits**
- **1 bunch artificial grapes**
- **2 stems with 1" fruits**
- **4 to 5 stems with small berries**
- **20 assorted 2" to 4" flocked velvet leaves**
- **14" to 18" grapevine wreath**
- **16" flat wire wreath frame**
- **1 pint Rolco Labs reflective beads**
- **24-gauge fabric-covered wire**
- **20-gauge 18" brown paper-covered stems**
- **Brown florist tape**
- **Bronze micro glitter**
- **Assorted metallic paints, 2 ounces each: Plaid Folk Art Bronze 663, Copper 664, Peach Pearl 674, Peridot 671, Periwinkle 669, Plum 668, Rose Shimmer 652, Accent Crown Jewels Imperial Antique Gold 2528**
- **Mod Podge (gloss)**

You'll also need:
hot-glue gun; 16-gauge steel wire; wire cutters; ⅝", ½", and ⅜" dowels; 1" foam brush; ½" flat soft-bristle brush; small sponge; X-Acto knife; candle and matches; wide-mouthed 1-quart container; large bowl; and twist-ties.

T O GIVE THE FRUITS ON THIS wintry grapevine wreath their lustrous appearance, I used two materials: a coat of iridescent metallic craft paint and tiny clear reflective beads. These inexpensive glass beads, sold for making reflective signs, are more sophisticated than the plastic "snow" usually used in holiday crafts.

The best fruit to use for this project is made of styrene. It's lightweight, durable, takes paint well, and is easily embedded with wire. Hard plastic fruit will also work, but soft, rubbery neoprene fruits don't hold the glass beads well.

The fruit surface must be smooth for the metallic paint layer to shine. Plastic peaches can be defuzzed easily by soaking, but unfortunately this method will not dissolve the glues used on styrene peaches. You can always smooth a fuzzy skin with several coats of gesso, but it's easier to avoid flocked peaches and use smooth-skinned nectarines instead. Some newer hard-shell fruits, especially those with a very matte della Robbia–style finish, are coated with a thin latex film that resists painting. It will be obvious immediately if your fruit has this coating when you prick it with a needle or an X-Acto blade tip. If the latex layer separates, lift and peel it off as a whole sheet. The painted surface underneath can then be painted with no further preparation.

For a visually interesting wreath, include fruits like pears and pomegranates that have distinctive silhouettes or details. Also use different sizes, including large and small versions of the same fruit. Although I didn't use them, limes and lemons are also suitable choices. Grapes or berries can be used in small clusters to add filler where needed. Finally, use velvet leaves to add a soft background. (If you want to make your own, *see* "How to Make Antique Velvet Roses," November/December 1995.)

To achieve a light and airy look, I used only 12 main fruits and arranged them around a grapevine base that was delicate rather than dense in appearance. To style my own wreath, I separated a few vines from a purchased wreath and wound them loosely around a wire wreath form. As you assemble your wreath, give each fruit "breathing room," and spin the tendrils toward the surrounding space. Finish the wreath with subtle highlights of bronze paint and glitter to camouflage any joins or blemishes and to give the wreath a dewy glow.

INSTRUCTIONS

Making the Fruits

1. *Make wire holders.* Cut twelve 12" lengths of 16-gauge wire. For each medium and large fruit, choose side with interesting details or contours to face outward on wreath, e.g., split of peach, belly of pear, stem of apple. Join wire to opposite side as follows: Curve end of wire slightly, heat curved section in flame, and push into fruit so it emerges 1" to 2" away. The hot wire will glide easily through the foam fruit. Let cool 5 minutes, then twist wire ends together. Use wire as handle when painting and paving fruits.

2. *Paint fruits.* Using ½" flat brush, apply metallic paint to each fruit (except grapes) according to its natural color. Let dry, then brush or sponge in shading and highlights. For example, paint a nectarine gold or peach and blush it with copper or rose; paint a pear green, then add gold highlights on one side to suggest sun ripening. Don't worry if shading does not blend realistically, since glass reflective beads will soften harsh lines. Paint small berries periwinkle. Hang fruits and let dry 1 hour.

3. *Pave fruits with glass beads.* Transfer glass beads to wide-mouthed container, to create a fan-shaped spill when poured. Using foam brush, spread Mod Podge evenly on one large fruit. With bowl underneath to catch excess, pour beads in gentle stream over wet fruit, turning it for complete coverage. Hold back glass dust at end of pour and discard it. Check that all areas are coated, then hang to dry. Repeat process for all fruits except berries; cut grapes into three or four small clusters and pave each cluster. Be careful not to nudge or disturb coated fruit, and do not let hanging fruits touch one another. Let dry overnight.

Making the Wreath Base

1. *Wind grapevines on wire wreath form.* Untwine grapevine wreath. If vines are extremely brittle and prone to breaking, soak entire wreath in basin of water for 1 hour or more, until more pliable. Wind a few vines around wreath form, just enough to give it some coverage while retaining light, airy look (*see* illustration A, right). Hold temporarily with twist-ties; if vines are wet, let wreath air-dry overnight.

Permanently secure vines to wreath form in four or five spots using wire and/ or hot-glue.

2. *Paint grapevine wreath.* Using ½" flat brush, apply antique bronze paint randomly to vines and wreath form. For lustrous effect, do not attempt to paint every surface. Let dry 20 minutes.

3. *Make tendrils.* Coil 18" brown paper-covered stem around dowel for 3" to 4", then coil back in other direction around dowel of different diameter. Push and pull finished coil to create natural-looking tendril. Repeat process to make 5 or 6 tendrils total. Set tendrils aside.

Assembling the Wreath

1. *Wire fruits to wreath.* Remove wire holder from each fruit and replace with 12" length of fabric-covered stem wire. Adjust so both ends extend evenly, then twist wires together close to fruit surface. Tentatively place 12 fruits around wreath, arranging them so like colors, sizes, and shapes are not adjacent. Once arrangement is set, wire fruits to inner or outer wreath to create undulating path. To secure each fruit, twist wires together at back of wreath, clip off excess, and bind with florist tape (illustration B). Fill in bare spaces with 1" fruits, grape clusters, and berries; to attach them, wind stems around grapevine for a few inches and bind with floral tape. Keep overall look open and airy, rather than lush or cluttered (illustration C).

2. *Add tendrils and leaves.* Attach tendrils and leaves in same manner as berries, by winding stem around grapevine and binding with tape. To extend or strengthen existing leaf stems, lay stem wire along existing stem and bind both stems together tightly with florist tape. Use leaves as camouflage to hide any exposed fruit wires, unattractive joins, or the wire wreath form. Position leaves so larger, darker leaves recede toward back and smaller, lighter leaves loft forward. Use longer stems to advantage to float leaves where you need them. To garnish a fruit, remove the plastic stem, insert the leaf stem in the opening, and rejoin the plastic stem with hot-glue. Wrap any areas of wreath form that remain visible with brown florist tape. Use short strips for easier handling, and wrap loosely to suggest woody vines (illustration D).

3. *Add sparkle.* Using flat brush and bronze paint, touch up any stem joins or other taped areas that could use camouflaging. Apply thin coat of Mod Podge at random to vines, tendrils, and leaf stems that are visible and easily reached. Sprinkle bronze micro glitter over these areas, rubbing pinches of it between your fingertips to release very light snowfall. To make a hanging loop, shape a brown paper stem and attach it to wreath back. ◆

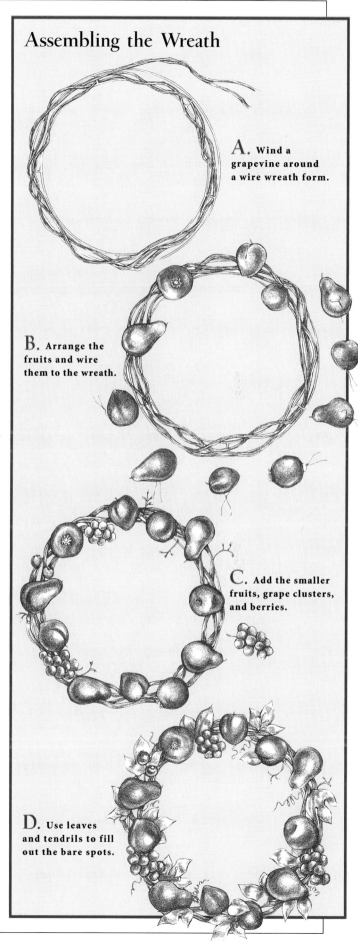

Assembling the Wreath

A. Wind a grapevine around a wire wreath form.

B. Arrange the fruits and wire them to the wreath.

C. Add the smaller fruits, grape clusters, and berries.

D. Use leaves and tendrils to fill out the bare spots.

Icicle Ornaments

Twist dazzling ornaments from child-friendly thermoplastic strips softened in warm water.

❧ BY MICHIO RYAN

Use coordinating shades of micro glitter to coat the uncolored sides of metallic-finish thermoplastic.

CUTTING
DIAGRAM

COLOR PHOTOGRAPHY:
Carl Tremblay

STYLING:
Ritch Holben

MATERIALS
Makes 20 icicle ornaments

- Five 1½" x 7" **Friendly Plastic strips, in metallic colors**
- **Micro glitter, assorted colors**
- **Thin gold elastic cord**
- **Mod Podge**
- **Acrylic spray sealer (gloss)**

You'll also need:
cutting diagram (left); low 4-quart stockpot; candy thermometer; X-Acto knife; self-healing cutting mat; awl; steel ruler; sharp scissors; paper clips or wire ornament hangers; string drying line; ⅜" flat brush; and scrap paper.

THESE ICICLE ORNAMENTS ARE made from Friendly Plastic, a thermoplastic with a low melting point that comes in both pellet and strip form. The strips are available in many colors and patterns, the best of which, in my opinion, are the mirrored-looking metallics. They come in glowing colors like fuchsia, hot pink, peridot, gold, and sky blue and resemble the shiny surfaces of hand-blown glass ornaments.

To begin, cut your plastic into tapered strips and heat a pot of water. Use a candy thermometer to maintain a water temperature of about 150 degrees, which is perfect for softening the plastic. If the water gets too hot, the plastic will become viscous, sticky, and impossible to shape. You can easily adjust the temperature by adding cold water or ice.

Working in sections makes it easier to shape the helix; practice the twisting on a few sample pieces until you get the hang of it. I curved my strip into a J-shape and heated and twisted one third at a time,

starting at the wide end and working down. This way, you can also avoid heating the ends that you hold, leaving them free from fingerprints or bends. The twisted sections will harden on their own, or you can hasten the process by dipping each finished section in cold water. If your twists end up uneven, you may be able to reheat and reshape your icicle a few more times.

To complete the ornament, use a small brush to coat the nonreflective back and edges with Mod Podge, then dust the surfaces with micro glitter. After the icicle is dry, seal it with a clear gloss acrylic spray finish to bind any loose glitter and heighten the mirror shine of the plastic finish, which tends to lose some luster during the hot-water dipping process. Avoid using lacquer, which will strip the glitter and the mirror finish.

INSTRUCTIONS
1. *Cut plastic.* Lay one plastic strip dull side up on flat work surface. Refer to cut-

ting diagram (left). Using X-Acto knife, steel ruler, and cutting mat, score strip in half lengthwise, then score diagonal line through each half, offsetting slightly so tapered end is blunt rather than sharply pointed. Cut on score lines with scissors. Cut straight across broad end to even up angles. Repeat process to cut 20 icicles total.

2. *Shape icicles.* Fill stockpot with water. Heat water to 150 degrees, monitoring temperature with candy thermometer. If water exceeds 150 degrees, remove from heat source and/or cool with ice cubes. Hold one strip by ends, broader end in your left hand and mirrored side face up, and flex into J shape. Lower bottom of J into water (do not submerge broad end) and hold for 10 to 15 seconds to soften plastic to al dente pasta stage. Lift strip, straighten it, then rotate ends in opposite directions for 1 to 1½ twists; do not overtwist. Hold under dribbling cold tap water a few seconds to set. Repeat process once or twice to soften and twist remainder of strip into a continuous helix. Repeat to twist each plastic strip.

3. *Apply glitter.* Using awl, pierce hole in broad end of each icicle. Suspend icicles temporarily using opened paper clips or ornament hangers. For each icicle, brush thin coat of Mod Podge on dull side and edges and sprinkle with coordinating glitter, catching and reserving excess on scrap paper. Hang icicles on string line and let dry overnight. Seal with acrylic spray, following manufacturer's instructions. To make permanent hangers, thread gold elastic cord through the hole and knot to make a loop. ◆

Diamond Cherub Ornament

Create Old English-style ornaments by combining stamped images, parchment paper, and gold accents.

❧ BY DAWN ANDERSON

MATERIALS
Makes one ornament

- 5"-long papier-mâché diamond ornament
- Medium-weight parchment paper
- Cherub charm (up to 2")
- 2" metallic gold tassel
- 10mm mesh-encased bead
- 2 gold seed beads
- Gold beading thread
- 2 ounces DecoArt metallic gold acrylic paint
- Gold pigment-based ink
- Clear embossing powder
- Yes Stikflat glue
- Multipurpose cement

You'll also need:
two rubber stamps, such as (1) G-clef staff with notes or (2) "Peace at Christmas!" script; thin craft foam; toaster (or substitute heat source); X-Acto knife with new blade; self-healing cutting mat; quilter's grid ruler; soft brush (for paint); stiff brush (for glue); T-pin; beading needle; white paper; scissors; and pencil.

L OOKING FOR A BEAUTIFUL ornament idea? Consider these traditionally styled ornaments that look as if they are covered with antique sheet music.

The background design for the face of the diamond is made by creating a horizontal pattern with two rubber stamps. Though I used one stamp with a line of holiday text and another with a few bars of music, you could combine other stamp motifs to create your own antique-look paper. Just think of the background as a wallpaper with a repeating symmetrical design. I recommend testing the stamps and working out the spacing on plain paper before applying the designs to the parchment paper.

To add the final touches, glue a cherub to the center of the diamond and thread beads and a glittering tassel through the bottom point.

Dawn Anderson is a writer and designer living in Bothell, Washington.

INSTRUCTIONS

1. *Emboss parchment diamonds.* Using papier-mâché diamond as template, lightly trace two diamond outlines on parchment; allow ample margins. Apply gold ink to craft foam, then load either rubber stamp. With ruler as guideline, stamp horizontally across diamond, going out beyond edges. Immediately, while ink is still wet, sprinkle embossing powder within diamond outline. Shake off and reserve excess. Repeat process to stamp both diamonds with alternating lines (*see illustration A, below*). To activate embossing powder, hold parchment a few inches above toaster and heat for 20 seconds, or

Cherub charms come in a wide array of styles. Consider making a gift set of four ornaments, each one featuring a unique cherub.

until powder melts.

2. *Assemble diamonds.* Paint sides and edges of papier-mâché diamonds gold (do not paint interiors, which will be concealed by parchment diamonds). Let dry 20 minutes. Apply second coat if needed. Using X-Acto knife, grid ruler, and mat, cut out each parchment diamond ⅛"

inside marked outline; use grid ruler to ensure that opposite edges are parallel. Turn parchment diamond facedown on white paper and brush thin coat of Yes glue across back and out beyond edges. Glue one parchment diamond to each side of papier-mâché diamond, pressing firmly to adhere (illustration B).

3. *Add trims.* Thread beading needle with 12" double strand of gold beading thread. String on seed bead, 10mm bead, and second seed bead. Push T-pin horizontally through bottom point of diamond to make two holes. Draw needle through both holes, go back down through beads in reverse order, and into tassel head. Repeat once more, going up through tassel head, through beads, through diamond, and back through beads (illustration C). Pull thread ends taut. Tie ends in square knot, draw knot down inside tassel head, and trim off tails. Use multipurpose cement to affix cherub charm to front of diamond. ◆

DESIGNER'S TIP

Try this stamping technique on the remnants of your parchment to create your own gift cards.

COLOR PHOTOGRAPHY:
Carl Tremblay

ILLUSTRATION:
Michael Gellatly

STYLING:
Ritch Holben

Making the Ornament

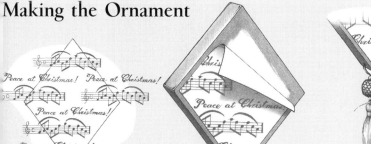

A. Stamp the parchment to fill in the diamond.

B. Glue the parchment diamond to the painted ornament.

C. Join beads and a tassel to the lower point.

Diamond Wreath with Kissing Ball

Use fresh boxwood and hot pink celosia to create a contemporary holiday wreath.

❧ BY DAWN ANDERSON

This diamond wreath form started out as a square. Try manipulating pliable, sturdy wire into wreath forms in other interesting shapes. For example, you could create an oval or a figure-eight form.

FOR A GRAPHIC TWIST ON THIS year's holiday wreath, try an angled shape—in this case a diamond—instead of the traditional circle. When I couldn't find a diamond wreath form, I simply shaped a square base into a diamond by pulling on two opposite corners until it elongated.

The greenery on my diamond wreath is boxwood, a hardy choice that will last for several weeks and dry to a soft green color. Celosia, known also as cockscomb because its broad flowers resemble the comb of a cock, is used to cover a kissing ball suspended from the apex of the diamond. The construction of the wreath is simple: Wrap small bundles of boxwood sprigs with wire, then bind them to the wreath form. The base of the kissing ball is a globe-shaped piece of foam that has been cut in half so that it will rest flat against the hanging surface. The foam has a base layer of moss and a top layer of celosia secured with hot-glue and wire.

If you plan to hang your wreath on an outside door, be sure to weatherize it. Cold temperatures can weaken the bond of hot-glue by causing the joins to become extremely brittle and break apart. A product called Hot-Glue Help Mate, applied at the same time as hot-glue, will continue holding even when

temperatures drop. Using hairpin-shaped wires in addition to glue will also stabilize the layer of celosia against the core. Sunlight can cause materials to fade so you may want to hang your wreath in a slightly shaded location like a porch or protected entryway. You might also consider spraying the celosia with Design Master color tool in raspberry to maintain its bright color. Select a ribbon that is colorfast and water-resistant so it will stand up to sunlight, snow, and rain.

INSTRUCTIONS
Making the Kissing Ball

1. *Glue moss layer.* Using serrated knife, cut foam ball in half; set aside one half for another project. Lightly spray-mist sheet moss for easier handling and less crumbling. Hot-glue sheet moss to remaining half-sphere, including flat cut surface (*see illustration A, right*).

2. *Attach celosia layer.* Cut two 20-gauge florist stems into 2" lengths. Using pliers, bend each wire into hairpin shape and crinkle the ends. Break celosia into small pieces. Secure celosia pieces to dome area of half-sphere using wire hairpins and hot-glue. Leave moss on flat back exposed (illustration B). For nonfading color, apply floral color spray to dome following manufacturer's instructions.

3. *Attach suspending wire.* Bend 18-

MATERIALS
Makes one 24" x 30" diamond wreath

- 4 to 5 bunches fresh boxwood
- 2 bunches hot pink celosia (cockscomb)
- Sheet moss
- Hot pink satin ribbon:
  1 yard ⁵⁄₈"-wide
  2¹⁄₂ yards 1¹⁄₂"-wide
- Hot pink wire-edged organza ribbon: 2¹⁄₂ yards 4"-wide
- 16"-square wire wreath form
- 3" Foam ball
- 18-gauge 18" florist wire stems
- 20-gauge 18" florist wire stems
- 22-gauge paddle wire
- 30-gauge paddle wire
- Green florist tape
- Design Master color spray (optional)

You'll also need:
hot-glue gun; needle-nose pliers; wire cutter; pruning shears; serrated knife; scissors; and spray mister.

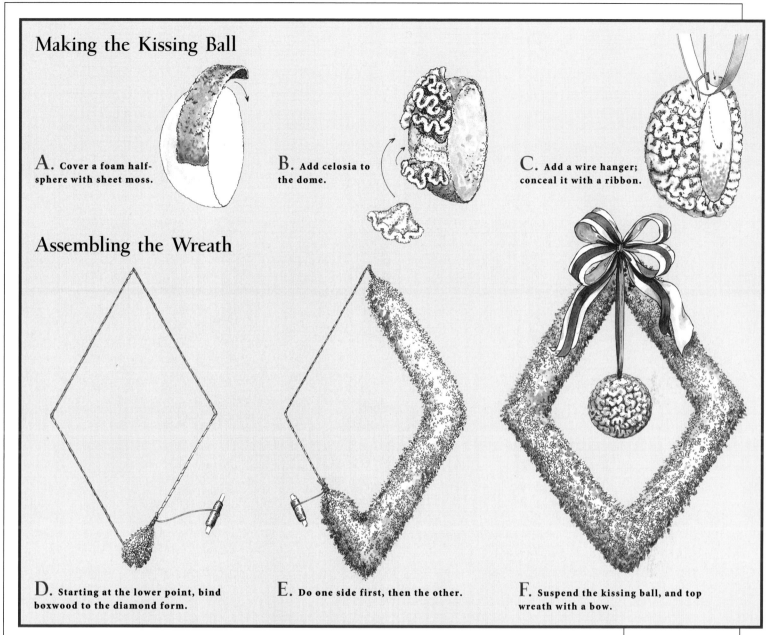

Making the Kissing Ball

A. Cover a foam half-sphere with sheet moss.

B. Add celosia to the dome.

C. Add a wire hanger; conceal it with a ribbon.

Assembling the Wreath

D. Starting at the lower point, bind boxwood to the diamond form.

E. Do one side first, then the other.

F. Suspend the kissing ball, and top wreath with a bow.

gauge wire stem 1½" from one end to make hairpin shape. Push longer wire end into center back of kissing ball, angling it to exit through dome ½" from edge. Pull snug to anchor hairpin at center back. Fold ⅝" pink ribbon in half, pierce small hole at fold with tip of wire, and slide ribbon down to kissing ball. Cut 5" length of 18-gauge wire. Using pliers, bend wire into a staple equal to ribbon width. Push staple into kissing ball to anchor ribbon in place (illustration C).

Assembling the Wreath

1. *Make diamond wreath form.* Grip two opposite corners of wreath form and pull apart, distorting square into a diamond 26" long and 18" wide. Bind diamond-shaped form with florist tape, stretching tape slightly as you go.

2. *Bind boxwood to wreath form.* Using pruning shears, clip boxwood into 6" to 8" sprigs. Hold 6 to 8 sprigs together and bind stems with paddle wire or florist tape. Repeat process to make about 40 bundles. Hold one bundle against lower wreath form so leaves "grow" down, concealing diamond point. Bind bundle to wreath form with paddle wire; do not clip wire (illustration D). Position second bundle about 1" above first bundle, concealing its binding; bind in place. Continue binding bundles up one side of form to create full, lush foliage; keep back flat for flush mounting. Stop when you reach top. Repeat process on other side (illustration E). Wire one more bundle to top center, so bound stems extend slightly above point.

3. *Suspend kissing ball.* For hanger, bend an 18-gauge wire stem in half and twist to form 1" loop. Hold loop flat against wreath behind apex of diamond. Wrap wire ends several times around frame, twist ends together securely, and clip off excess. Wrap kissing ball wire around base of loop so ball is suspended in middle of diamond. Draw loose ribbons up to conceal suspending wire and bind ends to hanging loop with paddle wire.

4. *Add bow with streamers.* Lay organza ribbon flat on work surface, layer satin ribbon on top, and locate middle. Observing midpoint and keeping satin ribbon on outside, make two continuous loops, each 14" long. Crimp at middle, bind with 30-gauge wire, and clip off excess (*see right*). To hide wire, wrap one layered ribbon streamer once around middle. Wire ribbon to top of wreath, allowing tails to hang free (illustration F). ◆

MAKING A DOUBLE-LAYERED BOW

Heirloom Giving Box

Decoupage a tzedakah box with artwork inspired
by fifteenth century manuscripts and ancient scriptures.

❧ BY ELIZABETH A. FISHBANE

Use color copies of the original artwork on pages 44 through 47 to make this beautiful tzedakah box.

COLOR PHOTOGRAPHY:
Carl Tremblay

MENORAH ARTWORK:
Judy Love

HEBREW CALLIGRAPHY:
Amy Fagin

STYLING:
Ritch Holben

T HE HEBREW WORD *TZEDAKAH* means charity. Tzedakah boxes are intended for use in the home to collect contributions for charity throughout the year. Although this triangular shape is not typical of most tzedakah boxes, I chose it to represent the three aspects of Jewish giving: charity, volunteering, and social action.

The lid of the box features a traditional Hanuka menorah on a parchment-like background. The edges contain blessings and prayers in Hebrew relating to righteous giving. Around the bottom, the words "Justice, justice, you shall pursue" are written with gold script. Inside, selected psalms line the walls.

The tricky part, especially for those not familiar with Hebrew, will be to position the panels in the correct orientation on the box. Be sure to follow the label key so the Hebrew letters are right side up and read from right to left. Test-fit the pieces before trimming at the crop marks. If you'd like to make two or more boxes, make additional color photocopies of the original panels before gluing them down.

Elizabeth A. Fishbane is a graphic designer living in Cambridgeport, Massachusetts.

MATERIALS
Makes one 7" x 4 1/4"-high box

- Basswood triangle box (each side 7" across x 4 1/4" high)
- 10 printed color panels (*see* page 44 to 47 for originals)
- Two 1" x 1 1/4" brass hinges
- Plaid Folk Art acrylic paint, 2 ounces each: Poetry Green #619, Sterling Blue #441, and Ivory White #427
- Mod Podge (matte)
- Shellac

You'll also need:
access to laser color copier; X-Acto knife; steel ruler; self-healing cutting mat; 220-grit sandpaper; small screwdriver; 1/2" foam brush; 1/2" soft bristle brush; watercolor palette; manicure scissors; pencil; spray mister; cotton balls; paper towels; wax paper; cardboard scrap; and newsprint.

INSTRUCTIONS

1. *Prepare box.* Pry off hinges, separate box and lid, and sand lightly, inside and out. Wipe dust with misted paper towel. Using foam brush, apply light coat of Mod Podge to seal lid top, lid outside wall, box inside wall, and box outside wall. Let dry 20 minutes. Mix equal amounts green and ivory paint, and dilute with drop of water to make wash. Apply wash with bristle brush to box underside. Mix and apply a blue-green wash to remaining unsealed areas in same way.

2. *Prepare color panels.* Make color photocopies of artwork. Use X-Acto knife, steel ruler, and mat to cut out 10 color panels; label wrong sides as you go. Test-fit pieces and adjust crops if necessary. Trim curved triangle points with manicure scissors. Lay panels face up on wax paper, apply thin coat of Mod Podge, and let dry 30 minutes.

3. *Glue triangular panel.* Lay panel 1 (triangle) face down on newsprint. Brush thin coat of Mod Podge on wrong side, going out beyond edges. Align panel on lid so top of menorah faces hinge edge. Rub cotton ball in circular motion to work out air bubbles and ensure firm adhesion. Swab any oozing glue.

4. *Glue side panels.* Organize remaining panels end to end in threes (Hebrew reads from right to left). Working in numerical order, apply Mod Podge to each panel in turn. Glue panels 2, 3, and 4 around outside lid, butting ends; at starting point, butt ends, or overlap slightly and trim off excess. Repeat process to glue panels 5, 6, and 7 to inside wall. Poke panels into acute corners using folded cardboard scrap. Glue panels 8, 9, and 10 to outside box, ending on hinge side. Let dry overnight. Seal with several light coats shellac. Rejoin lid to box using purchased hinges. ◆

Candied Citrus Peels

A simple cooking method and a roll in sugar transform citrus rinds into glittering confections.

COLOR PHOTOGRAPHY:
Carl Tremblay

STYLING:
Ritch Holben

🙠 BY EMILY GRIMES

FEELING NOSTALGIC FOR THE candied citrus peels your grandmother used to make? This recipe will create the sharp, zesty burst of flavor you remember. Essentially, there are only four steps: cutting the peels, boiling them in water, boiling them in syrup, and coating them with sugar.

When possible, choose fruits with thicker rinds—grapefruit, oranges, and lemons are all available with thick skins (though limes are not). For example, use navel oranges rather than the thin-skinned juice oranges. Collect the citrus peels over a few days so that your family can enjoy the fruit. The uncooked peels will keep well in a sealed plastic bag in the refrigerator for up to a week. When you're ready to make the recipe, start earlier rather than later in your day, since the peels require a fairly long simmering and drying time—about four to five hours from the time you begin cooking to the final sugar coating.

Traditionally, citrus peels are cut into long slices, but you can also cut them into holiday shapes using miniature tin cookie cutters (plastic won't cut through rind). Once the peels are cut, they are boiled in several changes of water to remove their bitterness. After that, they are boiled in a simple sugar syrup, then allowed to drain and dry out. The final step is coating them with sugar. If you prefer a softer, moister candy peel, place them in an airtight container immediately after sugaring. If you prefer a chewier peel, allow them to dry overnight before storing them.

Emily Grimes is a culinary instructor specializing in recipe development living in Raleigh, North Carolina.

INSTRUCTIONS

1. *Prepare peels.* Using paring knife, score each fruit into quarters. Carefully peel each quarter rind in one piece, reserving fruit for another use. Using teaspoon or knife blade, scrape white pith from each rind until remaining pith and colored rind layers are about equal. To cut shapes, press mini tin cookie cutter into right side of peel (use oven mitt to protect your hand). Cut remainder into strips ¼" to ⅜" wide.

2. *Boil peels.* Put each peel type (lemon, lime, etc.) in its own saucepan. Add water

to cover plus 1". Bring to boil over high heat, and maintain boil for 10 minutes. Drain peels and rinse under cold running water. Repeat boiling process with fresh water—once more for orange and grapefruit peels, twice more for lemons and limes—to remove all traces of bitterness. Drain, rinse well, and set aside.

3. *Cook peels in sugar syrup.* In each saucepan over medium heat, combine 1 cup water and 2 cups sugar, stirring until dissolved. Add food coloring if desired: 4 to 5 drops red for ruby red grapefruit, 1 to 2 drops yellow for lemons, and 4 to 5 drops green and 1 to 2 drops red for

limes. Stir in color, add peels, and bring to boil. Reduce heat, and simmer 1½ hours.

4. *Add sugar coating.* Remove pan from heat. Using slotted spoon, transfer peels to strainer. Shake strainer vigorously to drain off excess syrup. Arrange peels on cooling rack, in single layer and not touching, with baking pan underneath to catch drips. Let rest 1 to 2 hours, or until peels look dry and leathery. Using slotted spoon, transfer 4 or 5 peels to small bowl of sugar, toss lightly to coat, and set aside. Repeat process to sugarcoat all peels. Store in airtight container at room temperature; do not refrigerate. ◆

Candied citrus peels are perfect for after-dinner nibbling. They can also be chopped and added to cake and cookie batters or sprinkled over vanilla ice cream.

DESIGNER'S TIP

Don't discard the sugar syrup used for simmering the peels. It will be infused with a rich fruity flavor and can be used in other recipes. The lemon syrup, for example, can be used for lemonade. Try the orange syrup instead of honey in baklava.

MATERIALS
Makes 5 to 6 cups peels

- **1 medium grapefruit**
- **2 large navel oranges**
- **3 large lemons**
- **4 medium limes**
- **8 cups sugar, plus extra for coating**
- **Food coloring (optional)**

You'll also need:
mini tin cookie cutter(s); four 2- to 3-quart saucepans; oven mitts; 2 to 4 grid-style cooling racks; 2 to 4 baking pans; large strainer; large slotted spoon; wet and dry measuring cups; small bowls; paring knife; and teaspoon.

Natural Tree Garlands

Learn the best technique for stringing fruits, nuts, and spices into classic country garlands.

❧ BY ELIZABETH CAMERON

MATERIALS
Makes one 3' to 4' garland

- **24-gauge florist wire or nylon craft thread**
- **Choose any three:**
  4 to 5 fresh limes
  20 to 30 cinnamon sticks
  20 to 30 Brazil nuts
  20 to 30 filbert nuts
  20 to 30 shelled almonds
  20 to 30 walnuts

You'll also need:
drill with ¹⁄₁₆" bit; safety goggles; old telephone directory; sharp chef's knife and cake cooling rack (if using limes); long-nose pliers and wire cutters (if using florist wire); and crewel needle and scissors (if using nylon craft thread).

Nuts make wonderful beads because they have such a variety of shapes and textures. Linear cinnamon sticks add counterpoint.

DESIGNER'S TIP

To get more mileage from cinnamon sticks, string them the long way—just pass the wire through the coil. Alternate between cinnamon sticks and nuts, or, for a fancier look, add silver bead accents.

COLOR PHOTOGRAPHY:
Carl Tremblay

ILLUSTRATION:
Judy Love

STYLING:
Ritch Holben

THE SECRET TO THESE GARLANDS is simplicity. Originally I designed a single garland using a broad variety of natural elements but the result looked cluttered. I scaled back and chose six distinct shapes to work with, combining no more than three of them in one garland. Using three items keeps the visual configuration simple, yet makes it possible to create several distinct designs.

My choice of materials for these garlands included nuts, cinnamon sticks, and dried lime slices. Other natural items would work as well. For visual interest, combine items that have contrasting shapes and colors. You could try small dried pomegranates to add a little red, stacks of dried bay leaves for a feathery touch, or even popcorn. But don't automatically disqualify a garland made only of nuts. A garland made of three, two, or even a single nut may look uninteresting by itself but may be the perfect companion to a more lavish garland made of beads, pine roping, or cranberries.

To create a garland, three items are strung in a sequence that is repeated over and over. The most basic sequence uses one of each item—for example, walnut, lime, filbert nut. A more complex sequence will arrange the items symmetrically—for example, cinnamon stick, almond, lime slice, almond, cinnamon stick. If you choose this type of sequence, you will need more of some items than others to complete the pattern and fill out the garland.

The nuts are strung like beads on florist wire. Nuts and nutmeats are soft compared with wood and easy to drill through. I recommend resting the nuts on top of an old telephone directory and holding them with pliers while drilling. The telephone book makes a practical surface because it's easy to tell when you've drilled all the way through. The cinnamon sticks can be drilled through the center or threaded through the coil, depending on the look you want. Keep in mind that the sticks are less expensive bought in bulk from health food stores or by mail-order than purchased in small jars from a supermarket.

The best way to prepare the limes is to cut them into slices and let them air dry overnight on a cooling rack. This allows them to dehydrate and still retain their fresh green color. If you're in a hurry, you can dry them at a low oven temperature for an hour but you risk discoloration with this method.

The dried lime slices can be strung horizontally, so the rinds show, or vertically, so the sliced surface shows. For the vertical version, the entire garland is strung on a strong nylon line because it's less visible than wire across the sliced surface. Don't confuse nylon craft thread with monofilament sewing thread. Monofilament thread is used on the sewing machine to sew "invisible" stitches. Nylon craft thread is heavier—it resembles fishing line—and can be used for bead stringing and similar projects.

I recommend keeping each garland in the 3- to 4-foot range—long enough to go across a window or doorway, yet still lightweight and easy to manage. You can always hang several garlands end to end around a tree or drape them across a mantel to create the illusion of a longer garland.

INSTRUCTIONS
Getting Started
1. *Prepare lime slices.* Cut each lime into four or five ¼"-thick slices; discard ends. Arrange slices in single layer on cooling rack. Set aside to dry for 24 hours, or until surface of limes is no longer juicy. Limes can now be strung in garland; they will continue to dry further.

2. *Drill nuts.* Put on safety goggles. Use pliers to grip nut and hold it steady on top of old telephone directory or other drilling surface. Using 1/16" bit, drill straight down and through nut. Repeat process to drill remaining nuts. Make sure holes face same direction on like nuts.

3. *Drill cinnamon sticks.* Put on safety goggles. Lay cinnamon stick flat on drilling surface, grip one end firmly with your fingers, and rotate so one coiled section is atop the other. Using 1/16" bit, drill straight down middle of stick through both coiled sections. Repeat process to drill remaining cinnamon sticks.

To String Limes Horizontally:
1. *String garland.* Determine stringing sequence, beginning with nut—e.g., walnut, lime, filbert. String these items onto florist wire, using drilled holes; for lime, insert wire straight through pithy center. Do not cut wire from spool. Continue adding items in established sequence until all items are used up and/or desired length is reached; end with nut.

2. *Make hanging loops.* Bend wire back on itself 3" from end and insert into final nut (*see* illustration A, right). Push end of wire down into nut so it lodges inside. Twist wires together in tight spiral. Open up wire and shape into a circle (illustration B). Slide contents of entire strand snug against loop. At other end, clip wire from spool, leaving 6" tail. Form loop at this end in same way. Garland is now ready for hanging.

To String Limes Vertically:
1. *Make first hanging loop.* Determine stringing sequence—e.g., cinnamon stick, almond, vertical lime slice, almond, cinnamon stick. Thread needle with 6' length of nylon craft thread. Draw needle through cinnamon stick, then back down through same hole, forming loop. Tie overhand knot to define loop. Thread longer end through needle. Bring needle around cinnamon stick, through loop, and down through hole again (illustration C). Pull snug. Bring needle around other side of cinnamon stick and through hole (illustration D). Pull snug.

2. *String garland.* Begin stringing items on thread in established sequence, using drilled holes. To add lime, pass needle through slice from back to front along inside edge of rind. Gently pull snug, so lime butts previous item, and wrap once around standing thread (illustration E). Pull snug. At opposite edge, insert needle along rind from front to back, and wrap once around standing thread (illustration F). Pull snug. Continue adding items in established sequence until all items are used up or until desired length is reached; end with cinnamon stick. Form hanging loop and end off same as beginning. Garland is now ready for hanging. ◆

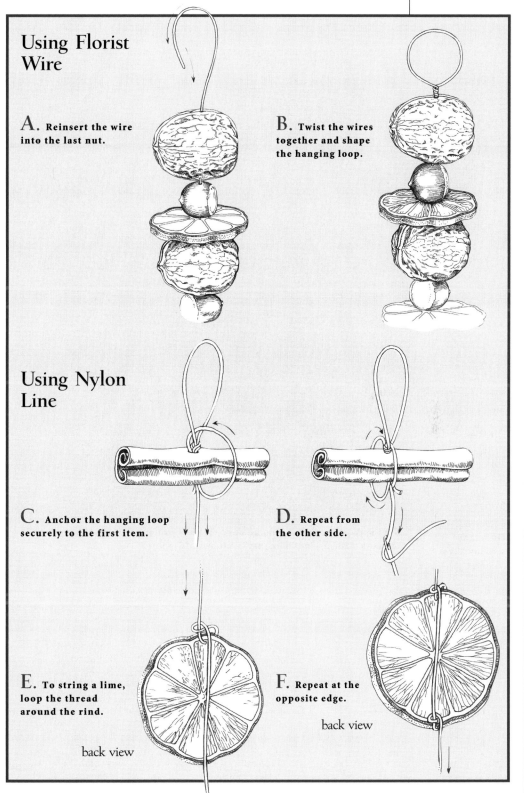

Using Florist Wire

A. Reinsert the wire into the last nut.

B. Twist the wires together and shape the hanging loop.

Using Nylon Line

C. Anchor the hanging loop securely to the first item.

D. Repeat from the other side.

E. To string a lime, loop the thread around the rind.

back view

F. Repeat at the opposite edge.

back view

Frosted Holiday Coasters

Use etching cream and adhesive lettering to transform plate glass squares into a smart set of coasters.

◆ BY ELIZABETH CAMERON

MATERIALS
Makes six coasters

- **Six 4" x 4" ¼"-thick plate glass squares, edges polished**
- **3 ounces Armour Etch glass-etching cream**
- **Assorted press type, ³⁄₄" to 1½" high**

You'll also need:
wooden burnishing tool; graph paper; ¼"-wide masking tape; 1"-wide bristle brush; old toothbrush; rubber gloves; splash goggles; spray glass cleaner; paper towels; and old newspapers.

With the right turn of phrase, these coasters will make the perfect gift for anyone—even the men on your list.

COLOR PHOTOGRAPHY:
Carl Tremblay

STYLING:
Ritch Holben

I LOVE TO GIVE UNUSUAL HOLIDAY gifts that have a personal touch—but it can be challenging to please everyone on my list. This year, however, these heavy-duty glass coasters fit the bill; with self-adhesive lettering, they can be etched with virtually any kind of message in about an hour of work-time.

To make these coasters, I purchased ¼"-thick plate glass squares, cut and polished on the edges by the glass supplier, for about $4 each. The thickness and weight of plate glass ensures a sturdy coaster that will not stick to the bottom of a perspiring glass. However, because plate glass has a higher silica content and a lower lead content than ordinary glass, making it harder and denser, it takes a little longer to etch than the three to five minutes typically required for wine goblets, mugs, or vases.

There are various brands of adhesive lettering (also called press type) from which to choose. For the best selection of typefaces and sizes, visit the graphics department of an art supply store. There you will find packages containing several 9 by 11-inch sheets of letters for $3 to $6. Stationery stores tend to carry the same product in smaller packages.

The fun is in using the lettering to create graphic designs on your coasters. Write out names, a toast, a favorite saying, or a line from a poem. Mix and match point sizes or change the orientation of different words to add graphic interest. For example, I spelled out "eat," "DRINK," and "be MERRY" on three different coasters, using letters ranging from ¾ inches to 1½ inches high.

The basic process is easy. Apply the self-adhesive letters to mask off words. Next, apply the glass-etching cream and let it set for 10 minutes. When you rinse the coasters and peel off the letters, you will have glossy sayings in a frosted field.

INSTRUCTIONS

1. *Design your coasters.* Plan message for each coaster. Keep in mind that you can mix and match point sizes and capital and lowercase letters.

2. *Affix letters.* Clean glass square with spray cleaner and paper towel. Set glass on graph paper, aligning corners with grid. Remove first letter from sheet. Use underlying grid lines as a guide; to center a word, position middle letter first. Continue in this way to position each letter in turn. When all letters are set, lay a sheet of paper over top of glass and burnish letters to ensure adhesion. Mask ¼"-thick glass edge with tape, and burnish down. Repeat for each square.

3. *Etch glass.* Read etching cream manufacturer's instructions. Place squares letter side up on newspaper next to sink. Make sure room is adequately ventilated and that room temperature is between 70 and 80 degrees. Wear long sleeves, splash goggles, and rubber gloves. Brush cream onto top glass surface, first in one direction and then in other, for smooth, even coverage. Repeat for each square. Let cream work 10 minutes. Rinse off cream under warm running water, scrubbing with old toothbrush to loosen tape and letters. Wash coaster in warm soapy water and let dry. ◆

Everlasting Herbal Garlands

Learn a foolproof technique for making garlands from herbal bouquets.

ð BY LAURA EPPERSON

COLOR PHOTOGRAPHY:
Carl Tremblay

ILLUSTRATION:
Mary Newell DePalma

STYLING:
Ritch Holben

THIS IS THE GARLAND YOU SHOULD make for the holidays. Not only is it graceful and fragrant, but you won't need to worry about shriveling leaves or falling needles—in fact, there's no need to dispense with this garland when the holidays are over. Just move it to the kitchen where you can pinch off bay leaves and rosemary for cooking, or hang it in your bedroom or bathroom where you can continue to enjoy the scent.

This garland is made by securing several small herb bouquets with florist tape. The bouquets are then wired to twine. Hemp twine provides a sturdy base and at the same time is flexible enough to be draped in any fashion.

The herbs you'll need for this garland are easy to obtain. You may even have some of them growing in your own yard. If not, rosemary and bay can be found in supermarkets, and lavender can be purchased from gift shops or mail-order sources. You'll need two to three stems of each herb per bouquet, and nine to 12 bouquets for each foot of garland.

If you end up with a surplus of materials, tie some sprigs together with a decorative ribbon to hang on a wall, use them to make a sachet, or save them for soap-making and other crafts.

Laura Epperson is a writer and crafter living in Milton, Massachusetts.

INSTRUCTIONS

1. *Make bouquets.* Select two or three rosemary sprigs of different lengths. Hold stems even at bottom and bind lower 1½" of stems with florist tape, stretching tape slightly as you wrap once or twice around. Select two or three bay leaf sprigs, place stems even with rosemary stems, and continue binding; do not tape beyond 1½". Bind in two or three lavender sprigs in same way. Tear off tape. Repeat process to make 36 bouquets.

2. *Prepare base.* At each end of hemp twine, make 2" to 3" loop and secure with overhand knot. Thread paddle wire through one loop, wrap once around, and twist wire to itself to secure. Tie loop to a doorknob (or similar setup) so you can pull twine toward you as you work.

3. *Wire bouquets to base.* Starting at doorknob, hold taped stem of one bouquet against twine so leaves extend onto

loop. Wrap paddle wire once around taped stem and pull tight. Repeat, wrapping down (toward you) so wire crosses 1" from base of stems. Wrap a third time, moving up stem (away from you) so it crosses taped stem between first two wraps (*see* illustration A, right). Pull very tight. Hold second bouquet against twine, leaves pointing toward loop and top of taped section even with standing wire. Repeat three-part wrap (illustration B). Continue in this manner to bind on remaining bouquets. Position each new bouquet to hide previous wraps so garland is full and lush from all angles. To end off, make a false tail and twist securely (illustration C). ◆

MATERIALS
Makes one 3' garland

- 4 feet ³⁄₈"-diameter hemp twine
- About 100 sprigs each:
  fresh rosemary
  fresh bay leaf (2 to 4 leaves each)
  dried lavender
- Florist tape
- 24-gauge paddle wire

You'll also need:
wire cutter; and flat-nose pliers.

This garland is made from pinelike sprigs of rosemary, silky deep green bay leaves, and sweet-smelling lavender stems.

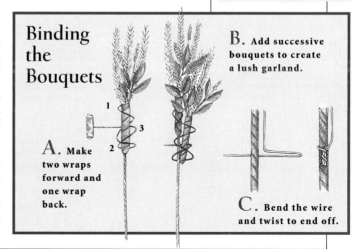

Binding the Bouquets

A. Make two wraps forward and one wrap back.

B. Add successive bouquets to create a lush garland.

C. Bend the wire and twist to end off.

Victorian Paper Angels

Make an angel ornament for your tree using a die-cut face, crepe paper, and ultrafine glitter.

☙ BY DAWN ANDERSON

Suspend a collection of angels dressed in different colored robes—or make just one as a perfect celestial tree topper.

PATTERNS
See **pages 31 and 43 for pattern pieces and enlargement instructions.**

COLOR PHOTOGRAPHY:
Carl Tremblay

ILLUSTRATION:
Judy Love

STYLING:
Ritch Holben

THESE ANGELS COMBINE THE sparkle of modern materials with the charm of old-fashioned paper ornaments. They are very easy to make, in part because the face and wings are purchased as die-cut pieces. The other materials—crepe paper, poster board, and glitter—are easily found in stationery and art supply stores. The technique of combining a realistic printed face with a handmade paper body was popular for home ornament making in the late nineteenth century, and printed die-cut faces were sold specifically for this purpose.

Today die-cut faces are easy to find and come in many styles, often with self-adhesive backing. Glue the paper face to poster board for extra support, then trim away any remaining white paper edges with manicure scissors.

The halo and the necklace are made from crinkle bullion, another old-fashioned material that is enjoying a revival today. Sold during the holiday season, crinkle bullion is a very thin wire crimped into a tight, slender spiral, like a slinky. By pulling on the ends, you can stretch it out to three to four times its original length for tree trimming, package

MATERIALS
Makes one 7½"-tall angel

- 1 die-cut paper face
- 4½" die-cut gold foil angel wings
- Colored crepe paper
- Ivory crepe paper
- Gold bullion crinkle wire
- White poster board
- Metallic gold poster board
- ½ yard ½"-wide gold mesh ribbon
- 9" narrow gold trim
- 4mm gold bead
- 2" head pin
- 28-gauge craft wire
- 12" x 6mm white chenille stem
- Ultrafine iridescent glitter
- Thread (to match crepe paper)
- Yes Stikflat glue
- White craft glue
- Multipurpose cement
- Acrylic spray sealer

You'll also need:
angel torso pattern and tunic cutting diagram (*see* pages 31 and 43); sewing machine; round-nose pliers; chain-nose pliers; wire cutter; soft brush (for diluted white glue); stiff brush (for Yes Stikflat glue); watercolor palette; ¾" dowel; eye pin; heavy books; transfer paper; white paper; scissors; manicure scissors; ruler; paper clips; and pencil.

decorations, and other uses. In this project, it is used unstretched. To shape the halo and necklace, I inserted wire through the middle of the corkscrew to act as an armature.

I recommend Yes Stikflat glue to assemble the paper components. With its low moisture content, Yes glue is ideal for crepe paper. (Wetter glues, like white glue, can bleed through and distort the paper's characteristic crinkle.) An alternative to Yes glue is a gluestick, but it can be tricky to apply in tight places and is less economical if you're doing a lot of gluing. For an even coat, apply Yes glue with a stiff brush. You'll also need diluted white glue to add glitter, and multipurpose cement to attach the halo stem.

The angels pictured here are made with dark pink and turquoise crepe paper and have gold accents, but you could try other color schemes; combine a white gown with blue or silver accents or a pale pink gown with magenta.

Dawn Anderson is a writer and designer living in Bothell, Washington.

INSTRUCTIONS
Note: Use Yes Stikflat glue unless another glue is specified.
1. *Cut crepe papers.* From colored crepe paper, use scissors to cut one 3" x 14" tunic, one 4" x 6" sleeve, and two 3" x 4"

torso rectangles, all with crinkle grain parallel to longer edge. Cut one 4¾" x 24" skirt, grain parallel to shorter edge. From ivory crepe paper, cut four 1½" x 10" strips on crosswise grain for arms.

2. *Make head.* Brush thin, even coat of glue across wrong side of girl's face. Glue face to white side of gold poster board. Weight under heavy books and let dry 20 minutes. Using manicure scissors, cut out head on hair outline. Trim away shoulders, but leave chest area intact to provide surface for gluing.

3. *Make two torsos.* Transfer angel torso (page 43) twice to white poster board. Cut out both torsos. For each, brush glue firmly across one side and adhere to torso rectangle, crinkle grain running lengthwise. Trim excess crepe paper ¼" from edge. Fold allowance to other side and glue down.

4. *Add sparkle to wings and head.* Dilute white glue slightly with water to make it more spreadable. Brush mixture onto front of wings, then sprinkle with glitter, using paper underneath to catch excess. Let dry 15 minutes. Funnel glitter back into container for future use. Repeat process for back of wings and back of head. Tap edges lightly to shed loose particles. Spray with clear acrylic sealer to prevent further shedding.

5. *Make arm piece.* Bend 12" chenille stem 3" from end, form ½" loop for hand, and twist remainder around existing stem. Repeat at other end to make 6"-long arm piece. Bend end of one ivory crepe paper strip around one loop, then wrap strip firmly around loop and up arm (*see* illustration A, below). Stop just past midpoint and tear off excess. Repeat from other side. Wrap each end of arm once again. Overlap and glue long edges of colored sleeve to make tube. Insert arm piece into sleeve and pinch at midpoint (illustration B).

6. *Assemble angel body.* Brush glue on chest area of head piece. Glue chest to wrong side of one torso so head appears above neck opening. Turn torso face-down and glue arm piece in position. Brush back of second torso with glue. Press both torsos together, matching outer edges (illustration C). Secure with paper clips, and let dry 20 minutes.

7. *Make tunic.* Referring to cutting diagram (right), slit center back of tunic and cut neck opening. Fit tunic on torso with opening at back. To close opening, overlap edges ¼" and glue together. Crimp tunic at waist, but let it flare out toward shoulders for bodice. Glue tunic to torso just below waist. Overlap and glue the side edges from the waist down (illustration D).

8. *Make skirt.* Machine-baste one long edge of skirt. Pull bobbin thread and gather waist edge to 6"; knot thread ends and trim tails. Starting at center back, wrap and glue gathered edge of skirt around angel's waist; make two complete wraps. To end off, fold edge under ⅜" and glue at center back. Trim tunic even with skirt hem (illustration E).

9. *Add gold trims.* Tie gold mesh ribbon around waist, making bow at center back. Thread 28-gauge wire through gold bullion crinkle wire for 7", crimp ends to prevent slipping, and cut off excess. Wrap one end around ¾" dowel or similarly sized object to shape halo; twist and crimp at starting point to secure. Using multipurpose cement, affix stem to head back so halo sits above face. Secure remaining wire around neck for necklace; twist to secure. For pendant, thread eye pin through bead. Bend down excess wire at right angle, trim to ⅜", and shape into loop with chain-nose pliers to attach pendant to necklace. (*See* "Making a Beaded Drop," page 9.) Cement ends of narrow gold cord to back of angel for hanging loop. Cement wings to back of shoulders. Gently stretch crepe paper at sleeve and skirt edges to create flare (illustration F). ◆

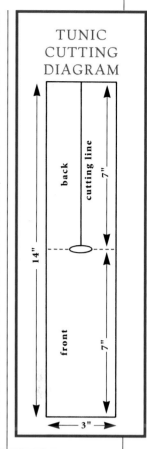

TUNIC CUTTING DIAGRAM

6"

Making the Paper Angel

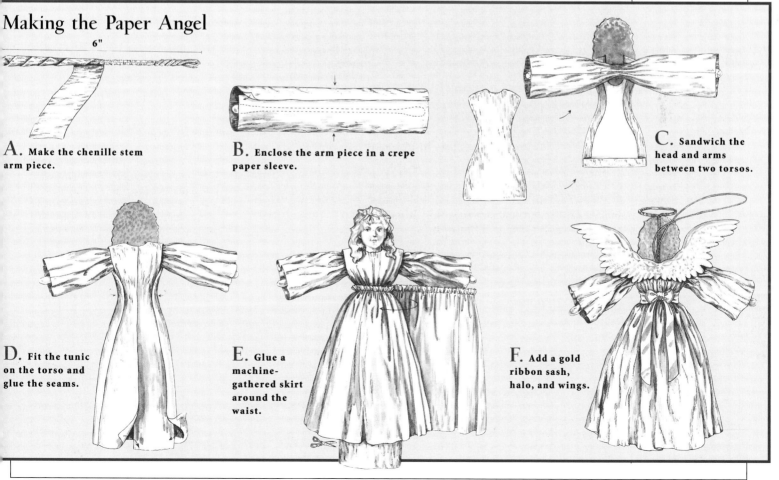

A. Make the chenille stem arm piece.

B. Enclose the arm piece in a crepe paper sleeve.

C. Sandwich the head and arms between two torsos.

D. Fit the tunic on the torso and glue the seams.

E. Glue a machine-gathered skirt around the waist.

F. Add a gold ribbon sash, halo, and wings.

Threaded Gift Boxes

Transform sheets of mat board into custom-sized gift boxes.

❧ BY MARY ANN HALL

Use wood, bone, or glass beads to accent the elastic cording.

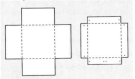

PATTERNS

See **page 42 for cutting diagrams.**

COLOR PHOTOGRAPHY:
Carl Tremblay

ILLUSTRATION:
Judy Love

STYLING:
Ritch Holben

IT'S OFTEN A CHALLENGE TO FIND sturdy, beautiful boxes in the right size when wrapping season rolls around. These unique gift boxes can be custom-sized and require no additional wrapping. The box floor can be square or rectangular and up to 10" across. The design is best suited for boxy, cubelike shapes up to 5" or 6" high.

The box is made by cutting two pieces, a lid and a bottom, from 2-ply mat board. No gluing or taping is required since the lid is held in shape by a decorative elastic cord. For a distinctive touch, I used black-core mat board. When used in picture framing, this type of mat board produces a black bevel instead of a white one, giving the framed work a dramatic look. Here, the black core elegantly delineates the outline of the box.

To use the box, wrap the gift in tissue paper and set it in the center of the bottom. Lift up the sides and slide the lid over them to hold them upright.

MATERIALS
Makes one gift box,
up to 10" x 10" x 5" high

- Two sheets 20" x 32" black-core mat board, in contrasting colors
- Elastic cord
- Two ornamental glass beads
- Two bell charms
- Fabric glue

You'll also need:
box and lid cutting diagrams (*see* page 42); utility knife; steel ruler; self-healing cutting mat; quilter's acrylic grid ruler; diamond holepunch; T-pin; and pencil.

INSTRUCTIONS

1. *Mark cutting diagrams.* Determine the length, width, and height you want, from 4" x 4" x 2¼" to a maximum size of 10" x 10" x 5". Substitute your numbers on the box and lid cutting diagrams (*see* page 42). Note that lid is ¼" larger than box and that lid height is set at 2".

2. *Draft and cut out box and lid.* Using grid ruler and pencil, draft box and lid diagrams on color side of mat board, using a different color for each diagram. Mark eight points on lid flaps ½" in from each end; mark two points, centered and ½" apart, on front flap. Lay each mat board marked side up on cutting mat. Using utility knife and steel ruler, score dash lines and cut through on solid lines, as per diagram. Use holepunch to punch 10 holes in lid flaps.

3. *Assemble lid.* Lay lid flat, color side up. Starting at front flap, insert elastic cord through one center hole and out adjacent side hole. Continue threading cord from flap to flap until you reach starting point. Trim cord, leaving 3" tails (*see* illustration A, below). Fold lid on score lines to square up flaps, and pull cord snug at center front (illustration B).

4. *Add beads and bells.* Tie cord ends together in square knot to secure lid flaps. Thread bead onto one cord and slide to knot. Thread bell on cord, stopping ½" below bead. Make two half hitches on the standing part, but reverse the second one for a decorative frog effect. Pull snug but not tight. Put a drop of fabric glue into lower bead hole. Trim off excess cord, then immediately use T-pin to push loose end into hole (illustration C). Let glue set 15 minutes. Repeat to trim second cord. ◆

Making the Box Lid

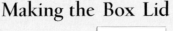

A. Thread elastic cord through the punched holes on lid flaps.

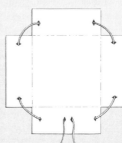

B. Fold down the flaps and square up the corners.

C. Tie the cord ends and add decorative knots and trims.

Silk Tree Trio

Make this whimsical trio of plump ornaments with an unpredictable selection of colorful silk fabrics and ribbons.

❧ BY DAWN ANDERSON

HANG THIS DYNAMIC TRIO OF stuffed silk trees from a door-knob, the mantel, or any-where you want a splash of holiday color. At seven inches high, each tree is large enough to brighten up the odd corner you might not normally think to decorate.

You will need to choose three key colors to make a coordinating set. My set uses fuchsia, tangerine, and a black-and-white combination. Make one tree in each color, then complete them all with accents that pick up one or both of the other colors. The resulting set will be unique because it avoids predictable matches. For example, the black-and-white component in my set shows up in a large-check tree, a mini-check ribbon hanger, and a polka dot hanger.

Once you've chosen a color scheme, the construction of the trees is simple. Just cut out, sew together, and stuff each tree. Then add decorative trim and a rib-bon hanger.

Dawn Anderson is a writer and designer living in Bothell, Washington.

INSTRUCTIONS

1. *Cut fabrics.* Using tree ornament pattern (page 42), cut two trees each from black-and-white check, fuchsia-pink, and fuchsia-gold iridescent silk. (To match checks, follow Designer's Tip on page 9.) Cut six trees from interfacing. Fuse inter-

Use tiny bells, Bakelite buttons, or bright glass beads to add ornaments to your silk trees.

facing tree to wrong side of each silk tree following manufacturer's instructions.

2. *Sew and stuff trees.* Pin two black-and-white check trees right sides together. Set machine for short stitch length. Starting at trunk, stitch ¼" from edge all around, pivoting at points and inside corners; leave lower edge open. Stitch again over previous stitching. Trim seam allowance to ⅛"; clip points and inside corners. Turn right side out, using point turner where needed. Press well. Tuck open edge ¼" to inside and press. Stuff fiberfill through opening, using point turner to reach points, until tree is firm. Slipstitch opening closed. Repeat to make remaining two trees.

3. *Add roses and leaves.* Hand-sew 7 green glass leaves to one side of black-and-white check tree as per pattern or as desired. Clip wire stems from 7 roses. Glue one rose next to each leaf. Repeat process to trim fuchsia-gold iridescent tree

with roses and leaves.

4. *Add ribbon hanger.* Cut 9" length of checked ribbon. Fold ribbon wrong side in and offset ends ⅜" (*see* illustration A, left). Fold extension under. Place folded end on back of fuchsia-pink tree just below peak. Tack in place, then use beading needle to tack glass bead through all layers (illustration B). Repeat process to attach fuchsia ribbon to checked tree and dotted ribbon to fuchsia-gold tree. Tie remaining checked ribbon into bow and tack to peak of fuchsia-pink tree. ◆

DESIGNER'S TIP

Try this tree design in other fabrics and trims. Ideas include blanket plaids with ecru wool pompons, cotton lace with rhinestone buttons, and panne velvet with star appliqués.

MATERIALS
Makes three 7" tree decorations

- 45"-wide silk dupi-oni, ⅜ yard each: black-and-white check fuchsia-pink iridescent fuchsia-gold (tan-gerine) iridescent
- ⅜"-wide ribbon: 18" black-and-white check 9" black-and-white dot 9" fuchsia
- 14 fuchsia silk roses, ½" across
- 14 green glass leaf beads, ½" long
- Thread to match fabrics
- ¾ yard 20"-wide fusible knit interfacing
- Fiberfill
- Fabric glue (quick-hold type)

You'll also need:
tree ornament pattern (*see* page 42); sewing machine; iron; small wire cutter; point turner; sewing shears; beading needle; hand-sewing needle; and pins.

PATTERNS
See page 42 for pattern pieces and enlargement instructions.

COLOR PHOTOGRAPHY:
Carl Tremblay

ILLUSTRATION:
Judy Love

STYLING:
Ritch Holben

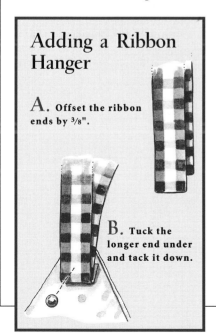

Adding a Ribbon Hanger

A. **Offset the ribbon ends by ⅜".**

B. **Tuck the longer end under and tack it down.**

Jewel-Encrusted Dragonfly

Paint die-cut insects with metallic colors and pave them with rhinestones.

🐛 BY DAWN ANDERSON

COLOR PHOTOGRAPHY:
Carl Tremblay

ILLUSTRATION:
Mary Newell DePalma

STYLING:
Ritch Holben

MATERIALS
Makes one ornament

- Two 5¼" foil dragonflies
- Flatback rhinestones:
  6mm or 7mm—4 sapphire, 4 aqua, 4 topaz, 2 ruby
  5mm—about 70 sapphire, 10 aqua, 30 topaz
  4mm—about 30 sapphire, 270 aqua, 80 topaz
  3mm—about 130 sapphire, 80 aqua, 120 topaz, 30 ruby
- Folk Art paints, 2 ounces each: Pure Gold 660, Blue Sapphire 656, and Blue Topaz 651 (all metallic); plus Brilliant Blue 641
- 9" narrow gold cord
- 1-ply chipboard
- Aleene's Design Paste
- Aleene's All-Purpose Primer
- Tacky glue

You'll also need:
palette knife; tweezers (preferably with angled arms); X-Acto knife; self-healing cutting mat; manicure scissors; ⅛" and ⅜" flat paintbrushes; heavy books; and pencil.

Use this technique to create other glittering creatures. Browse magazines and art books to find patterns for bees, frogs, snails, salamanders, or butterflies.

U SE THE SINUOUS FORM OF A dragonfly as the defining silhouette for this rhinestone-encrusted ornament. Though the overall shape appears large and dramatic, the actual surface area—the slender wings and body—is minimal, saving work time and materials cost.

To create the two-sided base of the ornament you will need two foil die-cut dragonflies, backed and stabilized with chipboard. After applying primer, use the body contours to sketch a guide for painting the colored sections. Each painted area is then encrusted with glass rhinestones in the same color. Use angled tweezers or the tip of a toothpick dipped in glue to lift and position the rhinestones. Then tamp each stone down with a fingertip or the clean end of the toothpick. For a children's project, use acrylic rhinestones.

Dawn Anderson is a writer and designer living in Bothell, Washington.

INSTRUCTIONS

1. *Make dragonfly body.* Remove and discard foil dragonfly hanging loops. Using palette knife, spread thin layer of design paste over wrong side of each dragonfly to fill hollows; let dry 30 minutes. Glue each facedown to sheet of 1-ply chipboard, weight with books, and let dry 1 hour. Using X-Acto knife, cut out both pieces. Glue dragonflies back to back, aligning edges and sandwiching stronger hanging cord in between (*see* illustration A). Weight and let dry overnight. Trim edges with X-Acto knife or manicure scissors.

2. *Paint body.* Brush primer on body and let dry 30 minutes. Sketch in guidelines to define body and wings. Using ⅜" flat brush, paint upper wings Blue Topaz (turquoise), middle wings and body Pure Gold, and lower wings 1 part Brilliant Blue mixed with 1 part Blue Sapphire. Let dry 20 minutes. Repeat to paint other side and edges. Apply second coat if needed.

3. *Glue down largest rhinestones.* Use small brush to apply glue and tweezers to lift and position rhinestones. Brush glue onto back of rhinestone or painted surface. Glue 7mm aqua rhinestone to each turquoise wing, centering it within fullest area. Repeat process on gold and sapphire wings, matching rhinestone to wing color. Glue two 7mm ruby rhinestones to head for eyes.

4. *Glue down medium rhinestones.* Filling one color section at a time, glue down 5mm and 4mm rhinestones, fanning out from larger stone (illustration B). Alternate ruby and gold rhinestones down tail section of body to create striped effect. Continue until all sections are encrusted with stones. Let dry 30 minutes. Turn dragonfly facedown and encrust back in same way, omitting ruby eyes.

5. *Glue down smallest rhinestones.* Glue 3mm rhinestones to edges of dragonfly, matching stone colors for stripes (illustration C). Let dry overnight. ◆

Making the Dragonfly

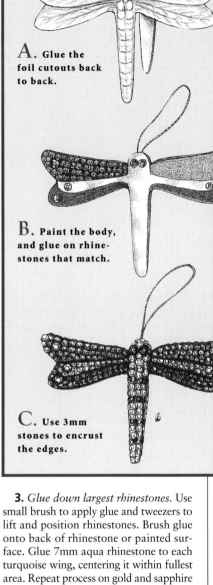

A. **Glue the foil cutouts back to back.**

B. **Paint the body, and glue on rhinestones that match.**

C. **Use 3mm stones to encrust the edges.**

Christmas Tree Vases

Wrap glass vials with wire and beads to make delicate hanging vases for your tree.

🐟 BY MARY ANN HALL

LOOKING FOR A UNIQUE HOLIDAY ornament? Consider using these miniature glass vials, which are actually recycled laboratory and pharmaceutical bottles. The ornaments are made by winding a decorative wire framework around each bottle and creating a curved ornament hook to suspend it. The bottles can be filled with water and used like bud vases to display fresh flowers or sprigs of holly. They can also hold colored sand, colored water, small pearls or glitter, or even a few drops of essential oil to scent your room.

Recycled bottles are inexpensive, sold in bulk, and come in many interesting shapes and colors. For instance, you can buy eight 20 ml amber bottles for $2; twelve 10 ml clear ampules for $2.40; or twenty 5 ml clear ampules for $3. Since you automatically purchase a quantity, you can create as many vase ornaments as you wish.

To maintain a natural color palette, I avoided red and green wire and colored beads and favored the colors of metal: copper, brass, silver, and black annealed steel. For harmony, I chose glass and metallic beads to complement the glass bottles and the metal wire. Choose two or three beads that will work in proportion to the bottles. For example, you might combine three silver beads on a vase: a small one to slip onto the hook, and a round bead and a teardrop bead to dangle from the bottom.

Cover your tree with miniature white roses or suspend a single bottle above a threshold and use it to hold fresh mistletoe.

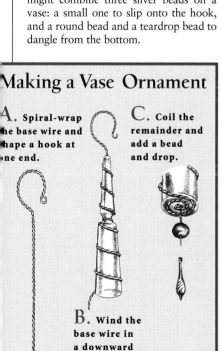

Making a Vase Ornament

A. Spiral-wrap the base wire and shape a hook at one end.

B. Wind the base wire in a downward spiral.

C. Coil the remainder and add a bead and drop.

INSTRUCTIONS

Note: Follow the instructions below to complete one vase.

1. *Prepare spiraled base wire.* Select wire that is 22-gauge or lower (thicker diameter) for base wire. Cut 24" to 30" length, depending on bottle/ampule volume. Relax coils but do not straighten wire. For wrapping wire, select contrasting wire, 24-gauge or higher (thinner diameter). Pinch ends of both wires together with fingers of one hand, hold thinner wire spool in other hand, and begin spiraling thinner wire around base wire in same direction as coil. Strive for rhythmic, evenly spaced wraps ⅛" to ¼" apart. Continue until you reach end of base wire. Clip wire from spool. Crimp wire ends to hold.

2. *Shape hanger hook.* Using needle-nose pliers, grip base wire ½" from top of bottle and make 90-degree bend. Use round-nose pliers to shape short end into loop. Make second bend 3" from loop. Bend section in between around dowel to form hook (*see* illustration A, left).

3. *Encircle bottle/ampule.* Hold base of hook against bottle/ampule neck. Starting at neck, wind base wire around bottle in downward spiral. (For an extra-snug wrap, wind counter to the spiral wire direction.) Follow the bottle's natural contours, making sure wire nips in at the waist for a secure hold. Be careful not to put excessive pressure on glass (illustration B).

4. *Add bead and drop.* When you reach lower edge, grip remaining wire 1" from end and make 90-degree bend. Shape section above it into coil. Slip base wire through bead (illustration C). Slide bead snug against coil, bend excess wire 90 degrees against bead, cut ⅜" from bend, and shape loop. Attach drop to loop. Gently tighten wire wrap at waist to draw coil snug against bottle base. ◆

MATERIALS
Makes one set of tree vases

- ■ **Your choice of: 20 ml amber bottles 10 ml clear ampules 5 ml clear ampules**
- ■ **Assorted beads and drops, approximately 3 per bottle**
- ■ **Assorted 18- to 30-gauge wires: Copper Brass Black annealed steel**

You'll also need: needle-nose pliers; round-nose pliers; wire cutter; tape measure; and ½" dowel (or substitute).

VARIATIONS

- ■ **Begin wrapping the base wire at the bottle neck. Add a separate hook in the same or a contrasting color of wire.**
- ■ **Slip a bead onto the hook before you loop the end.**
- ■ **Use a large bead with a small drop.**
- ■ **End off with a bottom spiral, and omit the bead and drop.**

COLOR PHOTOGRAPHY:
Carl Tremblay

ILLUSTRATION:
Mary Newell DePalma

STYLING:
Ritch Holben

Iridescent Pocketed Stocking

Use luscious fabrics and high-voltage colors to create dramatic Christmas stockings.

🐛 BY DAWN ANDERSON

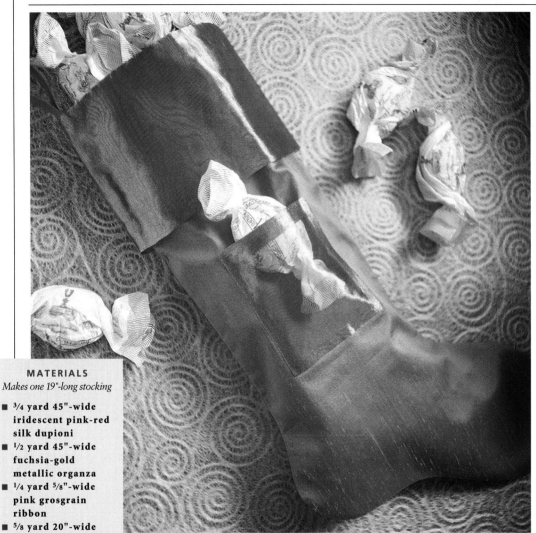

Use the sheer organza pocket to reveal "teaser" stocking-stuffers. It will easily accommodate a family photograph, a rolled necktie, or a handful of candies.

COLOR PHOTOGRAPHY:
Carl Tremblay

ILLUSTRATION:
Judy Love

STYLING:
Ritch Holben

TIRED OF PREDICTABLE HOLIDAY colors? Make this the year you venture beyond reds and greens to a brilliant pastel palette. I chose hot pink for my pocketed stocking design, but you could also use fuchsia, apricot, gold, chartreuse, or even teal. When sewn from shimmering iridescent fabrics—silk dupioni and sheer organza—these stockings will transform your hearth with their dramatic presence.

Making this self-lined stocking is easy, particularly if you keep in mind a few tips. For starters, don't try to cut the sheer cuff and pocket pieces using a rotary cutter. The ultrathin fabric tends to slip and distort, making it impossible to stay on grain. Instead, draw out lengthwise and crosswise threads to delineate the cuff or pocket rectangle, and then cut out each piece along the thread channels for perfect accuracy.

Most of the stocking assembly is done on the sewing machine, but for a fast finish, the sheer pocket is attached with fusible tape. Be sure to use a press cloth or heavy cotton fabric when ironing the tape to the organza. Without it, the heated glue may ooze through the organza, leaving a residue on your soleplate or ironing board cover.

Dawn Anderson is a writer and designer living in Bothell, Washington.

INSTRUCTIONS

1. *Cut cuff and pocket pieces.* Rough-cut one 12" x 16" rectangle from organza. Draw out thread close to one edge to mark straight grain. Repeat on perpendicular edge. Measuring from these two lines, draw out threads on the opposite edges to yield 10½" x 14½" rectangle for cuff. Cut out cuff on thread channels. Repeat process to cut one 4¼" x 5½" rectangle for pocket.

2. *Cut stocking pieces.* From pink-red silk dupioni, cut four stockings (reverse two). From interfacing, cut two stockings (reverse one). Fuse interfacing to wrong side of two stockings, following manufacturer's directions.

3. *Sew stockings and lining.* Pin interfaced stockings right sides together. Stitch curved edge, making ½" seam. Trim seam allowance to a scant ¼"; notch convex curves and clip concave curves. Pin two remaining stockings right sides together. Stitch curved edge, increasing seam allowance to ¾" around foot and leaving 4" opening on back seam. Trim seam allowance (*see* illustration A, right).

4. *Sew cuff.* Fold organza cuff in half lengthwise, wrong side in; press to set fold. Unfold, pin short edges right sides together, and stitch ½" from edge. Trim seam allowance to ¼"; press seam open. Refold along previous fold, and baste raw edges together (illustration B).

5. *Assemble stocking.* Press stocking seam open, turn right side out, and press well. Pin cuff to upper edge, matching back seam. Fold 6" length of ribbon in half, and pin ends, raw edges matching, over cuff seam. Hand-baste ³/₈" from edge all around. Slip stocking inside lining, right sides together (illustration C). Pin top edges together. Machine-stitch ½" from edge all around, trapping cuff and ribbon hanger in seam (illustration D). Pull stocking through opening and turn lining right side out.

6. *Add pocket.* Following manufacturer's instructions, fuse 4½" length of adhesive tape to corresponding pocket edge. Fold down edge ½" (even with tape) and press. Repeat to make double-fold hem for pocket top. Press three remaining raw edges ¼" to wrong side. Cut ¼"-wide strips of adhesive tape and fuse to folded edges. Fuse pocket to stocking front, as indicated on pattern. Slipstitch lining opening closed (illustration E). Push lining down inside stocking. Fold down cuff and press upper edge. ◆

Making the Iridescent Pocketed Stocking

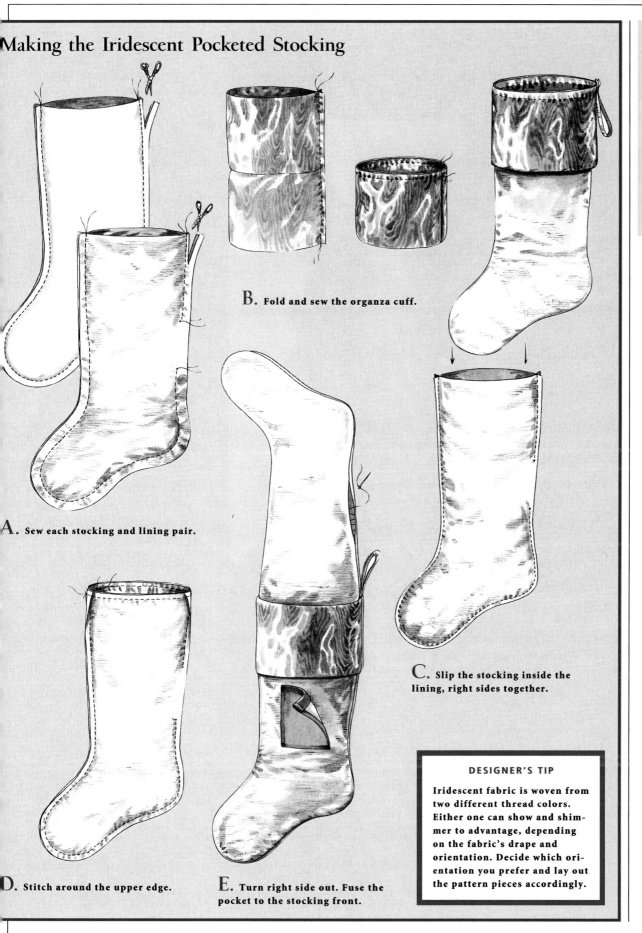

B. Fold and sew the organza cuff.

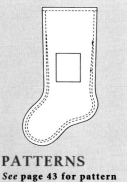

PATTERNS

See **page 43 for pattern pieces and enlargement instructions.**

A. Sew each stocking and lining pair.

C. Slip the stocking inside the lining, right sides together.

D. Stitch around the upper edge.

E. Turn right side out. Fuse the pocket to the stocking front.

DESIGNER'S TIP

Iridescent fabric is woven from two different thread colors. Either one can show and shimmer to advantage, depending on the fabric's drape and orientation. Decide which orientation you prefer and lay out the pattern pieces accordingly.

Spiral Wire Topiary

Recycle common household supplies into a glamorous holiday sculpture.

≥ BY MARY ANN HALL

Achieve a monochromatic effect by using lights and ornaments in a similar palette. This tree uses berry-colored lights with antique pink ornaments.

COLOR PHOTOGRAPHY:
Carl Tremblay

ILLUSTRATION:
Judy Love

STYLING:
Ritch Holben

I LOVE THE SLEEK APPEAL OF MODERN wire Christmas trees but the ones I've seen in catalogs and magazines have cost close to $100. With a little ingenuity, you can create the same look for about $6. Just shape a simple framework from vinyl-coated wire and decorate it with the dazzling ornaments of your choice.

The trunk of my tree is a 49-cent garden stake. To support the stake, I mixed up some plaster of Paris in a 1-quart yogurt container and embedded the stake directly in it. I hid the base inside a silver ice bucket. You might want to decide on your outside container first,

then select a disposable container that will fit inside. (*See* Designer's Tip on page 39 for more ideas.)

Use 14-gauge steel wire to hand-shape the conelike spiral of the tree. The type I purchased—sold for general household use—featured a clear, pale-green vinyl coating that was perfect for my holiday tree. Once you shape the coil, wrap it with a single strand of Christmas tree lights. I used pearl lights, which have small marble-sized bulbs, but any kind of minilights will look attractive. Fold the strand in half, and begin wrapping the folded end from the top of the tree.

The treetop is a lamp finial which, in

MATERIALS
Makes 30"-tall spiral tree

- **6" decorative container**
- **Strand of 35 pearl lights**
- **Assorted ornaments**
- **Velvet fabric scrap (for tree skirt)**
- **Lamp finial (or other topper)**
- **28" single-loop garden stake**
- **14-gauge green vinyl-coated steel wire**
- **1-quart disposable container**
- **Plaster of Paris**
- **Florist clay**

You'll also need:
flat-nose pliers; wire cutter; tape measure; masking tape; wet and dry measuring cups; and spoon.

addition to being decorative, clamps the wire spiral securely to the trunk. You can substitute a curtain finial or a large glass bead to perform the same function. To finish, I concealed the plaster base with a scrap of white velvet (you could also use reindeer moss), and I hung soft pink antique glass ornaments. Choose the ornaments for your tree from your own collection. For example, you may want to use the tree to showcase all your favorite miniature ornaments or combine different ornaments in a particular color scheme.

INSTRUCTIONS
1. *Prepare base and trunk.* Place 2 cups water in 1-quart disposable container. Add 4 cups dry plaster of Paris (or ratio that manufacturer recommends) and stir until dissolved. Set garden stake in container, loop end down. Crisscross strips of masking tape across container opening to hold stake upright and centered as plaster hardens. Let cure 30 minutes. Remove tape (*see* illustration A, right).

2. *Bend spiral.* Stand container inside coiled ring of 14-gauge wire. Using pliers, bend wire at right angle ¾" from end. Just above bend, cut through and remove plastic wrapping, exposing bare wire. Grasp bare wire and pull coil straight up around trunk. Bend wire in toward center of coil so that you can tape bare section to top of trunk (illustration B). To shape spiral, start at top and work down. Bend wire around trunk in open, airy spiral, making four or five revolutions that increase in size and spacing as you

Making the Wire Topiary

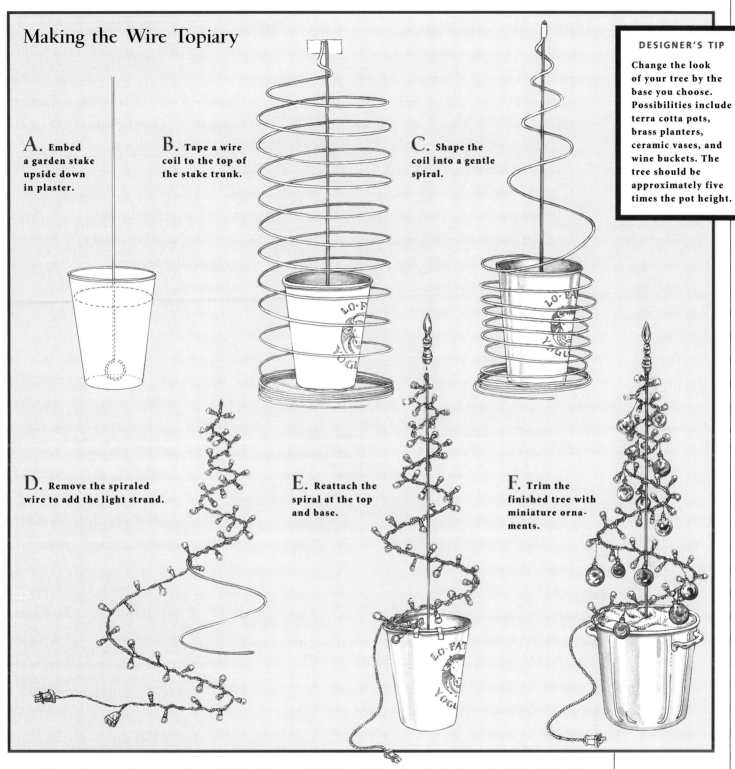

A. Embed a garden stake upside down in plaster.

B. Tape a wire coil to the top of the stake trunk.

C. Shape the coil into a gentle spiral.

D. Remove the spiraled wire to add the light strand.

E. Reattach the spiral at the top and base.

F. Trim the finished tree with miniature ornaments.

approach container rim. For a smooth, sinuous curve, bend short sections at a time in small increments; you can always go back and fine-tune the shape later (illustration C). Clip wire from coil a few inches beyond where it touches down on container rim.

3. *Add pearl lights to spiral.* Untape wire spiral and remove it from trunk. Fold strand of pearl lights in half so each light has a partner and plug end extends about 12". Part light strand slightly at fold, and lodge bent tip of spiraled wire between them. Wind double strand of lights around spiral wire. Adjust spacing as needed so end of strand coincides with end of spiral (illustration D).

4. *Reattach spiral.* Fit spiral around trunk. At top, slip finial onto trunk, then push exposed spiral wire up into base of finial until snug. At bottom, tape end of spiraled wire to container rim, letting socket fall to inside (illustration E).

5. *Trim the tree.* Conceal plaster container inside decorative container, stabilizing it with pieces of florist clay inserted at sides. Conceal top of plaster and socket with scrap of white velvet arranged as tree skirt. Hang ornaments from spiraled section, using light strand to keep hooks from slipping (illustration F). Plug in lights for the full effect. ◆

Striped Velvet Throw

Use this classic striped pattern to create a warm winter throw.

✍ BY CHIPPY IRVINE

This luxurious striped lap throw, designed in your favorite colors, will add glamour to any room.

MATERIALS
Makes one 53" x 53" throw

■ **56"-wide upholstery-weight velvet**
  3 1/2 yards dark red
  1 1/4 yards honey
  1 1/4 yards black
■ **Eight 3/4" self-covering buttons**
■ **Sewing thread to match fabrics**

You'll also need:
sewing machine; iron; velvet board; rotary cutter; quilter's grid ruler; self-healing cutting mat; scissors; hand-sewing needle; and light and dark marking pencils.

UPHOLSTERY-WEIGHT VELVET, a fabric not typically considered for a project such as this, turns out to be a lush and sturdy choice. This striped throw has substance and style; use it to keep warm on frosty nights or drape it casually over a comfortable chair or sofa.

To get started on this project, select three compatible colors of upholstery-weight cotton velvet. Two of the colors are cut and sewn into stripes, then used for the body of the throw, while the third color is used to form a mitered border. When selecting colors, pick one medium shade for the border, one lighter shade for one stripe, and a darker shade for the

second. I chose honey and black for the stripes and a rich red for the border. The throw is also backed with velvet—I used the same shade as the border. To finish, I embellished the corners with buttons.

This lap throw can be made using a variety of velvet types, including printed velveteen or embossed velvet. If you want to make a lightweight all-season throw, use a softer dress-weight or silk velvet. For a different look entirely, substitute damask or brocade fabric.

When you sew strips of velvet together, the fabric's pile often causes one piece to "grow," or wander. To prevent this, pin all the pieces together before stitching and pull gently on the fabric in front of

and behind the needle as you feed the pieces through the machine. You will need to pay special attention to the direction of the pile. On the vertical grain, parallel to the selvages, the pile will stroke smoothly in one direction and roughly in the other, making a wide variance in the richness of the color. The variance is less pronounced across the horizontal grain. For the most professional result, make sure all the pieces have the pile running in the same direction.

Chippy Irvine is a crafts designer living in Patterson, New York.

INSTRUCTIONS

1. *Cut velvet.* Using rotary cutter, grid ruler, and mat, trim one selvage from honey velvet, then cut four 9" x 42" strips along lengthwise grain. In same way, cut three 4" x 42" strips from black velvet. From dark red velvet, cut one 54" square, two 7" x 54" strips along lengthwise grain, and two 7" x 54" strips along crosswise grain. Mark arrow on wrong side of pieces to indicate nap direction.

2. *Sew honey and black stripes.* Lay strips face up on flat surface to form thick-and-thin stripes; make sure all nap arrows point in same direction. Turn black strip face down on adjacent honey strip, match one long edge, and pin. Machine-stitch 1/2" from edge. Press seam open from wrong side, using velvet board underneath. Repeat process to sew six seams total. Finished piece should measure 42" square (*see* illustration A, right).

3. *Attach dark red border strips.* Pin red strip cut on lengthwise grain to outside honey stripe, edges matching and strip extending evenly at each end. Make sure nap arrows correspond. Machine-

COLOR PHOTOGRAPHY:
Carl Tremblay

ILLUSTRATION:
Judy Love

STYLING:
Ritch Holben

Making the Velvet Lap Throw

A. Sew the velvet strips together in a stripe pattern.

B. Sew a border strip to each side edge.

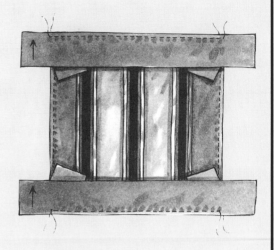

C. Sew a border strip to the top and bottom edges.

D. Fold the entire piece diagonally to miter the corners.

E. Stitch around the edges to join the backing.

F. Finish with topstitching and velvet buttons.

stitch seam, starting and stopping exactly ½" from ends of honey stripe. Sew companion strip to opposite edge (illustration B). Repeat to sew strips cut on crosswise grain to remaining edges; keep ends of first pair out of stitching path (illustration C).

4. *Miter corners.* Fold entire square in half diagonally, right side in, and align border seams and edges. Set edge of cutting guide along diagonal fold, and use marking pencil to extend line onto border strip. Pin strips together along marked line; trim off excess ½" beyond marked line. Stitch along marked line through both layers, stopping when you reach border seam. Miter opposite corner in same

way (illustration D). Refold on other diagonal to miter two remaining corners.

5. *Add backing and buttons.* Press border seams toward outer edge; press diagonal seams open. Piece should measure 54" square. Lay red velvet backing right side up on flat surface. Lay striped piece facedown on top, nap arrows corresponding and edges matching; pin edges together. Machine-stitch ½" from edge all around, leaving 12" opening for turning (illustration E). Clip corners diagonally, turn right side out, and slipstitch opening closed. To define edge, roll it between your fingers to expose seam, then pin through both layers. Topstitch 1" from edge all around.

Cover eight buttons with black velvet, following manufacturer's instructions. Sew buttons to border at each inner and outer corner (illustration F). ◆

> **DESIGNER'S TIP**
>
> **To prevent fabric "growth" and other misalignment problems, use your sewing machine's walking foot when sewing velvet. It works with the feed dogs to keep both layers of fabric moving in tandem.**

Holiday 1998 Patterns

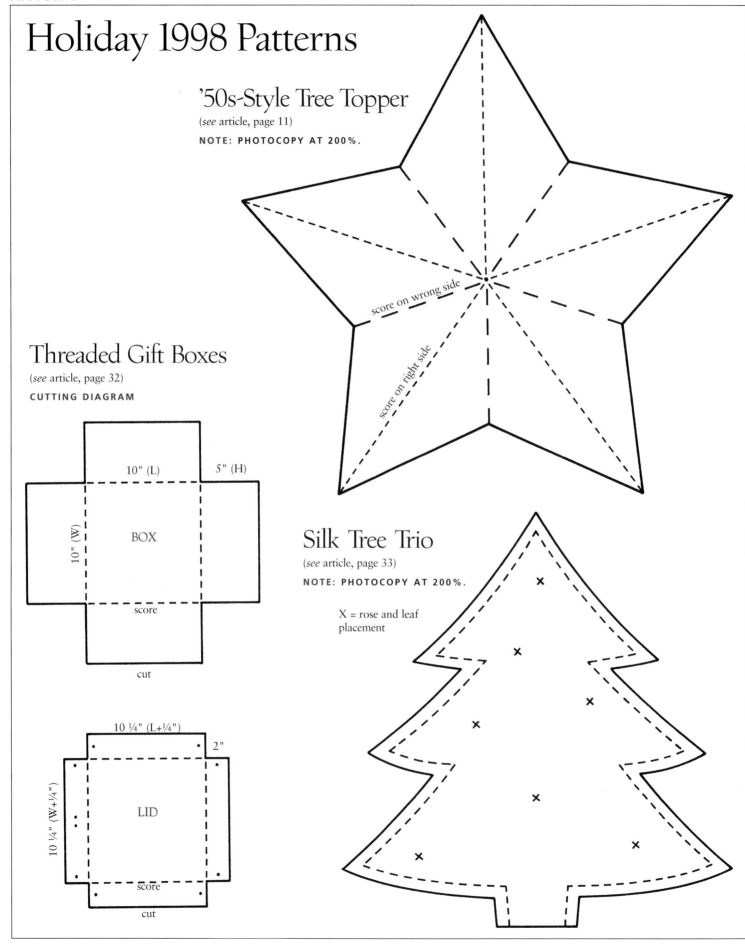

'50s-Style Tree Topper

(*see* article, page 11)

NOTE: PHOTOCOPY AT 200%.

score on wrong side

score on right side

Threaded Gift Boxes

(*see* article, page 32)

CUTTING DIAGRAM

10" (L)   5" (H)

10" (W)

BOX

score

cut

10 ¼" (L+¼")

2"

10 ¼" (W+¼")

LID

score

cut

Silk Tree Trio

(*see* article, page 33)

NOTE: PHOTOCOPY AT 200%.

X = rose and leaf placement

Check Your Stockings *(see* article, page 8)

NOTE: PHOTOCOPY AT 400%.

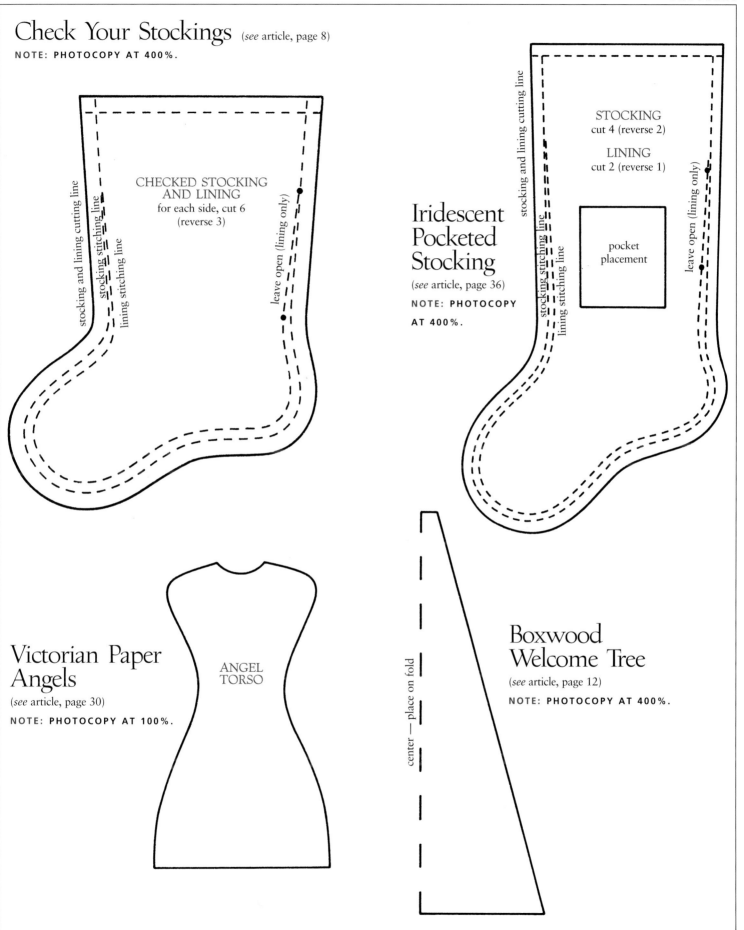

stocking and lining cutting line

stocking stitching line

lining stitching line

CHECKED STOCKING
AND LINING
for each side, cut 6
(reverse 3)

leave open (lining only)

STOCKING
cut 4 (reverse 2)

LINING
cut 2 (reverse 1)

stocking and lining cutting line

stocking stitching line

lining stitching line

pocket
placement

leave open (lining only)

Iridescent Pocketed Stocking

(see article, page 36)

NOTE: PHOTOCOPY
AT 400%.

Victorian Paper Angels

(see article, page 30)

NOTE: PHOTOCOPY AT 100%.

ANGEL
TORSO

center — place on fold

Boxwood Welcome Tree

(see article, page 12)

NOTE: PHOTOCOPY AT 400%.

Heirloom Giving Box

(*see* article, page 24)

8

crop

butt to 10

Justice, Justice, You

butt to 9

9

butt to 8

ou Shall Pursue...D

butt to 10

10

Deuteronomy 16:20

butt to 9

butt to 8

2

butt to 3

ברוך אתה, יי אלהינו, מלך העולם עשה מעשה בראשית: ברוך אתה, יי אלהינו, מלך העולם, אַ

כי~יהיה בך אביון מאחד אחיך באחד שערי

כי~פתח תפתח את~ידך לו והעבט תעביטון די מחסרו אשר יחסר לו: ברוך אתה, יי אלהינו, מַ

butt to 4

3

butt to 2

עולם, אשר נתן~לנו תורת אמת, וחיי עולם נטע בתוכנו: ברוך אתה, יי נותן התורה: השמים מספרים כ

ריך בארצך אשר~יהוה אלהיך נתן לך~לא תאמץ א

ינו, מלך העולם, מלביש ערמים: מזמור לדוד יהוה מי~יגור באהלך מי~ישכן בהר קדשך: הולך תמים

butt to 4

4

butt to 3

רים כבוד~אל ומעשה ידיו מגיד הרקיע: יום ליום יביע אמר ולילה ללילה יחוה יהוה~דעה:

ץ את~לבבך ולא תקפץ את~ידך מאחיך האביון:

מים ופעל צדק ודבר אמת בלבבו: יהיו לרצון אמרי~פי והגיון לבי לפניך יהוה צורי וגאלי:

butt to 2

שיר השירים אשר לשלמה: ישקני מנשיקות פיהו כי~טובים דדיך מיין: לריח שב
הגידה לי שאהבה נפשי איכה תרעה איכה תרביץ בצהרים שלמה אהיה כעב
בעדיי: נאוו לחייך בתרים צוארך בחרוזים: תורי זהב נעשה ~לך עם נקדו
אל~תאסף עם~חטאים נפשי ועם~אנשי דמים חיי: אשר~ בידיהם זמה וימינם
עמד ובמושב לצים לא ישב: כי אם בתורת יהוה חפצו ובתורתו יהגה י
~תדפנו רוח: על כן לא~ יקמו רשעים במשפט וחטאים בעדת צדיקים: כ
ובן~אדם כי תפקדנו: ותחסרהו מעט מאלהים וכבוד והדר תעטרהו: י
כליותי: שויתי יהוה לנגדי תמיד כי מימיני בל ~ אמוט: לכן שמח לבי ו
פנך ועמות בימינך נצח:עם~חסיד תתחסד עם~גבר תמים תתמם: עם~
יהוה רעי לא אחסר: בנאות דשא ירביצני על~מי מנחות ינהלני: נפשי ישוב

hinge side

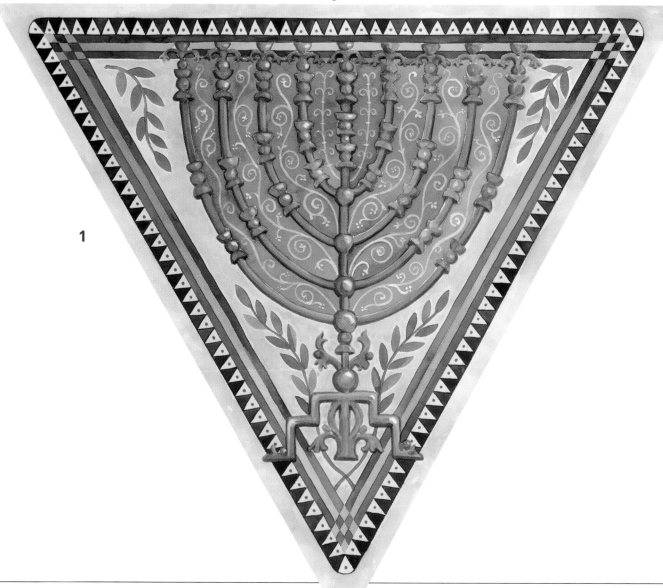

1

6

butt to 7

ריח שמניך טובים שמן תורק שמך על־כן עלמות אהבוך: משכני אחריך נרוצה הב
ה כעטיה על עדרי חבריך: אם־לא תדעי לך היפה בנשים צאי־ לך בעקבי הצאן
נקדות הכסף : ארחץ בנקיון כפי ואסבבה את־ מזבחך יהוה: לשמע בקול תודה
מינם מלאה שחד: ואני בתמי אלך פדני וחנני: רגלי עמדה במישור במקהלים אב
הגה יומם ולילה: והיה כעץ שתול על־ פלגי מים אשר פריו יתן בעתו ועלהו
ים : כי־יודע יהוה דרך צדיקים ודרך רשעים תאבד: כי־אראה שמיך מעש
רהו: יהיה מנת־ חלקי וכוסי אתה תומיך גורלי: חבלים נפלו־ לי בנעמים אף־נ
לבי ויגל כבודי אף־ בשרי ישכן לבטח: כי לא־ תעזב נפשי לשאול לא־ו
עם־נבר תתברר ועם־עקש תתפחל: כי־ אתה עם־עני תושיע ועינים רמות
ר ישובב ינחני במעגלי־צדק למען שמו: ידרך ענוים במשפט וילמד ענוים ז

butt to 5

7

butt to 5

בה הבי אני המלך חדריו נגילה ונשמחה בך נזכירה דדיך מיין מישרים אהבוך:
צאן ורעי את־גדיתיך על משכנות הרעים: לססתי ברכבי פרעה דמיתיך
תודה ולספר כל־נפלאותיך : יהוה אהבתי מעון ביתך ומקום משכן כבודך:
ים אברך יהוה: אשרי־האיש אשר לא הלך בעצת רשעים ובדרך חטאים לא
עלהו לא־ יבול וכל אשר־ יעשה יצליח: לא־ כן הרשעים כי אם־כמץ אשר
ר מעשה אצבעתיך ירח וכוכבים אשר כוננתה: מה־ אנוש כי־ תזכרנו
אף־נחלת שפרה עלי: אברך את־ יהוה אשר יעצני אף־ לילות יסרוני
לא־ תתן חסידיך לראות שחת: תודיעני ארח חיים שבע שמחות את־
מות תשפיל : כי־ אתה תאיר נרי יהוה אלהי יגיה חשכי: מזמור לדוד
עים דרכו : כל־ארחות יהוה חסד ואמת לנצרי בריתו ועדתיו:

butt to 6

Sources & Resources

Tips to Help You Find What You Need

Most of the materials used in this issue are available at your local craft supply store, florist, fabric shop, hardware store, or bead and jewelry supply store. Generic craft supplies can be ordered from catalogs such as Craft King, Pearl Paint Company, or Sunshine Discount Crafts. The following are specific sources for harder-to-find items, arranged by article. The suggested retail prices listed here were current at press time. Contact the suppliers directly to confirm prices and availability.

Check Your Stockings, *page 8*
Silk dupioni starting at $9.95 per yard from Super Silk.

Mosaic Seed Globes, *page 10*
Nonhardening modeling clay starting at $2.25 for a 1-pound package of assorted colors, available from Sax Arts & Crafts.

'50s-Style Tree Topper, *page 11*
Composition gold leaf starts at $4.20 for one book and gold size at $6.00 for 6.25 ounces, both from Pearl Paint.

Gold Mesh Ornament, *page 15*
Gold mesh ribbon (9" wide) for $23.75 per 10-yard spool from Craft King.

Sugarplum Wreath, *page 18*
Rolco reflective beads for $5.02 per pound from Pearl Paint. Contact Sein Imports for information on prices and availablity of artificial fruit. Assorted velvet leaves starting at $3 a stem from Tinsel Trading.

Icicle Ornaments, *page 20*
Friendly Plastic starts at 79 cents for a 1½" x 7" stick, from Sunshine Discount Crafts.

Diamond Ornament, *page 21*
Papier-mâché diamond ornaments for $9.00 per dozen from Packaging Specialties. Cherub charms starting at $2.40 for 12 from Craft Catalog. "Peace at Christmas!" stamp made by Peddler's Pack for $5.50 from Impress. "Musical Border" rubber stamp made by Double D (item no. D 1508) for $6 from Make An Impression.

Diamond Wreath, *page 22*
Delta Color Mist spray for $2.99 per bottle from Craft Catalog.

Heirloom Giving Box, *page 24*
Triangular wooden box (item no. 3208-1) for $18.94 from Walnut Hollow. Hinges (item # 81-2013), $2.49 for a package of four from Viking Woodcrafts.

Frosted Coasters, *page 28*
Assorted styles of adhesive lettering from $3 at Pearl, and Armour Etch glass-etching cream starting at $6.50 for 3 ounces, available from Eastern Art Glass.

Angel Ornaments, *page 30*
Die-cut paper angel faces, $2.43 for a pack of 12, and angel wings starting at 73 cents per pair, both from Craft King. Gold, silver, or copper bullion wire, $10.50 for three packs (15 strands) from Packaging Specialties.

Threaded Boxes, *page 32*
Assorted colors of mat board for $4.27 for 32" x 40" sheet from Pearl Paint.

Silk Tree Trio, *page 33*
Black-and-white check silk dupioni for $9.95 per yard from Super Silk. Fuschia-pink and fuschia-gold iridescent silk dupioni starting at $14.77 per yard from G Street Fabrics. Various leaf beads ranging from 5 to 30 cents each from Beads & Beyond.

Dragonfly, *page 34*
Dragonfly ornament (item # D8517S or D8517G), two for $7.50 from D. Blümchen & Company. Flatback Austrian crystal rhinestones starting at 7 cents each or $4.10 for ½ gram from Rings & Things.

Tree Vases, *page 35*
Amber bottles (item # 23126), eight for $2.00; 5 ml. clear ampules (item # 20958), 20 for $3.00; and 10 ml. clear ampules (item # 20964), 12 for $2.40, all from American Science & Surplus.

Iridescent Pocketed Stocking, *page 36*
Pink-red iridescent silk dupioni starting at $14.77 per yard from G Street Fabrics.

Metallic organza for $10.25 per yard from Super Silk.

Quick Projects, *page 49*
Buckle for 69 cents (item # 1646) from Tandy Leather & Crafts. D rings starting at $2.01 for one dozen, and end caps starting at $1.63 for one gross (144 pieces) from Fire Mountain Gems. Tree charms (item # 1071) for 25 cents each from Creative Beginnings. Toggle clasps starting at 75 each from Rings & Things.

Wire Mesh Shades, *back cover*
Paragon WireForm (all kinds) starting at $7.99 for a 16"x 20" sheet from Dick Blick Art Materials.

🐦 🐦 🐦 🐦 🐦

The following companies are mentioned in the listings above. Contact each individually for a price list or catalog.

AMERICAN SCIENCE & SURPLUS
Mail Order Warehouse; 3605 Howard Street; Skokie, IL 60076; 847-982-0870; www.sciplus.com

BEADS AND BEYOND
25 102nd Avenue NE; Bellevue, WA 98004; 425-462-8992

CRAFT CATALOG
800-777-1442

CRAFT KING
800-769-9494

CREATIVE BEGINNINGS
P.O. Box 1330, Morro Bay, CA 93443; 800-367-1739

D. BLÜMCHEN & COMPANY, INC.
P.O. Box 1210, Ridgewood, NJ 07451; 201-652-5595

DICK BLICK ART MATERIALS
P.O. Box 1267, Galesburg, IL 61402; 800-723-2787

EASTERN ART GLASS
201-847-0001

FIRE MOUNTAIN GEMS
28195 Redwood Highway, Cave Junction,

OR 97523; 800-423-2319

G STREET FABRICS
12240 Wilkins Avenue, Rockville, MD 20852; 800-333-9191

IMPRESS
120 Andover Park E., Tukwila, WA 98188; 206-901-9101

MAKE AN IMPRESSION
Gilman Village, 317 NW Gilman Blvd. #16, Issaquah, WA 98027; 425-557-9247

PACKAGING SPECIALTIES
515 South Michigan Avenue, Seattle, WA 98108; 206-762-0540

PEARL PAINT COMPANY, INC.
308 Canal Street, New York, NY 10013-2572; 800-451-PEARL (fine arts catalog) or 800-221-6845 x2297 (main store, craft dept.); 212-334-4530 (Rolco beads); www.pearlpaint.com

RINGS & THINGS
214 North Wall Avenue, Ste. 990, P.O. Box 450, Spokane, WA, 99210-0450; 800-366-2156; www.Rings-Things.com

SAX ARTS & CRAFTS
P.O. Box 510710, New Berlin, WI 53151; 800-558-6696; www.artsupplies.com

SEIN IMPORTS
150 West 28th Street; New York, NY; 212-255-6660

SUNSHINE DISCOUNT CRAFTS
800-729-2878; www.sunshinecrafts.com

SUPER SILK
P.O. Box 527596, Flushing, NY 11352; 800-432-SILK

TANDY LEATHER & CRAFTS
Call 800-555-3130 for the store nearest you.

TINSEL TRADING
212-730-1030

VIKING WOODCRAFTS, INC.
1317 8th Street SE, Waseca, MN 56093; 507-835-8043

WALNUT HOLLOW
1409 State Road 23, Dodgeville, WI 53533-2112; 800-950-5101

Quick Projects

In as long as it takes to tie the perfect bow, you can neatly secure your holiday packages using jewelry clasps, buckles, and charms.

Package decorations shown clockwise from left: gold buckle, toggle clasp, D-rings, and charms.

CLEVER CLOSURES

Add wit to your gift giving. These unique package closures are actually inexpensive findings used in leather crafts and jewelry making. They include two belt fixtures: a buckle and a pair of D-rings; and two types of jewelry findings: a toggle clasp, used for necklaces, and end caps, used for necklaces or bracelets. Raid your sewing kit, jewelry box, or junk drawer for fixtures to make your own clever wraps.

■ **Gold buckle with lime grosgrain ribbon:** Cut length of ribbon long enough to go around package plus 3". Make hole 3" from one end, centering hole across ribbon. Insert prong of buckle through hole, fold ribbon ends together, and secure with eyelet using eyelet tool.

Wrap ribbon around package, centering buckle on top. Insert remaining end of ribbon through buckle and pull snug. Mark location where prong of buckle hits ribbon. Remove ribbon and install eyelet at marked point. Install two additional eyelets along length of ribbon, 1 1/8" apart. Trim ribbon tail at an angle.

■ **Toggle clasp with red elastic cord:** Insert length of red elastic cord through loop on each side of toggle clasp. Knot ends of cord together. Stretch out loop of elastic cord by pulling each side of toggle clasp in opposite direction. Adjust cord so knot lies in center. Center package over cord; lift sides of clasp around package and hook together.

■ **D-rings with silk and velvet ribbon:**

Choose velvet ribbon with satin back in contrasting color. Insert ribbon through both D-rings and fold over. Use sewing machine with zipper foot attachment to stitch through both layers as close as possible to rings. Wrap ribbon around package, and insert end through both rings. Fold inserted ribbon back over first ring and then under second ring; pull snug. Trim ribbon tail at angle.

■ **Charms and end caps with satin cord:** Tie double length lime green satin cord around package in both directions and knot on top. Secure each double end of cord into end cap using tacky glue. Crimp with jewelry pliers. Attach brass Christmas tree charms to loops on end caps using jump rings. ◆

COLOR PHOTOGRAPHY:
Carl Tremblay

DESIGN:
Dawn Anderson

STYLING:
Ritch Holben

Wire Mesh Shades

Cut out light shades using a 5½" diameter cardboard circle as a pattern. Wearing work gloves, hem the circle's perimeter by holding a small saucer or tin lid ⅛" from the edge and bending the exposed mesh edge up 90 degrees. Work the saucer around the entire perimeter to make a perpendicular lip, then press the lip flat to make a fold. Repeat to make a double-folded edge.

Snip a ⅛" opening in the center of the circle and slide a light bulb into the opening, allowing the mesh to stretch at the point of entry. Crimp the shade around the base of the bulb holder. Use extended finger to create hills and valleys in the shade skirt.

COLOR PHOTOGRAPHY: **Carl Tremblay**　　STYLING: **Ritch Holben**　　DESIGN: **Elizabeth Cameron**